POPULAR PIETY AND ART
IN THE LATE MIDDLE AGES

THE NEW MIDDLE AGES

BONNIE WHEELER, *Series Editor*

The New Middle Ages presents transdisciplinary studies of medieval cultures. It includes both scholarly monographs and essay collections.

PUBLISHED BY PALGRAVE:

Women in the Medieval Islamic World:
Power, Patronage, and Piety
  edited by Gavin R. G. Hambly

The Ethics of Nature in the Middle Ages:
On Boccaccio's Poetaphysics
  by Gregory B. Stone

Presence and Presentation:
Women in the Chinese Literati Tradition
  by Sherry J. Mou

The Lost Love Letters of Heloise and Abelard:
Perceptions of Dialogue in Twelfth-Century France
  by Constant J. Mews

Understanding Scholastic Thought with Foucault
  by Philipp W. Rosemann

For Her Good Estate:
The Life of Elizabeth de Burgh
  by Frances Underhill

Constructions of Widowhood and Virginity
in the Middle Ages
  edited by Cindy L. Carlson
  and Angela Jane Weisl

Motherhood and Mothering
in Anglo-Saxon England
  by Mary Dockray-Miller

Listening to Heloise:
The Voice of a Twelfth-Century Woman
  edited by Bonnie Wheeler

The Postcolonial Middle Ages
  edited by Jeffrey Jerome Cohen

Chaucer's Pardoner and Gender Theory:
Bodies of Discourse
  by Robert S. Sturges

Engaging Words: The Culture of Reading in the
Later Middle Ages
  by Laurel Amtower

Crossing the Bridge: Comparative Essays
on Medieval European and Heian Japanese
Women Writers
  edited by Barbara Stevenson and
  Cynthia Ho

Robes and Honor:
The Medieval World of Investiture
  edited by Stewart Gordon

Representing Rape in Medieval
and Early Modern Literature
  edited by Elizabeth Robertson and
  Christine M. Rose

Same Sex Love and Desire Among Women
in the Middle Ages
  edited by Francesca Canadé Sautman
  and Pamela Sheingorn

Listen Daughter: The Speculum Virginum
and the Formation of Religious Women
in the Middle Ages
  edited by Constant J. Mews

Science, The Singular, and the Question
of Theology
  by Richard A. Lee, Jr.

Gender in Debate from the Early Middle Ages
to the Renaissance
  edited by Thelma S. Fenster
  and Clare A. Lees

Malory's Morte Darthur:
Remaking Arthurian Tradition
  by Catherine Batt

The Vernacular Spirit: Essays on Medieval
Religious Literature
  edited by Renate Blumenfeld-Kosinski,
  Duncan Robertson, and
  Nancy Bradley Warren

Popular Piety and Art in the Late Middle Ages
  by Kathleen Kamerick

POPULAR PIETY AND ART
IN THE LATE MIDDLE AGES

IMAGE WORSHIP AND IDOLATRY
IN ENGLAND 1350–1500

Kathleen Kamerick

palgrave

POPULAR PIETY AND ART IN THE LATE MIDDLE AGES
Copyright © Kathleen Kamerick, 2002

First published in 2002 by
PALGRAVE™
175 Fifth Avenue, New York, N.Y. 10010 and
Houndmills, Basingstoke, Hampshire, England RG21 6XS
Companies and representatives throughout the world.

PALGRAVE™ is the new global publishing imprint of St. Martin's Press
LLC Scholarly and Reference Division and Palgrave Publishers Ltd.
(formerly Macmillan Press Ltd.).

ISBN 0–312–29312–7

Library of Congress Cataloging-in-Publication Data

Kamerick, Kathleen, 1953-
Popular piety and art in the late Middle Ages : image worship and idolatry
in England 1350–1500 / by Kathleen Kamerick.
    p.   cm. – (The new Middle Ages)
  Includes bibliographical references (p.) and index.
ISBN 0–312–29312–7
   1, England—Religious life and customs.   2. Image (Theology)—
History of Doctrines—Middle Ages, 600–1500.   3. Christian art and
symbolism—Medieval, 500–1500.   4. Idols and images—Worship—
History.   I. Title.   II. New Middle Ages (Palgrave (Firm))
BR750.K35   2002
246'.0942'09024—dc21

                                                              2002020110

Design by Letra Libre, Inc.

First edition: June 2002
10 9 8 7 6 5 4 3 2 1

Printed in the United States of America

To my parents
Elaine and John Kamerick

CONTENTS

Series Editor's Foreword   ix

Acknowledgments   xi

Introduction   "Worship One God"   1

1.   The Cause of All Evil: Idolatry in Late Medieval England   13

2.   Diverse Doctrines: Religious Instruction and Holy Images   43

3.   "Fair Images" in the Parish   69

4.   Something of Divinity:
     Holy Images in the Community   107

5.   Art and Moral Vision:
     Julian of Norwich and Margery Kempe   131

6.   Staying the Senses: Image and Word in Prayer Books   155

Conclusion   "Things Tending to Idolatry"   191

Abbreviations   197
Notes   199
Bibliography   257
Index   285

SERIES EDITOR'S FOREWORD

The New Middle Ages contributes to lively transdisciplinary conversations in medieval cultural studies through its scholarly monographs and essay collections. This series provides new work in a contemporary idiom about precise and often diverse practices, expressions, and ideologies in the Middle Ages. In her monograph *Popular Piety and Art in the Late Middle Ages: Image Worship and Idolatry in England 1350–1500,* the twenty-seventh book in the series, Kathleen Kamerick challenges readers to rethink basic assumptions about late medieval ideas of religious art. Was religious art, as usually assumed, a "book" for the laity? Holy images, argues Kamerick, play complex roles in the negotiations between the institutional church and lay believers over devotional practices. Kamerick is interested in how the vigorous attempts of the post–Fourth Lateran English church to catechize its members, combined with increasing lay literacy and deepening lay participation in their parishes, altered responses to holy images. These responses to the visual power of "beholding" help us to understand both sides of the Lollard debate over image worship.

Bonnie Wheeler
Southern Methodist University

ACKNOWLEDGMENTS

It is a pleasure to thank the many people and institutions that have provided help with this project over several years. Katherine H. Tachau directed this work in its first stage as a dissertation. Constance Berman provided thoughtful critiques and, just as importantly, a great deal of encouragement. Rebecca Clouse very kindly read drafts of this work and offered pertinent criticisms. Questions and comments from Annemarie Weyl Carr's careful reading of the manuscript for *The New Middle Ages Series* helped me to rethink and sharpen several issues and arguments. I also thank Paul Lachance, Anne Clark Bartlett, Valerie Lagorio, Anne Roberts, and Sarah Hanley for their suggestions and support. The staff members of many libraries and archives have been unfailingly courteous and helpful. I thank the archivists and librarians at the Norfolk Record Office in Norwich, the Suffolk Record Offices in Ipswich and Bury St. Edmunds, the Public Record Office in London, the British Library, the Leicester University Library, the Newberry Library, the Library of Congress Rare Book and Special Collections Division, the Royal Library in Copenhagen, the Huntington Library, the Pierpont Morgan Library, the Bodleian Library, the Rijksmuseum Amsterdam, and the University of Iowa Libraries. During a semester in The Netherlands, Hans Bak and the English and American Studies Department at the Katholieke Universiteit Nijmegen generously gave me an office and library privileges. I would like to thank as well Alexandra Barratt, editor of *Mystics Quarterly,* for permission to reprint "Art and Moral Vision in Angela of Foligno and Margery Kempe." The Richard III Society, the University of Iowa Graduate College, and The Newberry Library Consortium provided financial support for research and travel.

My husband John H. Raeburn cheerfully accompanied me to churches, cathedrals, museums, and libraries in the United States, England, France, Denmark, Belgium, and the Netherlands. He joined wholeheartedly in my search for understanding holy images, and his thoughtful reading and editing improved this work considerably. Without him, this book would not have been written.

INTRODUCTION

"WORSHIP ONE GOD"

Holy images never completely shook off the taint of idolatry in the Middle Ages. Pope Gregory the Great (590–604) famously defended Christian art as a medium through which illiterates could learn their faith, but his notion that people could "read" in images what literate people learned through books could not quell the suspicions and doubts about art.[1] Despite medieval theologians' nearly ceaseless repetition of Gregory's argument, sacred art portraying the saints, Christ, and the Virgin Mary remained the focus of mistrust and anxiety that the simple laity would worship the art itself, rather than the holy people it represented. The malign and corrupting effects of such idolatry as it was understood in the late Middle Ages can be seen in a fifteenth-century manuscript illumination [plate I.1] that shows Moses holding up the tablets of the Commandments, while the oblivious and feckless Israelites dance around their newly minted idol of the golden calf. The richly colored gowns, stockings, boots, and caps, the handsome faces of men and women, the joined hands and the legs raised to take the next step, create a festive and joyous air. The small figure of Moses in the background seems almost negligible. The highly skilled illuminator who painted this scene understood how to please the eye, which only reluctantly descends the page to read the accompanying text, the First Commandment summarized in the single phrase "Worship one God," followed by a brief explication warning against idolatry, the invocation of demons, and divination.[2] This standard interpretation of the Commandment calls attention to the dancers' sinful worship, warning its fifteenth-century reader to beware emulating the Jews, who needed the Mosaic Law to restrain their notorious (to medieval Christians) tendency to idolatry.

Yet this illumination belonged to a traditional understanding of images that became less secure in the fifteenth century: It represents the standard medieval Christian notion that God's injunction against image worship in the Decalogue was necessary because of the errors of the Old Testament

I.1 Worship of the Golden Calf. Det Kongelige Bibliotek, Gl. Kgl. S. 1605, f. 20 recto. By permission of the Manuscript Department, The Royal Library, Copenhagen.

Jews, whose obvious and ridiculous sin was worshipping an idol, an animal made of gold. Such idolatry was foolish and (as the painting hints) somewhat licentious; one avoided it by worshipping God rather than idols. At the time this page was painted, however, idolatry was becoming a controversial topic, with its definition contested even among orthodox writers. Some claimed that idolatry meant not only idol worship, but also the improper adoration of Christian images. In England, for example, Lollards accused people of idolatry because they treated holy images as though these pieces of carved wood or stone embodied the Virgin Mary or Christ or the saints. Rather than learning from images, the Lollards charged that in their simplicity, folk mistook them for the holy people they represented. Lollard challenges to the standard interpretation of the First Commandment began to erode the traditional Christian understanding of images as substitutes for books. So too did increasing literacy among laypeople. The owner of the manuscript with the illumination of the idolatrous dancers, for instance, certainly read it, for it is filled with texts of prayers, explanations of the Seven Deadly Sins, the works of mercy, the gifts of the Holy Spirit, and so on. The greater part of this very beautiful manuscript would be incomprehensible to an illiterate, as would most of the books produced for laypeople in the fifteenth century.

The vocal and written opposition to holy images mounted by many Lollards stimulated an equally articulate defense of them by English churchmen. Orthodox treatises rebuilt the walls of protection around Christian art in order to defend against the attacks of their heretical opponents.[3] Yet as both sides engaged in the battle, the hearts and minds of the people they fought over seemed untouched. While churchmen repeatedly praised the didactic value of holy images, they often ignored the varied and creative uses that laypeople made of holy images. Laywomen and -men, literates and illiterates alike, made pilgrimages to wonder-working statues of the Virgin; gave money, lands, and jewelry to support and adorn favorite images in their parish churches and to commission new ones; and left money for lights to be placed in front of beloved statues of the saints as tokens of their continued reverence, even after death. Some made representations of Christ's Passion the focus of meditations and read prayer books that encouraged them to petition the Virgin Mary while gazing at her image. Few worried about idolatry. Holy images formed a crucial and completely commonplace element in their piety, as familiar material artifacts and as links to the supernatural.

This book began in my effort to understand the relations between late medieval people and the holy images that they saw in their parish churches, traveled to see at shrines, and looked at in their prayer books. Evidence of people's beliefs about and responses to holy images is sparse and usually indirect; these topics form, nonetheless, the heart of this work. This is by no means an iconographical study, although recurrent motifs and specific pieces of art receive some attention. My aim is to explore late medieval religious life by examining what was thought and taught about holy images, and what roles they played in the life of the parish and in devotional practices. Contemporary concerns about idolatry and attempts to work out its definition and implications, serve to bring to light various features of image worship. Throughout most of this study, fears about idolatry silhouette holy images, allowing us to discern the outlines of their position in late medieval culture.

Several problems complicate the process of understanding the position of holy images in the late Middle Ages. Artistic representations of sacred events and holy people—Christ, the Virgin Mary, the apostles, and the saints—in stained glass, carved statues, manuscript illuminations, wall paintings, and other forms, constitute perhaps the most tangible and appealing legacy of the Middle Ages. These holy images often appear to be our most engaging point of entry into the medieval era, as they show us how people then viewed their own world, conceived of the supernatural, and perceived the bonds between the two. Despite this promise of ready access to the past, holy images pose many puzzles for the modern viewer. Margaret Aston's comment that the religion of late medieval people "is impenetrable"[4] may overstate the case, but it reminds us of certain limitations. We cannot see this sacred art as medieval people saw it, for several reasons. Most obviously, much medieval art has been displaced. Many pieces now displayed in museums have been removed from their original context in churches. Today we often view a painting or statue outside the sacred space for which it was made, deprived of its immediate relations to other images nearby, abstracted not just from the time but also from the physical space and affiliations that initially gave it meaning.

A great deal of sacred art has also been damaged by attempts to destroy it, especially in England, the geographical focus of this study. Sixteenth- and seventeenth-century iconoclasts hacked, smashed, and shot at the holy images in English parish churches and cathedrals, so that today their remains only hint at the richly decorated interiors to which medieval people contributed and were accustomed.[5] Wall paintings, for instance, at one time dominated the interior of some parish churches, but now can be viewed only in the fragments recovered from the reformers' whitewashing. Piecing together what a fifteenth-century parishioner saw at Sunday Mass entails an elaborate reconstruction, a mental envisioning that reassembles the rood screen, wall paintings of the Last Judgment and lives of the saints, stained glass, small wooden statues, tabernacles, and even more.

Above all, most of us do not share with medieval Christians the belief that holy images are, first and foremost, referents to real supernatural prototypes. The power of images in late medieval religious culture depended on this bond, which was expressed in the medieval Christian theology of images but even more in the way people treated them.[6] While the exact nature of the relation between image and saint became a disputed subject, the argument itself points to the importance of that connection. Moreover, the aesthetic qualities that modern people often value in imaginative works of art were not always the primary concern of medieval viewers. Innovations in representation, for example, could be regarded as potentially dangerous because they risked inaccuracy and might mislead viewers into false belief. Because their ties to their prototypes were considered so significant, holy images were to depict the otherworldly reality as authentically as possible. Only their *accurate* rendition of holy people or scenes would allow images to fulfill their pedagogic function and instruct their viewers about the pious characters and glorious passions of the saints. For this reason the fifteenth-century author of *Dives and Pauper* felt compelled to excuse liberties taken with portrayals of various saints on the grounds that certain added elements contributed to the spiritual, if not literal, truth of the image. Thus, he said, the apostles were painted barefoot "in tokene of innocence and of penaunce" although the Gospel of St. Mark clearly records their footwear.[7] For the most part, however, holy images showed what medieval people were taught to believe was true about their subjects—Christ's physical suffering on the cross, the Virgin Mary's sorrowing over the body of her dead son, the saints triumphing over the physical tortures inflicted on their bodies.

Despite its saturation by holy images, late medieval religious culture was never free from anxieties about idolatry. Not only did Lollards attack holy images as demonic snares misleading ignorant people; even orthodox thinkers voiced uneasiness about the crowds that gathered to worship and make offerings to reputedly wonder-working statues and pictures, often of the Virgin Mary, at the many shrines that dotted the late medieval English countryside. Holy images became lightning rods that attracted suspicion because of the apparent superficiality and credulousness of the devotion that they inspired.[8] In addition, the period's didactic literature is suffused with tales of idolatry. Just as in the illumination of the worshippers of the golden calf, many moral tales construe idolatry as the chief sin of the ancient Jews and the impetus for the Law of the Old Testament.[9] Sermon *exempla* and lives of the saints also cast idolatry as the vile and depraved crime of the pagans who resisted evangelizing by the early Christians. The apostles, for instance, try to convert unbelievers to Christianity by destroying their idols and replacing them with the cross.[10] Late medieval people thus contended with conflicting views about what constituted idolatry and who could be identified as an idolater. Although most religious literature of the period models idolatry as the abiding error of those hostile to Christians, misgivings about contemporary devotions cast a shadow over this traditional definition, suggesting that Christians, too, could fall victim to this abhorrent sin.

Ironically, while critics suspected holy images of abetting an irrational and even superstitious attitude toward the supernatural among the laity, some people made them their primary focus for rapt concentration and reflection. Pictures in prayer books, especially, served as meditative objects for viewers who sought to deepen their empathetic understanding of Christ's sufferings in his Passion, or the Virgin Mary's sorrow over her dead son. Crucifixes, statues, and paintings in churches could also inspire their viewers to identify with and respond to the torments of Christ and the saints. Holy images apparently held the potential to enhance people's imaginative grasp on critical events in Christian history.

In addition, holy images remained deeply embedded in the world of mundane religious practice until uprooted by the Reformation. Pilgrimages to famous shrines like Walsingham form a notable and well studied element of medieval religion,[11] but the operations of daily life in the parish are, I think, a better gauge of people's beliefs and devout practices. Here holy images appear in multiple contexts: parish gilds often focused activities on the images of their patron saints; local shrines with miraculous statues brought in needed donations; sinners publicly reconciled with the Christian community through their obeisance to holy images; churchwardens recorded regular expenditures for the upkeep of parish statues; parishioners remembered favorite images in their final wills.

This study attempts to draw together the practices and theories about image worship, using them to illuminate late medieval religious culture, which much recent scholarship has demonstrated to be rich, vibrant, and diverse.[12] In particular, the laity's beliefs and practices form the focus of this work. The term "laity," of course, glosses over the variety of social ranks, economic conditions, levels of education, and numerous other factors that distinguished the plowman from the merchant woman from the knight. Yet it remains a useful term, and one that late medieval lay people understood to position them within their church.[13] In theory they were subject to clerical authority; in fact they sometimes shrugged off this assertion of power if it interfered with their religious activities. Because image worship was always a worrisome and contested activity, its study is particularly useful in revealing this interplay between clergy and laity, as both groups tried to reconcile contemporary practice with what the church hierarchy considered theologically permissible.

The evidence about image worship—from episcopal orders, ecclesiastical courts, manuals of religious instruction, sermons, and parish records—

charts a dynamic and fluid relationship between the late medieval laity and their church. Tensions often arose because the laity insisted on pursuing activities they regarded as pious, but that the clergy disapproved of. Laypeople, for instance, sometimes responded to reports of miraculous images by making pilgrimages to cult statues, ignoring clerical censure. Yet the men of the church did not present a united front on such issues, and where a bishop condemned an unauthorized pilgrimage, a pope might award it an indulgence. Theologians and writers of religious manuals repeated ancient precepts on images as useful pedagogic tools and warned against worshipping them improperly, but other clerics actively encouraged people to venerate statues and paintings. Late medieval critics of the clergy implied that in pursuing their own gain, cynical priests manipulated holy images in order to elicit donations from the gullible laity. While I have found some examples of this kind of predatory behavior, there is more evidence of the clerical hierarchy responding to, not directing, popular practices. Indulgences issued by popes and bishops for visiting statues and relics, for instance, most often seemed to confirm preexisting devotions, rather than initiate pious activities. In these particulars, the relationship between church and laity appears to have been open to negotiation.

The spread of lay literacy in the late Middle Ages distinguishes it from earlier periods and was crucial in reshaping image worship. By the fifteenth century growing numbers of laywomen and -men made reading part of their devotions, signaling the end of the clergy's traditional monopoly on literacy. The exact contours of the late medieval laity's literacy will always remain stubbornly vague. We have no tool to measure precisely how many people could read, nor in what language—English, French, or Latin—nor with what degree of mastery.[14] Yet religious books of various kinds—prayer books, religious manuals, dialogues, meditations, and so on—became more available in the fifteenth century, a trend that gathered speed with the beginning of printing in the second half of the century. The connection between how people regarded holy images and how written texts treated them is tenuous but suggestive. Several vernacular texts taught people how they should venerate holy images, probably responding to Lollard critiques of image worship. These texts generally repeated the orthodox apologia for images as instruments for teaching the laity, and warned against regarding them as if they embodied God or the saint whom they merely represented. Yet the ambiguity inherent in holy images also complicated their literary presentation. This pedagogic and rational treatment of images contended with another one, found in sermon *exempla* and popular saints' lives, offering stories of wonder-working and animate images. These tales seemed to encourage readers to regard holy images as the conduits of supernatural power.

Laypeople also owned prayer books containing image-related devotions. In the fifteenth century English book producers could scarcely meet the demand for prayer books, and many of these—especially Books of Hours—encouraged readers to pray before statues and paintings, and to look at them intensely while considering their spiritual and moral significance. In addition, reading seemed to soften the supposedly hard distinction between clergy and laity. Laywomen and -men and priests might read the same texts and pass books among one another.[15] Even Books of Hours, commonly associated with laypeople, were owned by priests, who might receive them as legacies from parents, siblings, cousins, and friends. Prayer books with devotional images that carried indulgences for looking at them as one prayed, and with holy images attached to charms, were commonly owned by both priests and laity. Many devotional practices linked to images do not separate clergy from laypeople, but bind them together.

Laypeople's literacy also challenged the ancient notion in the West that holy images served above all a pedagogic purpose in teaching the illiterate laity the essentials of their faith. Gregory the Great's statements supporting pictures in churches were not the first to propose the idea that art could be "read" like a text,[16] but they became the basis for the Western notion of religious art as a "book for laypeople." This was the definitive explanation and defense of art in the Middle Ages, and it remained current into the sixteenth century, although Gregory's precise meaning always lay open to varying interpretations. Certainly preachers continued to use church art to remind audiences of the pains of hell, the virtues of the saints, or Christ's agony in his Passion. Yet increasing literacy made a substitution of images for texts unnecessary, as more and more people had access to both. The traditional opposition of holy images and sacred texts suggested by Gregory the Great's words breaks down in the late Middle Ages. As literacy spread, holy images remained popular, receiving such attentions as pilgrimages, donations, and final bequests of money and jewels. People were eager for both text and image, a desire that culminated in late medieval prayer books in which images and texts attain a perhaps unique position of parity, merging praying and beholding into a single pious act.

In addition to making reading a part of their pious activities, a significant number of late medieval laywomen and -men became energetically engaged in creating the material culture of their religion.[17] The parish church offers the clearest examples of this, as people raised money for their church's upkeep, to pay for additional services, and to adorn it with artwork. Canon law made the laity responsible for the church nave, a duty partly discharged through the office of churchwarden, who collected money from parishioners to spend on the church.[18] Among their duties, churchwardens had to hire carvers, painters, and gilders to make and decorate the parish images. In the late-fourteenth and fifteenth centuries, parish churches also underwent a massive rebuilding program to enlarge them, making them higher, wider, and lighter. Wealthy people donated stained-glass windows, gilds provided for altars and images of their patron saints, and many parishioners made small bequests of money for lights before their favorite statues.[19] By the fifteenth century, what parishioners saw at church (apart from the mass itself) was the result of their own efforts and those of their parents. The altars, paintings, stained glass, and statues that adorned the late medieval English church reflected the parishioners' religious desires and their means.

Although this material expression of their piety was fundamental to the laity's religion, it tended to be dismissed, misunderstood, or condemned by writers who debated the value of holy images. Orthodox churchmen who defended sacred art focused on its pedagogic function and its value in reminding people of God. The Lollards objected to statues as lifeless lumps of wood and stone, deriding people who would give to insensate matter the affection and devotion that belonged to God, and the money that should go to his poor. Yet laypeople found a vital connection between these pieces of wood and stone and the supernatural, one that was more than pedagogic or commemorative. The written testimonies of two women, Julian of Norwich and Margery Kempe, show how the crucifix and the pietà provided inspiration for visions and ecstasies. Julian and Margery belonged to a mystical tradition in which sacred art was a conduit for apprehending God, but they were also women of late medieval England whose experiences were informed by the material culture and pious practices of their contemporaries. Their writings both reflect and illuminate their particular historical milieu.

Finally, the material nature of holy images formed their connection to other integral physical elements of late medieval religious culture. Traditionally, holy images have been linked to relics and reliquaries,[20] but by the fifteenth century their most powerful bond was to the consecrated Host, the most sacred object in Christianity. The kinship of Host and image is attested by gild provisions, prayer book devotions, sermon *exempla,* and their ability to evoke ecstatic responses. This affinity suggests that medieval people perceived in or through holy images the same supernatural presence that they believed was embodied in the Host.

The Plan of the Book

The sources on images are diffuse, and my approach to discovering the teachings, attitudes, and activities centered on them is, of necessity, multipronged. Each chapter constitutes a separate investigation of one aspect of

holy images based on a discrete set of sources, although the concerns outlined above link one to another. The first chapter probes the various meanings of idolatry in the late Middle Ages, specifically addresses the charge of
idolatry leveled by Lollards, and examines the arguments used to rebut it,
focusing on the treatises written by the Dominican Roger Dymmok and
the canon Walter Hilton. Neither side in this debate put forth consistent
arguments. Both Dymmok and Hilton approve of images as mnemonic
and pedagogic tools; they echo each other's lines of reasoning, use the same
terminology, and rely on the same authorities, St. Thomas Aquinas, St.
Basil, and St. John of Damascus. Yet the two men display such different approaches to the "simple laity" who engaged in image worship that their
treatises demonstrate the divergent and complex positions toward images
that existed even among the orthodox. On the other side, Lollards appeared no more harmonious. Neither Lollards nor clergy could even agree
on what constituted "idolatry," but both were determined to rescue the
laity from falling into it.

The literature of religious instruction that flourished in the fourteenth
and fifteenth centuries reflects this battle over idolatry and image worship.
The second chapter examines the manuals for parish priests, instructional
and devotional works read by laity and clerics, and sermons that define
how images should be regarded and used. To remain innocent of idolatry,
for instance, the devotee was told to adore a saint's statue with the low
form of worship called *dulia,* rather than the highest form reserved for
God himself, called *latria.* Treatises like Dymmok's explicated and insisted
on the significance of these different forms of worship, and their treatment
by vernacular works shows that they became a crucial ingredient in refuting Lollard charges of idolatry. In contrast to such overtly rational teachings on image devotion, however, sermons and saints' lives also conveyed
traditional tales of wonder-working and animate images, statues of the Virgin Mary that come alive, and crucifixes that bleed when struck. The dis-
junction between these two presentations of image worship contributed
both to the multivalence of late medieval images and to the difficulties
faced by the Church in teaching a coherent doctrine of images.

Chapters 3 and 4 move beyond the theological and literary discussion
of images to their social context. Chapter 3 looks specifically at their place
in the parish. Several hundred wills from eight locales in East Anglia (the
counties of Norfolk and Suffolk) provide testimony from the laywomen
and laymen whose activities were so much debated by Lollards and clerics. This chapter analyzes the number and kinds of bequests made involving holy images, pointing out the differences between those of women and
men, and between those of willmakers in Norfolk and Suffolk. As the only
documentary trace left by many medieval people, wills offer useful testi-

mony about individual piety and, in this case, about how late medieval people regarded the familiar statues of saints, paintings, and crucifixes in their churches. This valuable but still limited information is supplemented by chapter 4, which considers the public functions of holy images. Whereas final bequests typically sketch private and personal ties to images, these same parish images were also the center of events such as pilgrimages, gild rituals, and penitential rites. Ecclesiastical records—including papal letters, bishops' registers, and churchwardens' accounts—delineate images' diverse public functions and roles. Their symbolic and practical uses are brought to the fore in the investigation of the dispute over the statue of the Virgin Mary in Foston, Yorkshire, a quarrel that caused Archbishop Greenfield of York to allude to the dangers of idolatry when he tried to settle the matter. The events surrounding that image—including theft and assault, quarrels over offerings to it, and threats of excommunication for worshipping it—underscore the economic, doctrinal, and customary accretions that attached to individual images, and provide a basis for examining the seriousness of concerns over idolatry.

The final two chapters examine the linked issues of the use of holy images in private devotions, and the validity of their descriptor as "books of the laity." Although individual testimonies are rare, the two most famous holy women of late medieval England both wrote about holy images. Julian of Norwich's *Showings* and Margery Kempe's *Book* describe their authors' heartfelt and bodily reactions to sacred art, particularly to the crucifix and the pietà. Both women found in these artifacts catalysts for deep contemplation and emotional identification with the suffering Christ and his mother. Chapter 5 locates their profound responses within the tradition of late medieval mysticism, connects them to the admonitions and directives of late medieval vernacular religious texts, and positions them within the context of medieval scientific theories about the construction of the human eye and the mechanics of vision. The body was never thought to be purely or merely material; all the senses exhibited moral qualities, so that seeing or beholding holy images constituted an act at once physical and virtuous, a creative mingling of body and spirit.

Finally, chapter 6 focuses on devotional images and their accompanying texts found in prayer books. Many late medieval prayer books contain rubrics instructing readers how to look at and pray before an image; they usually provide the required prayer, and often supply the image as well. The intricate braiding of rubrics, prayers, and images in these books reveals an unusual and short-lived harmony between text and image that dispels the traditional concept of images as the illiterate's replacement for the written word. Yet some prayer book images, like their counterparts in churches and shrines, became connected to special indulgences and even charms, at times acquiring a near-magical potency in protecting people from the terrors of storms, shipwreck, or sudden death. Such associations made the prayer book devotions involving holy images suspect by early reformers, who condemned them as idolatrous. In fact, because of their wide audience, early-sixteenth-century prayer books became one site for the increasingly heated quarrels over images and accusations of idolatry.

Statues and paintings of Christ, the Virgin Mary, and the saints were integral to the devotions, rituals, and economies that shaped fifteenth-century religion. Their literal visibility made them ideal objects for attack by heretics armed with scriptural condemnations of idols carved by human hands. Although these holy images are found at nearly every critical juncture in both private and public piety, little agreement emerged on the purpose of these artworks or on how people should, or did, regard them. Their ubiquity, the diversity of their uses, and the ongoing quarrels and fears related to images and their allied sin, idolatry, offer a penetrating view of the variety, contentiousness, and vitality of late medieval religious life.

CHAPTER 1

THE CAUSE OF ALL EVIL:
IDOLATRY IN LATE MEDIEVAL ENGLAND

The idols of the Gentiles are silver and gold, the work of the hands of men.
They have mouths and speak not: they have eyes and see not.
They have ears and hear not: they have noses and smell not.
They have hands and feel not: they have feet and walk not:
neither shall they cry out through their throat.
Let them that make them become like unto them; and all such as trust in them.

—*Psalm 113*[1]

Worschippyng of ydolez is cause of al yuel

—*Rosarium Theologie*[2]

Demons in the Image

In 1429 a woman named Johanna Clyfland testified to a remarkable and strange comment made by one Margery Baxter, who was then on trial for heresy in Norwich. The previous winter as the two women had sat before the fireplace sewing, Margery began to question Johanna about what she did in church every day. Johanna responded that she first genuflected before the crucifix and said five *Our Fathers* in its honor, then as many *Hail Marys* in honor of the Blessed Virgin, presumably before an image of the Virgin Mary, although Johanna did not say so. Margery then began to upbraid Johanna, claiming she did wrongly to genuflect and pray before images, and saying that such crosses and images were made by "lewed wrightes of stokkes" and that "lewed peyntours glorye thaym with colours. . . ." Instead, telling Johanna to "look," Margery extended her arms out, saying "this is the true cross of Christ. . . ." and declared that it was pointless to go to church to adore or pray to "any images or dead crosses." With this dramatic bodily posture imitating the crucified Christ, Margery began to preach to Johanna on the falseness of various doctrines and practices, including the Eucharist, the cult of St. Thomas of Canterbury, the sacrament of baptism, and the custom of fasting on holy days. Margery's criticisms and ideas, and her praise of the condemned heretic William White, all marked her as a Lollard, and she urged Johanna to learn more by joining at night in secret meetings where Margery's husband would read the law of Christ from a book. Returning to the question of holy images, Margery then made a claim that was apparently alien to both orthodox and standard Lollard beliefs, saying:

> people honor devils who fell with Lucifer from heaven, certain of which devils, when falling to earth, entered into the images standing in churches, and lived in these continuously and still reside there lurking, so that the people adoring the same [images] thus commit idolatry.[3]

Margery Baxter's conviction that people committed idolatry in venerating statues and other paintings of Christ, the Virgin Mary, and the saints, was widely shared by Lollards, who frequently protested images and pilgrimages as part of the cult of the saints, which they opposed. Yet the most common Lollard complaint about images was that their inanimate nature made them unworthy to receive human devotion; they were simply "stocks and stones." Made by human hands, these "dead" artifacts deserved no more adoration than a piece of wood or a stone. Baxter herself said this at first to Clyfland, but her later description of demon-inhabited statues did not derive from contemporary Lollard iconomachy. Most Lollards worried that people would confuse an image with its prototype, and take the crucifix for Christ, or suppose that a pietà *was* the Virgin; while harmless in themselves, images offered the faithful the all-too-easy possibility of misbelief and idolatry. Rooted in the Bible, Lollard hostility to holy images focused on the error of venerating these human-made objects as if they somehow contained the spark of holiness, when in fact they were lumps of lifeless material.

Margery Baxter's curious idea that demons inhabited images of the saints was thus at odds with the common Lollard complaints about image worship. Still, while Lollard texts did not usually protest holy images because they might house demons, neither did they ignore the possible association of the devil with images. The Wycliffite *Rosarium Theologie,* a compilation of texts for preachers on subjects ranging from absolution to "ymage," declared in the latter entry that a "stok" or a figure or any other human work could not perform miracles; still the devil "bigileþ many" to believe that such a miracle occurs, but this is "clene deceyuyng" [pure deception].[4] In discussing the various arguments for and against image worship, *An Apology for Lollard Doctrines* mentions that those who defended the worship of Christian images rejected analogies between holy images and those biblical idols that "vnfeiþful men worschipid as þer god, and in wilk þei worschipid deuel. . . ."[5] Baxter could therefore have developed her notion of demons living in images from talks with other heretics, but she could just as easily have come to her conclusion by paying attention to completely orthodox sources. Both the Old and New Testaments are, of course, replete with condemnations of idolatry. The warning of Psalm 113 against idols (cited above) reappears several places in scripture, and nowhere more powerfully than in the thundering of the Book of Wisdom (13:10) against those "unhappy" ones whose hope "is among the dead, who have called gods the works of the hands of men, gold and silver, the inventions of art, and the resemblances of beasts, or an unprofitable stone the work of an ancient hand."[6] Sacrificing to idols was the fundamental error of the gentiles, proving their ignorance or rejection of the one true God and their basic irrationality in attributing superhuman powers to what they themselves had made. Old Testament Israelites also repeatedly committed idolatry, most famously in their worship of the golden calf, but at many other times as well. Some New Testament passages also linked these idols or sculpted objects to demons. St. Paul (1 Cor. 10:14–20) urges Christians to "fly from the service of idols," and declares that when heathens sacrifice to idols, they sacrifice to "devils, and not to God." The Apocalypse of St. John (Book of Revelation) (9:20) condemns men who did not repent of "the works of their hands, that they should not adore devils, and idols of gold, and silver, and brass, and stone, and wood, which neither can see, nor hear, nor walk. . . ."

Some early Christians argued that statues were inhabited by evil spirits who delighted in sacrifice. The second-century Christian apologist Athenagoras identified these spirits as devils.[7] In the *Octavius* of Minucius Felix, a debate about the virtues of paganism and Christianity, the character Octavius denounces demons as the source of evil rumors about Christians, and comments that they "find a lurking place under statues and consecrated images, and by their breath exercise influence as of a present God. . . ."[8] After his conversion to Christianity, Justin Martyr also saw the "spiritual forces of evil in heavenly places" behind the familiar sculpted figures of the Roman gods and goddesses. Elsewhere he explains that Christians do not honor the objects made by people, set in temples and named gods, because "we know that they are lifeless and dead," and that they "have the names and shapes of those evil demons. . . ."[9] Tertullian begins his *De Idololatria* by defining idolatry as the "chief crime of mankind, the supreme guilt of the world. . . ." He declares, "all sins are found in idolatry and idolatry in all sins." This may be explained in another way:

> since all sins are directed against God and everything directed against God is allotted to the demons and impure spirits, to whom the idols are subject, it is beyond doubt that everybody who sins makes himself guilty of idolatry, for he does that which is in the realm of the masters of the idols.[10]

In *The City of God* St. Augustine also considered the nature of demons, their origins and purposes, and their hold over humankind. While people either worshipped demons as gods or as intermediaries between the gods and humans, Augustine argues that Christians must realize they are spirits who intend harm. Demons dwell in the air, having been "cast down from the upper heights of heaven as a reward for their irremediable transgression. . . ." Many of these demons can be found in statues. Augustine cites the legendary Hermes Trismegistus as saying that "certain spirits have been induced to take up their abode" in idols, and from this position these spirits can either harm or please their worshippers. Augustine explains that:

> When Hermes talks of gods being made by men, he refers to a kind of technique of attaching invisible spirits to material bodies, so that the images dedicated and subjected to those spirits become, as it were, animated bodies. This, he says, is the great, the marvellous power of creating gods, which has been given to men.

To expose the full horror of Hermes' ideas, Augustine then cites a passage from *Asclepius,* a work that portrays Hermes rhapsodizing about "Statues endowed with souls" that could "foreknow the future, and foretell it," could cause disease and cure it, bestow "sadness or joy, according to deserts." Hermes acknowledges that only by going astray in their notion of the gods did human beings learn the art of forcing "the souls of angels or demons" to inhere in sacred images, but regrets nonetheless the eventual loss of the skill. Augustine does not question Hermes' account, but names the demon-inhabited idols "products of this abominable art" that the true religion of Christianity will abolish. For Augustine, the animate statues that human hands created were not humanity's servants but its captors. The demons bound to the images by this "wicked art" forced the souls of their worshippers into a fellowship from which only the true faith could free them.[11]

Augustine's account contains all the elements that appeared in Margery Baxter's description some thousand years later, with the exception, of course, of Baxter's identification of images of Christian saints as idols. Idolatry continued to concern the Christian Church after Augustine's time, and various medieval sources describe demon-inhabited idols. Early medieval penitentials, for example, sometimes prescribed severe penalties for those who honored demons or their idols.[12] Demons dwelling in statues are also found in Celtic and Byzantine sources: St. Patrick expelled a demon from the great idol of Ireland.[13] In 1402 Eastern bishops bearing crosses reportedly drove out a demon living in a nude statue of Aphrodite in the Marneion at Gaza.[14] Citing Augustine, Thomas Aquinas acknowledged that demons could work in images to produce "certain strange effects," so that it was thought "something of divinity resided in them."[15]

In late medieval England, vernacular sermons described the wonders worked by early Christian saints who cleansed statues of their demonic dwellers; St. Bartholomew, for instance, was said to have successfully ordered a demon to exit and then demolish its idol. So too did the Apostle St. Thomas, who suffered martyrdom for this deed. These sermons could draw on Jacobus de Voragine's popular *Golden Legend* among other sources, and laypeople might also read such stories for themselves, particularly once William Caxton printed an English version of the *Golden Legend* in 1483.[16] The dramatic possibilities inherent in these scenes did not escape artists; thus, the manuscript known as the *Great Book of Hours of Henry the Eighth* contains an illumination of idols falling headfirst off an altar at the approach of St. Philip, who carries a large cross; a winged and horned demon flies off, escaping from the overturned statue.[17] [plate 1.1] Writing in the 1440s, the English Bishop Reginald Pecock cited Augustine's comments on Hermes Trismegistus, and with astonishing sympathy explained how heathen men made fair, rich, and precious images so that good spirits would descend into them, a misguided effort to achieve a sensible god that Pecock compared to the Christian belief in Christ's Incarnation. In the event, the heathens failed because, as Pecock explains, wicked spirits moved into the images.[18] Finally, images other than pagan idols were popularly associated with demons. A thirteenth-century Latin collection of the miracles of the Virgin includes the tale of a Cistercian abbot who visits a heretic and finds a stone statue of the Virgin inhabited by a devil; by producing the consecrated Host, the abbot causes the destruction of all but himself and a fellow monk.[19] The late-fourteenth-century encyclopedia called the *Omne Bonum,* compiled by an English royal clerk, expresses the common notion that astronomical and necromantic images were linked to demons; indeed, the latter were made "expressly for the invocation of demons."[20] The medieval Christian tradition thus supplied a rich treasury of diabolic affiliations with many kinds of images.

1.1 Demon flees idol at the approach of St. Philip. The Pierpont Morgan Library, New York, H. 8, f. 177. By permission of The Pierpont Morgan Library.

English writers in the fourteenth and fifteenth centuries sometimes acknowledged that confusion might arise in distinguishing pagan idols occupied by demons from Christian images deserving reverence. The fourteenth-century canon Walter Hilton, aware that idols with demons might be confused with holy images of saints, took pains to distinguish them. He describes the adoration of demon-inhabited images as the idolatrous sin of the Old Testament gentiles. Even though they understood that the images were only wood, the gentiles adored them in order to communicate with evil spirits. "Whence deservedly," wrote Hilton, "because of such aversion to God and conversion to demons, the demons received the power to deceive them through their deceitful responses and empty lies. This adoration of images was idolatry." It is different among Christians, said Hilton, who do not adore images of the cross or saints in order to hear a response, but so that their minds will "be recalled to divine and spiritual things."[21]

In his popular fifteenth-century handbook for preachers known as the *Destructorium Viciorum,* Alexander Carpenter produced a painstaking examination of the eight ways to commit idolatry as part of his larger discussion of superstition.[22] Each of these idolatrous acts errs in crediting the "dead" material object with the attributes of a living spirit. By bestowing names on images, swearing by them, putting faith or hope in them, loving them, adoring them, devising idols or praying to them, the idolater shows his "foolishness." As a rational creature, the idolater should be ashamed to pray or speak to a "dead idol," for he is asking for help, health, and life from an insensible object that, in the words of the psalm, can neither hear, nor walk, nor see. Carpenter then reviews the origins of idols, and cites for authority Augustine, the Dominican Robert Holcot, and others who say that demons live in such idols. This history, says Carpenter, leads to doubt as to whether Christians should be permitted to adore any image. Carpenter more fully expresses his own qualms about the veneration of holy images in his discussion of the proper way to pray. Here he censures people who ask for help from "the dead images of saints"; even if they are indeed healed, these people are deceived if they attribute this cure to the "virtue and power of the image." Rather, it is likely that such healing is accomplished through "an illusion of the devil," whose actions God allows on account of the "unbelief" [*incredulitatem*] of the people.[23]

Carpenter's disquisition exemplifies the vexed issues raised by image veneration in the late Middle Ages, and the contradictory efforts to resolve them. Lollards and orthodox theologians alike agreed that idolatry violated the First Commandment:[24]

Thou shalt not have strange gods before me. Thou shalt not make to thyself a graven thing, nor the likeness of any thing that is in heaven above, or in the earth beneath, nor of those things that are in the waters under the earth. Thou shalt not adore them, nor serve them. (Exodus 20:3–5)

Yet defining idolatry itself was no simple task. Was idolatry the deliberate or even accidental worship of demons in idols? Or the improper worship of images of saints? Could holy images *be* idols? Did people indeed believe that spirits—albeit beneficent ones—inhabited such statues? All contributions to the debate seemed riddled with contradictions. Margery Baxter could assert the Lollard view that images were nothing but pieces of wood and stone, but also insist that they were inhabited by demons. Alexander Carpenter suggested the same thing, without noting any inconsistency. The *Omne Bonum* agreed that the Old Testament showed that demons had entered material forms and responded to people's questions; nonetheless, while its entry on "Idolatria" acknowledges the danger of idol worship, the author maintains that one may commit idolatry in numerous ways that have nothing to do with idols: through unworthy reception of the Eucharist, for example, or through rebellious disobedience or greed, or paying attention to sooth-saying and divination.[25] Most orthodox apologists simply assumed their images of saints to be free of any pagan taint, and instead elaborated arguments about how the proper mode of worship warded off idolatrous sin. In this, they missed the point of the Lollard objections and never fully answered them.

Although few of her contemporaries seemed to agree with Margery Baxter that demons dwelled in the ubiquitous statues of the saints, the persistent Christian condemnation of idols created an abiding suspicion of any devotion to sculpted or painted objects. The paradox posed by carvings, paintings, and other visual representations of God, the Blessed Virgin Mary, and the saints, tantalized late medieval thinkers: These images could give rise to great devotion and yet might also incite damning acts of idolatry. How could the Christian Church promote the first and prevent the second of these possible consequences? This question became increasingly urgent in England in the fourteenth and fifteenth centuries, as Lollards repeatedly accused the clergy of promoting idolatry and the laity of simple-minded acquiescence in this grave sin.

This problem lay at the heart of the controversy swirling around images in late medieval England. The denunciation of image worship became standard in Lollard criticisms of contemporary religious practice, but their protests against images as occasions of sin soon met a wall of resistance in the treatises penned by churchmen justifying the traditional custom of image veneration. No one denied the potential for sin; the biblical specter of idolatry, resurrected by the Lollards, loomed large in these centuries, and only fools ignored its threat. Defending holy images required, therefore, more than the simple reiteration of custom. Apologists for sacred art had to define, clarify, and justify the Church's position on several interlocking issues: the nature of visual representation and its relationship to the invisible deity; whether contemporary Christians must obey God's commands to Old Testament Jews; and perhaps the most pressing concern, how closely must the beliefs and practices of laywomen and laymen conform to the teachings of the Christian Church. The authors of these works often disagreed, and these treatises thus disclose various late medieval understandings of the intellectual, aesthetic, and social components of religious practices and identification.

Few of the arguments regarding images' dangers or their benefits were new. Lollards and image defenders alike repeated—knowingly or not—opinions and judgments about religious art that were developed centuries earlier. Sacred art had often sparked controversy among Christians. Early Christian apologists decried pagan idolatry, and many demanded that Christians reject art. In the second century, Clement of Alexandria worried about art's deceptive powers. Origen proclaimed the Old Testament prohibition against making images to be binding on Christians, and said that reverencing statues led men to believe they were gods. Eusebius, the early church historian, protested any representations of Christ in art.[26] Still, by the fourth and fifth centuries, wall paintings and other artwork were integral to the Christian Church's efforts to teach the faith. Like relics, crosses became common devotional aids.[27]

The most enduring and best known statement from the West championing sacred art for its pedagogic value came from Gregory the Great, who reasoned that illiterates could learn from images, or "read" in them, what literate people read in books. So many later writers adopted this apology that the concept of images as *libri laicorum* or "books of the laity," became a commonplace in the Middle Ages.[28] Iconoclastic controversies riddled the Eastern Church in the eighth and ninth centuries, provoking the Western response in the *Libri Carolini,* in which Carolingian theologians sanctioned images only as church ornaments and reminders of saintly heroism.[29] In the following centuries cathedrals, churches, monasteries, and wealthy laypeople continued nonetheless to acquire holy images. Yet misgivings always adhered to sacred art; the ancient fear of paganism never died, that people would commit idolatry by worshipping an image as a living and divine being. St. Bernard of Clairvaux's famous invective against art derided "the thoroughly beautiful image of some male or female saint," which people believe to be "the more holy the more highly colored the image is." Bernard chastised the church as "radiant in its walls and destitute in its poor. It dresses its stones in gold and it abandons its children naked." St. Bernard's complaints about the deceptive nature of images and the so-

cial damage they caused by drawing money away from the poor anticipated the arguments voiced by English Lollards a few centuries later. Yet
Bernard also spoke to monks, launching his objections primarily at art in
the monastery; it was different for bishops, he wrote, who had to "stimulate the devotion of a carnal people with material ornaments because they
cannot do so with spiritual ones."[30]

Despite such qualms and criticisms, holy images became central to
Christianity. In late medieval England, as elsewhere in Europe, holy images
permeated every aspect of religious ritual, popular belief, and devotional
practices.[31] As parish churches grew up and out in small-scale versions of
the great cathedral building campaigns of the twelfth and thirteenth centuries, laypeople filled their interiors with works of art that they then venerated. Men and women acting individually or as members of religious gilds
endowed churches with stained-glass windows, paintings, and gilded and
painted statues carved in wood or stone. The rich also possessed their own
religious statues and commissioned fabulous prayer books illuminated with
paintings of scenes from the lives of Christ, the Virgin Mary, and the saints.
Famous images drew kings, merchants, and peasants to renowned shrines
like Walsingham in Norfolk, but images reputed to perform miracles could
also lead people to obscure corners like the village churches at Foston in
Yorkshire and Kersey in Suffolk. This widespread veneration of images, the
money lavished on them, and their integration into the material and spiritual fabric of the English Church, made them ripe for Lollard attack.

"Near of Kin to Idolatry": The Lollard Dissent

While Lollards embraced a variety of not always uniform beliefs, Margaret
Aston points out that they were consistently hostile to images, although
their views ranged from simple criticism to outright iconoclasm.[32] Lollards
tended to focus disdain on exterior shows of piety, like pilgrimages and offerings to shrines, promulgating instead what they considered to be a more
interior devoutness. Most Lollards founded their rejection of images on the
First Commandment, which they believed explicitly forbade the making
and worshipping of images. The echo of the prohibition in Exodus rever-
berated through Lollard discourse, and they also cited warnings against
idols from Psalms and the Book of Wisdom, proclaiming their doctrinal
grounding in the Bible. Against images, for example, the priest Richard
Wyche cited the Decalogue, Psalm 96, and Wisdom 13:10.[33] John Burell,
tried for heresy in Norwich in 1429, testified that his brother had taught
him the Decalogue in English, and that the First Commandment instructed him that no honor was to be shown to images sculpted by men's
hands, "ne likened after hem in hevene above ne after hem that be in water

benethe erthe, to lowte thaym ne worsshipe thaym."[34] Sixty years later in 1491 John Tanner of Steventon, in Salisbury diocese, abjured his belief "ayenst wurshipping of ymagis seing that we shall wurship no stokkis ne stonys ne nothing made or graven with mannys hand of no lykenesse of thingis in heven ne erth." Another man admitted that he learned to spurn holy images

> aftir the doctrine of a Boke of Commaundementis which I have had in my keping wherin is wreten that no man shall worship eny thing made or graven with mannys hand, attending the wordis of the same litterally And not inclynyng to the cense of the same.[35]

From such literal interpretations of the biblical injunction arose the Lollards' rationalistic condemnations against worshipping images, and there was much in Christian tradition to support their view. The Commandments were not easily dismissed, and the Decalogue provided ammunition against religious art both for early Christians fighting paganism and later for iconoclasts in the Eastern Church.[36] Yet not all Lollards believed the Old Testament ban on images to be absolute, and this position also had authoritative backing. Repeating the formulation of Gregory the Great, for example, some Lollards conceded that images might perform a limited educational function as "signs and tokens" from which laypeople could learn as clerks did from books. The leader of the 1414 Lollard rebellion, John Oldcastle, confessed his belief that images could only be "calendars to lewed men to represent and bryng to mynde ye passyon of oure lorde Jesu Cryste and martyrdom and good lyvyng of other seyntes. . . ."[37] John Wycliffe himself found images acceptable as *libri laicorum,* although he also thought that they could be dangerously misused by the laity. In his Latin commentary on the Commandments, he wrote that images could be put to both good and evil purposes; images might excite the mind to worship God more devoutly, but could also lead one astray from the faith.[38]

Despite Wycliffe's words, most Lollard men and women simply seemed to oppose images, protesting repeatedly that holy images of the saints, the Virgin Mary, and even the crucifix were nothing but "stocks" [wood] and stones, their words deliberately emphasizing the inanimate nature of the images. Because wood and stone were characterized by the absence of spirit or life, Lollards particularly objected when these material objects were revered as though they were alive, as if images somehow embodied holy persons rather than simply representing them. The gift of life belonged only to God; thus attributing life to anything made by human beings defined the essence and evil of idolatry. In their protest against reverencing what is only matter, Lollards repeated an objection that was voiced by pagan Greeks, later adapted by Christians to condemn pagan idolatry, and then by Eastern iconoclasts determined to eliminate icon worship. Like these predecessors, Lollards complained that reverence owed to God was misdirected and degraded in being given to material objects.[39] At his trial for heresy in 1429, the chaplain Robert Cavell admitted that he had believed that trees growing in the woods were of greater virtue and deserved adoration sooner than stone or "dead wood" carved in the likeness of a human being, an idea he likely learned from the condemned William White, who was earlier charged with asserting the same thing. White itemized devotions to holy images by saying that trees deserved to be adored by "prayers, genuflections, oblations, pilgrimages, and lights" more than did the "dead idols" in churches.[40] Some Lollards in Lincoln diocese were said to believe that it was as worthwhile to kiss the stones lying in the field as the feet of the figure of Christ on the crucifix in church, the latter clearly referring to contemporary practice.[41] *An Apology for Lollard Doctrines* eloquently recalls the biblical litany of the various incapacities of images: If they fall to earth, they cannot rise; if any set them up, they shall not stand; they cannot ordain a king, nor give riches, nor "quit" evil; they cannot deliver a man from death, nor restore the blind to sight, nor help a man in need; they will not have mercy on the widow, nor help the fatherless; they cannot shine as the sun nor give light as the moon. Images have neither the miraculous powers of God, nor the sovereignty of a king, nor the ability to perform the simple acts of charity that any human being can do.[42]

Another Lollard tract repudiating images and pilgrimages repeatedly contrasts the "deade ymagis" and "dede stones and rotun stokkis" to the "quicke ymagis of God, þat ben pore folc." This writer excoriates those "lewid folc" who believe that images perform miracles, and are in fact the saints themselves, so that they address the images by name, as the "swete rode of Bromholme" or "oure dere lauedy of Walsyngham." He condemns those verbal addresses and physical postures of worshippers that presumed the presence of saints in their statues, saying they

> cleuen sadly strokande and kyssand þese olde stones and stokkis, layying doun hore grete offryngis, and maken avowis riȝt þere to þese dede ymagis to come þe nexst ȝeer agayn, as ȝif þei were Crist and oure Lauedy and Ion Baptist and Thomas of Caunterbery and siche oþer.[43]

Lollards abhorred this practice of stroking and kissing statues and naming them as one would a person, so that the statue assumed an individual character. The rhetorical contrast of the "dead" and "quick" images of statue and human being intensified the insinuations of idolatry. Biblical passages made clear that worshipping a "dead thing" constituted idolatry, and a statue was indisputably lifeless, unable to see, breathe, hear, feel, or walk.[44] Using this terminology, Lollards accused Christian holy images of kinship to the forbidden idols of the biblical gentiles. At the Norwich heresy trials held in the early fifteenth century, Hawisia Mone confessed that she had believed the crucifix and images of Our Lady and other saints to be idols, and that worship and reverence were due only to the "ymage of God, whiche oonly is man." Likewise John Skylan declared that the cross should receive no more reverence than a gallows, "for al suche ymages be but ydols and the makers of hem be acursed." William Hardy's description of the cross as "the signe of the Antechrist" proposed a further association between holy images and the devil.[45]

Rejecting the emotional attentions and economic offerings bestowed on images, Lollards urged instead that people should redirect these to the "quick" images of God, their fellow human beings. Poor people were more truly created in God's image than any human-made statue or painting could be, so the money and gifts lavished on images should rightfully go to the relief of the poor. At his 1429 trial in Norwich, the wright John Pyrye confessed that he thought that the money people squandered on "worthless pilgrimages" should be spent on poor people who were the "images of Christ."[46] *An Apology for Lollard Doctrines* orders those who would worship the image of God to do well to a man "þat is maad to þe ymage of God" by giving him honor and reverence, and performing the works of mercy: providing meat to the hungry and drink to the thirsty, clothing the naked, ministering to the sick, welcoming the stranger and visiting the imprisoned. In fact, says the *Apology,* the person who *could* perform these deeds but does not, shall be thought to "do despit to þe ymage of God."[47]

Anticlerical sentiments contributed to Lollard definitions of idolatry, which cast clerics as greedy for both money and undeserved reverence. Some Lollards suspected that unscrupulous clerics used images to enrich themselves by promoting belief, for example, in the miraculous powers of an image and thereby inspiring the awe and capturing the offerings of pilgrims. In 1491 William Carpenter confessed to an episcopal court that he said it "were better to geve a poreman a peny" than to go on pilgrimage to an image, and that offerings to images "be made but only for the availe and lucre of the pristis" and not for the benefit of the soul. The *Apology* went further, warning readers about those prelates that commit the "werst idolatri" by taking to themselves the honor that God should have; people should obey, trust, and serve these prelates only so far as God allows, for if they obey orders or trust words that are contrary to God's, they will commit idolatry with these priests.[48]

Perhaps the most deliberate and extensive accusations of idolatry launched against the worship of Christian images came from the *Twelve Conclusions of the Lollards,* a document posted on the doors of Westminster Hall and St. Paul's during the 1395 session of Parliament.[49] The *Twelve Conclusions,* says its author, would inform the lords and commons of Parliament about "certeyn conclusionis and treuthes for þe reformaciun" of the English church, the degeneracy of which is blamed on the "proude prelacye." The fourth conclusion charges the sacrament of the Eucharist, "þe feynid miracle of þe sacrament of bred," with inducing "ydolatrie," for innocent people are taught to believe that God's body is enclosed in "a litil bred" by the words of the priest. Here the Lollard writer indicts as idolatrous the belief that a lump of material, the bread, contained the presence of the sacred. The eighth conclusion also protests belief in the holiness of physical artifacts, now emphasizing their lack of sensory power—they are blind and deaf—and thus their inanimate and inhuman nature. It then declares that pilgrimage, prayers, and offerings made to these images are "ner of kin to ydolatrie. . . ." Calling this "forbidin ymagerie" a "bok of errour to þe lewid puple," the writer underscores the Decalogue prohibition of graven things, and sarcastically refigures the Gregorian defense of holy images as *libri laicorum.* Needy men, he claims, are a closer likeness to God than stock or stone because God did not say he made wood and stone to his image and likeness but he made men so.

Turning from biblical sources, the Lollard author then opposes images by repudiating standard orthodox defenses of image veneration, which referred to the different species of worship itself. Clerks name the high worship due to the godhead alone *latria,* while the "lowere worchipe" that belongs to men, angels, and lower creatures, is *dulia.* The corollary, he insists, is that the twice-yearly service of the cross is "fulfillid of ydolatrie," for if the rood tree, nails, and spear and crown of God should be worshipped in so holy a manner, then so would be the lips of Judas, if available. Clearly, this untenable conclusion must be averted by the rejection of all image worship.

The impact of this scornful and somewhat cryptic argument depended on its audience's knowledge of the kinds of worship distinguished by theologians. In the thirteenth century Thomas Aquinas had argued that one worships God with the highest adoration of *latria,* which should also be directed to the cross and to images of Christ. People should extend *latria* to images of Christ because the honor or worship given to images reaches to the prototype, to that which is represented by the image. Since Christ was adored with *latria,* so too should be his image. Thomas argued further that *latria* was due to the cross for two reasons: because it represents the figure of Christ extended on it, and because the true cross had contact with

Christ's limbs and was drenched with his blood. Thomas named *dulia* the honor reserved for purely rational creatures; the special veneration called *hyperdulia* is reserved to the Virgin Mary, in recognition of her special status as the mother of God.[50]

Fourteenth- and fifteenth-century Lollards strenuously objected to this classification of the three kinds of worship, each with its appropriate objects. In their view, this ridiculous system turned the rational order upside down, requiring the divine worship of *latria* for a mere piece of wood shaped into a cross, while granting human beings only the lesser reverence of *dulia*. Lollards remained unappeased by the argument, as Thomas explained it, that "no reverence is shown to the image of Christ in so far as it is an independent reality—a piece of wood, carved or painted—for reverence cannot be given to any but a rational being." Thus, says Thomas, the reverence shown to this cross "has in view its function as an image." In other words, the person looking at the cross understands it is mere representation, and is in truth venerating its prototype, Christ himself.[51]

Not all theologians agreed with Aquinas. His fellow Dominican Robert Holcot, for one, had expressed reservations about these gradations of worship. In his influential commentary on the Book of Wisdom, Holcot shows why objections might be raised against giving *latria* to images of Christ. While agreeing that a viewer might really be worshipping the person who was represented by the image, he questions the accepted usage that permitted the "same honor" to both the image and the "God who is imaged."[52]

While numerous Bible passages provided authority for the Lollards' condemnation of images, their own observations of the contemporary practices of image worship stimulated their allegations of idolatry. Lollards did not believe that their contemporaries, who knelt before statues weeping and stroking them, were venerating the unseen deity or saint. No matter what the theologians might say, these people worshipped the stone or wood itself. Image worship constituted idolatry, not because people misunderstood the distinctions of *latria* and *dulia,* but because these worshippers credited dead material objects with life and spirit. While other Lollards did not share Margery Baxter's idea that demons lived in holy images, it nevertheless pointed to the crux of the problem: these statues seemed alive. As the early-fifteenth century Lollard treatise *The Lanterne of Liȝt* contended, "þe peyntour makiþ an ymage forgid wiþ diuerse colours til it seme in foolis iȝen as a lyueli creature."[53]

Roger Dymmok's Reply to the *Twelve Conclusions*

Lollard objections to traditional religious thought and practice concerning holy images produced a counterwave of treatises aimed at elucidating and justifying the position of images in Christianity. Among these, the work written by the Dominican Roger Dymmok, doctor of theology and regent of the Dominican house in London after 1396, is notable for its detailed and voluminous response to each issue raised by the *Twelve Conclusions,* and also because the author wrote it for laypeople. Dymmok dedicated his treatise to Richard II and intended it, at least nominally, for a wide audience, which it likely did not receive.[54] Yet his conventional arguments in favor of holy images included both learned and popular explanations of their history, authorization, and purposes, and his work thus forms a digest of contemporary orthodox views regarding sacred art. In addition, the theological discussions and terminology that Dymmok reviewed appeared in abbreviated forms in vernacular religious literature. While Dymmok's work itself was an unlikely source for this more broadly disseminated literature, it provides a useful introduction to the orthodox arguments in favor of image veneration in the late Middle Ages, and illustrates as well their limitations.

Instituted by God: the Old and New Testaments

Dymmok wrote sixteen chapters defending images in his *Liber contra xii errores et hereses lollardum,* aiming in the first five to demolish the dangerous accusation of idolatry. These chapters, devoted to proofs that "Images of the crucifix and the salvation-bringing cross of Christ are to be adored with the adoration of *latria* by the faithful of Christ," assert God's authorization for artistic renderings of the holy, investigate the nature of visual representation, and prescribe the correct stance for worshippers to assume before holy images.

Dymmok's first statement in chapter one repudiates Lollard protests that holy images violated the First Commandment by asserting that "the custom of the church in the making of images was useful and instituted by God."[55] Stories from the life of Christ furnish the particulars of the divine sanction of images, although these incidents lack biblical foundation. One concerns a certain King Abgar who dispatched an artist to paint Christ's likeness. The brightness of Christ's face made it impossible for the painter to look at him or produce the portrait; instead Christ impressed his image on a cloth by holding it to his face, and sent this cloth to Abgar. The veil of Veronica is another example of the "divine authority" of images; Christ was believed to have left the imprint of his face on the veil that she offered him as he carried the cross to Cavalry, and this veil—Dymmok reminds his readers—could be seen in Rome. Finally, he cites as further proof the legend of St. Luke as an artist who "painted images of Christ and the glorious Virgin."[56]

Dymmok believes these examples establish that images of Christ and the saints were "usefully and validly introduced." Christ himself made two of them, and St. Luke the third. Dymmok further undermines the authority of the Decalogue prohibition of images when he reasserts the historical origins of holy images in the New Testament and claims that the apostles established many things in the early church not found in scripture. As St. Paul wrote, tradition was taught by word as well as by letter (2 Thes. 2:14).[57] Dymmok implies that Lollards erred and revealed their own biblical illiteracy when they ignored both the transmission of Christian teaching by word and scripture's acknowledgment of its own lacunae.

Although Dymmok places the historical birth date of holy images in the "time of Christ and the Apostles," he also shows that God ordained certain images for the use of Old Testament Jews. To refute the Lollard contention that the Decalogue prohibition forbade humans to make any image, he recalls that God permitted the ancient Jews to make images such as the carved cherubim that overshadowed the mercy seat on the top of the Ark of the Covenant. Was this not the work of human hands [*nonne opera manuum hominum*]? And the Temple in Jerusalem—was it not also built by human art [*nonne manufactum et hominum arte constructum*]?[58] Later Dymmok also notes that at God's command Moses erected a brass serpent in the desert (Num. 21:8). Holy Scripture objects *not* to these sanctioned images of the Jews, but to the sacrifices made by Greeks and gentiles to demons. The sculptures of the Greeks were the "images of demons" and thus detestable and condemned. These Old Testament examples prove that God did not forbid all images in his commandment. Instead, the Decalogue prohibited images being made either "for the purpose of adoring them as God" or, just as importantly, for picturing God, who at that time in human history was incorporeal and thus could not be represented by any bodily likeness.[59] The Incarnation of Christ marked the beginning of legitimate images of God. Once God had taken on a human body and lived on earth, then he could be represented in bodily likeness. Even the Trinity could be represented in various forms in order to express the spiritual truth of the unity of the three persons.[60]

In each of his efforts to challenge the Decalogue's seemingly absolute prohibition against images, Roger Dymmok drew on defenses of art that had emerged in the early Christian era and evolved in the face of opposition to art in both the East and West. His appeal to unwritten tradition against Lollard biblical fundamentalism reiterated a cherished iconodule argument from the Eastern Iconoclast controversy, which stated that many church practices, like the use of icons, were hallowed by long practice.[61] Similarly, Dymmok's references to divinely sanctioned Old Testament images echoed another defense of images developed in the Eastern church;

as early as the seventh century, Leontius, Bishop of Neapolis in Cyprus had cited God's orders to Old Testament Israelites to create certain images, and John of Damascus later took up this line of reasoning: God himself had broken the prohibition in Exodus. In 787 the Seventh Ecumenical Council at Nicaea used several Old Testament texts to establish the validity of venerating icons.[62] For most image defenders, however, the crucial argument centered on Christ's Incarnation. Images of Christ show the historic fact of God made man, and thus teach the doctrine of the Incarnation. Among Byzantine iconophiles, this point reigned supreme, not only justifying images, but demanding them.[63]

Dymmok's taxonomy separates pagans, Jews, and Christians according to the kinds of images each group constructed. Pagan "Greeks" or "gentiles" worshipped sculptures of demons as gods, an abominable practice. God gave the ancient Jews the First Commandment to prevent them from committing the same offense, but he allowed—even ordered—them to make and use various images in their religious practice, although never likenesses of the divine. After the birth of Christ, however, Christians were permitted to figure the divinity, and holy images became a lawful and beloved part of Christianity. Lollards were thus mistaken in understanding the Decalogue to prohibit Christian images. Indeed their hatred of images linked them to contemporary Jews, who were popularly reputed to despise the crucifix and other sacred art. Dymmok relates two tales from *The Golden Legend* in which crucifixes bleed when Jews strike them, causing the astonished Jews to convert to Christianity and turn their synagogues into churches.[64] Dymmok's implication is clear: holy images can save even God's enemies, heretics and Jews.

The Nature of Images

God ordained holy images for his church because of the superiority of visual depiction over verbal representation. An image "speaks more certainly to us and, like a sign, impresses more firmly on the memory what is to be understood than does the written book." Images are more powerful than words because of the nature and organization of the human bodily senses; Dymmok cites John Chrysostom (d. 407), who claimed we learn better through seeing than hearing because the ears are less disciplined and educable than the eyes; the ears' placement opposite each other shows this, as if what enters through one exits through the other.[65] In championing the pedagogic power of images over words, Dymmok repeated an idea with origins in pagan classical thought, later adapted by Christian writers. Chrysostom himself had drawn upon a tradition that emphasized vision's importance for understanding and memory. In his *Metaphysics* Aristotle had declared that the sense of sight is above all the other senses because it "makes us know and brings to light many differences between things."[66] In Cicero's *De Oratore* the poet Simonides is credited with the discovery that "the keenest of all our senses is the sense of sight"; perceptions are better retained if received "by the mediation of the eyes" than by other senses.[67] Martianus Capella (fl. after 410), whose work *De nuptiis Philologiae et Mercurii* transmitted the ancient art of memory to the medieval world, linked memory to vision when he wrote that "the remembrance of things is held by the images, as though they were letters."[68] When Pope Gregory the Great compared holy images to books, he relied on this classical notion to confirm for Christians the validity and value of sight and image in teaching the faith. Arguing against iconoclasts in Byzantium, John of Damascus and other iconophiles insisted on the primacy of sight in apprehending God.[69] In the West, Peter Lombard affirmed that feelings of devotion were better aroused "by things seen than by things heard"; and in the thirteenth century St. Bonaventure declared that "those things which are only heard fall into oblivion more easily than those things which are seen."[70]

Having argued that vision is preferable to hearing, Dymmok then maintains that the arbitrary nature of nouns, which are simply accepted conventions, also argues for the superiority of visual images, which actually bear some likeness to what they represent. The intimate and above all truthful bond of image and prototype cannot be matched by words. A depiction of a man whipped and crucified, he says, more forcibly reminds us of the Lord's mercy than letters that tell of the same thing. While acknowledging that sacred writings teach us what we should believe, Dymmok believes that images teach the same things "more clearly and immediately."[71]

Finally, their nearly universal audience makes images better teachers than letters. Letters "speak and are signs only to clerics and experts" while an image "is a sign indiscriminately to clerics and laity."[72] Dymmok later expands on this notion of the all-embracing nature of images. Holy Scripture was produced for the benefit of all. Christ's deeds on earth—his miracles and sufferings, crucifixion, resurrection, and ascension—were written down "for our memory and knowledge," so that those "not seeing, hearing and believing might obtain the blessing of the Lord." Yet, despite this gift of scripture, not everyone has the ability or leisure to read; therefore, the Fathers contrived to have these holy things depicted in images "for swift memory."[73]

Dymmok's strong arguments favoring images over letters were perhaps meant to curry favor with his semi-literate audience, while maintaining the general clerical mistrust for scripture reading by the laity.[74] Dymmok suggests that looking at holy images is a valid substitute for reading Holy Scripture.[75] By advocating not just their general instructional value but also their superiority to letters, Dymmok broadens the concept of images as *libri laicorum*. Along with their pedagogic function, images have a mnemonic one, bringing to mind Christ's life and passion in a fashion that letters cannot imitate. Further, he admits an unusual, but not unprecedented, parity between priest and people by insisting that images can be worthwhile to clerics and laity alike.[76] Dymmok's investigation of the nature of images asserts their power to impress their viewers, their close relationship to sacred truths or events, and their accessibility to both literate and illiterate.

Latria *and* Dulia: *The Dynamics of Devotion*

Having demonstrated the divine authority for images and their pedagogic usefulness, Dymmok then establishes how worshippers should regard them. The Lollard *Twelve Conclusions* objected that people offered *latria* to images, the adoration that belonged only to God. Deriving his explanation from Aquinas and the authorities Aquinas in his turn had adduced, Sts. Basil and John of Damascus, Dymmok explains that honor paid to an image passes to its prototype, the person who is imaged. Because Christ is to be adored with *latria,* so too are his images. The corollary is that people do not honor the material image in itself, but what it brings to mind.[77]

Lollards condemned this understanding of *latria* as directing higher honor to "dead" images than to living men who were the "quick" images of God. Dymmok counters with a dissection of the technical workings of *latria*. The rational nature of human beings is worthy of honor on its own merit, but directing *latria* to humans would not lead to the honor of God. On the other hand, *latria* directed to the "dead image" that is "worthy of no honor in itself but only because of him of whom the image is," does not rest in that image, but "completely redounds to what is imaged." Dymmok believes that *latria* shown to a rational nature somehow lodges there; conversely, because insensible wood and stone are incapable of receiving and holding any honor, they pass *latria* on to the one depicted. Turning the Lollard argument on itself, he argues that *latria* given by one man to another leads the adorer to idolatry and the recipient to pride. Because images (as Dymmok needlessly points out) are not prone to pride, these wretched consequences are avoided by proper worship. The conclusion, which grated against the Lollard sense of the high value of human beings, is clear: Images of God deserve the highest honor of *latria* and human beings do not.[78]

The images of saints must be treated differently from the crucifix or other depictions of God. Dymmok affirms that relics of the saints may be venerated as parts of bodies that were once "instruments of the Holy Spirit" and that would be rejoined to the saints themselves at the Last Judgment. God confirms the sacredness of these relics by frequently revealing the burial sites of saints and performing miracles in those places. Dymmok then conflates "relics and images," reflecting widely held views about their similar natures, and allowing images to share in the sacral quality that inhered in the bones. He argues that Christians honor both image and relic as substitutes for and representatives of the absent saints. Saints are pleased by offerings to their relics and images, and these oblations also testify to Christians' subjection to the saints. Further, as signs of "reverence and honor" these gifts are in harmony with the lesser worship called *dulia,* appropriate to the saints.[79]

Pilgrimages and offerings at shrines were among the "exterior signs" criticized by Lollards, who believed such devotional superficialities absorbed people at the expense of true spirituality. "And now men shulden be more gostly and take lesse hede to siche sensible signes," wrote one Lollard.[80] On the contrary, Dymmok argues that these "exterior signs" are necessary and desirable. Precedents for pilgrimage exist in the Old and New Testaments, but ordinary human behavior provides an equally strong justification: "Nor indeed does it suffice for the lover to hide his love on the inside, but rather he should strive to reveal it by exterior signs, with service, that is with tributes and honors."[81] Gifts and bodily prostrations, moreover, are signs of reverence owed by inferiors to superiors. Further, Aquinas taught that human beings learn from what is "sensible" (that which the senses can perceive), so it is natural, says Dymmok, that they use "sensible" things to honor God. Although it is proper to offer sacrifices to God, there is no possible danger of idolatry in these acts venerating saints' images and relics, because of their relationship to the Creator, and because this devotion receives approval from the Bible, from social custom, and from the workings of human reason.[82]

In his understanding of the relationship between an image and its prototype, and of the hierarchy of veneration, Dymmok's arguments again repeated those elaborated in previous conflicts over images. As early as the third century, Origen had distinguished between honor and veneration, and Augustine himself had clearly defined the difference between *latria,* due only to God, and the respect owed to men.[83] When eighth- and ninth-century iconoclasts accused image worshippers of idolatry, icon defenders in Byzantium opposed them by pointing to the different forms of veneration given to God, to men, and to material items; they also pointed to the relationship between image and prototype. In complex and subtle polemics, John of Damascus, Theodore the Studite, and others argued that despite the "difference in essence between image and prototype, there is an identity of likeness" so that the two are venerated in the same way.[84] Although Carolingian bishops in the West first rejected the image defenses developed by the Eastern Fathers, by the twelfth century Western canonists and theologians had rediscovered the Greek arguments and integrated them into their standard justifications for the now flourishing cult of images in Western Europe.[85] Christian image defenders insisted that honor is never paid to wood or stone, but to God and the saints, of whom the images remind the viewer. At the same time, Christian tradition also admitted that images—like relics and other holy items—could be conduits for divine power.[86]

Dymmok's defenses of images were based in a textual tradition that had developed over centuries, and for the most part he overlooked the practices that incited Lollard disapproval. Where Lollards worried that image veneration was charged with improper emotion and shadowed by misunderstandings of basic Christian truths, Dymmok spoke of an intellectual process that neatly aligned forms of adoration with their appropriate objects. He dismissed idolatry as irrelevant to Christian devotion. The dynamics of image devotion worked out by the Greek and Latin fathers and their successors taught that when a Christian honored an image, that honor reverted to the prototype, God or saint. This rendition of image worship ignored Lollard descriptions of people stroking, kissing, and speaking to statues as though they were alive. Concerned to defend the theory of image worship, Dymmok shrugged off problems that arose in its practice, displaying a grand indifference to pastoral care and to the commonsense truths of Lollard complaints. Nowhere is this clearer than in his response to Lollard protests against images of the Trinity as misleading people into thinking of the Father as an old man and the Holy Spirit as a bird. This bothers Dymmok not at all, who says disparagingly, "And if the laity imagine something false on account of that picture, it is to be blamed on them, not the image"; they are like heretics who misconstrue Holy Scripture to develop their heresies, although scripture in itself is good and faithful.[87]

Walter Hilton: "If they knew better"

No writer revealed more fascination with this delicate interaction between image and viewer than the Augustinian canon Walter Hilton, who responded to Lollard activities and denunciations with a treatise on images written in the late 1380s or early 1390s.[88] In contrast to Roger Dymmok, Hilton understood and sympathized with the psychological and emotional appeal of images, the pull on mind and heart that could nudge a viewer from orthodox adoration into sin. While the two defenders of images often use the same arguments and cite the same authorities,[89] their attitudes toward the laity and image worship differ dramatically. Dymmok fends off charges of idolatry by referring to the doctrines of *latria* and *dulia,* but he explains each only in terms of its object, and not by the spiritual and physical stances that distinguished the two. In contrast, Hilton carefully describes how *latria* and *dulia* differ, but also asserts that people who adore Christian images are sanctioned, whether or not they worship in the approved manner. Whereas Dymmok censures the laity who fabricate false ideas from images, and compares them to heretics, Hilton repeatedly stresses that errors committed in ignorance will be forgiven.

Hilton's sympathy for the laity's need for holy images springs from his sense of the historical moment in which they (and he) live. Members of the early church were few in number but nearly perfect, whose strength in faith needed no exterior signs for support; likewise, at the end of time, when the faithful will see God face to face, all signs will be abolished:

> In the early church, the few faithful who believed in Christ were almost all perfect, always prepared to submit to martyrdom for the faith. Nor did they need to be drawn to devotion through the exterior signs of images or other corporeal signs, because with the memory of Our Lord glowing freshly in their hearts and with the grace of the Holy Spirit visiting them in greater abundance, they were completely ready for all the torments to be sustained in Christ's name; and therefore in the time of the early church there were few signs.[90]

During this middle era, however, "cause, means and end" recommend the use of images in churches: "The cause, indeed, is the benefit and salvation of the simple, carnal, and weak in the Church." The means is the signification of past and absent things, and the end is eternal happiness. Although Hilton acknowledges that images are offered "to the eyes of the laity and clergy for contemplation," it is the link between defective human nature and the need for material signs that forms the basis of his reflections on how and why Christians adopted images. Few believers are perfect; indeed, in the early Christian centuries so many people received the faith that the church was "almost swamped." Among this "multitude of believers" were many who were "imperfect, carnal, and ignorant," who had little notion of "spiritual things" because they were yet "joined to earthly things. . . ."

> And therefore because weak human nature is always prone to evil and disposed to the vanity of this visible life, quick in forgetfulness of that which pertains to the future life, the church considering this, like a pious mother . . . ordains suitable remedy against the weakness of the flesh, namely the use of corporeal signs, through which the obstinate are humbled and the idle are exercised, taught, and instructed, and the feeble are led to the internal and spiritual knowledge and love of God.[91]

Enlarging on his conception of the simple laity [*laicos simplices*] as weak, carnal, and childlike, Hilton describes them as "poor in faith and tepid in love" who need to "drink from the milk of corporeal signs." In contrast, the perfect sons of the church have matured beyond their need for this "milk of corporeal signs" because "with the solid food of truth and spiritual adoration, they feast from within."[92] Although their feebleness leads the church to nourish her weakest children with the material "food" they crave, Hilton scorns neither them nor their hunger. Physical artifacts like images can be pathways to spiritual truth, and to reinforce this point Hilton repeatedly compares images to the sacraments. The metaphor of images as spiritual food also links them to the consecrated Host, a bond emphasized when Hilton notes that the crucifix placed above the altar represents the sacrifice reenacted on the altar.[93] The crucifix presents visually the body of Christ, who is actually present but unseen in the Host. Further, Hilton insists that the weakest have a right to their place in the church, because Christ called to the "banquet not only the strong, the healthy, and the unscathed" but also, to fill his house, "the weak, blind, and crippled." The church holds these latter through corporeal signs, because removing them would allow these children to "be destroyed by hunger. . . ."[94]

Hilton also uses historical time to delineate the error of the Jews, and to clarify the differences between their images and those of Christians in his own day. Just as Jews used rituals and corporeal signs to recall the past benefits of God, so the Christian Church ordained "images of Christ crucified and his saints" so that these carnal objects would teach viewers to recall the "spiritual benefits" shown to humanity. The Judaic signs, however, were both "memorials of the past favors of God" and also prefigured the future, namely the coming of Christ. Once Christ had appeared in the flesh, these signs should have been eliminated; "whence the Jews err, still vainly observing these figures." In contrast to these Jewish figures, Christian images either commemorate the past or denote "the presence of hidden things," as do all sacramental signs, which provide visible forms to invisible grace.[95]

Like Dymmok, Hilton appeals to authority and custom, but his most impassioned defense of image worship arises when he describes precisely how it works. He admits that out of ignorance the "the simple and laypeople" may "direct all their affection and thought around the viewing and adoration" of images, but as long as their intent is good, as long as they "want to include themselves in the bosom of the universal church through faith, humility, and love" they will be excused. To clarify this point, Hilton explains that those who are lettered and learned, as well as the devout laity [*litterati et docti et deuoti laici*]—those who see that an image is nothing but wood or stone, have no affection or reverence for its material substance, but use such images only for recollection—keep the "explicit intention" of the church. They may fall down before images to pray to God and the saints, but the images themselves may be forgotten. An image may stir the memory of divine things for the learned or devout person, or may hinder his or her prayer. With the ring of experience Hilton describes how "those who wish to pray spiritually usually close the exterior eye or avert it from the object of the image, lest the purpose or attention of the mind be diverted through the sensory apprehension of the object."[96]

This ideal behavior cannot be expected from the "simple laity," who still keep the "implicit intention" of the church in their image worship. Hilton confronts and admits the truth of the charge that images distract these people from thoughts of God; a "pretty image skillfully painted and preciously decorated" can lead their minds by "a certain carnal reverence" to adore this image more than another, and to occupy their intellect and emotion in their exterior senses rather than in God. Nonetheless, Hilton contends in his principle argument, "their intention is habitually directed to God" in whose name they adore the image, because their "affection for the sensual and carnal is diverted and regulated according to the form and manner" established by the church. The church forgives their imperfect and blameworthy adoration, if they submit to her "faith and intentions."[97]

Hilton reiterates this major point—that good intentions will make up for ignorance and error in image worship—because its significance extends beyond the immediate concerns about idolatry. Dymmok explains with excruciating and unconvincing exactitude how people worship with *latria* here and *dulia* there, but Hilton faces the fact that people will blunder. He resolves the dilemma by insisting on the ascendance of faith and love. Should image worshippers never attain "explicit knowledge of the faith," yet they will be saved, for despite their errors they "implicitly" grasp the faith of the church and this is enough. Hilton says, "it is sufficient to believe as the Church believes," and declares that those who adore images believe that they are acting in harmony with the rules of the church. They should be judged by this intention, and not by their deeds.[98]

Ideally, adoration should vary according to its object. Due only to God, *latria* consists on the interior of "faith, hope, and love," and is evidenced on the exterior by "reverence, obedience and sacrifice." *Dulia* is the reverence and submission given to both temporal and spiritual lords and the saints. The faithful, says Hilton, are criticized for showing improper adoration to images because of the "exterior disposition of the body" that they display. Yet "simple people and laity ought not to fear idolatry in such adoration of images" even though both exterior sense and interior emotion are concentrated in their external reverence to images. They believe they are acting according to the customs and intention of the church. "If they knew better," says Hilton simply, "they would wish to do better. . . ."[99]

The Widening Circle of Debate

By writing in Latin, Walter Hilton ensured that his treatise on image worship would not be widely read by the laity. His work and Roger Dymmok's belong to the discussion of idolatry and image worship that took place among churchmen in the late Middle Ages in response to Lollard critiques.[100] Hilton's and Dymmok's writings reveal two distinct points of view regarding image worshippers rather than a single or monolithic response to the Lollards; fuller investigations of other contributions to this debate might uncover other theories about images and their worship. The wide variety of opinion about images in late medieval England is also evident in other kinds of works that aimed at influencing laypeople's beliefs and practices. The linked issues of idolatry and images were never limited to being topics of merely academic discussion. Lollards, as we have seen, discussed them in vernacular treatises, in private conversations, and at their trials. Idolatry and image worship also appear as subjects in preacher's manuals, vernacular treatises of devotion, and even poetry.

Roger Dymmok's reasoning about image worship perhaps carried abstraction to an extreme; the lack of concern for human emotion or intent that characterizes his writing finds little echo in other works. More commonly, writers plunged into the ambiguities of human behavior, as did Walter Hilton, in order to understand the boundaries of idolatry. Alexander Carpenter's *Destructorium Viciorum* repeats most of the arguments used by Dymmok, but unlike him, considers their problematical results as well. On the idea that *latria* should be offered to images of God, Carpenter cites Holcot's work and the opinions of Sts. Basil, John of Damascus, and Thomas Aquinas in reaching a conclusion. Clearly troubled about offering "true adoration" to stone or wood because this means that "something other than God" can be called "God"—the very definition of idolatry—Carpenter offers this resolution instead: In speaking freely it is said that we adore the image, but "it seems to me that it must be said that I do not adore the image of Christ" but instead that "I adore Christ before the image of Christ," and "because it is the image of Christ, it inspires me to adore Christ." Carpenter thus accepts the Lollard point that carved or painted images had the power to move their beholders, but still rescues image worship from total condemnation through refining his reading of the authorities.[101]

Hilton's and Carpenter's efforts to understand what really happened and what should ideally happen when a believer looked at an image, is paralleled by a work written in English but with the Latin title *bonus tractatus de decem mandatis*. This work insisted on the deadness of insensate images, but also admitted their legitimate veneration. Images can be made well and ill, says the author; images can stir "þe soules of goede cristene folke" to devotion, but can also be the occasion of error when they are "worscheped as god." Like Carpenter, the author says that he worships Christ "by fore þe ymage of crist." Then he proposes the correct actions and postures of image veneration. When first entering the church, we should kneel upon the ground, and if the "holy sacrement of þe auter," which is Christ's body in the form of bread, is above or upon the altar, then "worschepe it wiþ al þyn heorte, soule, and mynde." Then when you see the cross, you must think with "gret sorowe and compunccioun of heorte" on the death he suffered for mankind. "And so byfore þe cros þat meueþ þe to deuocionn worschepe þou crist wiþ al þy myȝt." The author's hierarchy descends from the consecrated Host to the cross then continues with a consideration of images of saints. By "ymages and peynture," he says, you can know how holy saints loved almighty God, and how they suffered for love of him. St. Lawrence is painted and graven holding a griddle in his hand, "bytoknyng and schewyng how laurence was yrosted upon a gredel." So too St. Katherine's wheel and sword demonstrate the means by which she suffered. By the sight of saints' images our devotion is moved "þe more deuouteloker to worschepe god." Should we mistakenly offer to the saints or their images the worship that belongs only to God, they will be offended.[102]

The author of the *bonus tractatus* links Host and cross, then cross and saint's image, and distinguishes the reverence owed to each. Only the Host, which *is* Christ, receives the worship of heart, soul, and mind, the total devotion of which the believer is capable. The cross evokes an emotional response, stirring the heart to sorrow and remorse. In contrast, the saints' images teach how the saints suffered, so that inspired by their example beholders would increase their own devotion to God.

The *bonus tractatus* clearly demonstrates an effort to educate people in proper image behavior, and numerous late medieval works of spiritual instruction and guidance made similar attempts. People's tendency, which Walter Hilton so clearly recognized, to veer from the straight and narrow path of sanctioned image veneration, was one impetus for the transmission of orthodox defenses of images from the pages of academic Latin treatises to the vernacular works read by parish priests and literate laypeople, considered in the next chapter. The discussion of the problems that seemed inherent in image worship spread beyond the writings of theologians and their Lollard antagonists. Orthodox defenders of images responded to the heretics' cries of idolatry by articulating a range of arguments that supported image worship. Sermons and vernacular works of religious instruction, in turn, carried the defense of images to the laypeople whose behavior was, after all, the heart of the issue. If they were the "fools" who thought that a saint's statue spoke to them, if they venerated images with the highest worship possible, then they must be instructed differently. To

eliminate idolatry, laypeople must learn, for instance, the difference between *latria* and *dulia*. Lay education in image worship was thus one result
of Lollard iconomachy.

Yet the relations of church and laypeople were clearly not in the fifteenth century what they had been in the time of Gregory the Great. In
particular, increasing literacy, briefly nodded to by Hilton in his reference
to the educated layperson, meant that many laywomen and laymen no
longer had to depend on holy images as religious primers. Once they
could read, what need had they for substitutes for books, for images as *libri
laicorum?* The laity did not, however, dispense with holy images in their devotions; they seemed, if anything, ever more attached to the statues, paintings, and stained glass that they encountered in their parish churches and
visited at shrines near and far.

Many laypeople whose supposed illiteracy formed an essential part of
the orthodox justification of images could now in fact read how holy images should work for them as described in the poetry of Thomas Hoccleve
and John Lydgate. Neither Hoccleve nor Lydgate reduced images to simple *libri laicorum;* both detailed a process of looking that was more complex
and exalted than this descriptor suggested. In his 1415 *Remonstrance Against
Oldcastle,* Hoccleve, a fervent defender of orthodox views, attacks Lollard
condemnations of images, calling it "greet errour" to hold against image
making. He avows that images stir good thoughts and cause men to honor
the saint "after whom maad is that figure." Scoffing at the notion that anyone might mistake an image for the real person of the saint, Hoccleve flatly
denies a major Lollard critique of image worship. Men do not worship the
image, "For this knowith wel euery creature / þat reson hath, þat a seint is
it noght." He uses a homely metaphor, and one that readers would most
appreciate, to explain how image worship works:

> Right as a spectacle helpith feeble sighte
> Whan a man on the book redith or writ
> And causith him to see bet than he mighte,
> In which spectacle / his sighte nat abit
> But gooth thurgh / & on the book restith it;
> The same may men of ymages seye.[103]

Hoccleve suggests that images help their viewers to perceive and appreciate more fully—to "see" better—the holy people and events represented
by images, and his poem also illustrates a key point of the orthodox defense, that honor passes through an image to its prototype.

Where Hoccleve outlined the mechanics of image veneration, John
Lydgate detailed their potentially salvific or redemptive effects. His poem

on the "Image of Pity" or pietà, urges readers to "behold and se / The moder of Cryst." This sight should bring beholders to rue the pain Christ suffered, to pray to the Virgin Mary, and to confess to a priest "whill this is in thi mynd" and thus be cleansed from sin and saved from the devil. If tempted to sin "Thynk how thow sest Cryst bledyng on þe tre" and the temptation will cease. By these means, even the weakest creature can ward off the fiend and "saffe hym-selffe in sole and body sure." Lydgate's poem teaches that looking at an image and keeping it in remembrance can move its viewer to contrition, prevent further sins, and be the means to salvation. After this forceful proclamation on the power of images, Lydgate concludes somewhat feebly but still insistently:

> To suche entent was ordeynt purtreture
> And ymages of dyverse resemblaunce,
> That holsom storyes thus shewyd in fygur
> May rest with ws with dewe remembraunce.[104]

Views about holy images spanned a wide spectrum in the late Middle Ages, ranging from Margery Baxter's habitations of demons to Hoccleve's spectacles for improved vision. The contrary opinions and argumentative voices still sputter and boil from the documents left behind: Fools think the statue lives, no creature of reason considers stone or wood to be alive; simple people treat images as God, putting all their hope and trust in them; if their intent is good, people do not sin. Idolatry is conceived, variously, as the unintentional worship of demons in images of saints, the deliberate worship of any image, the misplaced offering of *latria* to a saint's image, the belief that an image is animated by a holy person, or the trust that image devotions will reap spiritual rewards.

The single thread that links these diverse and contradictory notions about images and idolatry is the attitude toward the "simple laity," as Walter Hilton dubs them. Every voice raised—from common people on trial for heresy to the Dominican Roger Dymmok—spoke as though apart from this great amorphous mass of people, whose actions were, depending on one's point of view, appalling or forgivable or sinful, and also ostensibly the cause of the commotion about idolatry. These (presumably) orthodox laypeople did not contribute to the polemics they inspired, and their silence amplifies the sound of the voices raised in contention about the meaning of their devotions. Despite their literary muteness, however, their relations with holy images can be explored in the scattered documentary and artifactual evidence they left. In their contributions to parish churches and religious gilds, in their wills and in the prayer books they read, the laywomen and -men of late medieval England paid homage to the images of God and the saints, regarded them as symbols of social and political identification, employed them as sources of inspirational meditation, and made other varied uses of these statues and paintings, unacknowledged and perhaps unseen by either orthodox defenders of images or their Lollard opponents.

CHAPTER 2

DIVERSE DOCTRINES:
RELIGIOUS INSTRUCTION AND HOLY IMAGES

> þer beþ so manye bokes & tretees of vyces and vertues & of dyuerse doctrynes, þat þis
> schort lyfe schalle raþere haue anende of anye manne þanne he maye owþere studye
> hem or rede hem.[1]

Readers interested in the issue of holy images could find a great number of vernacular writings that, like Hoccleve's and Lydgate's poems, took up the defense and definition of proper image worship. Many kinds of late medieval English texts abounded in talk of holy images, from stories of miraculous crucifixes to prescriptions for proper veneration of a saint's statue. Vernacular sermons, lives of the saints, explications of the Ten Commandments, and manuals for devout living present a dizzying array of demon-inhabited idols replaced by Christian statues, holy statues, and pictures that spring to life to defeat their desecration by Jews, as well as reasoned arguments about how Christians might properly venerate sacred art.

Spurred by the Fourth Lateran Council of 1215, medieval bishops and councils in England worked to improve lay religious education. In time their efforts spawned a multitude of instructional manuals, sermon collections, and treatises grounded in canon law and moral theology, explicating basic Christian tenets such as the Ten Commandments.[2] Many of these works, perhaps originally intended for clerics with pastoral duties, became available in the vernacular and were read by laypeople. This literature did not only preach a simplified Christian doctrine, although the intent of reaching a wide and unevenly educated audience shaped its organization and topics. It also participated in contemporary discussions about religious belief and practice, including the vexed issue of the worship of holy images.

Some of the Middle English works of religious instruction clearly drew on the Latin polemics produced by the image defenders like Dymmok. Latin remained the language for an educated, if not purely clerical, audience, but increasing vernacular literacy in the late Middle Ages demanded texts in English. Vernacular religious literature repeated in abbreviated form key arguments about the nature of images and their proper veneration, and also reflected the theologians' real concern over erroneous, albeit innocent, uses of images. These texts mirrored an abiding uneasiness about the laity's apparently large and indiscriminate appetite for the quasi-magical qualities often associated with holy images. Manuals of religious instruction took part in an effort to quell this appetite by educating laypeople in some of the finer points of image theology, intending to produce a more intellectual and acceptable image veneration. Treatments of the subject range in length from a few sentences to several pages, encompassing diverse approaches and showing little agreement on how to resolve the multiple problems that images presented.

While certain Middle English religious texts tried to teach their audiences proper image veneration, others—notably sermon *exempla* and saints' legends—recycled centuries-old tales of wonder-working crucifixes and animated statues of the Virgin. These images appear as the *loci* of supernatural powers, performing miracles, speaking, and moving. Their heavenly prototypes work through them, and the formal relationship between the image as the signifier, and the saint who is the signified, fades as the two become one. The apparent simplicity and even naiveté of these stories can deflect serious investigation of them, but increasing attention to their content has demonstrated their importance in delineating cultural attitudes. Thus late medieval vernacular literature presented strongly contrasting views of holy images. Efforts to inculcate in clerical and lay readers the theologically correct approach to images confronted ancient and folkloric elements that encouraged viewers to regard holy images as the embodiments of heavenly figures.

Explicating the First Commandment

Instructing the laity in the Ten Commandments was a basic pastoral duty, so Decalogue commentaries commonly figured in the manuals of religious instruction. The First Commandment's ban on worshipping graven images provided the occasion for commentary on image worship, although similar discussions sometimes appear in treatments of the Seven Deadly Sins or of idolatry. Writers confronted an essential problem: How could Christians venerate holy images in the face of the clear prohibition in Exodus? Many authors acknowledged that contemporary image devotions seemed to be at odds with the apparently absolute interdiction. Several interpretations arose to bridge the gap between Commandment and practice: One argued that God intended the Commandment only for the Old Testament Jews because of their notoriously bad behavior; since Christians were not given to such sins and excesses, this law did not apply to them; a second pointed to scriptural exceptions to the prohibition as evidence of its lack of universality; yet a third argument rested on translation, stating that the Commandment only forbade worshipping images, but allowed their veneration. This last explanation was grounded in the distinction between *latria,* the worship appropriate to God alone, and *dulia,* the reverence allowed to others.

A major point of contention in the debate centered on the relationship between images and what they represented. Lollards claimed that worshippers confused images with their prototypes, and for this reason credited the images with supernatural powers or even supernatural being. The orthodox response—that people who worshipped images in fact adored their prototypes—was problematic; it seemed more to prescribe ideal behavior than to describe common practice. After all, who could determine whether image worshippers addressed the image or the person it represented? In addition, images acquired miraculous associations from their identification with supernatural beings, so that dismantling any notion of images' wonder-working capabilities became a priority among churchmen. This had been a concern even prior to Lollard accusations. A fourteenth-century Decalogue commentary, perhaps the work of the mystic Richard Rolle (ca.1300–1349), emphasized the First Commandment's negative force in prohibiting witchcraft, charming, sorcery, divining by stars or dreams, and "mawmetryse" or idolatry. This standard interpretation of the First Commandment thus links images to magic, but Rolle insists that holy images deserve reverence. Men should love holy crosses, he insists, for they are the "syngne of Cryste crucyfiede." Images should be given the "louynge" that is due to those whom they represent, and "ffor þat Entent anely þai are for to lowte" [for that reason only they are to be reverenced].[3] Rolle states in the simplest terms what theologians discussed at length, the relation of the image as signifier to the holy person as signified. "Reverence" and "respect" are all that is owed, however, implying that more emphatic emotional displays violated the Commandment's spirit. Images must remain symbols, pointing their beholders to their prototypes. This restraint on the nature of images and their veneration anticipated later and lengthier discussions.

The bond between images and magic reappears in *Jacob's Well,* an early-fifteenth-century collection of sermons that instructed readers on all subjects they needed to consider in order to make a good confession. In *Jacob's*

Well image veneration belongs to a discussion of the Seven Deadly Sins, falling under blasphemy, a subdivision of wrath. The author condemns people who "grucchyst" or speak against God in their tribulations, who set "no pryse be pylgrimage to sayntes & to ymages," and who mistrust the church's prayers and suffrages because they are not instantly delivered from their troubles. The author emphasizes that the church's rituals are neither magical nor superfluous; turning against them is a serious sin.[4] *Jacob's Well* divides the laity into two groups: those who lacked respect for the external rites of pilgrimage and image veneration, and their polar opposites, those who expected images, pilgrimages, and church rituals to respond to their needs and became angry when they did not. The author regards images as part of a larger category of religious devotions liable to misunderstanding, for which the blame rests on laypeople. The rituals and holy objects of the church were intercessory in nature, providing the places, moments, and sensory apparatus through which humans might beg for the prayers of the saints and God's mercy and grace. Expectations for automatic results were completely misplaced and mistook these devotions as akin to magical exercises.

Pedagogic works like *Jacob's Well* tended to condemn misunderstandings in faith or defects in religious practice; no doubt the genre encouraged this attitude. Rather than adopting Hilton's charitable view that errors in image worship were trivial offenses, many Middle English works promoted precise mental postures toward images as the only way to avoid sin. The best example may be the *Speculum Christiani,* a compilation of materials for religious instruction, popular in the fifteenth century, which focuses on the "dangers of ignorance."[5] The issues of image worship and idolatry appear, not in its First Commandment explication, but in an appended commentary offering a detailed albeit confusing exposition of image orthodoxy. The author condemns all the standard idolatries, including the worship of deviltry, the sun, moon, planets, stars, elements, men, irrational beasts, and also images or any other man-made work. Idolatry is "a grete synne" because it takes worship away from God and gives it to an unworthy creature. Specifically, idolaters give to the worshipped object what only God deserves—the veneration of *latria,* the "commune subieccyon of fre seruise and worschipe owght to god." *Latria* is distinct from *dulia,* the "subieccyon of seruise and worschip doon to man and to eny other."[6] Idolatry is thus defined as misdirected *latria.* The worshipper, through accidental error or sinful choice, has given the highest adoration of *latria* to an undeserving recipient that merits only the lesser honor of *dulia.*

This exposition of idolatry finds parallels in several First Commandment commentaries. The popular *Book of Vices and Virtues,* for instance, a Middle English translation of the influential thirteenth-century *Somme le*

Roi, asserts that the First Commandment teaches us that we make a false god and commit deadly sin if we honor, serve, or love anything more than God. A variant manuscript expands on this, saying that gluttonous men make their bellies their God, and that men set themselves up as God through their pride and desire for worldly worship and vain glory.[7] Idolatry could mean more than misguided image worship, so that the intensity of the *Speculum Christiani'*s focus on images suggests increasing anxieties about them.

The strong condemnation of idolatry stakes the *Speculum Christiani* author's claim to authority and orthodoxy in discussing images, which he excuses from any blanket denunciation. "Note here wele," he says emphatically, that the commandment forbade the worship of images with *latria* but not with *dulia.* Although "Moses forbeed grauynge[s] [graven things] and similitudes of false goddes to be worschiped and prayede to," his intention was not "to for-bede vtturly" their making. Moses himself had the carved cherubim made for the Ark of the Covenant. Therefore, the Decalogue prohibition never banned "ymages and portrature" for the purpose of bringing to mind the lord God. Indeed, "this es not drawynge to ydolatry, bot rather reuokynge fro ydolatry." Having cracked the door of image worship open this far, the author then almost slams it shut again, in his care to back away from the precipice of error toward which images might lead. "Bot to make ymages bi cause to worschipe hem only, it es forbedden vtturly," he declares, underscoring this prohibition by citing a litany of authorities—Wisdom, Isaiah, Augustine, Jerome, and others—on the perils of idolatry.[8]

The *Speculum Christiani'*s ambivalence toward images confuses its message. Legitimate image worship depended on the devotee understanding the distinction between *latria* and *dulia.* The potential pitfalls appear so numerous, however, that it seems unlikely anyone understood or used this information. What was the reader or listener of this text to understand about *latria* and *dulia?* It is silent concerning the interior and exterior states that mark each form of worship. Further, not all theologians supported the *Speculum Christiani'*s divisions. Thomas Aquinas, for one, had argued that the crucifix was in fact due the highest worship of *latria.* Since honor paid to an image went to its prototype, said Aquinas, the crucifix was due *latria* because it reached to Christ, but saints and their images do not receive this highest worship.[9] The *Speculum Christiani* ignores such difficulties, moving instead to reconcile the biblical prohibition of images as improper objects of worship with the common medieval practice of image devotion, and bridging the perceived gap between the two by discussing the varieties of worship as embodied in the *latria/dulia* duality. The text aims to affirm the Decalogue prohibition, teach the proper worship of religious images, and deny Lollard charges of idolatry. Yet its incomplete, even incomprehensible, instruction on *latria* and *dulia* results in a muddle.

Ineptness often accompanied determination in teaching these forms of worship. One collection of sermon materials for parish priests, the *Speculum Sacerdotale,* alludes to the problem that the saints themselves, like their images, presented potential occasions of sin; a believer might displace God by giving a familiar saint primacy in her private pantheon. The *Speculum Sacerdotale* offers a hierarchy of different forms of worship as a preventative. We do not intend, says the author in the introduction, that offerings and sacrifices to saints' altars and chapels are for them; they are for Him who "is God of hem and of vs bothe." We give saints the same devotion we give to living holy men; offering *latria* to any but God is idolatrous. *Latria* is defined by this tautology: "Therefore the Lord God oweth only to be worschipid with sacrifice and worschip in the effect of the worde 'latria', whiche worschip is only propirde to the godhede." People commit "punyschable" and "dampnable" idolatry when they offer to a martyr, saint, or angel the worship that belongs to God alone. Should *latria* be offered to saints or angels they will refuse it, says the *Speculum,* knowing themselves to be only servants of God.[10]

The lack of substantive or meaningful definitions for these terms must have made it difficult for parish priests to teach them to parishioners. *Latria* and *dulia* remained, nonetheless, a part of religious instruction, receiving perhaps their most complete vernacular exposition in *Dives and Pauper.* This fifteenth-century work is shaped as a dialogue between Dives, a worldly and critical layman, and Pauper, a defender of the clergy and orthodoxy. *Dives and Pauper* addresses images and the forms of worship in a First Commandment commentary longer than 100 pages that covers much of the late medieval spectrum of image theory.[11]

Dives and Pauper begins with Dives provoking Pauper by declaring that the First Commandment clearly forbids any image worship as idolatrous. Pauper responds by citing Old Testament image uses, concluding like the *Speculum Christiani* that God forbade "vttyrly" only that men worship images as gods. Unimpressed, Dives advocates that all images be burned. Pauper's answer asserts the three primary rationales for religious images promoted by late medieval theology: They stir people's minds to think of holy events like Christ's Passion and the lives of the saints; they move viewers' affections and hearts to devotion, for people are more often moved by sight than by hearing or reading; finally, they were ordained as books to common people so that they could "redyn in ymagerye and peynture þat clerkys redyn in boke. . . ."[12]

Pauper's apologies for holy images echo the arguments developed over the centuries in Christian theology and often repeated by the anti-Lollard image defenders. All three justifications for images avoided the thrust of the criticism that simple people mistook images for their prototypes. Dives asserts just this, claiming that people pray to the images themselves:

> For þei staryn and lokyn on þe ymage wyt wepyngge eye. þey heldyn vp here hondys, þey bunchyn here brestys and so be here eye and here contenaunce, me thynky3t, þey doon it al to þe ymage.

> [For they stare and look on the image with weeping eye. They hold up their hands, they beat their breasts and so by their eye and their countenance, I think, they do it all to the image.][13]

Using the analogy that the priest says mass in front of but not *to* a crucifix, Pauper explains how the behavior that Dives describes may be done in front of an image, but not to it. This debate is finally irresolvable because Pauper's position refers to the interior mental or spiritual state of the image worshipper. He points to what worshippers should think and feel, but Dives describes how they act, treating images as though they were alive and graced with miraculous powers.

To dispel a major difficulty in defending image worship—the credulity of the laity—the author of *Dives and Pauper* turns to the variety of forms of worship. Pauper seizes on the linguistic confusion bedeviling interpretations of the First Commandment. The word "worship," he explains, encompasses several kinds of devotion: first, the divine service of *latria;* next, *dulia,* which belongs to rational beings; and finally the "veneration" due to holy objects such as books, chalices, vestments, and images. Performing this veneration does not subjugate the devotee to the object, so reverencing images in this way cannot be idolatrous.[14]

Pauper's nomenclature of worship is driven by the author's conviction that the laity must understand the subtleties of *latria, dulia,* and "veneration," in order to avoid sinning out of ignorance. A more theologically adept laity must conform itself to these differences, and their behavior will also stop the criticism of images, which are harmless if properly used. *Dives and Pauper* thus joined the *Speculum Christiani* and other late medieval works in combining traditional defenses of images, especially that they were books for the illiterate laity, with an insistence on this division of worship. Each kind of adoration must be matched to its appropriate object. *Quattuor Sermones,* printed by Caxton ca.1483, provides a succinct blending of these rationales for holy images. "Lewd men" learn from images whom they should worship and imitate, it says, just as clerks learn this from books. But "to doo Goddys worship to ymagis euery man is forbede." The worshipper seeing the cross should have "mynde in the

passyon." Then he or she should look at the images of the saints, not believing in these images but so that the sight of them will bring to mind the
saints in heaven, whose lives one should imitate.[15]

Dives and Pauper also acknowledges images' emotional impact. Whereas
Dives reiterates Lollard complaints that people weep over, kiss, and caress
images, Pauper notes the tender sentiments that images should arouse.
When Dives asks how he should read in the "book of peynture and of
ymagerye," Pauper details the proper response to the sight of a crucifix. His
answer shapes a protocol of image worship, directing the onlooker where
to focus, what to think, and how to feel. Generally, the beholder must
think of Christ and his sufferings. More particularly Pauper says one must
"take heid" from the image how the crown of thorns went into his brain,
and the blood "brast out on euery syde" to destroy pride. "Take heid" from
the image how Christ's arms were spread and drawn on the tree "tyl þe
senuys and þe veynys crakyddyn" and how the hands streamed blood, all
to destroy the "wyckydde werkys" men and women do with their hands.
Further graphic descriptions order one to note the wound in the side,
Christ's heart cloven in two, the scourging that left his body without any
"hool place," and the blood flowing from his feet. Each limb of the holy
tortured body carries its reminder of Christ's suffering for human sins.
Then Pauper elucidates the spiritual meaning of the image. Look again, he
says, at how the head of the image is "bowyd doun to the, redy to kyssyn
the. . . ." His arms and hands spread out on the tree show that Christ is
ready to embrace you, kiss you, and take you to his mercy. His side is open
and his heart cloven in two to show that his heart is always open, ready to
love and forgive. His feet nailed to the tree show that he will not flee but
will abide with you forever. Pauper urges Dives

> On þis maner, I preye the, rede þin book and falle doun to grounde and
> thanke þin God þat wolde doon so mechil for the, and wurshepe hym
> abouyn alle thyngge, nought þe ymage, nought þe stok, stoon, ne tree, but
> hym þat deyid on þe tree for þin synne and for þin sake, so þat þu knele, ȝyf
> þu wylt, aforn þe ymage nought to þe ymage.[16]

Pauper's vivid sketch of the dynamic between image and viewer strains
the boundaries of the bland prescription that images should "bring to
mind" Christ's Passion or the lives of the saints. In noting each wound,
drop of blood, and every mark of suffering that the image shows, the onlooker identifies with Christ in his Passion and also reaches a deeper spiritual knowledge of Christ's mercy.

Dives and Pauper offers an unmatched description of the interwoven emotional and spiritual power produced by looking at holy images. Few works

attempted this, but *The Pore Caitif,* once suspected of Lollard sympathies, as was *Dives and Pauper,* also develops a psychology of image veneration. A popular work read by clergy, nuns, and laypeople, *The Pore Caitif* is a compilation of religious tracts explaining the Creed, the Commandments, the Pater Noster, the gifts of the Holy Ghost, and similar topics.[17] The First Commandment is interpreted to prohibit witchcraft, charms, and conjurations, and to warn against loving any vice more than God. On images, however, *The Pore Caitif* proposes a different argument. The author admits that God forbade people to make images if they intended to put their trust in them or to do "goddis worship" [God's worship] to them. Significantly, though, God made this prohibition because the Jews were "so false in beleeue" that some worshipped an object made of gold, and gave the worship due to God to "symylitudis & licnessis" that they made themselves. Indeed, Christians owe all ten of the Commandments to the frailty of the Jews' faith. Because of their great idolatry, Jews were forbidden to make any similitude or likeness. Without pause, the author then adds that in many places the old law teaches that all such similitudes and images should be "kalendris to lewid folc" who can learn by images what clerks learn through books.[18]

The Pore Caitif's view of the Jews' idolatry, which they displayed in their worship of the golden calf and which distinguishes them from Christians, is typical of late medieval religious writings. Although the two peoples shared the Old Testament, they differed in their relationship to it and to Mosaic Law. For medieval Christians, the Gospels proclaimed a New Law that superseded the Old Law. In vernacular religious literature, the conflict between idolatry and image worship symbolized and confirmed the gulf between the Old Testament Jews and contemporary Christians. The Israelites' inclination to idolatry was widely accepted among medieval Christians. Thomas Aquinas argued that the Israelites' lack of culture made them unable to understand the idea of incorporeal modes of being, and thus they tended to idolatry, from which Moses tried to redirect them.[19] A visual presentation of this idea in a miniature in a fifteenth-century Flemish commentary on the Decalogue depicts worshippers dancing around the golden calf, while in the background Moses stands posed with the two stone tablets in his hands. [plate I.1] The burden of the Commandment's prohibition on making graven things thus fell on Jews, not Christians, who were excused from it by their faith and innocence of idolatry. Indeed, his determination to blame the necessity for the First Commandment's anti-idol provision on the Jews blinded the author of *The Pore Caitif* to the potential of this analysis for undermining the force of the other nine Commandments for Christians.

The Pore Caitif's allusion to images as "calendars" to simple people simply repeats the old formula of *libri laicorum.* More significant is its description of the psychology of image worship. Like *Dives and Pauper,* this author directs viewers on how to respond to images. Like *Dives* again, this response transcended simple notions that people learned from art the basic precepts of their faith. *The Pore Caitif* instead depicts image viewers as spiritually transported. When men first enter the church they should look to the high altar to see "goddis bodi in foorme of breed. . . ." Then they should direct the eye of their soul to heaven, thanking God that he should come every day for their soul's health. After this devotion to the Host,

> if þei seen ony licnesse of crist don on þe cros: haue þei þanne mynde vpon þe bittir peynes & passioun þat he suffride for saluacioun of mannes soule & herteli þanke þei him þerfore / and aftir þat if þei seen ony licnesse eþir ymage maad in mynde of ony oþir seynt: rere þei vp þe mynde of her soule to heuene / preiynge alle þe seintis þat ben þere to be meenes & preiers to god for hem. . . .

> [if they see any likeness of Christ crucified on the cross, they have mind of the bitter pains & passion that he suffered for salvation of man's soul & heartily thank him for it. And after that if they see any likeness or image made in remembrance of any other saint, they lift up the mind of their soul to heaven, praying all the saints that are there to be the intercessors & prayers to God for them. . . .][20]

This passage establishes a visual hierarchy that places the Host, as God's body, at the apex, then descends to the crucifix, and finally ends with saints' images. Images, including the crucifix, are distinct from yet validated by their association with the Host. All three of these material objects draw one's thoughts toward heavens, although the Host and the crucifix direct one's thoughts toward God, while other images lead only to the saints. Readers are warned against believing in image magic; saints' images cannot cure a person of spiritual or bodily illness, or give or deprive one of help or riches, or rescue a man from death, or restore a blind man to sight. They can only "teche men be þe siȝt of hem to haue þe better mynde of hem þat ben in heuene," and encourage people to imitate the actions of the saints' earthly lives, which won them heaven.[21]

This antimagic warning does not rid the images, however, of the associative power of the supernatural qualities of the Host. Michael Camille has commented on how the belief in the "real presence" of Christ in the consecrated Host influenced the way medieval people perceived images. The Host was a "visible thing . . . capable of becoming and not just signifying its prototype." The Consecration of the mass miraculously converted the bread into the body of Christ; what had been indeed the work of human hands became the holiest object in the universe. This metamorphosis was visualized most concretely by worshippers in miracle tales and by some medieval saints who saw the flesh or body of Christ rather than the disc of the Host at mass.[22] The growing cult of the Host in the late Middle Ages encouraged its adoration, and likely that of images as well.

The similarity of image to Host as sketched by *The Pore Caitif* presented problems. As physical objects for contemplation, both image and Host could lift one's thought to higher realms. Yet people's spiritual posture was supposed to acknowledge the distinction between the two, and *The Pore Caitif* tries to instill a sense of difference by setting limits to images' power, emphasizing their incapacity to perform miraculously. The tension caused by the ambivalent nature of images—whether they are purely material objects or whether they, like the Host, share in some essential quality of a supernatural being—finds expression in different versions of the above passage that exist in variant manuscripts of *The Pore Caitif.* One such manuscript protests any suggestion that the Commandments are not still in effect for Christians, for he says, "And þe same god þat was þanne is now wiþ þe same comaundementis." Nonetheless, there is room for images, for according to a "gret doctour" images "doon boþe good and harm." They are useful for men to whom they act as books, to teach them to love God more than they would otherwise. But images do harm to men who "sette her hope" or "scaterit her loue folily" in them, sins committed by the lewd and the learned alike. Furthermore, the greed of priests is the source of much of this error.[23] Perhaps this writer had Lollard sympathies, but orthodox believers too found images problematic. Neither good nor bad in themselves, the validity of interactions with images rested in the intent of the beholders. Blaming images made no sense, as it seemed to credit them with a power that all parties in the image dispute were concerned to deny.

The Pore Catif variant follows up this critique with another that is both moral and aesthetic. It complains about those "ouerlewid and to beestly" folk who rely heavily on images. Incapable of bringing to mind the goodness of God, or Christ's Passion, or the holy living and patient suffering of the saints without carved or painted images, these people can be led astray because the images are often created "amysse and contrarie to oure feiþ eiþer bileeue." These human-created objects should be replaced with those of God's, the diverse and wonderful workings and creatures that God himself created.[24] This version of *The Pore Caitif* echoed Lollard fears that images misled people by their inaccurate depictions, such as portraying Christ and the apostles as wealthy men. The more common version of *The Pore Caitif,* however, does not judge images themselves to be dangerous, but concentrates on educating the eye of the beholder, instructing readers how to cultivate the appropriate mental posture.

These works of religious instruction promoted the education of the laity beyond an ability to recite basic tenets of the Christian faith. Stung by Lollard descriptions of simple people venerating statues and pictures as sources of supernatural power, just as pagans and then Jews had supposedly worshipped their idols, these Middle English religious manuals acknowledged images' potential dangers while working to dispel those dangers. Advocating a rational approach to images, these works drew on subtle distinctions that not even theologians agreed upon to differentiate the varieties of worship. Lollards complained that image adoration represented an all too common superficiality in devotion as well as a profound misunderstanding of doctrine in a religion excessively devoted to exterior pomp and ritual. By insisting that worshippers first understand the differences between *latria* and *dulia* and simple reverence, and then reflect these in their practice, the works of instruction recast image worship as an interior movement of the spirit. Never explicitly stated, it is implied that the exterior behaviors of those venerating images is unimportant. What matters is not that people weep over or touch or caress the crucifix or statue of the Virgin, but how they think of it. Their devotions remain blameless so long as they understand the completely representational nature of the image, and do not attribute to it supernatural being or magical powers.

The efforts of these vernacular texts to inculcate a more intellectual and cautious approach to holy images, while still admitting their power to stir beholders' emotions, paralleled the Latin treatises written to refute Lollard attacks. Both the vernacular works and their Latin models faced enormous difficulties in reconciling the apparently absolute Decalogue prohibition of images with common religious practice, in which images were often treated as sources of power rather than as simple likenesses. Furthermore, this attempt to instruct laypeople in image worship met a strong countervailing force in other forms of popular religious and pastoral literature, primarily sermons and saints' lives.

Images in Exempla

Late medieval English sermon *exempla* and saints' legends teem with stories about holy images. These narratives about statues and paintings that console sinners, reconcile enemies, bleed when struck, and perform other miraculous deeds were usually borrowed from the collections of miracles associated with the Virgin Mary, *The Golden Legend,* or from popular compilations like the *Dialogus Miraculorum* of Cesarius of Heisterbach, the *Speculum Historiale* of Vincent of Beauvais (both from the thirteenth century), or from English works like the *Alphabetum Narrationum*. Medieval preachers customarily used brief moral tales within their sermons in order to teach doctrine and illustrate lessons in vivid and memorable ways. Historians today find these stories important sources for exploring what one has called "the commonplaces of their time," and recent studies have exploited *exempla* in order to examine such topics as medieval notions of gender and attitudes toward Jews.[25]

These tales recycled for their readers and auditors a vast lore about miraculous and animate images that posited these "works of human hands" as the sites or agents of active supernatural intervention in the quotidian world. Over and over, these wonder-working crucifixes and animate statues of the Virgin Mary convert skeptics to true faith and iconoclastic Jews to Christianity. Free from the qualms displayed by *Dives and Pauper* and the *Speculum Christiani* about the thin line separating idolatry from image worship, these stories instead encouraged their audiences to consider images as potential incarnations of their heavenly prototypes. These *exempla* and legends, which received continual retellings throughout the Middle Ages, are permeated by a view of holy images in complete opposition to that found in the prescriptive religious manuals discussed above. They are rooted in the conviction that pagan statues are evil idols while Christian images are divine emissaries, mediators of heavenly grace and justice. While scarcely reliable descriptors of popular belief or practice, these tales still reveal an entirely different stream of teachings about images, idolatry, and iconoclasm with which their audiences must have become quite familiar. Indeed, some *exempla* were so well known that key scenes from them were depicted in Books of Hours produced for the Bohun family around 1370. The three or four pictures that relate each *exemplum* accompany the standard prayers for Matins, Prime, and the other hours, but no other text explains them. Presumably the readers/viewers of these books needed no words to identify the familiar moral tales.[26]

Exempla offer plentiful evidence for late medieval anti-Semitism, reflecting general Christian hostility and especially the animus of the preaching friars toward Jews. Whereas *The Pore Caitif* and other didactic works picture Old Testament Jews as great idolaters, the Jews in *exempla* appear as iconoclasts seeking to destroy precious Christian images. In both cases, however, Jews' behavior in regard to images defines them and sets them apart from Christians. The Jews of the *exempla* invariably defile holy images, committing outrages that are followed by either death or conversion. This abuse of holy images parallels the infamous medieval stories of the Jews' violations of the sanctified Host, tales that became firmly rooted in *exempla,* in saints' legends, and also in secular literature and in late medieval chronicles.[27] The presentations of Jews as image-defilers and Host-desecrators served similar purposes, underscoring the holiness and power of the profaned objects and the anti-Christian nature of those who injure them.

One Middle English tale tells the simple story of a Jew who damages an image of the Virgin Mary and is instantly struck dead.[28] A more complex *exemplum* in the preacher's manual called *Mirk's Festial* repeats a story from *The Golden Legend* about a Jew who is incited by his great "envy" of Christ to enter a church and stab the figure of Christ on the cross with his sword. Blood spurts out of the image, soaking the Jew's clothes; these stains lead to the discovery of his crime and then to his conversion. In a fuller version of this tale in the *Speculum Sacerdotale* a Jew in Constantinople steals an image of Christ from the porch of St. Sofia, and "for the cursede enuye þat he hadde to this ymage" smites it though the middle with a sword and casts it into a pit. But his clothes are bloody, and the pit water also turns red. The pit is drained to uncover the image "fro the whiche there was blood flowynge oute vncessyngly. . . ." The emperor, presented with the image, instantly perceives that "som Iew haþ done this dede," and orders a search for the guilty one. The Jew is found, then confesses and converts, convinced of Christianity's truth by the bleeding image. The blood continues to perform miracles.[29]

One final variation on this story elaborates the basic motifs and emphasizes the image's relations to its prototype and its tormentor. A Christian man in the city of Beritus (Beirut) forgetfully abandons a crucifix in his house when he moves. The Jew who takes his house is accused of being a Christian when his neighbors discover the crucifix. An angry crowd beats the Jew and then turns on the image, declaring that they would do to Jesus' image what their fathers did to Jesus' body. They bind the figure, beat it, crown it with thorns, and nail it "fote and hond to þe cros." Finally they choose the strongest man among them to "take a sper, and wyth all his myght þrost hit to þe hert," making the image bleed. Finding the blood has curing properties, the Jews take it to the bishop, who in turns sends packages of it to various churches. This is the origin of the holy blood of Hailes, the famous pilgrimage site in England.[30]

These grotesque stories of bleeding images reframe medieval image worship. Rather than defending images by asserting their pedagogic value in replacing books or their mnemonic value in bringing God to mind more readily than do written texts, these tales reverberate with images' emotional, sensual, even primordial appeal. The crucifix *is* Christ on the cross, for both Christian defenders and Jewish attackers. The overt anti-Semitism of these *exempla* reinforced their listeners' negative views of Jews, while establishing which behaviors toward holy images distinguish Jews from Christians: Christians worshipped holy images, Jews attacked them. Still, Christians and Jews both perceive images to be more than representations, church decorations, or devotional aids. These *exempla* emphasize that Jews attacked crucifixes as though, or *because,* they made Christ present. The images prove their embodiment of Christ's humanity by gushing miraculous blood, just as the Host did when it was stabbed or torn by Jews. Should medieval audiences not accept literally the tales of bleeding crucifixes, they could still have learned that the desecration of holy images marked a despised people who hated Christ. Iconoclasm as a badge of anti-Christian sentiment could be a useful weapon in the battle against Lollardy in late medieval England.

Whether or not these stories of iconoclastic Jews helped to inflame audiences against the Lollards (there is no evidence for this), their anti-Semitism served specific purposes. Whereas Old Testament Jews fell into idolatry by worshipping improper objects like the golden calf, the *exempla* propose that Jews living since the time of Christ disclose their wickedness by attacking Christian images, usually the crucifix. Behavior attributed to Jews thus revealed both of the major if antipodal sins—idolatry and iconoclasm—connected to images. Like the Jews who defiled the Host, iconoclastic Jews performed a useful function for Christians, by showing the true nature of the images that can perform miracles when attacked. In contrast to these offenses of the Jews, Christians worship the proper objects in the correct manner; indeed, in the *exempla,* reverence for holy images often defines the Christian. The *exempla's* hostility toward the Jews becomes an act of Christian self-definition: Christians are the opposite of Jews, iconolaters as opposed to iconoclasts.

Exempla were familiar and customary points of reference across both time and space, since first Latin and then the vernacular languages of Europe repeated them for centuries, providing distant audiences with a common set of events, figures, and attitudes.[31] The origins of these image tales are usually unknown, although some can be traced to the early Middle Ages or late antiquity. Yet the historical production of one *exempla* or another is occasionally illuminated, reconnecting these seemingly trivial bits of literature to a specific social world. For example, the Middle English *exemplum* of the bleeding crucifix of "Beritus" clearly links the image to the incarnate Christ; the image suffers the same violence as had Christ, and then bleeds miraculous blood. Hans Belting ties this legend firmly to the famous crucifix of Lucca known as the *Volto Santo.* A version of the tale was mentioned at the Council of Nicaea in 787, and the icon that was its origin was brought from Beirut to Constantinople in 975. A ninth-century Latin account claims the icon was painted by Nicodemus, who witnessed the Crucifixion. The *Volto Santo* legend of Lucca traces this image's move from the Holy Land to Tuscany, and also transforms it from icon into crucifix. The treasury of San Marco in Venice held an ampulla of Christ's blood, believed to come from the image of Beirut, and this ampulla was joined in the thirteenth century by another miraculous cross that bled from knife "wounds." Belting emphasizes that the exalted rank of Lucca's *Volto Santo* among images stems partly from its supposed creation by Nicodemus and its Eastern origins; like the Veronica, this image has the authenticity of a relic.[32]

Miri Rubin has termed the Host-desecration tale a "blueprint for action," and shown the connection between literary narratives about Jews and their actual slaughter at the hands of Christians who heard and read these tales.[33] The effects of the *exempla* concerned with Jewish image-attackers are less known, but one case from Italy suggests that these stories might also foster violence. In 1493 a Jew was convicted and mutilated for defacing images of the Virgin Mary in Florence. He allegedly covered one statue of the Virgin with filth, ruined a pietà, then stabbed the face of the marble Virgin at Or San Michele, a deed strikingly similar to the Jews' actions in these *exempla*. Legally punished by having his hands amputated and his eyes removed, he was then given over to a crowd that completely mutilated him. The mob's savagery toward the Jew indicates the enmity and brutality that such stories might help to engender.[34]

Hostility to crucifixes and to images of the Virgin Mary forms a significant part of the image lore presented in the *exempla*. Animate images like the bleeding crucifixes in these *exempla* protest or thwart their own destruction, signifying their sanctity by their actions. No less dramatically, however, images in the *exempla* also instruct worshippers on how to regard them. One such *exemplum* concerns a knight who decides to forgive the man who killed his son. On Good Friday the two men are together in a church where they venerate the image of Christ on the cross. The image looses its arms from the cross, embraces and kisses the knight, saying, "I forȝeue þe, as þow hast forȝeuen for me."[35] Another *exemplum* recounts how a priest hoping to reform a prostitute gave her money to say five *Aves* in front of the Virgin Mary's image. As she does this, the prostitute sees the Virgin's statue speak to the carved infant Jesus in its arms. Astounded at hearing the two holy images/people talk, the prostitute is moved to reformation and confession, then immediately dies in anguish for her sins.[36] A third widely retold tale with multiple variants concerns a young man devoted to the Virgin Mary, who places his ring on the finger of the Virgin's statue. The hand closes on the ring, preventing its removal. When the youth later decides to marry, the image reminds him that he is already betrothed, so he leaves his bride-to-be and becomes a monk.[37]

Finally, an *exemplum* that combines the conversion motif with the sense of wonder that images supposedly invoked, recounts how a monk on pilgrimage to Jerusalem fell into dispute with a Jew, who refused to believe that a maid could bear a child. Yet because the monk praised the Virgin

Mary so highly, the Jew asked him to make an image of her that he might see it. The monk drew a "wondur fayre ymage of our lady, and hur chylde in hur arme, and a lytel feyre pappe on hur brest." The Jew was struck by her beauty, and as he looked at the image, he saw the child take the nipple in his hand and suck milk. The Jew was immediately converted to Christianity, admitting it was less marvelous for a maid to bear a child than for the image to do what he had seen. After baptism, the Jew turned to converting others.[38]

Many *exempla* celebrate the power of images' beauty to move their viewers, an aesthetic appeal noted and disparaged by Lollards and orthodox critics. A striking instance occurs in a Middle English version of the miracle of the Virgin known as the "Jew of Bourges." A Jewish boy who goes to church at Easter with his Christian friends is overwhelmed by the lamps, tapers, and beautiful images, especially that of a seated queen with a blissful babe on her arm. The boy feels ravished by the joy that the sights inspire. (In some versions he receives the Eucharist.) Later, when his angry father puts him in a hot oven as punishment for this trespass, the Virgin Mary rescues him. He, his mother, and all the town's Jews are converted. Despite this testimony to the power of a statue's comeliness, beauty was secondary to supernatural affiliation. In one tale, when a clerk scorns a roughly made statue of the Virgin Mary in a London church, it comes down from its pedestal and reproves him.[39]

These animated images perform on multiple levels. The images' movements and speech naturally inspire wonder and deference in the knight, the prostitute, the youth, and the Jew, just as the crucifixes' copious blood flow did in the iconoclastic Jews. This literal coming-to-life dramatizes how images might seize the attention of a casual viewer, while also instructing the *exempla*'s audience in proper devotion. Reverential awe befits the image worshipper, who may be struck by the image's lovely colors and delicate sculpting, as well as its embodiment of supernatural power. The holy images also affirm standard doctrinal lessons: God forgives those who forgive others; even the worst sinner may win salvation through the intercession of the Virgin Mary; Christ's mother miraculously combined virginity and motherhood. Such stories thus invoke the power of images to reveal God's will toward humans. In this context, finally, these *exempla* implicitly refer to and derive authority from the most significant medieval precedent for animated images—the crucifix in the church of San Damiano from which St. Francis of Assisi heard the voice ordering him to rebuild the house of God.

The *exempla* recommend praying before images, because this activity provides the devotee direct contact with the saint. A clerk who lived an incontinent life of "fleschely lustes" nevertheless prayed each day to the Virgin Mary before an image of her. When he dies he is allotted a lonely grave in a distant part of the churchyard, as punishment for his wicked life. But the Virgin then orders the archbishop to rebury the clerk among other holy men, as his prayers to her have saved him.[40] Another example concerns a pretty nun who runs away with a young man, placing her sexton's keys before the Virgin's image when she goes, commending them to the Virgin's keeping. For several years the Virgin performs the sexton's offices. When the disgraced nun returns to the convent, she discovers what has happened and falls down before the Virgin's image full of self-recrimination. The Virgin appears to her, and tells her to put on her habit and return to work.[41] A boy who lives in an abbey eats his meal in front of an image of the Virgin and child, and is one day rewarded when "the ymage of the chylde Ihesu came downe from his moders lappe & sat wyth hym." The boy and the image eat and speak together, but when the boy later tells the abbot of this, the image refuses to come to him again until the boy promises he will in the future come to dine with the image. Observing this, the abbot asks the boy if he too might go to that dinner, and the two "yelded vp theyr soules to God" on Christmas day.[42]

Even more than by their animation, images display their power by their effective intercessions for humans. When a plague incurred by the Emperor Justinian's heresy ravages the land, an image of the Virgin taken in procession cures the plague and the heresy.[43] A merchant of Constantinople borrows money from a rich Jew, and pledges surety by going with the Jew to a church where he holds the hand of the Virgin's image (or, in another version, the merchant pledges the image itself as surety). After a year the merchant, who has become rich in Alexandria, places the money in a chest and throws it into the sea, praying the Virgin to be its "schip and mast." She conducts the chest to the Jew, but he later denies receiving it. The two men go to the church where the merchant had first sworn on the image, and the image speaks, revealing where the Jew hid the money.[44]

The *exempla* and miracle stories fight a different enemy than do the works of religious instruction like the *Speculum Christiani* and *Dives and Pauper*. Positioning their Christian audience as anti-iconoclasts, the *exempla* encourage listeners to treat images as holy beings, a fusion of spirit with wood or stone or paint that is manifested by their movement, speech, bleeding, and powers to effect desired results. In contrast, the pedagogical manuals, recasting anti-Lollard theological arguments, battle charges of idolatry by their efforts to educate their audience in non-idolatrous behavior. The *exempla* are unconcerned with idolatry because this characterized only the worship of pagan statues and not Christian images. Medieval tales never confuse the two.

Images and Idolatry in the Legends of the Saints

Where the image *exempla* highlight the evils of iconoclasm, the popular presentation of idolatry can be found in another group of religious stories, the lives of the saints. Legends of the saints existed in a rich variety of forms in the late Middle Ages. Today the best known collection may be Jacobus de Voragine's *Golden Legend,* written in the thirteenth century and later translated in whole and in part into English and other languages.[45] Many other verse and prose collections of saints' lives and miracles also circulated, so that legendaries formed one of the most popular sources of reading material among the laity. Collections of saints' lives were owned by monks, Oxford fellows, and parish rectors, but also by kings, knights, ladies, masons, and fishmongers.[46] The popularity of one Middle English collection of saints' lives, the *South English Legendary,* continued for over two centuries, from its origin in the thirteenth century to the late fifteenth century.[47] Several fifteenth-century English writers produced new lives of the saints, including the prolific Augustinian John Capgrave of Norfolk, and Osbern Bokenham, an Austin friar of the convent of Stoke Clare in Suffolk. In addition, sermons recycled condensed versions of saints' lives from *The Golden Legend,* and incidents from these stories formed the subjects of miniatures in prayer books and paintings on church walls. While the sermons and legendaries include some medieval saints, there are many more missionaries and martyrs from Christianity's first centuries. These legends define early Christian heroics in large measure by the destruction of idols.

As their Middle English lives recount, the first Christian missionaries found idol demolition a necessary prelude to the work of conversion; indeed, it was at times the only work required for preparing pagan peoples to accept Christianity. Pagans are cast as idol worshippers and tormentors of Christians, two characteristics that fully denote their ungodliness. Pagans typically torture and kill the Christians, whose major crime is refusing to sacrifice to idols. The battle over idols, and their eventual removal or destruction, encapsulates the entire conversion process. St. Andrew is martyred for his refusal to offer to "mawmets," as are St. Lawrence and St. Eustace. St. John is exiled to Patmos for refusing to sacrifice to idols. St. George fights his dragon but then undergoes torture rather than worship idols. By his prayer, a heathen idol of Apollo is melted and its temple destroyed. Mary Magdalen convinces the heathen inhabitants of Marseilles that their idols are deaf, dumb, and therefore powerless.[48] Even the youthful Jesus destroys idols; the early-fifteenth-century verse *Life of Saint Anne* recounts how he caused all the "fals godys" in an Egyptian temple to fall down, leading to the conversion of the city.[49] In Persia, Sts. Simon and Jude try to destroy belief in an idol by commanding the devils living in it to leave: "And a-noon two grete blake and nakyd gyantis passid oute of þe symilacres. . . ." They are nevertheless put to death for refusing to worship idols. Preaching in India, St. Bartholomew exposes another idol-residing fiend who had fooled people into believing it was a god.[50]

The Middle English tales of evil spirits living in idols derived from ancient sources (see chapter 1). Yet none of these legends suspects any kinship between Christian images and pagan idols. In their universe, the categorical opposition between pagan and Christian meant that Christian images naturally lacked this capacity to house demons, and could therefore safely replace idols. Although images replace idols as conversion proceeds, and although people pray to these images as once they did to idols, nonetheless an absolute antagonism separates the two objects just as it does their prototypes, the Christian saints and the pagan deities. The idol denotes falseness, evil, and deviltry; whereas the image betokens truth, good, and ultimately God's grace. Several legends deploy this duality. Both *Mirk's Festial* and the *Speculum Sacerdotale* describe how the Roman Pantheon, originally furnished with "fals ydoles," was reconsecrated to the worship of Mary and the saints (presumably with images) by Pope Boniface: "And so the temple that was made for alle fals ydoles is nowe i-halowyd for alle holy seyntis. And where that the multitude of ydoles were i-worschipid is nowe loued and worschepid a multitude of holy seyntis."[51] Even more tellingly, St. Philip was said to replace the idol of Sythia with the rood, or cross, which bested the idol in curing the sick and for this reason converted the idolaters.[52] The saints' legends are unconcerned with worshippers' mental attitudes toward statues; only a statue's pagan or Christian identity (and source of power) matters.

Idolatry is nowhere more essential in defining paganism than in the legends of the early virgin martyr saints. Several of these female saints, such as St. Katharine and St. Margaret, were especially popular in the late Middle Ages, when their lives received frequent retelling. The legends portray these young women who felt drawn toward Christianity as surrounded by a hostile pagan culture. The virgin disobeys a father or a tyrant, or rejects the advances of a particularly lustful idolater, and then suffers torture for refusing to sacrifice to his idols. The conflict between chaste Christianity and idolatrous, often libidinous, paganism can only be resolved by the violence, graphically described, inflicted on the virgin's body. Idol-hating virgins are boiled in oil, whipped, torn by knives, put on wheels, have their breasts torn off, are buried at sea, enrolled in brothels, hung upside down on gibbets, branded, and usually decapitated.[53] In Osbern Bokenham's *Legendys of Hooly Wummen,* composed in the 1440s, the narratives of Sts. Katharine of Alexandria, Margaret, Christine, Faith, Agnes, Dorothy, Cecelia, and Agatha are fueled by the women's rejection of idols.[54] These virgins mock the idols as nothing but "gold or syluyr, stonys or tre," made by humans, powerless to walk, speak, hear, or see; one calls idols "deuelys dennys," suggesting their function as abodes for demons; they mock pagan statues as "doum ydols," and as "ueyn stonys."[55] St. Agnes disparages idols made of brass, a material better used for "caudrons . . . or pottys and pannys" or other useful and inexpensive items, and claims those of stone would be better used to pave muddy roads. St. Christine's prayer destroys an idol of Apollo, and St. Dorothy's call to God brings down angels who "vyolently" wipe out a hideous idol and the high pillar on which it stands.[56]

Bokenham's legends of the virgin martyrs clearly link idol worship to uncleanness, lust, cruelty, anger, and madness. St. Katherine's torturer, the emperor "Maxence," makes a proclamation "in hys fers rage" ordering sacrifices to the god. St. Christine is imprisoned and tortured by her father, who is a "cruel tyraunth, ful of vnpyte," angry, and lacking "wyt and vndyrstondynng." Dacian, who attempts to seduce St. Faith to idolatry, is overcome by the "rage of woodnesse [madness]" when she refuses him. St. Agatha's antagonist "Quyncyan" is described as not only ignoble,

> But he eek was a ful vycyous man,
> And specially he was lybydynous
> Thorgh fleshly lust, & þere-to coueytous,
> Fals of byleue & an ydolatour,
> Wych to mammettys doth godly honour
> And uery god in heuene doth denye.[57]

Idolatry crowns this pile of errors, but is also the structure on which paganism itself is built. Once a pagan rejected idols, the other traits of paganism disappeared.

These legends carry rhetorical echoes of the image critics in the fourteenth and fifteenth centuries. Lollards condemned images as simply stone and wood, blind and deaf, and complained that the money lavished on images would be better spent on the poor; they would have approved of St. Christine, who broke her father's idols of gold and silver and threw the pieces out a window, calling poor men to come for this distribution of wealth.[58] Although the saints' legends, like the Old Testament, may have provided critics with a vocabulary for attacking images, in fact these stories remained innocent of mounting a critique of holy images. Instead, they propose that the object of worship distinguished Christians from pagans. Pagans adore idols, Christians venerate images. Idolatry marked pagans as a fallen and despised people, just as iconoclasm marked the Jews as outcasts.

Perhaps the only substantial challenge to this image-idol dichotomy that was mounted in orthodox vernacular religious literature is found in *The Life of St. Katharine of Alexandria,* written in the 1440s by John Capgrave.[59] In his version of the life of this popular saint, Capgrave maintains the basic outlines of the Katharine legend: The wise, beautiful, and idol-hating virgin rejects the advances of the idolater Maxentius, who orders his philosophers to debate with her. Katharine wins the contest, converts the philosophers, and is then tortured and finally killed by the emperor. Unlike other Middle English versions of this legend, however, Capgrave's philosophical debate contains a lengthy and detailed consideration of the nature of idols, in which the author shows his familiarity with the arguments of the image debate carried on by Lollards and their orthodox opponents. Capgrave slyly overturns the conventions of the saints' legends by showing how the late medieval defenses of images could be easily transferred to pagan idols.

Capgrave's knowledge of and attitude toward Lollards and their image critiques may be inferred from his biography and his historical work. Born in 1393, probably in Norfolk, he entered the Augustinian order in Lynn, and was ordained about 1416. He studied theology first in London from 1417 to 1422, and then at Cambridge. His extant scholarly works include commentaries on Genesis and Exodus, as well as vernacular lives of St. Augustine, St. Norbert, and St. Gilbert, but many Latin works no longer extant are also attributed to him. Capgrave was elected Provincial Prior of the Augustinian Order in England in 1453, and lived in Lynn until his death in 1464. Lollard communities were active in East Anglia, and their preaching and then trials for heresy could have provided Capgrave ample opportunity to become familiar with their criticisms of images; also, his extensive education probably led him into contact with the anti-Lollard image treatises produced by Oxford and Cambridge theologians in the late fourteenth and fifteenth centuries.[60]

Capgrave's *Abbreuiacion of Cronicles* reflects a determined hostility toward Lollards. He first mentions an Augustinian friar who "felle in þe secte of Wiclefistis" and grew so great in malice that he put "letteris" on St. Paul's door, slandering his order and his brethren. This gave great joy to the Lollards, who were called "hodid" men because they would not remove their hoods in the presence of the sacrament. Among the worst of these men was John Montagu, "a gret distroyer of ymages," who was said to have received the sacrament in the church, and then "voyded it to his hand, bare it hom, and ete it with his oystres."[61]

Capgrave abhors notices set up by Lollards in 1394 at Westminster and St. Paul's as filled with "abhominable accusaciones" against clerics. In his account for the year 1401 he discusses the Lollards' "schamful conclusiones." Capgrave names the Lollards "tretoures to God and to þe kyng," and he calls the Earl of Salisbury, who died in an uprising against Henry IV, "a gret fauorer of Lollardis, a despiser of sacramentis. . . ." Finally, in recounting the history of the Lollard leader Sir John Oldcastle, Capgrave denounces Lollards as those who "condempned þe teching of þe prophetis, þe gospel, and þe aposteles. . . ."[62]

Despite this evidence placing him firmly in the anti-Lollard ranks, Capgrave's *St. Katharine* suggests that his antipathy to Lollards did not prevent him from seeing the justice of some of their comments. Karen Winstead comments on Capgrave's "ambiguous position between orthodoxy and heterodoxy" in his *St. Katharine,* arguing that he "champions an informed, examined faith," even though encouraging questioning among Christians carried potential dangers.[63] Capgrave used the familiar life of this saint to reexamine the late medieval controversy over holy images through Katharine's debate with Maxentius' pagan philosophers, although the ostensible focus of this dispute are pagan idols. He audaciously has his saint, the font of Christian wisdom, voice the same denunciations of statues that could be found in many Lollard critiques.

When the emperor Maxentius first orders Katharine to honor his idols, she alludes to the doctrine of *latria* by refusing on the grounds that this would take from Christ his "hy honour" and give it to "maumentys" [idols]. Echoing Lollard objections to saints' images, Katharine points out that Maxentius' gods are only material and without animation, as they can neither sit nor rise, eat nor drink, have mouths without speech and hands that cannot do work. She asserts the power of the true God and claims Maxentius will receive no help from his idols.[64]

Maxentius orders fifty learned men to rebut Katharine on the questions of idols, and the arguments they devise mirror those of the late medieval image defenders. One sage assures Katharine that she is correct about the impotence of pagan idols. He explains that the idols are "but figures, representynge other-maner thyng." They are "tooknes" [tokens] of the gods, to whom the pagans give with "grete honore," not on account of the idols themselves, but for those whom they represent. The makers of these idols intended only "that to hyere deuocion men shuld goo therby."[65]

This wise man thus excuses idols in the same way that Capgrave's contemporaries defended images, as mere representations that direct honor to their prototypes, and are intended to inspire devotion in onlookers. Katharine does not concur with this argument. She regards the pagan idols as shams, made of stone and tree. Pagans err because they "wurshep the shadwe and leue the substauns."[66] When Maxentius, besotted by her beauty, offers with extraordinary tactlessness to make her his queen and set her image of stone and gilt in the marketplace to be worshipped, Katharine ridicules the projected statue as insensible and useless. Who will make the statue's limbs move, its tongue speak, or its eyes see, she demands. She emphasizes the statue's lack of dignity by pointing out that birds will leave dung on the image's face and dogs will defile it every day. Finally, reiterating the warning from Baruch and *The Pore Caitif* that holy images cannot cure illness, give riches, restore sight, or prevent death, Katharine proclaims the statue's impotence:

what shulde it profyte
On-to my soule? me thenketh, it coude not plese
No good man; for though it were to the sight
fful delectable, with colouris shynynge bryght,
On-to oure dayes it shulde ȝeue noon encrees,
On-to oure siknesse it shulde be no reles,
On-to oure lyf it shulde be noo myrthe,
On-to oure deth it shulde noo comforte bee,
N[o]n avayle to ende ne to birthe.

[what should it profit / Unto my soul? I think it could not please / Any good man; for though it were to the sight / Very delectable, with colors shining bright / Unto our days it should give no increase / Unto our sickness it should be no release, / Unto our life it should be no mirth / Unto our death it should no comfort be / No avail to end nor to birth.][67]

Capgrave's *St. Katharine* resoundingly rejects the standard defenses of holy images, and cleverly has a saint declaring her own image to be worthless. St. Katharine herself adopts the vocabulary and concerns of the late medieval image debate; like the *Speculum Christiani* she worries that image worship leads to misplaced *latria;* like *The Pore Caitif,* she rejects all notions of images' magical abilities. St. Katharine goes even further, however, in finding the materiality and beauty of the pagan idols to be misleading; the one true God cannot be found in these pathetic human creations.

By placing orthodox arguments supporting holy images in the mouths of the pagan philosophers, Capgrave breaks through the image-idol dichotomy that sustains other saints' legends. He reveals the dangerous similarities between pagan idol and Christian image. Clearly neither Lollard nor iconoclast, Capgrave acknowledges the practical wisdom and appeal of Lollard criticisms of images. Churchmen argued that people adored the holy person represented by the image, and could be protected from sin by adopting the proper mode of worship that used the physical object simply as a springboard to higher devotion. As the Lollards recognized, however, images, like idols, attracted adoration through their very materiality and appeal to the senses; through the ability to be, as St. Katharine says of her statue, "fful delectable, with colouris shynynge bryght." By their glamour and allure, Capgrave suggests, they lead people astray. His *St. Katharine* emphasizes that the material and formal kinship of pagan idol and Christian image—both are statues in human shape—makes them equally susceptible to misperception by their viewers, who will see them as the vital embodiments of divine (Christian or pagan) power.[68]

Conclusion

Middle English religious literature comprises a large and varied group of texts, many as yet unedited and relatively unknown. This survey on the issue of holy images is not, and cannot be, all-inclusive. Yet it shows that this rich body of work clearly presents two distinct and contradictory approaches. Works like *Dives and Pauper* drew on the Latin treatises of theologians to present rational and doctrinally sound defenses of images. These didactic treatises acknowledged some problems with using holy images, and promoted education as their solution. Idolatry was simply improper and ignorant devotion. Orthodoxy decreed that devotees approach images with the appropriate worship of *latria* or *dulia,* accepting them as devices for reminding and teaching the observer about the unseen universe of God and the saints.

This image theology could not seal over the ancient well of image lore. The definition of idolatry as a defect of one's spiritual state contended with the explanation offered by the image *exempla* and legends, that idolatry plainly meant the worship of pagan idols. Treating holy images as powerful agents in the work of salvation, the *exempla* encouraged the very attitudes toward holy images that the more theologically adept treatises condemned. More than representations of supernatural prototypes, the holy images in these stories partake in the essence of the holy people, as they show by bleeding, moving, and speaking. Rather than inspiring the memory of the deity and the saints, the statues and pictures in the *exempla* are the conduits for Christ's and the Virgin Mary's active participation in the world.

The relations between these textual presentations of images and the particular contours of image worship are not easily discerned. Did people who heard or read these tales believe them? No clear answer exists to this, yet the following chapters adduce evidence for late medieval people's attitudes toward images by examining the image practices of two English mystics, Julian of Norwich and Margery Kempe, and of parishioners in several localities in Norfolk and Suffolk, the native counties of John Capgrave and Osbern Bokenham. The internal oppositions of this literature also illuminate its possible meaning for its medieval audience. The divisions over image worship and idolatry in vernacular religious texts signal a significant problem in lay religious instruction. The works of religious instruction tried, if ineptly, to teach the laity the proper rationales for and approaches to images, but they contended with traditions that encouraged an emotional response to images as numinous objects and potential sources of miraculous activities. The theology of image worship also met resistance, according to one Lollard homilist, in people's practice. Insisting that orthodox image defenses misunderstood people's real behavior, he dismissed the notion that devotees believed images to be only representational. People lie, he proclaimed, in saying that they do not believe there is virtue in images, but only in God. For if the image they seek is stolen, they will stop their pilgrimages, although God is still mighty and the place where they would have gone is still there. These actions prove their trust was "in þat ymag[e]," and not, by implication, in its supernatural prototype.[69]

The failure to develop a believable, comprehensible, and consistent defense for the veneration of images left them vulnerable to criticism. The late medieval effort to reduce images to simple devotional and mnemonic aids foundered, thwarted partly by the enduring and vigorous literary tradition of presenting images as embodiments and agents of heavenly powers, a direct contact with the supernatural with which traditional believers seemed loathe to part.

CHAPTER 3

"FAIR IMAGES" IN THE PARISH

In the late sixteenth century, with England's religious course set firmly in Protestantism, a gentleman in Long Melford, Suffolk, wrote his farewell to the traditional faith of his youth in a mournful memoir of his parish church. Roger Martin (ca. 1527–1615), always a resolute Catholic, voiced his sadness for the loss of his faith's physical manifestations in tabernacles, lights, processions, and images. His deep affection for certain images in the church illuminates his description of them, and even moved him to rescue a table depicting the crucifix and the two thieves on crosses, which he took to his home, in the hope that his "heires will repaire, and restore again, one day." A "fair gilt" tabernacle had contained "a fair image of Jesus," who held "a round bawle in his hand, signifying, I think, that he containeth the whole round world. . . ." Most lamented was

> a fair image of our Blessed Lady, having the afflicted body of her dear son, as he was taken down, off the Cross, lying along in her lapp, the tears, as it were, running down pitifully upon her beautiful cheeks, as it seemed, bedewing the said sweet body of her son, and therefore named the image of our Lady of Pitty.[1]

Martin's memory of these images contains two potentially contradictory elements. He interprets the image of Jesus holding the ball metaphorically, reading it for theological meaning. In contrast, he bestows on the pietà a warm regard and tenderness that are signified by his verbal rendering of the statue as—almost—a living being. The short phrases "as it were" and "as it seemed" both suggest the image's vivid realism and deny the reality of its animation; the image may "seem" to cry, but of course does not. Martin knows the image is just that, a piece of carved wood, but his fondness for it almost overcomes this rational view. As an educated man, Roger Martin understood the pedagogic value of these carvings, but he also felt their pull on his sentiment and their power to envelop him in their depictions of climactic scenes such as Christ's death or the Virgin Mary's mourning over the dead body of her son.

Roger Martin's description evokes the vanished adornments of his church, his devotion and response to its statues sketching a final salute to these once esteemed and well-loved figures that stood in the niches and on the pillars of every parish church in England. Laymen and especially laywomen formed distinctive relations with their parish church images, particularly the painted and gilded wooden or alabaster statues that played a far more consistent and important role in their lives than did better known pilgrimage statues such as Our Lady of Walsingham. As Roger Martin's memoir attests, these carvings could stake strong claims upon the affections of their habitual beholders, largely on account of their vivid portrayals of physical and emotional humanity in their rendering of skin, tears, death, and mourning.

The spiritual dangers of these images lodged precisely in their seeming reality, their ability to deceive the "simple" who might, in the flickering candles of the church, see the Virgin Mary's tears as real drops. The written discourses discussed above, both scholarly and more popular, lay out the arguments and methods for teaching about holy images so that such error might be prevented, but in fact these works tell us far more about the apprehensions of their clerical authors than the beliefs and practices of laypeople. Direct evidence of how late medieval people reacted to and thought about images is meager. The late medieval writer, pilgrim, and mystic Margery Kempe described how seeing a crucifix and a pietà elicited from her loud cries and sobs. By her own account, though, she so astonished everyone who saw her that she seems unlikely to exemplify the more typical fifteenth-century layperson's response to sacred art.[2] Aiming for a broader and more representative scope, this chapter considers the ties between parishioners and the familiar holy images in their parish churches by assessing the evidence of wills, the documents most often left by the men and women of late medieval England.

East Anglia

Since at least the seventh century, Roger Martin's home county of Suffolk formed with its northern neighbor Norfolk the heart of a distinct geographical unit in England called East Anglia. The two counties have often been treated as one district politically and ecclesiastically; together they made up the medieval Diocese of Norwich, which comprises the geographic focus of this and the following chapters. East Anglia enjoyed a rich and varied religious culture in the late Middle Ages. Although Norfolk and Suffolk may have formed a stronghold of "old-style Catholicism," with important monastic centers and pilgrimage sites and the highest density of parish churches in the country, contrary voices were raised there as well. Lollard activities and sentiments, including hostility to images, existed in East Anglia, and several people suspected of Lollardy were tried for heresy in Norwich in 1428–31.[3] Several important late medieval writers came from Norfolk and Suffolk, including the mystics Julian of Norwich and Margery Kempe, as well as John Capgrave and Osbern Bokenham—all of whom figure prominently in describing the place of images in late medieval religion.

These East Anglian writers, mystics, and heretics articulated a range of beliefs about and criticisms of holy images, and sometimes exhibited startling behaviors in regard to them. Yet these people must be viewed in some measure against the mundane background of the quotidian practices of their less vocal contemporaries, the laypeople whose convictions and conduct were at the core of the late medieval controversy over images and idolatry. This chapter aims to sketch this context using the evidence from wills, although these are notably problematic sources. These wills come from eight localities: Great Yarmouth, Great and Little Walsingham, Swaffham, and Wymondham in Norfolk; and in Suffolk from Ipswich, Walberswick, and Mildenhall. Great Yarmouth and Ipswich, substantial towns in the late Middle Ages, each had a population of probably a few thousand.[4] Both are port towns, and their citizenry included merchants whose trade connected them to foreign countries as well as to towns in East Anglia's inland. Ipswich possessed a popular cult statue of the Virgin Mary, as of course did Walsingham, which was one of the great pilgrimage shrines of Europe.[5] Mildenhall, in the breckland area of Suffolk near the fens, is the furthest west and provides a geographical counterpoint to coastal Ipswich and Walberswick. The religious institutions in these towns and villages varied: Wymondham was dominated by a Benedictine abbey; Great Yarmouth and Ipswich each hosted several orders of friars; Little Walsingham had Augustinian canons and a house of Franciscans that the canons had tried unsuccessfully to keep out. Mildenhall, Walberswick, and Great Walsingham give no evidence of any religious houses; Swaffham may have had a hospice.[6] These towns and villages thus incorporate several key features of the region, including coastal and inland areas, villages and large towns, famous shrines, and localities with and without major religious institutions besides the parish church.

Many East Anglian parish churches reflect the region's increased wealth in the late fourteenth and fifteenth centuries, much of the new prosperity flowing from the trade in woolen cloth. This is a well-known story. As the export of raw wool became less profitable in the fourteenth century, merchants turned to manufacturing and exporting woolen cloth instead. By the late fourteenth century, rural cloth production in Suffolk (and other counties) was growing, tapping first into local, then national and finally international markets. In the fifteenth century cloth took the place of wool as England's major export. Lavenham, Long Melford, and many another village rebuilt and beautified their churches with the profit from this trade. This success, however, did not apply to all of East Anglia or even to all of Suffolk. Mid-fifteenth-century tax records indicate that Ipswich suffered economic decline at this time, whereas Walberswick and Mildenhall appeared not to.[7] The Norfolk worsted cloth industry declined by the mid-fifteenth century, yet Norwich itself, its capital city and a center of both trade and industry, apparently flourished from the late fourteenth to early sixteenth centuries. While both Norfolk and especially Suffolk grew richer in the late Middle Ages, the whole area did not experience the tremendous prosperity of Lavenham, and this simple fact testifies to the importance of local distinctions, which we will also see in the patterns of religious giving outlined in the wills.[8]

Most architectural historians believe that the late medieval rebuilding of parish churches in East Anglia resulted from the area's economic good fortune, although an alternative theory proposes that money spent on churches more likely reflects religious devotion than prosperity.[9] It seems safe to say that the laity's religious needs demanded certain changes in their churches, and their wealth helped to finance structural and decorative alterations, most of them in the Perpendicular style that dominated from the mid-fourteenth to early sixteenth centuries. In the fourteenth century many churches were greatly enlarged and bigger windows made their interiors brighter; the fifteenth century saw even more radical changes, with some churches—as at Long Melford—pulled down and completely rebuilt to suit new tastes and devotional styles. Throughout East Anglia significant building changed the churches, and those in the eight locales that are our focus here exemplify many regional trends. St. Peter and St. Paul in Swaffham, for instance, rebuilt its chancel in the fifteenth century, and from 1507 to 1510 built its steeple and rebuilt its north wall. The new popularity of roodlofts demanded that nave walls be raised, clerestories added, towers built higher. New towers were added at a great rate; Walberswick built a tower between 1426-ca.1441, and a parochial west tower was added at Wymondham as a rival to the central monastic tower, creating an oddly two-towered building. The popularity of chantries and gilds, each requiring its own altar, led to additions and the widening of aisles. Walberswick added its north aisle in 1507; St. Mary at the Elms in Ipswich has a perpendicular nave and north aisle; St. Nicholas in Ipswich has fifteenth-century chancel chapels and tower. Little Walsingham's St. Mary has Perpendicular chancel chapels as well. Open timber roofs, often the beautiful hammerbeam roofs for which East Anglia is famous, spanned the new broader naves.[10] In Swaffham, for instance, the church of St. Peter and St. Paul has a double hammerbeam roof decorated with angels.

Overall, these changes made the late medieval parish churches in East Anglia longer, wider, higher, and brighter, with additional windows, aisles, and side chapels. In addition to these dramatic structural changes in parish churches, their interiors were at the same time altered by new fashions for adornment, which also reflected certain devotional trends or preoccupations. Parishioners made contributions for images, rood screens, stained glass, and other works to beautify their churches, and to provide items that they found important for their religious practices. From the late fourteenth century, for instance, rood screens became common in England, separating the laity in the nave from the clergy at the altar, a change emphasizing the priest's central role in the miracle of transubstantiation while ironically making it harder for the laity to see the consecrated Host.[11]

Another innovation was the introduction of benches in the fifteenth century. Until then seating was sparse, but the increased wealth of the period allowed this luxury, and East Anglian bench ends often featured intricately carved figures, both sacred and profane, contributing to the beauty and visual appeal of the churches. Carved fonts of high quality and new designs, many showing the Seven Sacraments, also appeared in fifteenth-century Norfolk and Suffolk, as did larger stained-glass windows, often of exceptional beauty and liveliness.[12]

The testamentary evidence of this period shows as well a concern with the wooden and alabaster images in the parish church, to which a significant number of people left small donations. Because of the general use of "ymage" to denote these sculptures, as well as paintings and perhaps even stained glass, we cannot always know precisely what kind of artwork was referred to in any given instance. Alabaster carvings were numerous in England from the mid-fourteenth century to the sixteenth century. Quarries located around Nottingham provided much of the stone, and the earliest alabaster effigy, dating from the early fourteenth century, is in a nearby parish church. Nottingham itself produced many alabaster carvings, but other towns, such as York, also manufactured them. References to alabaster carvers and their works abound from the late fourteenth century until much of the industry died under the impact of reforming anti-image legislation in the sixteenth century. During this time alabaster was used for tombs, altarpieces, figures of saints, and panels showing religious scenes. In Suffolk, for example, Long Melford church contains an alabaster panel of the Nativity showing the Virgin on a bed, the Christ Child, and various worshippers. Brilliantly painted alabaster carvings decorated churches and wealthy homes and depicted God, the Virgin Mary, scenes from Christ's

Passion, the twelve Apostles, John the Baptist, and many another saint, but the special favorites appear to have been St. Katherine, St. John the Baptist, and the Archangel Michael, among others.[13]

Parish churches held carved wooden images of the saints as well, painted and even gilded, like the image of a "riding George" commissioned in 1519 from two "gravers" working in Wymondham. This statue of St. George on his horse, and no doubt with dragon, was intended for the parochial nave of the abbey church there.[14] Typically made of oak, such images would have been produced for many centuries and—unlike alabaster—not just at the end of the Middle Ages. Few are left. Iconoclastic fury found oaken images easy to burn, so that almost every one of the many thousands of these statues that enlivened the niches of parish churches at the end of the medieval era has disappeared. Still, we know that parishioners commissioned these, left money for them in wills, and that they were essential components of the church interior.

Overall, then, the parish church of the late fourteenth and fifteenth centuries changed significantly. Not only was it larger and lighter, its interior became visually more intricate. Rood screens separated and defined the space between chancel and nave, but also contained dazzling paintings of saints below, while holding above statues of the Virgin Mary, St. John, and the crucifix. Alabaster images now supplemented wooden ones, providing colorful narrative scenes of holy events or portraits of individual saints. Stained glass showed Christ as the Man of Sorrows displaying his wounds or the Virgin mourning her dead son, as well as the wealthy donors of the parish. Carvings on fonts and bench ends contributed as well to what may seem a continual increase of decoration. Parish churches in Ipswich, Mildenhall, Yarmouth, and elsewhere became filled with angels above in the roofs, the gleaming figures of saints in windows, carvings, and paintings, and the figures of parishioners in brass, alabaster, and glass, whose wealth had created this treasury of forms, color, and light.

Late medieval parishioners thus changed their churches, contributing money to their rebuilding and adornment. Sometimes they recorded their own largesse by inscriptions in the church. For most people, however, the only trace we have of their gifts to the church resides in a final will and testament, and these bequests form the basis for the rest of this chapter. Whether they lived in village or town, near an abbey or house of friars, the most immediate, consistent, and frequent contact that most laypeople had with their religion came through their parish.[15] Despite their reverence for renowned pilgrimage statues, laypeople like Roger Martin almost invariably formed their most enduring attachments to those familiar images that they saw regularly in the parish church. Using their final bequests as a guide, this chapter tries to understand what these images meant to laypeople. Interpretation of their final bequests must begin with an attempt to reconstruct what late medieval parishioners encountered when they attended church, that is, with the physical context of the parish church and especially its adornments.

The Parish Church

At the north end of the same altar, there was a goodly gilt tabernacle, reaching up to the roof of the chancell, in the which there was one fair large gilt image of the Holy Trinity, being patron of the church, besides other fair images.[16]

The East Anglian countryside today is still crowned by the flint churches of the fourteenth and fifteenth centuries. A Suffolk tourist brochure boasts that each of the county's five hundred medieval churches is worth a visit, and Norfolk has even more.[17] From the graveyard of one parish church the spires of others are often visible. None of these hundreds of churches remains today in the condition in which its medieval parishioners would have known it. Time has altered them: Iconoclasts from the sixteenth and seventeenth centuries destroyed windows and shot at angel carvings on the roofs; the death watch beetle ate into timbers; liturgical and confessional changes over the centuries demanded the modification of altars, the removal of decorations, the addition of texts painted on the walls. Victorian restoration attempts not infrequently destroyed what they sought to recover. The medieval presence is strong in some churches but erased in others. Still there remain enough pieces of rood screens, outlines of wall paintings, a few headless statues, and other decorations, both to suggest the variety and richness of holy images held by a medieval East Anglian church and to outline the visual experience of its parishioners.[18]

The precinct of the parish church is entered through the churchyard, perhaps past a stone figure of the Virgin Mary or a cross on the wall encircling the yard. A porch juts out from the main body of the church, its arched doorway topped by niches containing the carved images of Christ, the Virgin Mary, popular saints like St. Katherine and St. James the Greater, and the church's patron saint—perhaps Peter, Margaret, Andrew, or the East Anglian Etheldreda. In the spandrels of the doorway St. George combats the dragon, the lance of faith thrusting into and defeating evil. Upon entering the church itself, one sees a massive baptismal font. Some East Anglian fonts were octagonal, each side carved with a representation of one of the seven sacraments, the eighth with the Crucifixion. Other fonts might alternate angels with the symbols of the evangelists. The font in St. Matthew's, Ipswich, displays the joys of the Virgin, reflecting this theme's popularity in late medieval prayer.[19]

St. Christopher, patron of travelers, dominates the large wall painting that looms before the eye as one enters the church, a prominent position accorded him perhaps because of the belief that one who saw his image and invoked his aid would be protected that day from all harm, especially sudden death. Near him appears St. George again, patron saint of England.[20] Looking toward the front of the church, one's gaze travels down the length of the nave to the choir. Overhead is a hammer-beam roof, the beams and their supporting spandrels richly carved with images drawn from the Bible and from saints' lives. Angels with outspread wings are fixed to several beams, appearing to hover over the congregation. The carved angels carry shields depicting the instruments of Christ's Passion—the nails, lance, cross, and other implements of his torture—that medieval people believed angels would bear as they accompany Christ at his Second Coming.[21]

Paintings cover the nave walls. Familiar scenes from the early life of Jesus show the Nativity, the adoration of the Magi, the presentation in the temple. Other paintings depict the moments from the lives of the saints by which these holy yet companionable people were best known: St. Francis preaches to the birds, St. Katherine suffers her wheeled torture. The Seven Deadly Sins and the Seven Works of Mercy were favorites, perhaps because of their everyday settings and presumably familiar activities. The Doom, or Last Judgment, threatens over the chancel arch, a warning no one could avoid seeing. An angel's trumpet brings the dead rising from their graves; devils bear away the damned while the saved join the blissful saints and angels in heaven.[22]

Stained-glass windows of exceptional beauty, skillfully produced in fifteenth-century East Anglia, filter the light. Adam and Eve mingle with the Annunciation to the Virgin Mary. Beloved saints revel in their moments of glory and martyrdom: St. Katherine triumphs over the pagan philosophers, St. Luke in his role as a portraitist holds an artist's palette and brush, St. George wields his sword. The likenesses of wealthy church patrons who paid for the glass also fill these colored spaces, with written reminders to pray for them and their families. As Our Lady of Pity, the Virgin Mary cries plentiful tears that cascade down her cheeks, like the cherished statue described by Roger Martin.[23]

A screen and roodloft separate the parishioners from the sanctuary. The bottom part of the screen contains several panels with paintings of saints. The Virgin Mary and Mary Magdalen appear, as do the Church Fathers Jerome, Augustine, Ambrose, and Gregory. Local interest is represented by the East Anglian St. Edmund, martyred by the Danes in the ninth century, and St. Etheldreda, the seventh-century founder of a double monastery at Ely. Devotion to newer saints produced panels depicting the pious King Henry VI and the mysterious Sir John Schorne, a fourteenth-century rector renowned for his miraculous ability to cure gout. Roger Martin remembers the rood-screen of Melford Church as "fair painted with the images of the twelve Apostles." The gilded portraits gleam with bright colors visible even in the interior dimness of the church.[24] Above the screen rises the loft on which stands the crucifix and the rood group figures, the Virgin Mary and St. John, lit by the candlebeam. Above the rood arches the canopy of honor, a colored and gilded section of the ceiling that halos the entire group.

Other images may embellish the church; sacred and secular figures decorated font covers and bench ends. Torches and tapers illuminated the bright reds, blues, and golds of the paintings, glass, and carved images. Even the beams and the rafters might be colored. Despite the new large windows, church interiors still seem dark. The candles so frequently bequeathed by medieval parishioners were often needed to see the church images. Yet the parish church could be a treasure house of art; like a fine reliquary made large, holy images met the eye in every direction.

Of all the artwork in paint, glass, and carved wood and stone that bedecked the parish churches, East Anglian wills most frequently mention the small statues of the Virgin Mary and the saints that were set around the church. These figures, mass produced in the late Middle Ages in alabaster and wood and painted to emphasize their life-like qualities, stood in tabernacles or on gild and chantry altars that lined the side walls of the nave. Statues may also have been placed on the columns separating the nave from the side aisles, standing on the shelves where the pillars meet the arches, and slightly above the heads of parishioners. Roger Martin mentioned a pietà, or "our lady of Pitty," which struck him with great force, and this was a popular representation of the Virgin Mary in the fifteenth century. Other statues portrayed the familiar figures of John the Baptist, St. Nicholas, St. Andrew the Apostle, St. Thomas Martyr, and the Holy Trinity (a figure particularly detested by Lollards). Parishioners could choose which saints would stand in their churches. Only a wealthy person could imitate Sir Robert Throckmorton of Coughton, Warwickshire, who had images of Our Lady, St. Gabriel, St. Raphael, St. Michael, and the Trinity, all painted and gilded, set up on altars and pillars in the church where he would be buried.[25] Still, several wills from East Anglia reveal testators of more modest means who left money to have specific images carved or painted for their churches. These small statues have fared badly over the centuries, although alabaster images have survived in greater numbers than wooden ones. This is no coincidence, as the very attributes that led Roger Martin's forebears to make bequests to these statues and Martin himself to mourn their loss, finally attracted the destructive attention of iconoclasts.[26]

The scattered and battered remains of late medieval English statues make it difficult to appreciate the formal qualities that stirred parishioners to respond to them in a heartfelt manner, although apparently people did so. We cannot see these carvings in their medieval settings, and must speculate on the physical relations between them and their beholders. Some of the statues were perhaps crude and ill-proportioned, others displayed the carelessness and blandness that resulted from the quick production needed to satisfy a large demand.[27] These figures, nonetheless, held people's attention. Three-dimensionality and a painted face could transform even a clumsily sculpted statuette into a life-like and sympathetic or inspiring figure, an impression intensified by its child-like height of two to three feet and its visual accessibility in the church. These were not monumental stone statues, but relatively small figures placed at eye level or just above, where medieval parishioners might easily see them during mass. Should parishioners repeatedly stand or sit in the same spot within the church, a habit reflected by wills ordering a testator's remains to be buried "where I was wont to sit," they would have constant proximity to and unrestricted views of some statues during services, whereas others would be invisible to them. This regular closeness could engender the almost possessive feelings of intimacy evidenced by Roger Martin and stimulate final bequests of money and other goods to these statues.

A number of alabaster images remain from late medieval England, but given the scanty and damaged remnants of the once common wooden figures in England, it seems permissible to look to the more complete medieval survivals on the Continent to supplement our understanding of such statues. In the Low Countries, Germany, and Brittany, museums and some parish churches preserve wooden statues of the saints dating from the fifteenth and sixteenth centuries. Flemish sculptors likely influenced late medieval English carving, suggesting that the English statues of this period were similar to those extant in the Low Countries.[28] The following discussion, therefore, will focus on some English alabasters [plates 3.1–3.3] and Flemish wooden statues [plates 3.4–3.5] in order to explore and understand the qualities that could attract the devotion and affection of late medieval parishioners.

The alabaster images are more complex than the wooden statues; Francis Cheetham has rightly said that some alabasters might be considered as "three dimensional pictures rather than as pure sculpture."[29] Although an alabaster might represent a single saint, panels frequently depicted scenes with multiple figures. In Plates 3.1 and 3.2, the figures of St. Eloy and St. Michael do not return the look of the beholder, as each is occupied with his work. Eloy shoes the hoof of a horse's severed leg. The horse and its owner stand to his left, awaiting the miraculous reattachment of leg to horse. St. Michael raises his sword against the dragon and simultaneously weighs a soul—a demon's head pops out of the weighing pan on his left,

3.1 Alabaster of St. Eloy. Victoria & Albert Museum. Courtesy of the V&A Picture Library.

3.2   Alabaster of St. Michael the Archangel. Victoria & Albert Museum. Courtesy of the V&A Picture Library.

attempting to alter the scales (part of this is missing) and seize the soul. To Michael's right stands the Virgin Mary holding a rosary, the weight of which she places on the beam of the balance in order to influence the scale in favor of the soul whose fate is being decided. Only traces of color remain on these alabaster carvings, so they appear less vivid than they would have five hundred years ago. Like the wooden statues, though, these alabaster depictions are made familiar and companionable through homely details—St. Eloy's blacksmith shop, for example, with its anvil, wooden frame, and four horseshoes, suggests that he works there regularly. The alabaster-carver also created a realistic horse, saddled and roped to a post, piebald and its face marked with a blaze. The realism of the scene underscores its relevance for the viewer; Eloy performs this miracle in humble surroundings, showing how the supernatural worked in everyday life.

The alabaster Trinity [plate 3.3] is missing the dove, which represented the Holy Spirit, and although much of the paint remains, the colors that would have picked out the eyes of the figures and given them expression are gone.[30] Despite missing important features, this carving still shows how a fifteenth-century artist might configure the supernatural in stone (to the perturbation of some). The six angels, the golden throne, and his crown emphasize the majesty and authority of God the Father, who literally holds the souls of the saved in his hands. Gilding on his crown, hair, and beard emphasizes his splendor. Christ is shown on the cross, below and in front of the Father, reminding viewers of his human nature. Yet the souls in the napkin seem almost to rest on Christ's head, a physical relationship that expresses the spiritual truth that their salvation is made possible only by his body, and his sacrifice of it. This Trinity invites the consideration of its various parts, asking the beholder to examine the placement of souls, crucifix, God the Father (and, once, the Holy Spirit) in order to understand better the drama of human redemption and to contemplate the mystery of the Trinity.

The two Flemish figures of St. Catherine and St. Sebastian [plates 3.4 and 3.5] are fine examples of the simple, inviting, almost doll-like characteristics that made such statues appealing. These two saints were well known in England and throughout Europe in the late Middle Ages. St. Catherine was usually easily identified by the wheel on which she was tortured (perhaps this statue once had one); St. Sebastian typically appears as he does here, with the arrows of martyrdom piercing his body.[31] These iconographical identifiers, however, are not the statues' most important attributes. Both are painted to heighten their realism and make them lifelike; their cheeks have a rosy glow, color defines and heightens their lips and eyebrows; and blood flows from Sebastian's wounds. Sebastian, nonetheless, seems to gaze into space, not feeling the pain of torture, but

3.3 Alabaster of the Trinity. Victoria & Albert Museum. Courtesy of the V&A
Picture Library.

3.4 Statue of St. Catherine. Meester van Koudewater, ca. 1470. Courtesy of the Rijksmuseum Amsterdam.

simply enduring it. His humanity is made vivid by the careful sculpting of his muscles and bones, the tinting of his hair, eyes, cheeks, and lips. His sanctity is evident in his transcendence of physical pain; the arrows do not disturb his calm certainty of salvation. St. Catherine gazes serenely at those below her. She is a picture of late medieval affluence, wearing a fur-trimmed cape and a gold chain, her head encircled by a carved garland, and she has the high forehead, plucked eyebrows, and slightly pursed lips of the beauty. She seems not to notice the king under her feet, likely the Emperor Maxentius, who had her martyred. Like Sebastian, her face expresses a soul-deep tranquility. These statues show perfectly the meaning of sainthood as the intersection of the ethereal and the physical. Their composure is otherworldly, but their postures, coloring, clothes, and three-dimensionality render Catherine and Sebastian life-like and approachable; like their viewers, they are clearly human, suggesting that sanctity and heaven are attainable and not completely alien.

The late medieval parish church overflowed with holy images that were commissioned and maintained by the people of the parish. Of them all, none commanded more individual affection and attention than the small wooden statues that have now disappeared from England, and the alabasters of saints and holy scenes. These artifacts also formed the targets for the most severe Lollard censures of idolatry. The following analysis of East Anglian wills sketches the place of these artifacts within the parish church, and in so doing tries to understand what they meant to their fifteenth-century viewers.

The Evidence from Wills

Historians of late medieval religion in England have found the testamentary documentation of the fourteenth and fifteenth centuries a particularly thorny rose. Its abundance entices and frustrates: By far the most common late medieval source offering direct evidence of laypeople's religious concerns, wills remain problematic and defy easy interpretation.[32] Both women and men made testaments to enumerate their last wishes and bequests, although married women theoretically needed their husbands' consent.[33] Wills also exist from late medieval inhabitants of cities, market towns, and villages all over the country. Caveats must, nonetheless, signal wills' deficiencies and the purely suggestive nature of conclusions built upon them. Testators typically dictated their wills to clerks, who created a standardized format not always reflective of individual piety, if not in opposition to personal wishes. Far more men than women made wills; no group of wills represents the sexes equally. Many wills are not extant; gaps of decades may occur for a given locality; lack of consistency in the provisions of wills

3.5 Statue of St. Sebastian. Mechelen, ca. 1520–1525. Courtesy of the Rijksmuseum Amsterdam.

makes it difficult to determine the status or wealth of individual testators. Clive Burgess has pointed out that will analysis tends to emphasize individual religiosity, thereby obscuring the predominantly corporate nature of late medieval popular piety.[34] Most important, as Philippa Maddern argues, wills were not the single repositories of their makers' hopes for their afterlife or for the future disposition of their goods. Instead, the will marked one stage in a testator's ongoing spiritual and worldly transactions.[35]

The following exploration of East Anglian wills cannot avoid all the pitfalls inherent in the nature of the evidence. This discussion narrows the scope of inquiry to the bequests that illuminate the place of holy images in daily life, and such a tight focus somewhat distorts the nature of religious practice in these places, where reverence to images formed just one part of a larger complex of devotions surrounding the saints and the deity. The communal context for these wills—the relationships of parish and gild to holy images—is discussed in the following chapter. Here the emphasis is on the value of wills as mediators between personal piety and communal religion; individual people made specific choices for the benefit of their own souls and for the good of the community of the living, from which they were soon to depart.

Fourteenth- and fifteenth-century wills are usually brief, often occupying less than half of the large page of a will register. Will makers frequently mentioned only their pious bequests, leaving their souls to God, the Blessed Virgin, and the saints, their bodies for burial in the churchyard or, less often, within the church itself, and money for "forgotten tithes" to the parish church. Bequests for the repair of parish churches are so numerous that the scribe's prodding not to forget the building program seems almost audible. Many testators distributed some household goods, personal belongings, and land. No gifts are universal, however, and despite the intervention of the scribal hands that recorded these wills in the registers, people made personal choices about the disposition of their goods.

The brevity and near-formulaic nature of most wills heightens the significance of the less common bequests, indicating their importance to the testator and giving voice to particular preferences, hopes, and piety. The image-related bequests can be counted among these, as only a quarter of the will makers in this sample included such legacies. Yet clear patterns emerge here as well. Bequests to holy images included small amounts of money left to the roodloft and candlebeam and to votive lights before a statue or picture, money left for making an image, jewelry or clothes given to dress a saint's statue, and requests to be buried near an image. What moved people to remember pieces of sacred art in their final document? What did they hope for from such memorials? Answers, if tentative, can be sketched by comparing differences among the testators themselves, examining their positions within the parish, and probing their relations with both the living and the dead.

The Will Makers: Gender Differences

The wills that form the basis of this study date from 1371 to 1500, but the great majority—693 of the total 883—come from the half century after 1450. This general increase in willmaking during the decades from 1450 to 1500 included the multiplication of women's wills, so that women comprise a significant proportion of the total number of testators.[36] The eight Norfolk and Suffolk localities studied here included 883 testators, of whom 224 (about 25 percent), mention images (table 3.1).

Significant differences existed between groups of testators. Women named images in their wills more often than either clerics or laymen. Almost a third of the female testators made such bequests, while less than a quarter of the laymen did so. Women made image bequests even slightly more often than did clerics. In addition, women are modestly overrepresented in the group of testators who made bequests involving holy images. Women comprise only about 19 percent of all testators, but constitute 23 percent of all those who name images in their wills. Clerics are also overrepresented, but by a slighter margin than women; clerical wills form about 10 percent of the entire group, while clerics who name images compose 12 percent of the image testators (table 3.1).

Female testators, who were often widows, were comparatively rare, and thus likely to be less representative of their sex than were male testators. Nonetheless, other evidence reinforces the close association between women and images sketched by these wills, suggesting a general predilection among women of this era. Medieval women's emotional attachment to images was noted by their contemporaries. John Wycliffe thought statues of the Virgin decorated in gold and silver and paint attracted women; over a century later, Thomas More seemed to agree with this impression when he described women in London staring at the Virgin by the Tower until they believed the image smiled at them.[37] While these comments reveal less about the nature of women's devotion than the male intellectual's distaste for what he thought it was, they still highlight a perceived gender difference. Men may have believed women to be especially attentive to holy images; in 1516 a man of Salisbury Diocese commented on how "wemen" would place their candles "a fore atree, the Image of Saynt Gyles."[38]

The standard medieval explanation of images as *libri laicorum* would suggest that these parish church images functioned as texts for women, more likely to be illiterate than men. Unable to read, women turned to art to learn about their religion, completing this education with final bequests to honor the images that taught and inspired them. No evidence, however, supports this unsatisfactory argument. Wills rarely indicate whether their makers were literate, but clerics surely formed the most educated group of testators, leaving far more books than either laymen or laywomen. Yet clerics made image bequests at about the same rate as women did. Further, a study of religious practice in late medieval Norwich found that bequests to votive lights increased steadily until 1532,[39] a period when lay literacy in general and probably female literacy in particular were both increasing.[40] Literacy obviously did not preclude image devotion, and in fact, late medieval prayer books (discussed in chapter 6) included texts that encouraged people's attentions to images.

Women's ardent responses to sacred art have been explored by scholars of Italy, the Rhineland, and the Low Countries, who propose several interpretive frameworks for understanding the evidence of women's special affection for images. These explanations cover, broadly speaking, psychological, institutional, social, and religious grounds, although these modern divisions falsely separate motivation or causation of a single experience into distinct categories. A combination of them may approach most closely the experience of the medieval woman's devotion. Overall, most scholars emphasize the significance of physicality, suggesting diverse reasons why women's bodily experiences drew them to material images. Christiane Klapisch-Zuber, for example, describes Italian women's need for visual and physical connection with images, which gave them "immediate access to the child Jesus." For their trousseaux, lay- and religious women in quattrocento Florence received "holy dolls" as props for their devotion. They performed rituals with these dolls that allowed them to identify with the Virgin Mary, thereby transforming the disappointments, unsatisfied yearnings, or tensions of convent life or the married state into a spiritual catharsis that gave them visions of sacred truths.[41]

Margaret Miles also stresses the power of images to make their beholders participants in the lives of holy people, and to encourage worshippers to identify their lives with sacred events. In addition, images of female saints provided models of spirituality freed from a "life ordered by biology. . . ." These idealized virgin saints, immensely popular in fourteenth- and fifteenth-century art and literature throughout Europe, operated as symbols of freedom from the maternal and domestic responsibilities that confined most women for the better part of their lives. Women had special incentive to turn to these images as sources of inspiration for reimagining their lives "as containing potential for spiritual growth, meaningful rather than arbitrary suffering, and a degree of individuation."[42]

Perhaps the most detailed consideration to date of women's veneration of specific images is Joanna E. Ziegler's study of Beguines' devotion to the

Table 3.1 Testators with Image Bequests/All Testators[*]

	Women	Laymen	Clerics	Total
L. Walsingham	7/11	17/40	4/11	28/62 [45%]
Gt. Walsingham	1/6	9/21	0/6	10/33 [30%]
Wymondham	4/18	11/84	0/7	15/109 [14%]
Swaffham	13/16	23/37	4/13	40/66 [61%]
Gt.Yarmouth	11/21	43/74	16/22	70/117 [60%]
Norfolk totals	36/72 [50%]	103/256 [40%]	24/59 [41%]	163/387 [42%]
Walberswick	3/17	2/50	0/2	5/69 [7%]
Mildenhall	1/12	6/105	0/7	7/124 [6%]
Ipswich	12/63	35/218	2/22	49/303 [16%]
Suffolk totals	16/92 [17%]	43/373 [12%]	2/31 [7%]	61/496 [12%]
Totals: Norfolk and Suffolk	52/164 [32%]	146/629 [23%]	26/90 [29%]	224/883 [25%]

Note: All percentages are rounded

[*]The wills in this study are registered copies proved by 1500 in the Norwich Consistory Court, and the courts of the Archdeaconry of Sudbury, the Archdeaconry of Suffolk, the Norwich Archdeaconry, and the Norfolk Archdeaconry.

pietà. She finds that the material nature of the Beguines' lives and especially their "heightened sensitivity and active engagement in matters of touch" gave them a particular view of religious sculpture (but one that many medieval women would have shared). The predominance of tactility in the Beguines' daily work of cleaning, baking, knitting, and other manual activities shaped their experience of images; their highly developed sense of touch allowed them to recognize specific qualities in material substances. Beguines approached the pietà, the sorrowing mother holding her sacrificed son, through their physical senses; by seeing, touching, feeling, they identified with the sculpture.[43]

Women's special devotion to holy images may also have been nourished by the interpretive freedom that art offered, providing women a direct contact with the holy that appeared unmediated by men (although image makers were more often male than female), and unmarred by the common misogyny of sermons that labeled women as vain, lustful, and garrulous.[44] Unlike sermons, legendaries, or devotional works, sacred art offered neither clerical authorship nor the directive force of the written or spoken word instructing the reader or auditor on how to pray or meditate. Once painted or sculpted, an art object was open to the emotional, intellectual, and spiritual perceptions of the individual beholder. Because they could be venerated or provide a focus for pious meditation without the immediate intermediary of priest, husband, confessor, or preacher, images granted women a unique freedom from male intercession in their religious activities. Floating free from the constraints of verbal interpretation, holy images were hospitable to women's spiritual longings.[45]

In addition, the East Anglian women who made these wills occupied an inferior position in the corporate religious life of the parish. Although women joined parish gilds, most gild officers were male, as were most parish officials such as churchwardens.[46] Thus men dominated not just the liturgical rituals of the church, but also the extra-official activities that bound the parish together. Like their Continental counterparts, East Anglian women could only pursue their spiritual callings with male approval. Margery Kempe's life shows this clearly: A businesswoman and mother, she began her spiritual questing only in midlife, and even then needed her husband's consent, which he gave reluctantly. Despite her discussions with holy women such as Julian of Norwich, Margery's spiritual advisers were men. A bishop had to give her permission to wear the white clothes she wanted; she relied on various male spiritual advisers to sanction her unusual life; the two scribes who wrote down her story were male. In a life dependent on male approval and hedged with male restrictions, Margery Kempe's dramatic emotional identification with a pietà (and other images), the sight of which caused her to cry out loudly and uncontrollably, proclaimed her spiritual freedom.

Medieval women might well have taken the images of female saints as symbols for their own spiritual potential. The heavenly hierarchy did not subordinate female to male saints. St. Catherine of Alexandria, so popular in late medieval England, was a powerful and learned virgin martyr whose images frequently appeared in East Anglian churches. Of the surviving English alabasters, more depict St. Catherine and scenes from her life than any other saint. A fourteenth-century wall painting in Sporle, Norfolk, shows twenty-seven scenes of her passion. St. Margaret of Antioch, a virgin martyr believed to help women in childbirth, became another English favorite whose images appeared in several East Anglian churches.[47] Carvings and paintings of these saints were visual reminders and models of strong, virtuous, and, indeed, sanctified womanhood. The triumphant virginity that characterized so many of the female saints (Catherine, Margaret, Dorothy, and Barbara, for example) need not be considered an example that late medieval women strove to imitate, as Eamon Duffy points out, so much as the acknowledged guarantee of their intercessory power with the deity.[48]

The will data support the notion that women identified with images of women: Of the seventy-eight bequests women made to named male or female saints (including Jesus and the Virgin Mary), forty-six, or 59 percent, were to images of females. Men also made more bequests to female images than to male ones, but their legacies were directed overwhelmingly to images of the Virgin Mary. Women favored the Virgin as well, but in addition made bequests to images of St. Catherine, the early martyrs St. Petronilla and St. Barbara, Mary Magdalen, and St. Helen, mother of Constantine, revered for finding the True Cross, and popularly believed to be of British origin.[49] This concentration on female saints from the early Christian era is found as well in literary sources such as Bokenham's *Legendys of Hooly Wummen,* and in the suffrages of saints in late medieval prayer books.

The Will Makers: Geographic Differences

Geographic differences in image bequests are even starker than gender differences. Norfolk testators were far more likely to leave money to images than were Suffolk people. Wills from the five Norfolk locales—Great and Little Walsingham, Wymondham, Swaffham, and Great Yarmouth—constitute about 44 percent of all wills in the study. Yet image testators from Norfolk far outnumber those from Suffolk: 163, or 73 percent, of all image testators came from Norfolk, compared to sixty-one, or 27 percent, from Suffolk (table 3.1).

The strongest contrast appears in comparing the wills of Mildenhall in Suffolk with those of Great Yarmouth in Norfolk. The paucity of images in Mildenhall wills would suggest a mass conversion to Lollardy and the widespread rejection of images, if other evidence supported it. Only about 7 percent of the Mildenhall testators made image-related bequests, compared to 60 percent in Great Yarmouth. What accounts for this disparity? Each town was graced with a fine church containing many chapels and altars. Mildenhall's church of St. Mary remains one of the loveliest in Suffolk, a county famed for its medieval churches, and its images drew the attention of seventeenth-century iconoclasts who defaced the roof angels with buckshot and arrows.[50] Perhaps the ambitious fifteenth-century building program left people with little money or desire to give even more money to the holy images in their church, although parishioners in other areas made bequests to images despite their contributions to new construction in their churches.

From 1370 to 1500 a majority of Great Yarmouth testators directed their image bequests either to the light of the Virgin Mary in the church of St. Nicholas, or to the light of "Our Lady of Arneburgh." The image of the Virgin in St. Nicholas was a special object of devotion for a long time, as was the image of Our Lady of Arneburgh that was housed in a chapel of the same church, attended by a gild bearing her name. Associations with the sea probably contributed to the popularity of the cult of our Lady of "Arneburgh" in this port town. Yarmouth men brought it to England after their participation in the naval battle at Sluys under Edward III in 1340. After the battle, Edward had gone to nearby Aardenburg to give thanks for his victory, in keeping with his habit of visiting both greater and lesser Marian shrines.[51]

Once established in Yarmouth, this cult was probably unknown beyond the radius of a few miles; such local and obscure shrines and saints contributed many pieces to the mosaic of the fifteenth-century spiritual landscape.[52] Their traces may be faint, but they produced distinct variations in religious activities. Placing the image bequests of Norfolk and Suffolk within a larger devotional context yields some insight into reasons for their significant differences. Just as image bequests were most often intended to solicit help after death in attaining salvation for the testator (a point discussed more fully below), so too were many other kinds of bequests, such as leaving money to friars. Norfolk testators made bequests to friars more often than did those of Suffolk, perhaps indicating again the former's closer attention to the afterlife (table 3.2). However, Suffolk bequests to friars were double its number of image bequests: 25 percent of testators made legacies to friars, compared to 12 percent who mentioned images. Both laypeople and clerics left money to the friars for prayers or trentals (a set of thirty requiem masses). The local presence of a house of friars was unnecessary to generate these legacies; Mildenhall contained no house of friars, so people left money to friars in Thetford, Ixworth, and especially

Babwell. Swaffham testators left money to friars in Lynn. The Suffolk testators clearly trusted more in the spiritual efficacy of the friars' prayers than in their own attentions to saints' images.

The springs of such devotional differences between Norfolk and Suffolk or between the people of one parish and another are difficult to trace, but they are suggestive of the diversity of religious life in the late Middle Ages. The more frequent image bequests in the Norfolk parishes could be due to a greater number of chantries in these churches. A wealthy magnate or a group of church parishioners or a religious gild, could hire one or more priests to celebrate masses for the welfare of the souls of the dead and for other intentions. The services typically took place in a chapel within the church or at a side altar, usually adorned with a tabernacle and holy image. The multiplication of chantries within a parish church made these peripheral areas and their artifacts more central to the religious practice of the community. A lack of firm evidence about the number of chantries in each parish studied here, however, and the difficulties of computing chantries for any locale, must render this merely a conjecture about the differences between Suffolk and Norfolk practices.[53]

Norfolk devotions were also likely shaped by the international shrine of the Blessed Virgin Mary at Walsingham in the northern part of the county. Princes, queens, members of the nobility, and common people flocked to Norfolk to visit this shrine, the attractions of which included a replica of the Holy House of Nazareth but also, and more importantly, the statue of the Blessed Virgin, which was the most revered holy image in England. Most of these pilgrims traveled established routes dotted with chapels on their way to honor this renowned statue, popularly called "Our Lady of Walsingham." The consciousness of this shrine and its image was widespread in Norfolk. Anne Harling of East Harling, Norfolk, for example, divided her rosary among Our Lady of Walsingham and three other shrines, and both Norfolk and Suffolk people requested pilgrimages be made to Walsingham on their behalf.[54] In the commonplace book he compiled in

Table 3.2 Testators with Bequests to Friars/Total Number of Testators

	Laymen	*Clerics*	*Women*	*Total*
Norfolk	107/256 [42%]	10/59 [17%]	24/72 [33%]	141/387 [36%]
Suffolk	86/373 [23%]	11/31 [36%]	25/92 [27%]	122/496 [25%]

Note: All percentages are rounded
Total bequests to friars: 263 [30%] of 883 wills. Norfolk: 141 [54%] of 263; Suffolk: 122 [46%] of 263.

the 1470s, Robert Reynes of Acle, Norfolk, listed the images that could be found at the shrine in Walsingham: "Gabriel gretyng Our Lady; in the myddes of the tabyll at the avter stante Our Lady, on eche syde of her stante an angel; Seynt Edward, Seynt Katheryne on the ryght hande, Seynt Edmond, Seynt Margarete on the lefte hande; alle clene gold."[55] The last three words emphasize the wonder of these images, their "clene" or pure gold epitomizing Walsingham's grandeur. Towns such as Great Yarmouth that lay along the pilgrimage routes must have been especially attuned to Walsingham's influence, and local and particularized devotional fashions, like Yarmouth's cult of Our Lady of Arneburgh, may have been in part echoes responding to the influence of the great shrines of national and international stature.[56]

The placement, architecture, and adornment of parish churches also shaped the particular contours of local piety. Commenting on the fifteenth-century church at Walberswick, Suffolk, Colin Richmond has remarked that people participated in and in some ways even created the religion offered to them in their parish churches. Men and women gave their money for new construction, for chantries, for images, for services.[57] A saint might be reverenced in one area and not another. The cult of Thomas Becket, for example, generally declined in the fifteenth century, but people in nearly all of these parishes left money to his gild or image.[58] Among the eight localities studied here, only the people of Swaffham venerated the Anglo-Saxon St. Guthlac, because of their proximity to Crowland in the fen country, where his cult was centered. Guthlac was an important saint for the Swaffham parishioners, as they left money to his image and to the local chapel and gild named for him.[59] Each bequest contributed to the development of the cult, as the maintenance of the statue, the wealth of the gild, and the lights in the chapel would attract more worshippers. Such variations in chantries, gilds, altars, and images, modulated the devotions of the people, who in turn shaped the next generation's piety through their bequests left most often, not to Rome or Canterbury or even to Norwich, but to their parish church.

Will Provisions: Votive Lights

Variations among bequests relating to holy images reveal different intents and relationships between testator and image. Some people wanted their bodies buried near or in front of a holy image. Others left money for making new images or for repairing old ones. A few women gave veils and jewelry to adorn statues. Most common of all, the will maker stipulated a small amount of money to purchase lights before an image in the parish church.

Votive lights cost little. Most bequests providing for these lights allotted sums under 20d. and many gave only 2d. or 3d. In contrast, wills often record gifts to friars of several shillings, nor was it unusual for the well-off testator to designate 10s. to each of three or four houses of friars.[60] Image bequests also came in multiples. The most common, found in each parish and in every decade, was a few pence given to the lights of the Blessed Virgin, and many people supplemented this offering with money for images of other saints. In 1423 Julian Medel of Swaffham provided 6d. for the light of the Virgin and also small amounts of money—2d. or 4d.—for each of eleven other images, including those of St. Jacob, St. John, St. Katherine, Mary Magdalen, St. Mary "pietà," St. Nicholas, and the Annunciation, or "salutacionis beatae Marie." In evaluating Julian's attachment to holy images, however, we must also note that the will provides 6s. 8d. for the church bell.[61] While it may be misleading to calculate the importance of individual bequests by the amounts of money granted to each, it is a simple fact that holy images rarely consumed as much of a testator's wealth as other presumably "pious" legacies, and might therefore have been made more casually.

Gilds typically maintained votive lights before the image of their patron saint, a point emphasized in the wills. John Fuller of Swaffham left 6s. 8d. to the lights of the four gilds to which he belonged, to be divided equally among them.[62] In 1498 Agnes Marteyn of Wymondham left 3d. to the light of the Blessed Mary on condition that the gild accept her as a member; since wills were usually drawn up close to the time of death, Agnes presumably wanted the burial ritual that gild membership would guarantee her.[63] Bequests to votive lights were not simply hidden bequests to these gilds, however, as many testators donated money to both image and gild. Gilds tended to receive more money than did images. For example, in 1488 Simon Sawer of Wymondham left 12d. to the light of Blessed Mary, but 6s. 8d. to the gild of St. Peter.[64] Similarly, William Heron of Great Yarmouth gave a generous 12d. to the light of the Blessed Mary, but an even more liberal 10s. to the gild of the Holy Trinity.[65] No doubt devotion to the patron saint of one's gild prompted some bequests of votive lights. In 1488 Nicholas Merchowse of Great Walsingham, for instance, left 8d. to the gild of St. Jacob and money to the lights of St. Jacob in All Saints Church there. Yet he also gave money to the light of St. Katherine there, and to the gilds of the Holy Trinity and St. John the Evangelist in another church.[66] While a parish gild usually supported a particular image, it was clearly important to keep their assets distinct. The Black Book of Swaffham, for example, specifically distinguishes land given to the light of Blessed Mary from land of St. Mary's gild.[67] Overall, the bequests to images and gilds display only partial correspondence, as shown by the comparison of images and gild

Table 3.3a Comparison of Gilds and Images Found in Wills: Little Walsingham

Gilds	Images
Assumption of the Virgin Mary	Blessed Virgin Mary[*]
Purification of the Virgin Mary	Blessed Virgin Mary[*]
Annuciation of the Blessed Virgin Mary	Blessed Virgin Mary[*]
Our Lady's Chapel	Blessed Virgin Mary[*]
St. Katherine	St. Katherine
St. Thomas martyr	St. Thomas of Canterbury
Holy Trinity	Holy Trinity
St. Anne	[no images found]
John the Baptist	[no images found]
St. Peter	[no images found]
St. Jacob apostle	[no images found]
St. George	[no images found]
[no gilds found]	St. Erasum [Erasmus][**]
[no gilds found]	St. Elene [Helen]
[no gilds found]	St. Edmund
[no gilds found]	St. Wulfstan
[no gilds found]	St. Christopher

[*]This image may or may not have been linked to one of the gilds of the Virgin Mary.

mentioned in the wills from Swaffham and Little Walsingham (tables 3.3a and 3.3b). People could leave money to images and not their supporting gilds, or to the gilds alone.

As the Black Book of Swaffham indicates, although the lights before images customarily received only small amounts of money, they could also be endowed by more permanent and valuable gifts. Hamond Pulham, burgess of Great Yarmouth, was a rich and pious man with a troubled conscience; his 1476 legacies include 40s. "to our lady lyght in sent Nicholas cherch for the duty I have nott payed." Besides this lavish sum, he also left an estate to his wife to be sold, with half the income left to her and part of it for various pious purposes including "to help our lady lyght in sent Nicholas cherch. . . ."[68] Even this unusually generous gift could be surpassed by grants of land to lights. In 1483 Simon Dixburgh left one acre of land to the light of Blessed Mary in Swaffham's church, adding to the considerable property already given to the image of Mary, which a 1454 entry in the Black Book lists as four acres and three rods.[69] More exceptional is the grant by John Broun of Ipswich, who gave income from land to sustain lights forever before the sepulcher of the lord in three churches: St. Margaret, St. Mary at the Elms, and St. Peter. These bequests to churches

Table 3.3b Comparison of Gilds and Images Found in Wills: Swaffham

Gilds	Images
John the Baptist	John the Baptist
St. Gregory	St. Gregory pope
St. Guthlac	St. Guthlac
Ascension of the Lord	Ascension of Jesus Christ
St. Thomas martyr	St. Thomas martyr
St. Mary	Virgin Mary
St. Helen	St. Helen queen
Sts. Peter and Paul	St. Peter
Finding of Holy Cross	Holy Cross
Corpus Christi	[no images found]
Holy Trinity	[no images found]
Nativity of the Lord	[no images found]
[no gilds found]	St. Nicholas
[no gilds found]	Bd. Jacob
[no gilds found]	Mary pietà
[no gilds found]	St. Savior
[no gilds found]	St. Herasum [Erasmus]
[no gilds found]	St. Christopher
[no gilds found]	All Saints
[no gilds found]	St. Katherine
[no gilds found]	Mary Magdalene
[no gilds found]	Salutation of the Virgin Mary
[no gilds found]	St. George

outside his own parish testify to Broun's attachment to the custom of the Easter sepulcher, which represented Christ's tomb and might contain a crucifix or a consecrated Host.[70]

In his discussion of late medieval Norwich wills, Norman Tanner argues that bequests to votive lights formed an important source of income for parish churches.[71] Perhaps so, but if we consider them from the parishioners' point of view, these bequests appear puzzling at first glance. What purpose could these lights serve for the newly dead person? The same men and women who left a few pence for candles in front of a favorite image also gave money to the church for "forgotten tithes," for repair of the church fabric, for building the belltowers that were increasingly fashionable, for the priest to pray for them, and for other purposes as well. All of these gifts added more to the parish funds than the customary amount of 2d. or 4d. left to pay for a simple light; and it seems that if parishioners on the verge of death wished to give money to the church, they did so.

A person in the midst of health and life who provides lights for a holy image combines pragmatic and spiritual aims: A flame illuminates the artwork so that the devotee may see it better while praying, no small consideration in a dark church. The lit candle may express the gratitude for favors received from the saint, like the ex-votos found at shrines. Multiple and frequent lights could testify to the power of a saint or a particular image, and encourage others to worship. Testators, however, would never see the candle flames lit by their gifts of money. These lights may have been a final call for the help of saints whose intercessions, once helpful on earth, might now be beneficial in the progress from earth to purgatory to heaven. The lights also reminded the saint of the donor's past devotion to the image and, by illuminating a favorite image for living parishioners, permitted the dead a continued participation in the parish. Most crucially, though, the lights represented the donor before the representation of the saint. The holy image was now faced not by the praying devotee, but by the flickering candle standing in for the absent person, who could thus worship the saint even after death. A modern "Prayer of the Light" addressed to the image of the Virgin Mary expresses this relationship: "The flame of the candle, witness of my passage, the sign of my presence, will continue my prayer near you. . . ."[72]

Bequests of lights to images took part in the pious economy of requests, assistance, and thanks that formed the relations between late medieval people and the saints. Providing such lights on a permanent basis by donating lands to that purpose extended this dynamic of giving and receiving, so the testator believed, in perpetuity, that is until the Last Judgment, after which all souls would be beyond the help of any intercession. Alertness to this economy, and to its dual bases in the material and spiritual worlds, informs the 1380 declaration by Henry of Playford. To maintain a light in the church of St. Michael of Coslany, Norwich, he granted lands "of the goodes which the same God the Lord of all Lords have gyven unto me in this world" in the hopes that he may "obteyne hys grace and mercye in hys extreme judgement and to se hym wyth glorye in the lyght of hys magestye."[73]

Will Provisions: Burial

Medieval people usually designated a site for burial in their wills, although this was often no more specific than the parish cemetery, where most parishioners could expect their bodies to be interred. In this group of East Anglian wills, clerics requested burial inside the church, usually naming the chancel or choir, more often than did laypeople. Several testators stipulated burial in a chapel or before an altar in either their parish church or, more surprisingly, another church. Seventeen people named the chapel and altar of the Blessed Virgin Mary, by far the most popular; three selected St. Katherine, two the Holy Trinity, and one each St. Thomas and St. Francis.

Noting the frequency of church entombments in pre-modern Europe, despite repeated prohibitions by Church councils, Philippe Ariès called churches "veritable cities of the dead."[74] Indeed, lay burials within churches became more common in the fourteenth and fifteenth centuries, and in England at least official objections against the practice became less stringent.[75] Against Ariès' claim that burial inside church was the "customary procedure" for Christians until the eighteenth century, however, the East Anglian wills show that most testators settled for, if they did not prefer, the graveyard. In the entire group, fewer than 20 percent of these women and men asked for burial in the church, although almost half of the clerics did and women were slightly more likely to do so than laymen. Status and wealth clearly played a part in the place of one's grave in the late Middle Ages; those with high social standing and money could request burial in prominent locations inside the church. In London, for example, burial fees were higher for such prime spots as the chancel, and poorer parishioners were interred in the less expensive churchyard.[76] This was likely true for East Anglians as well, although the will evidence is inconclusive. Yarmouth laymen who described themselves as burgers opted for both churchyard and church. The cost of church burial was clear: Robert Ayssleton of Yarmouth asked for burial in St. Nicholas "in owr lady qwer" for which "sepultur berying & brekyng of þe grownds I geve and beqweth vjs. viijd."[77] Anne Newporte of Ipswich left the same amount of money for "brekyng of þe pament and the grownd" to make her grave in front of the crucifix in St. Mary-le-Tower.[78] On the other hand, Geoffrey Curson of Swaffham included many bequests that indicated he was not a poor man: His 1462 will provided money for the lights of the Ascension of the Lord, St. John the Baptist, St. Gregory, and others; he provided 6s. 8d. for a chapel window and another 20s. to the church fabric; he also left money for a trental. Despite his evident wealth, he chose burial in the cemetery.[79]

Holy images played only a small role in the selection of burial sites. Again, clerics and women made this request more often than did men, although the numbers involved are so few that no clear-cut conclusion can be drawn from them; only eighteen people, about 2 percent of the total, specified a burial spot near a holy image.[80] Surprisingly, no one named an image of the Virgin Mary. A woman from Ipswich and another from Walberswick requested burial before an image of the Holy Trinity.[81] One Ipswich woman wanted her grave before the image of St. Nicholas, and a layman asked to be interred by an image of St. Leonard, patron of pregnant women and prisoners of war.[82] People who either opted for or were consigned to the cemetery could also choose to be near images. Bartholomew Elys of Great Yarmouth ordered his burial in the cemetery of St. Nicholas next to the cross, and Joan Freborne of Ipswich specified the cemetery of St. Lawrence, next to the window of St. Christopher.[83]

The order to bury one's body near an image of the Holy Trinity or of St. Nicholas suggests that in this final act the testator completed a long-standing devotion to the deity or saint, but this pious request also emphasized the belief in the intertwined spirituality and physicality characteristic of both human and holy image. Christian theology taught that the corpse would be resurrected, so its immediate decay did not render it void of future meaning. Even more, as John Bossy comments, the "common-sense view" held that a dead person's soul resided where the corpse did. Thus the body's placement near the saint's image presumed that the numinous quality of the statue or picture would, like earlier Christian burials near the bodies of the saints, assist the dead person in attaining salvation.[84] Burial near a holy image constituted an act of hope in one's future salvation and a statement of belief in the continuity of one's self as an integrated whole of body and spirit.

Rarely, however, did the choice of burial location represent only one concern. The cross and the crucifix, for example, received several mentions for burial sites in the East Anglian wills. As the most powerful of images, the cross was linked in popular belief to great power and numerous miracles. It evoked the remembrance of Christ's suffering, of course, but even more pertinently to those on the edge of death's abyss, it symbolized redemption and resurrection. A crucifix was held up before the eyes of a dying person in order to ward off the demons threatening the soul.[85] Burial by the cross signified hope in its spiritual promise, but as the cross occupied the most prominent place in the church, burial before it could also proclaim personal prestige.

Some of these burial instructions likely acted as both statements of piety and directional aids. Anne Newporte of Ipswich, for example, ordered "my body to be buryed" in the church of St. Mary-le-Tower "in þe gret aley before the crucifixe."[86] Such directional requests also aimed at continuity, an element most clear in wills like that of the shipwright Robert Peteman of Ipswich, who had his body buried in St. Clement's church, "by fore my seete" where "I was wont to sitte;" and Sibyl Cruse, who likewise ordered interment "byfore the pewe that I am wonte to sytte in heryng the divyne servyce off god."[87] These burials within the church underscore the notion that one still belonged to the parish community after death, a "place" that the position of the body, living or dead, created and defined in the consciousness of other parishioners.[88]

The general indifference to the saints and their images in selecting burial sites may appear surprising, given the lively saint worship of the period as exemplified by the numerous gilds and images dedicated to the saints in these parishes. Near the end, however, people tended to find their families more important than the saints. Many more testators asked to be buried next to a spouse, parent, or child than by an image or an altar. Johanne Rokysby of Great Yarmouth demonstrates the influence of family graves in choosing a burial spot, as she asked that her body be placed "in the church by William Brimsted late my husband or ellys in the Churche yard by my father and mother."[89] Philippe Ariès claimed that this phenomenon became widespread only in the fifteenth-century in France and expressed "the rise of a feeling that transcended death" in the testator's sense of the authority of the family.[90] In addition we might understand it as an avowal of belief (or hope) in the continuity between the earthly world and the afterlife, that like the body and social relations, familial affection and intimacy would also endure the coming transition.[91]

Will Provisions: Gifts to Images

Most medieval people signified their devotion to holy images through the gift of money for votive lights, but many made other legacies to pictures and statues of the saints. Sometimes the bequest was simply a sum of money, left to the image as though to a person, and with no more explanation. Joan Atgoor of Ipswich, for instance, left 3s. 3d. to the image of the Blessed Virgin Mary in the church of Freston (a village south of Ipswich) where she had previously lived, witness to a particular image's hold on affection and memory.[92] Had Joan wanted only to show devotion to the Virgin, she could have left money to a picture or statue in her current parish church, St. Mary-le-Tower in Ipswich, where she would be buried. These legacies crossed gender lines; both men and women gave to the images of male and female saints. Isabel Sextayn gave 10s. in 1489 "to þe peyntyng of seynt petyr," and Cecilia Bukke of Walberswick left 6s. 8d. to be equally divided between the images of St. Andrew and John the Baptist. The gifts of 6s. 8d. from Thomas Chyldyrston of Mildenhall and 40d. from Henry Bencroft of Ipswich joined those of many men and women who left money to images of the Virgin, the object of most such legacies.[93]

Testators often intended particular uses for their money, dictating the painting or repair of an old image, or even the creation of a new one. Margaret Boty of Walberswick ordered that the image of "Saint Mary pety" (that is, "pity," or pietà) be painted with gold, like the image of the Blessed Mary "pety" in nearby Southwold.[94] Similarly, Robert Dolfynby of Walberswick gave precise instructions: "I wyll have made seynt John Evangelyste and þe tabernakyl þerto acordyng to the makyng off seynt John Baptyste and also I wyll that bothe be paynted at my coste."[95] Since it is unlikely that he wanted the two saints to look alike, presumably his intention was to duplicate the style, size, coloring, or gilding of John the Baptist. Other bequests to tabernacles of St. Nicholas, All Saints, St. Peter, and other structures meant to contain and exhibit an image, indicate their importance in the church and the desire to enhance the image itself.[96]

A few women left garments—perhaps veils—to images of the Virgin Mary. Alice Nelyng gave one each to the two images of the Virgin in Wymondham's church, and Joan Williamson left one for every image of the Virgin in the Church of St. Peter in Great Walsingham.[97] Katherine Genyngham of Walberswick bequeathed jewelry: "Item I bequeth to our lady in þe chirche of Walberswick ii Rynge of Siluyr and gilt."[98] These gifts reflect the medieval custom of decking out statues of the Virgin Mary according to the liturgical calendar. Our Lady of Halberton (a shrine statue in the west country, north of Exeter), for instance, was adorned with mantles, beads, and silver rings.[99] Statues of other saints might also receive clothes or jewelry; one York widow left a ring, girdle, and beads to an image of St. Anne, for example.[100] These legacies endured longer than votive lights and emphasized the human qualities of the statues, which like their female donors could "wear" clothes and jewelry. (The sentiments that inspired these legacies persist today, as modern people continue to contribute to the wardrobes of beloved statues.[101]) Genyngham's gift of rings also suggests the presence of the saint in the statue by recalling the well-known tale of the youth who lightheartedly placed his ring on the finger of an image of the Blessed Virgin; when he was later about to marry a human bride, the image prevented the union by reminding him that he was already betrothed.[102]

While these gifts may signify their owners' sense of identification with a saint and their fondness for a statue, they also had an economic value. Rings were portable wealth, as were the buckles, pendants, brooches, beads, and other items that Robert Whiting enumerates as early-sixteenth-century oblations to the Rood at Crediton.[103] Holy images that attracted such gifts might be financial assets for a parish, which could use the added wealth for building or social programs, and for that reason might encourage at least local pilgrimages to a favored statue. Indeed, disputes sometimes erupted over the right to such gifts, lending support to the idea that some images received oblations worth a significant amount. (Chapter 4 discusses some of these disputes.) Yet the precise value of offerings to any given image remains elusive, partly because of gaps in the records. Some images clearly received more than others, and the parish church that housed a statue reputed to perform miracles might count on additional income from pilgrims. The East Anglian will makers, however, generally gave to images money or items of relatively little value.

Executing the Wills

Wills stake out their makers' claims on the earth after they have left it, but their desires and hopes might easily be thwarted. It would be a mistake to calculate the income of a parish church, to conjecture its adornments, or to figure the placement of graves on the dictates in wills. The gifts of rings, veils, votive lights, money for painting of statues, and other image bequests in these wills were likely fulfilled because of the trifling amounts usually involved, but medieval testators had reason not to trust the living to respect their final wishes. Despite the testators' promises of money to executors for their labors, things could go astray, and contemporary literature warned will makers about the untrustworthiness of executors. In the 1499 episcopal visitation, eleven people in Norwich Diocese were charged with detention of testators' goods.[104] People tried to prevent such occurrences by either appealing to the affection of family and friends, or threatening them with curses, and also by devising systems to ensure that their executors carried out their wishes.[105] Few people could have followed the lead of Margaret, countess of Norfolk, who in 1398 obtained a papal threat of excommunication for anyone who interfered with the disposition of her property as set forth in her will.[106] Less powerful people also feared that even their parish church might misdirect their much smaller legacies and they tried to prevent this, although their methods were less effective than those of the countess. Agnes Garard of Ipswich, for one, wrote in her will: "Also I beqweth to the tabernakyll of our lady at þe hey awter x marc upon a condycion that þe seyd x marc shall go to seyd tabernakyll or ell not."[107]

Bequests for church adornments to be paid out over several years often involved higher sums than those for image lights, the high altar, or painting a statue, and these amounts appeared to increase their jeopardy. John Newman, for example, left ten pounds for the repair or restoration of a cross in All Saints Church, Great Walsingham, to be paid when the money was available from his goods, trusting this to be done "according to the discretion of my executors."[108] Even more generous and at risk was Thomas Cachecrost's gift of forty pounds for a roodloft in the collegiate church of Our Blessed Lady in the Field in Norwich, to be paid at the rate of five pounds per year after his wife's death. In 1501 Thomas' heir, Simeon, agreed with Robert Honywod, dean of the college, that the vagaries of time might prevent the fulfillment of the bequest; in place of the original gift, Simeon would pay the college ten pounds immediately, another ten pounds later, and so conclude the bequest. Thomas' pious wish for a new roodloft was not forgotten, as the dean and canons promised "they shall with in the space of iiij yere next after the date of this endenture do make and set up a sufficient rodeloft in the middes of the body of the church of the seid college as well and as sufficiently as the seid money wole extende to. . . ."[109] Thomas Cachecrost's forty-pound bequest was thus halved, and his roodloft correspondingly reduced. Nonetheless, the detailed and lengthy document needed to change the legacy points to the respect accorded his bequest in word if not in deed.

Conclusion

The early-nineteenth-century historian of Norfolk, Francis Blomefield, said about the votive lights in the medieval church in Great Yarmouth that "so zealous was the superstition of those times, that there was scarce a will made, but a bequest was bestowed on this species of Popish parade."[110] Blomefield's characterization of votive lights as "superstitious" reflected, of course, a Protestant inheritance that rejected the practices of the pre-Reformation church in England, and also restated the Lollard objection to image worship as idolatrous. The analysis here of Great Yarmouth wills supports his impression, if not his interpretation, for 60 percent of Yarmouth testators made image bequests, the majority for lights before an image. Yarmouth was unusual, however, for among the entire group of East Anglian testators considered here, 75 percent made no mention of holy images. This number suggests either that images gripped people's imaginations and affections less tightly than was feared by both the theologians and Lollards who worried about idolatry, or simply that people satisfied their desire for image devotions in ways other than final bequests. Will evidence is not conclusive, and pious remembrances made at death's approach do not infallibly sketch a testator's spirituality. Yet nothing indicates that bequests were inconsistent with testators' usual devotions.

Some of the wills studied here support other material that documents late medieval people's ties to particular carvings and paintings. Roger Martin's loving evocation of the holy images at Long Melford, for instance, arose in part from his recollection of the distinctive features of these artifacts, such as the life-like tears of the Virgin. His fondness for individual images finds echoes in the words and actions of others whose attachments seemed drawn more by the image than the saint it represented. An odd but not unique witness of this affinity comes from an altered painting in Earl Stonham in Suffolk that originally depicted the martyrdom of St. Thomas Becket. Following Henry VIII's 1538 order to eliminate all images of Becket, the head of the saint in this painting was made female.[111] The church retained its image at the cost of shifting devotions to another saint. Joan Atgoor's bequest to the image of the Virgin in her previous parish (see above) also underscores her fondness for the image itself. Similarly, Crystiana Hayll, who wanted burial in the cemetery of St. Lawrence in Ipswich, left money for the lights of the Virgin Mary and John the Baptist in the church of Blakenham, where presumably she had once worshipped.[112] Hayll's devotion to these holy people could have been satisfied with votive lights to their images in St. Lawrence. Like Roger Martin's memories and Earl Stonham's effort to preserve its image, Atgoor's and Hayll's bequests express nostalgia for their pasts as well as affection for a specific piece of art. Following the human tendency to become attached to the particular rather than the abstract, people prized pieces of sacred art for themselves, as well as venerated them for the saints they represented. Artists created varied representations of the supernatural in wood, stone, and paint, and people naturally found some more appealing than others.

Image bequests articulated private devotions, but these coexisted with a public and corporate religion to which both male and female testators paid attention through numerous bequests to their gilds and parish churches; these outnumber the final gifts to holy images. Gilds dedicated themselves to the care of their patronal image or altar, but just as importantly they provided prayers and services for members. As part of the pious economy of salvation, these wills show that most East Anglians entrusted their hopes for the afterlife to their membership in these communities of gild and parish and to the prayers of the friars. Yet the significant number who insisted that their ultimate and perhaps only earthly document testify to their devotion to holy images reveals the persistence of the individual spiritual life within a predominantly communal framework.

CHAPTER 4

SOMETHING OF DIVINITY:
HOLY IMAGES IN THE COMMUNITY

The Case of the Foston Virgin

In 1313 the Archbishop of York, William Greenfield, commanded an end
to the gathering of simple people who came to venerate an image of the
Virgin newly placed in the parish church of Foston, as if "something of divinity appeared more in this image than in other similar images." In his
written order, Greenfield suggested that he feared that their naiveté could
allow these faithful ones to be dragged into idolatry and error; for this reason he ordered an inquisition into the "causes, reasons, and motives" that
drew them to this image, and he also threatened the disobedient with excommunication.[1]

The twentieth-century editor of Greenfield's register inferred from this
order that the archbishop considered the worship of this image at Foston
to be "sheer idolatry."[2] The incident has also been cited as an example of
how newly acquired or freshly repainted statues of the Virgin Mary gave
rise spontaneously to cults that flowered briefly and disappeared almost
completely in the Middle Ages, leaving behind few traces.[3] Such interpretations underline the credulousness of the common people, ready to see
miraculous powers in something new to them. Guarding these gullible
ones against their own impulses stands the rational voice of the great man
of the church, who reins in their superstitious tendencies and puts an end
to the unwarranted, even perilous, worship. Indeed, Greenfield alluded to
the dangers of "error and superstition," but significantly he applied these
descriptors to the Old Testament Israelites, who had burnt incense to the
brass serpent built by Moses, and which Hezekiah finally destroyed (4
Kings 18:4). The archbishop reserved final judgment about the fourteenth-
century Christian laypeople under his pastoral dominion until his inquisition produced its findings. In fact, Greenfield was less concerned about the

laity's activities, no matter how potentially superstitious or idolatrous, than about other disruptions in his diocese, which also centered on the Foston Virgin.

In his injunction forbidding veneration of this image of the Virgin Mary, Archbishop Greenfield also mentioned that this image was the cause of quarrels between the prior and convent of Bridlington on one side, and Joan, widow of Thomas of Poynton, on the other. Further disputes between these adversaries might occur, wrote Greenfield, unless suitable remedies were taken. Both Greenfield's order for an inquisition into the cult of the image and his threat of excommunication were partly directed toward settling this disagreement; tracing the dispute between Joan Poynton and the monks of Bridlington provides a fuller history of the Foston Virgin and from this context we can better understand what part idolatry played in the case.

Prior to Greenfield's 1313 mandate, a Yorkshire inquisition (held sometime between 1300 and 1309) documented the arrival of an image of the Virgin Mary in Foston and the genesis of the quarrels that soon surrounded it. Because the inquisition's findings contain the seeds of much that followed, it is worth reprinting here in full:

> Thomas de Poynton bought an image of the Blessed Virgin Mary in the parts of Scotland, and carried it to a chapel in Fraisthorp, co. York, where it stood for five years in his lifetime. The chapel is annexed to the church of Kernetby, whereof the prior of Briddelington is rector, and during the said five years God worked for the said image, so that several offerings came there, whereof the prior received twopence and the vicar of Kernetby the third penny by grant of the prior. After the death of the said Thomas, Joan his wife took away the image, and sold it to Robert le Conestable, parson of Foston. The prior, claiming property in the image, obtained divers writs to the sheriff of York to replevy the same, who sent Geoffrey de Eston with sufficient warrant to deliver it. The said Geoffrey went to the manor of the said Robert, parson of Foston, and found the image in his house, and delivered it to William de Wynstowe in the name of the prior.[4]

This document highlights several key themes in the history of the Foston Virgin. The phrase "God worked for the said image" implies that the statue became associated with miracles, and on this account brought in money for its owner(s). Several people claimed ownership of the Virgin, including Joan Poynton, the Foston parson, the Kernetby (or Carnaby) vicar, and the prior of Bridlington, although it is not clear whose right should prevail. The image was the object of legal action, as the prior had it seized under warrant from the house of the Foston parson, Robert le Conestable. Finally, the Foston Virgin was remarkably peripatetic, traveling from Scotland to Fraisthorp (by Carnaby), then to Foston, from where it was taken by the prior of Bridlington's man, who likely returned it to Fraisthorp.

In 1310 an argument erupted over pious donations to an image of the Virgin in Fraisthorp chapel. The Bridlington Priory cartulary contains a decree settling a dispute between one William de Bolum, vicar of Carnaby and Fraisthorp, and the prior and convent of Bridlington, over "new offerings" arisen "suddenly and unexpectedly" to a "certain new image of the said Virgin." Each side claimed the gifts, but in the end "it was arranged for the sake of peace and quiet" that "all offerings at the said image" would be divided, with the prior and convent receiving two parts and the vicar one part.[5]

This 1310 image was doubtless the same one investigated by the first inquisition, the statue brought by Thomas de Poynton from Scotland. The allotment of the offerings was identical in both cases; the second settlement duplicated the first one that pertained between Bridlington and Fraisthorp (before Joan Poynton sold the image to the Foston parson), in which Bridlington received two-thirds of the offerings and Fraisthorp one-third. We know that the first statue had been returned to the control of Bridlington and, probably, to Fraisthorp chapel. Apparently by 1310 this same image, possibly refurbished, had begun to attract offerings again. Or perhaps the offerings had remained constant and it was the quarrel over oblations that was resumed between Fraisthorp and Bridlington. The cartulary is unconcerned about the motives for the gifts to the image; in fact they are assumed to be "in honour of God and the most glorious Virgin Mary." The dispute centers on money and, by implication, the control of Fraisthorp chapel.

This was the background to Greenfield's 1313 decree, but the events and motives surrounding the Foston Virgin are still puzzling. In 1310 the Virgin's image was at Fraisthorp, having been taken from the Foston parson by the prior of Bridlington's man. But in 1313 Greenfield named an image "newly placed" [*noviter collocatam*] in Foston church. How did it get there? Two miracle-working images of the Virgin in this small vicinity, both attracting crowds and gifts, seem unlikely. Later documents indicate that only one statue was ever at issue, and they offer explanations for its perambulations.

Greenfield's mandate was dated 5 *ides* April, 1313. In September of 1313, a commission of oyer and terminer was formed on the complaint of Robert Conestable, parson of Foston Church and purchaser of the image from Joan Poynton. Conestable claimed that Gerard, prior of Bridlington, along with several other men whom he named, "broke his doors and houses at Foston . . . assaulted him, and carried away an image of the Virgin Mary and other goods of his."[6]

Whether or not Constable's allegation of theft was true, between 1313 and 1314 the miraculous image had evidently moved from Foston to

Bridlington. A second order issued by Archbishop Greenfield in early 1314 concerned "all those who adore the image of the blessed virgin in the monastery of Bridlington." Greenfield announced that he had sent letters to the deacon of Dickering, which encompassed Foston and Bridlington, forbidding adoration of the Virgin's image either at Foston, where the statue was placed at the time he sent the letters [*ubi quedam ymago beate virginis tunc extitit collocata*], or at another church where the wandering image had meanwhile been transferred. This second church was at the monastery of Bridlington itself. Greenfield also ordered that the prohibition against adoring the image and making offerings to it be made public in all churches in the archdiaconate, and especially at the conventual church of Bridlington.[7] Although the archbishop alluded again to idolatry as a snare of the devil, it is plausible that his major concern was to end the dispute among his warring clergy by simply banning all offerings to the statue.

Greenfield's efforts to settle the squabbles over the Foston Virgin failed. The quarrel outlived him and Prior Gerard of Bridlington. After Greenfield's death in 1315, Gerard's successor appealed for a relaxation of the interdict against venerating the image, and was likely successful. The new bishop ordered the rector of Foston and other interested parties to appear before him if they had "reasonable cause why the prohibition should not be relaxed."[8]

Some kind of peace seemed to prevail between Foston and Bridlington, and the monastery must have consumed the claims of Fraisthorp, which disappeared. In the autumn of 1315, the prior and convent of Bridlington were licensed to grant a pension of 40s. to Thomas le Conestable, nephew of Foston's rector, Robert, for the sake of reinstating peace and harmony between his uncle and the religious house.[9] A few years later, however, in 1319, a letter from Pope John XXII to the Archbishop of York named Foston among those benefices refused by various candidates "as being of too little value and disturbed by conflicts."[10] Although Foston's role in the case ends here, the image of the Virgin Mary became the object of theft once again. In 1331 another commission of oyer and terminer was formed, this time on the complaint of Robert, prior of Bridlington. Robert claimed that during Prior Gerard's time one Roger Grimston, his brothers, and other men had broken the "doors of the chapel, house, and church of the priory at Fraysthorp, co. York, and carried away an image of the Virgin Mary worth 60*l.*, which was in the chapel."[11] It is not recorded where Grimston took the image.

The final disposition of the Foston Virgin is unknown, and the quarrels it provoked are perhaps no easier to untangle today than they were 700 years ago when Archbishop Greenfield first attempted it. Allusions to idolatry in Greenfield's two mandates suggest that improper worship caused some worry, but even so this anxiety was overwhelmed by the opposed and rancorous assertion of economic rights in the Virgin by the participants. All sides coveted the offerings made to the image. The division of these gifts resolved the dispute between the vicar of Fraisthorp and the prior of Bridlington. The pension granted to Robert le Conestable's nephew seems a likely settlement of the Foston claim to some portion of the income brought by the wandering image. The Virgin's image may have been, in fact, only the temporary focus for a squabble between Bridlington and Foston that began long before Thomas of Poynton introduced the statue to Yorkshire. The Bridlington cartulary records a letter from Pope Nicholas III (1277–1280) that confirms the settlement of an earlier dispute between the Bridlington convent and Robert de Scardeburg, then rector of Foston, "respecting certain tithes and other things."[12] For at least several decades, then, the monastery at Bridlington and the parish of Foston squabbled over money, and the offerings to the image of the Virgin Mary that each claimed constituted one source of their broader conflict.

The events surrounding the Foston Virgin in the early fourteenth century anticipated many of the contradictions and dilemmas that enveloped the public use of holy images in the succeeding two centuries: The clergy fought each other for the image's income, the laity worshipped it for the miracles they believed it performed, and the archbishop's uncomfortable duty was to mediate among the conflicting claims on the image. Various powers—religious and secular, legal and physical—entered into the dispute, as the antagonists wrestled for control of the holy image. Greenfield surely intended his 1313 temporary interdict on offerings to the Foston Virgin to cool the heated quarrel between Bridlington and Foston, as much as to banish the potential of idolatry. His successor, not pausing at all to consider the dangers of idolatry, seemed disposed to reverse this ban, although we do not know his final decision. Only Archbishop Greenfield ever hinted at the perils of improper worship, and whatever his real pastoral concerns may have been, idolatry also formed a convenient rhetorical blind that allowed him to exert his authority over the Bridlington-Foston fracas.

While the case of the Foston Virgin provides no clear picture of the extent of the clergy's apprehensions about idolatry, it offers plentiful evidence that laypeople labored under no such worries, and furthermore that they consistently disregarded their archbishop's orders to cease venerating the image. Despite warnings of excommunication, people continued to give to the statue and their oblations fostered the ongoing feud between the parish and the monastery, and between the monastery and its chapel at Fraisthorp. Had the offerings stopped, as Greenfield enjoined, the holy image would likely have remained in one place—no longer revered, it would no longer be fought over. The history of the Foston Virgin points to the powerlessness of the church hierarchy to halt a cult's momentum. Defying the interdict, people sought out this image; even its multiple migrations among the churches of Foston, Fraisthorp, and Bridlington did not diminish the image's power of attraction.

As the gift of Thomas de Poynton to Fraisthorp church, the Foston Virgin illustrates the laity's involvement in adorning and enriching their parish churches, a crucial strand in their bond with holy images. A saint's statue was a familiar presence to parishioners, who were responsible for its upkeep—cleaning, painting, or regilding—and removing an image could disrupt the dynamics and economics of worship in the local community. Yet the same image could act simultaneously as an object of cult devotion, as did the Foston Virgin, even attracting pilgrims and money from afar, and in their wake inviting disputes over oblations and over local, episcopal, or even papal power. Issues of authority and control also arose when holy images became emblems of regional, spiritual, and indeed political identity. While they were the objects of individual devotion, holy images simultaneously and literally stood in positions—in churches—that gave them public roles and communal significance. They were encircled by concentric rings of meaning, which might include belief in an image's miraculous powers, economic activities centered on the image, attacks on a saint's image, and efforts by secular or religious authorities to prescribe proper behavior toward images. The innermost ring simply denotes locale; a holy image acquired significance partly through its association with the place where it stood, and for that reason we turn first to images in the parish.

Images in the Parish: Church, Gilds, and Land

While some laypeople made final bequests evidencing their attachment to specific pieces of sacred art and to the saints they represented, not all relations between images and worshippers were so personal. The laity also encountered these same images as members of the parish community. The corporate character of the laity's religion was evidenced in many ways in the late Middle Ages: The mass, for instance, was (and is) considered a communal offering by the parish. Most parishes probably had religious gilds that allowed smaller associations within the congregation to practice group devotions centered on the images of saints. The collective nature of parish life also manifested itself in such everyday practicalities as the maintenance of the parish church and its ornaments, a responsibility of parishioners established by the Fourth Lateran Council of 1215. This duty was frequently cited in reminders to congregations; for example, a 1425 papal bull addressed to the parishioners of Ringwood in Winchester diocese adduces "the custom introduced in the realm of old" that parishioners provide for the fabric, buildings, and repair of their church.[13] Parishioners' obligation for this upkeep sometimes led to disputes. In Norwich diocese, for example, members of St. John the Baptist's parish in "Tyryngton" claimed freedom from the burden of repair and other duties related to St. Clement's, the church on which St. John's had once been dependent. St. Clement's protested, but the matter was settled for St. John's in 1402 by papal decree.[14] As this case indicates, laypeople willingly accepted obligations only for their immediate church.

All parishioners were responsible for the continual costs involved in maintaining images. Late medieval churchwardens' accounts show that parishes regularly spent money on buying, gilding, repainting, and repairing images.[15] The accounts for Walberswick, Suffolk, record several such expenditures. In 1463 the parishioners paid to have the cross mended and images cleaned, and in 1466 spent 5s. "ffor payntynge of the ymage of oure lady," as well as 8d. for a base for that image, and 6s. 10d. "ffor the taburnakiylle peyntynge of our ladye."[16] A cross purchased in 1470 cost 5 nobles 15d.; smaller amounts were spent on altars and coverings for the images of Sts. George and Andrew, for the windows of Sts. Christopher and Walstan, and for the tabernacles of Sts. Thomas and John.[17] In 1492 they paid 13s. 4d. "for peynting of owyr lady," perhaps referring to refurbishing the same statue that had been painted in 1466.[18] The churchwardens spent the comparatively large sum of 11l. 10s. for painting a new crucifix and the ceiling (presumably as a canopy of honor), although these were only the last of several expenses for this image. Two 1496 items indicate the effort and resources needed to install the crucifix, as the churchwardens list payments for "bryngyng hom of the crwsyfyx and mete and drynk," and for "mete and drynk for settyng vp of the crwsefyx."[19] The accounts also list money from the parish's young women who had banded together to raise money for "peytyng of king herry tabyll."[20]

The Walberswick accounts for these years are unusually full, but records from other East Anglian churches show similar expenditures. The acquisition and upkeep of images formed a significant part of the churchwardens' duties, and their accounts help to sketch the market for holy images. For example, in 1474 churchwardens of All Saints in Tilney, Norfolk, spent 13s. 7d. for making a tabernacle for the Blessed Virgin, and 26s. 8d. for a picture for the tabernacle.[21] The accounts of Cratfield, Suffolk, list payments for the painting of images and tabernacles and for their covers.[22] The Mildenhall churchwardens' accounts show several payments for images, including painting the roodloft in 1506–07, for the painting "of our lady," and for the "crowene of owyr lady" in 1508–09.[23] The parish of Shipdam, Norfolk, spent money on painting crosses and setting up images of St. Katherine and

St. Margaret.[24] Churchwardens in Swaffham, Norfolk, paid a Norwich goldsmith to mend the best cross, paid another man to make a mold for it, and a third for leather for a case for this cross, which was perhaps used in processions.[25]

These examples could be multiplied to show the regular amounts of money paid for the roodloft and its images of the crucifix, the Virgin Mary, and St. John; for cloths used to veil images during Lent; for the candle holders and candle wax needed to illuminate images; and all the other expenses associated with the statues and paintings in a church.[26] The money came from the church fund fed by tithes and by those last bequests made so universally for the upkeep of the parish church. Parishioners supported their local church's images in this way, or through specific legacies, and there is no indication (apart from Lollard complaints) that they begrudged this expense. Because the parish was a source of local identification and the church a focus for community responsibility, parishioners would have taken pride in keeping images freshly painted and gilded, their cloths mended, and their tabernacles in proper condition.[27] Indeed, the records from late medieval religious gilds bespeak an eagerness among the laity to contribute even more to favorite images, to tighten their spiritual bonds with the saints through group devotions, and to demonstrate the vitality of their fellowship.

The religious gilds of late medieval England probably numbered in the thousands, although no exact count exists. At one time or another most parishes probably had at least one gild, and many parishes had several; late medieval wills show that Swaffham and Little Walsingham had at least a dozen each over the course of a century (Tables 3.3a and 3.3b). Membership lists and account records of some gilds are extant, but we know about others only because members named them the beneficiaries of small legacies. Some gilds survived for decades or longer, while others were more ephemeral.[28] Their purposes, customs, and activities varied so much that the word "gild" encompassed many diverse associations. Parish gilds often formed to provide burial services and masses for their dead members, in this way acting as communal chantries.[29] In addition, some gilds provided help for indigent members, and over the decades many evolved from their origins as burial and prayer societies to organizations that sponsored, directed, or supplemented parish activities such as processions, ales, the support of charitable institutions, repairs to the church, and more.[30] Many gilds arose out of the veneration of a saint's image, which continued to occupy a central position in their enterprises, and to which members dedicated their money and their devotions.

In 1388 Parliament demanded information on the foundations, forms, and possessions of gilds throughout England. Responses from 1389 are extant from 165 Norfolk and 39 Suffolk associations, and these returns elucidate the diverse functions of images in gilds.[31] A few societies that appeared eager to avoid being labeled as a "gild" declared that they began simply in order to provide candles to burn before images. The Yarmouth society of St. John the Baptist claimed *not* to be a gild partly because its sole purpose was to provide a candle before the image of its patron; similarly, a group of Yarmouth cobblers echoed this protestation because they aimed only to maintain a candle before the image of the Blessed Virgin of Arneburgh.[32] Dozens of fifteenth-century Yarmouth will makers left money for lights to burn before the popular image of St. Mary of Arneburgh; whether or not it was a gild, the cobbler's society, which emphasized its lack of possessions, probably originated so that poor people unable to afford even a candle might combine their meager resources to provide for the image's light and thus participate in the popular local cult. On the other hand, declarations of poverty by parish groups may have been a simple tactic to avoid potential taxation, one purpose for the 1388 parliamentary survey.[33]

In contrast to these Yarmouth associations, other societies formed for the express purpose of providing candles for images accepted the appellation of gild. In Bury St. Edmunds, Suffolk, the gild of St. James declared its sole object to be procuring thirteen candles to burn before the image of St. James on Sundays and holy days.[34] The Bury gild dedicated to the Assumption of the Blessed Virgin Mary had no regulations other than to proffer twenty-six candles to burn before the Virgin's image on Sundays and feast days.[35] Similarly, a newly founded gild in Stradishall, Suffolk, declared its only purpose to be the provision of four torches to burn in the church in honor of God, the Blessed Virgin, and St. Margaret.[36] A gild might also be born of the interest surrounding a new image, as happened in Spalding, Lincolnshire, where in 1358 John de Rughton painted an image of St. John; he and some friends then provided a light for it.[37]

While most gilds either embraced other objectives from their beginnings or eventually expanded their activities far beyond the mere provision of candles for images, this practice remained a common stipulation in gild regulations.[38] Some gilds assessed their members fines in wax for breaking regulations, and donated the wax to the light of their patronal image; others made contributions to the light a condition of membership.[39] The societies' expectations or hopes for returns on their investments in images are sketched by the record of the gild of the Holy Cross, Stratford, which promises that its candle before the Holy Cross would burn daily at every mass, so that God, the Blessed Virgin, and the Cross would "keep and guard all the bretheren and sisteren of the gild from every ill."[40]

Fulfilling their part of this spiritual contract was not the sole reason for the religious societies' persistent use of candles. Illuminating a statue directed attention to it, granted its viewers a better sight, and also marked a visually distinct space within the church. The gild candles usually burned only on Sundays and on the feast days when the gild had mass said at its patron saint's altar, if one existed. The lit candles thus defined both the spatial and temporal dimensions in which gild rituals operated. Lights before an image notified the community of the gild members' special devotion and bonds to its patron saint, and distinguished them, in a particular place and time, from other parishioners. The simple and quite common devotion of providing lights before an image therefore helped to create a sense of identification and cohesiveness among gild members.[41]

The 1389 returns also show how some gilds associated their images with the consecrated Host or with miracles. Members of the gild of St. John the Baptist in Barton, near Mildenhall, supported "a candle to burn before the image of St. John Baptist in the same church and a torch to burn at the elevation of the body of Christ every feast day."[42] St. Peter's gild in Lawshall, Suffolk, pledged five torches to burn during the elevation of the Host at the high altar and eight candles before St. Peter's image.[43] Three gilds in Tilney seemed to vie with one another over providing the most torches during the elevation and before their saints' images: St. Laurence's offered six candles for the elevation, and two before the image; Holy Trinity said it provided four candles for the elevation and one before the image, as did St. Edmund's, which also maintained a candle at the sepulcher of St. Edmund in Bury.[44] In their parallel treatments of image and Host, gilds announced their devotion to both holy objects and intimated their kinship, ignoring the doctrinal distinction between the two, which held the consecrated Host *to be* Christ's body, while an image was merely a representation.

Nonetheless, the gild records include no inkling of idolatry, no mistaking of an image for its prototype, even in the face of miracles. A gild in King's Lynn, Norfolk, pledged itself to maintain a light before the image of its patron, the Holy Trinity, which had attracted "a multitude of people" because of the miracles that occurred "before the said image and also indeed many were often cured of their illnesses and feebleness. . . ."[45] No one claimed that this image performed miracles—a potentially troublesome declaration, as the case of the Foston Virgin proved—but gild officers who supplied the information connected their society with supernatural events. The Holy Trinity image did not work miracles but marked their site, and through their candles and rituals the gild members associated themselves with this exceptionally sacred spot in the church.

In addition to money from bequests and gilds, images received support from the profits of so-called lamplands, donated by parishioners for lights in the parish church. The plots of land given to endow such lights were usually small, a few roods or at most a few acres, but this common practice could eventually lead to the dedication of several acres within the parish.

The Suffolk historian V. B. Redstone lists many such endowments among Suffolk chantry certificates, although it is clear that the "chantry" often consisted only of the endowed light.[46] These gifts of land for lights were not restricted to parish churches. When Bishop Alnwick in neighboring Lincoln diocese, for example, held a visitation at Ramsey Abbey in 1439, Brother William Caumbridge complained that although the light before the image of the Blessed Mary was endowed with temporal property so that it should burn continually day and night, it was in fact being extinguished between seven at night and seven in the morning. The sacristan was held to blame for this, and ordered to change the practice, under pain of fasting upon bread and water.[47] The attempt, if such it was, to redirect some of the money from this endowment must have appeared practical to the sacristan—why light a candle that no one would see? Yet the bishop's judgment reinforced the donor's intention of placing the land in the service of the image and asserted the spiritual and not the earthly intent of lamplands.

By 1546, when royal commissioners compiled a list of chantries and lamplands only in order to dissolve them, the donations' origins were forgotten or obscured. Icklingham, Suffolk, for example, was listed as having two acres and a rood "gyven by whome or to what Intente or purpose wee know not"; the profits of the land "hath bene alweys employed about the finding of three tapers before the Image of our Lady" in the parish church.[48] The report's formulaic disclaimer of knowledge about the sources and purposes of these land grants was partly disingenuous; although ignorant of the original donor's name, the authors must have known that this common practice had a pious purpose.

Most lamplands provided simply for a light in the parish church, but some Suffolk churches received endowments for the Easter sepulcher, the roodloft, or saints' images.[49] Norfolk churches also had endowed lights, and the profits of some lands maintained gilds which, in turn, most likely used the money for their patron saints' images and altars.[50] This ligature between holy images and plots of earth in the parish marked spatial distinctions outside the church walls, as the gild lights in front of images did within the church. Profits from small parcels of land were dedicated also to anniversaries, obits, alms, and other pious purposes. Holy images in this way took part in the spiritual mapping of a community's territory; as integral parts of parish life, they were bound not only to private devotions and communal rituals, but to the land itself.

As Archbishop Greenfield's order concerning the Foston Virgin indicated, separating the devotional uses of images from their economic context may be impossible. Parishioners expressed their affection for statues and pictures of the saints through gild-sponsored lights, processions, and masses, but also through financial transactions like bequests, land donations,

gild fines, and paying for their repainting, regilding, cases, veils, and tabernacles.[51] Whether or not images were credited with transcendent qualities
like those of the consecrated Host or linked to miraculous healings, they
were deeply integrated into the life of their communities. Removing an
image was not inconsequential, for it would have disrupted the ritual life
of the parish, perhaps altered some part of its income, and diminished the
bond between this particular piece of earth and heaven.

Images and Shrines

The gathering of simple people who venerated the Virgin Mary's statue at
Foston and then at Fraisthorpe had many counterparts, of course, both in
the "multitude" who sought help from the image of the Holy Trinity in
King's Lynn and the people who flocked to the many shrines, famous and
obscure, that thickly dotted the East Anglian landscape in the late Middle
Ages. The most celebrated among these was Walsingham in Norfolk. Frequented by royalty who bestowed lavish gifts upon it, thronged by poorer
folk who contributed their pennies and bought badges depicting the
renowned statue of the Virgin Mary enthroned with the infant Jesus, the
shrine of Our Lady of Walsingham held a place of honor among the great
pilgrimage destinations of Europe. Although the original chapel was believed to replicate the house in Nazareth where the Annunciation had taken
place, and had miraculous associations, the chief attraction was the image of
Our Lady of Walsingham. The image was often petitioned for help; in the
1340s, for instance, some fishermen prayed that "by reverence of the image
of Blessed Mary at Walsingham and by the merits of St. Edmund" they
might recover their nets. The image of Our Lady of Walsingham acquired
such precious gifts as money for a gold crown from Henry III and a ring
with diamonds given by Lady Elizabeth Andrew in 1474. The 1535 *Valor
Ecclesiasticus,* which detailed the resources of English churches, recorded offerings at the chapel of the Virgin at 250 pounds, almost five times those to
the relic of the holy milk of the Virgin Mary at Walsingham.[52]

"Our Lady of Ipswich" was another acclaimed East Anglian image.
Early printed pamphlets record miracles at its shrine in Ipswich, and the
image was visited by such luminaries as Princess Blanche in 1402 and
Catherine of Aragon over 100 years later. While less widely known than
Our Lady of Walsingham, the statue in Ipswich was notorious enough in
the eyes of iconoclastic reformers to merit burning in London in 1538, as
one of a group of "notable Images vnto the whiche were made many spe-
ciall Pilgrimages and Offerynges. . . ."[53]

The two statues—"Our Lady of Walsingham" and "Our Lady of Ipswich"—received their names from the locales where they stood, as did so

many images of the Virgin in Europe. Some clerics worried, however, that this nomenclature pointed to different *beings,* not just images; they feared that people might believe there was both a Virgin of Walsingham and a Virgin of Ipswich (to say nothing of many other beloved Virgins). Such anxieties arose from suspicions, discussed by Roger Dymmok and Walter Hilton, among others, that simple people would confuse an image with its prototype. In the fourteenth century Archbishop Fitzralph warned of "a certain danger from the veneration of images which some frequently and wrongfully call by the name of those they are intended to represent. . . ."[54] In the *Destructorium Viciorum,* Alexander Carpenter explained that there were eight ways to commit idolatry, of which the first was "by bestowing the name of the thing imaged on the image." People who fall into this form of idolatry include those who "call wood or stone images by the names of the saints" whom the images depict.[55] Sixteenth-century reformers claimed that this practice revealed faith in the image of Ipswich or Walsingham, rather than faith in the Virgin herself.[56] These objections censured the naming of images as an idolatrous action that sought to personify or incarnate them, transforming representations into real holy persons; the multiplication of images and names of the Virgin Mary in particular suggested that a separate genius or spirit resided at the site of each of her images. Yet the custom of identifying statues by place-names also recognized the close bond of image and place, an intimacy between artifact and locale that was dramatized by miracles.

In the constellation of East Anglian shrines, Walsingham shone as the brightest star, but many lesser chapels and churches were also visited for their relics and images, for the sake of indulgences, and for their miracles. Control of shrines was critical, not so much because of concerns about spiritual dangers like idolatry and superstition, but for economic reasons. Pilgrims' offerings could be crucial for maintaining a church or convent fallen on hard times. For example, the Rood of Bromholm, believed to be a piece of Christ's cross, inspired pilgrimages to the Bromholm priory in Norfolk in the thirteenth and fourteenth centuries. By the fifteenth century the priory was in trouble; perhaps to shore up its fortunes the pope granted an indulgence to those visiting and giving alms to Bromholm. Another papal bull granted special power of confession to the priests there, since among "the multitude" who resorted to the church on account of the "true wood of the Cross" were some people who, presumably because of their sins, were "unable perfectly to look upon the said piece, thereby sometimes incurring infirmities of divers sorts." The "multitude" was likely more hoped for than real, as Bromholm had lost its earlier popularity, although it claimed (at least in the sixteenth century) to hold the additional attractions of the girdle and milk of the Virgin Mary. The two bulls contrived to make pilgrimage to and confession at Bromholm more desirable, perhaps bringing in pilgrims whose money offered to shrine and confessors, to say nothing of payment for lodging, food, and souvenirs, would help to sustain the priory.[57]

Papal and episcopal encouragement in the form of indulgences for pilgrimages and alms-giving to poor churches and chapels was common in late medieval England. In 1411 a papal bull granted indulgence for visiting and giving alms on certain feast days at the parish church of St. Mary the Virgin in the Marsh in Norwich, for its "repair and conservation."[58] In 1440 another papal indulgence for visits and offerings supported the chapel of St. Theobald in the parish church of Thirsford in the diocese of Norwich, "which is in a state of ruin."[59] Examples could be multiplied for Norwich diocese and for all of England. Despite the benefactions of Yarmouth testators, the shrine of St. Mary of Arneburgh was "in ruin" according to a 1430 papal bull, and warranted an indulgence for pilgrimage and alms.[60] Even the renowned shrine of the Cistercian monastery of Hailes in Gloucestershire, famed for its relic of Christ's blood, received such indulgences in the early fifteenth century because of its poverty.[61]

The insistence on poverty and ruin was formulaic and probably overstated at times; it is at odds with reports of the "multitudes" traveling to churches and chapels because of their relics and miracles. Penitents who visited the Norwich collegiate church of St. Mary in the Fields "and its relics" and made contributions to its repair and conservation could receive the generous indulgence of the "Portiuncula."[62] So too could the "great multitude of people" who resorted to the Cluniac priory church of Castel Acre, Norfolk, "in which are divers relics of saints. . . ."[63] The miraculous potential of these relics attracted people, and papal letters of indulgence often refer to their marvels. St. Etheldreda's smock was preserved in the parish church of her name in Tesford in the diocese of Norwich, where "God shows many notable and wonderful signs."[64] An Augustinian priory church in Winchester diocese possessed "very many most precious relics of saints, including the finger of St. John Baptist with which he pointed to the Saviour of the human race"; a "multitude of people" flocked to this church because of the "frequent miracles which the most High has often deigned to work there by the intercession of the said saints. . . ."[65]

Norwich Diocese had its share of those holy images that, like relics, became linked to miracles. The records of the gild of the Holy Trinity in Lynn, discussed above, emphasized miracles that took place before its patronal image. Another example appeared earlier in the fourteenth century, when in 1327 the Bishop of Norwich was ordered to grant indulgence to penitents who contributed to the completion of a chapel at a place named "Ypeçug," "where a representation of the Blessed Virgin was found underground, and where divers great miracles have been wrought." More than 100 years later, in 1464, Pius II granted an indulgence for visits and alms to the parish church of St. Mary "de Pietat(e)" in Kersey, Suffolk, where there were "infinite miracles which by the merits and intercessions of the same Virgin had been and were being wrought daily by Almighty God at a certain image of her in the said church. . . ." Already there was a "great resort of the faithful" to Kersey. Images of the Virgin were the kind most often associated with miracles, in Norwich diocese and elsewhere. An image of the Virgin in a chapel of the Cistercian monastery of Tintern in Wales could not be moved "although the attempt has more than once been made"; for this miracle (and for the sake of daily mass) "a very great multitude" frequented the chapel. In the diocese of York, a picture of the Virgin Mary in the chapel of Stayner attracted the faithful in the mid-fifteenth century because of the "great and innumerable miracles which God has worked and daily works there by the merits of the said Virgin."[66]

"Multitudes" of people also visited holy images purely from their deeply felt devotion, according to the papal letters. Devotion "to a certain crucifix" drew a "great multitude" to the parish church of Drypole, York, on the feast of the Exaltation of the Holy Cross.[67] A 1399 bull speaks of the "great devotion" to a pietà in Worcester diocese; another from the 1470s grants indulgence for visiting a chapel in the monastery church at Ambresbury, Salisbury diocese, that housed an image of "the Saviour crucified" to which "Thomas de la Mare, knight, lord of Aldremanston" and other faithful had great devotion.[68] Only a few saints' images enjoyed the attention and honor usually given to the crucifix or statues and pictures of the Virgin Mary. The convent of St. Michael without Stamford, for instance, received about five shillings a year in offerings to an image of St. Michael.[69] An indulgence was attached to the image of St. Edmund in the priory chapel of Hoxne, Suffolk.[70] Generally, though, people seemed to perceive a saint's intercession as more powerful when they prayed at a relic than an image. In contrast, images of the Virgin and Christ were imbued with sacral qualities, signifying not only their prototypes' higher celestial status but also the relative paucity of their relics.[71]

Far from worrying about idolatry, the papal and episcopal records indicate that the church authorities usually approved of offerings and pilgrimages to images, although problems and disputes naturally arose from time to time. Perhaps the Bishop of Lincoln was concerned about idolatry when in the 1380s he condemned the adoration of a statue "vulgarly known as Jurdon Cros" erected in Rippingdale, where miracles had been reported. Nonetheless, the bishop's refusal to allow a chapel to be built on the site was reversed by papal bull, which accepted the account of the miracles and encouraged devotion to the cross.[72]

Such local cults must frequently have risen and fallen without interference or note. Some images entered the written record when, like the Foston Virgin and "Jurdon Cros," they became the focal points for arguments about money and authority. For example, in 1418 the pope addressed the Bishop of London concerning his suit over the offerings at a picture of "St. Mary the Virgin *de Graciis*," located in the nave of the cathedral. The bishop's opponents were the cathedral's dean and chapter, who had initially prevailed when the issue was brought before the archbishop of Canterbury.[73] In a 1492 case with less exalted participants, the rector of St. Magnus the Martyr, London, charged two men with taking the offerings left at an image of the Virgin recently erected on London Bridge. The accused men were "masters of works and possessions of London bridge," but the rector claimed the offerings because the image stood within the boundaries of his parish.[74]

The offerings of the faithful at popular shrines presented severe temptations that were not always resisted. In his chronicle of the late fourteenth century, the Augustinian canon Henry Knighton reported an incident that pointed to the economic value of images and relics:

> At that time robbers and thieves flourished in the kingdom, and robbed churches, and the shrines of saints, and carried off relics, namely from Thornton Abbey, the image of Our Lady from her chapel at Merivale, and the image of Our Lady at Monks Kirby, and things from many other places, and many of them were captured and hanged.[75]

"The desire of gain" was also held to be the culprit in a dispute that erupted in 1478 in Cornwall over relics and "other sacred things" in the chapel of St. Buryan the Virgin. These holy objects were exposed on certain days for "the devotion of the people," but motivated by greed both clerks and laity took them, ran about the diocese with them "in indecent places," and received alms and oblations, which they put to "their own damnable uses."[76] In another, albeit less egregious example from the late fourteenth century, Meaux Abbey in Yorkshire tried to capitalize on a crucifix, but the plan backfired. Abbot Hugh had a new crucifix made by a craftsman who fasted on bread and water and "worked from a nude model standing before him." The result was a "beautiful image to adorn the crucifix" through which God "performed manifest miracles. . . ." The chronicler, Thomas Burton, recorded the consequences:

> It was accordingly thought that if women had access to the crucifix it would increase popular devotion and also bring great benefit to our monastery. The abbot of Citeaux . . . thereupon gave us permission to admit men and honest women to see the said crucifix. . . . With the authority of this license women often came to the crucifix, especially when devotion had grown

cold in them. But it was to our damage, for they came in such numbers to see the church that entertaining them increased our expenses.[77]

The women's offerings at the crucifix were clearly insufficient to balance their costs to the monastery. The monks' disappointment in the outcome of this venture is as palpable as their calculation in launching it.

Special indulgences assigned to certain statues and pictures, the quarrels over their oblations, and the miracles associated with them, all underscore the economic significance of holy images. While some of these disputes likely masked deeper grievances—as we might suspect in the case of the Bishop of London who fought with the dean and chapter of the cathedral—nevertheless, holy images could provoke mercenary impulses, venality, and even conflict. Churches promoted their holy images in the hope of increasing their incomes, for some perhaps a necessity for staving off dilapidation and ruin. Certainly the Lollards protested what they perceived as the economic evils of images, accusing priests of encouraging idolatry in order to increase their offerings, which Lollards believed should have gone as alms to the poor.[78]

Yet these disputes over images should also be seen as part of a larger ongoing struggle to define areas of control and responsibility in the daily operations of the Christian Church that often pitted laypeople against priest, or one clergyman against another. In the fourteenth and fifteenth centuries, parish priests found themselves at odds with their parishioners, clerical superiors, and other clergy, over a number of issues. Laypeople not infrequently refused to pay tithes or mortuaries, for instance, because of uncertainty about parish boundaries, immoderate demands by the clergy, or for other reasons, and these clashes could drag on for decades in the church courts. Tithes also caused arguments between clergymen.[79] At episcopal visitations, parishioners sometimes complained that their priests neglected their duties in offering the sacraments, or behaved improperly or even immorally, fathering bastards, playing dice, spending their time in alehouses.[80] Friars and parish clergy fought over the friars' right to bury laypeople in their churches and cemeteries and to receive the money for this service that would normally go to the parish church. Because they preached and heard confession, friars could divert the laity's attention and loyalty from the parish as well as their money, and so undermine the authority of the secular clergy.[81] Further clashes occurred in the fourteenth and fifteenth centuries when dependent chapels tried to secede from their parish churches; both lay churchwardens and parish incumbents might defend the rights of the parish against the attempts of parishioners in outlying areas to direct their parochial obligations to a nearby chapel.[82]

Papal bulls, episcopal intervention, and church court decisions led to the peaceful settlement of many of these disagreements, but a few—like the quarrel over the Foston Virgin—descended into violence, with antagonists coming to blows. The underlying springs that fed these passions are not always clear, but certain themes emerge from these events. Disagreement over money was a consistent issue in contests over tithes, mortuaries, burial fees, and offerings to images. Overlapping and conflicting jurisdictions caused confusion and gave rise to rival claims of authority and rights to offerings or other moneys.[83] In addition, laypeople's determination to shape their religion—by offering to images they believed powerful, by demanding that parish priests provide the services they needed, by trying to establish chapels that would constitute new parishes, by refusing to pay tithes or other fees they considered dubious—brought down on their heads criticisms, legal challenges, and sometimes threats of excommunication, to all of which they seemed remarkably impervious.

The disputes over images open one window onto this complex and continuous process of negotiation that was integral to late medieval religion. How clerics used or even manipulated pictures and statues is only one side of this process; on the other are the people who went in "multitudes" to reverence images and relics. All of the women and men who traveled to the greater and lesser shrines of East Anglia—to Walsingham and Ipswich, to the images of the Virgin at Kersey, Thetford, Stoke, Chipley, and Lynn, the image of St. Edmund at Hoxne, the Holy Rood at Bromholm, St. Walstan at Bawburgh, and many others now unknown[84]—belonged to parishes where holy images played a vital role in daily devotions, and that these people supported through gilds, tithes, and testamentary bequests. Their visits to images outside their own parishes may have been inspired by the desire to earn indulgences, to benefit from miracles, to rekindle devotion, or to view an object renowned for its beauty. Yet if they believed, as Archbishop Greenfield suggested, that the sacred inhered more in one image than another, more in this place than in that,[85] this conviction was nourished by a parish life where images helped to demarcate hallowed times and places. In addition, an intimate relationship with the statue of St. George, for instance, could be formed by one's gild membership; a pregnant woman might pray more often before the image of St. Margaret who helped one in childbirth; and a man might work the land whose profits went to sustain candles before the image of St. Walstan; so that for any individual, one image could indeed carry more meaning than another. The widespread veneration of renowned cult images such as Our Lady of Walsingham gave credence to Greenfield's assertion that people believed "something of divinity" could be found more in one image than another, but this behavior was first shaped by people's habitual interactions with images in their own parish church.

The pervasiveness of holy images in the lives of late medieval Christians helps to explain their locational denomination. The jeweled splendor of Our Lady of Walsingham distinguished it from the no doubt simpler, but likewise miraculous statue of the Virgin in the small hilltop church perched above the village of Kersey in Suffolk, but so too did geography. Each image was firmly rooted to its site. The enduring importance of images (and the pragmatic economy they engendered) in their communities is indicated by churchwardens' accounts, which show that parishioners preferred to refurbish old images than purchase new ones. Furthermore, shrine images were rarely exceptional by virtue of the persons represented. Every parish, for instance, must have had a statue of the Virgin Mary, and regional favorites like St. Edmund or St. Etheldreda would also be found in several parishes. One image of the Virgin varied from another by shape, color, size, expression, and skill of execution, but location was the unique distinction of each.[86] Perhaps we may see those images that refused to be moved, like Tintern Abbey's Virgin, as dramatic expressions of this conceptual unity of image and place.[87]

Images, Allegiance, and Identification

The ties that bound image and locale, as well as the public nature of shrine and church images, made them ideal bearers of local and regional identification. Images could also signify political allegiance.[88] Every area pledged loyalty to local saints, naming churches after them, painting them on rood screens, displaying their statues, depicting their deeds in stained glass, and organizing gilds under their names. East Anglia was rich especially in Anglo-Saxon saints. St. Etheldreda (d. 679), for instance, whose smock was associated with wonders in Tesford, was the daughter of a king of East Anglia and founded the monastery at Ely. Her image adorns several rood screens in Norfolk and Suffolk, and is also found in carvings, alabaster, and stained glass.[89] St. Walstan was a Norfolk favorite to judge by donations to his shrines in Bawburgh and his image on rood screens there, but he was elsewhere unknown and his very existence is now considered dubious.[90]

Political figures posthumously renowned for their holiness received similar attention through their images, as though they were saints. Popular belief in their sanctity probably derived from the ancient and common desire to see such men as bearers of divine as well as earthly powers. Creating holy images of them was also an expression of political sentiments. In the fifteenth century, the ill-fated Lancastrian king Henry VI was the object of cult attention that arose both from anti-Yorkist views and genuine belief in Henry's holiness.[91] Pilgrims made their way to the abbey at Chertsey, where Henry VI was first buried, and when his body was later moved to Windsor, they followed. Many people claimed to be cured of disease or otherwise helped by Henry VI, and under the Tudors his miracles were collected as evidence for a canonization that never took place. In the areas of the country not favored by one of his tombs, images of him appeared as substitute objects of pilgrimage. In 1479, during the reign of Henry VI's successor and antagonist, Edward IV, the Archbishop of York forbade further offerings to the statue of Henry in York Minster, evidence of a heavy-handed effort to snuff out the cult.[92]

Despite Yorkist hostility, however, the images of Henry VI scattered across the country proved a national interest in his sanctity. East Anglian contributions to the cult included pictures of Henry on several rood screens, his statue erected in various churches, and chapels dedicated to him in Norwich and Yarmouth.[93] In 1497 the maidens of Walberswick collected 6s. 4d. for painting King Henry's table in the parish church; there was a light of Henry VI in the Norfolk parish of Horstead. The gild of St. Michael in Lynn added Henry's name as a secondary dedication in the early sixteenth century.[94] Some East Anglian prayer books included fifteenth-century prayers addressed to Henry, and miniatures of him as well.[95]

Because he had been the king of England, Henry VI's cult offered devotees a satisfying blend of national pride and religious feeling, just as St. Louis' did in France. But as a deposed and perhaps murdered king, Henry VI was also a potent emblem of Lancastrian, and later, Tudor loyalty. His statues and pictures encouraged pious public exercises, such as saying prayers and lighting candles to him, which could also serve as advertisements for anti-Yorkist feeling. Archbishop Booth's attempt to eradicate devotions to Henry VI's image was therefore an act embedded with mingled political and religious meaning. His effort to control a cult image appeared to arise from motives as mixed as those of his predecessor, Archbishop Greenfield, in the case of the Foston Virgin, over 150 years earlier.

While the public nature of church and shrine images gave them an extra-religious character by allowing them to become representatives of regional and political allegiance, it also made them effective symbols of reconciliation in ecclesiastical rites. The episcopal records of late medieval England catalogue numerous instances of laypeople who atoned in part for their transgressions by performing penances witnessed by their communities. Not uncommonly, a sinner was compelled to signal his or her interior rapprochement with the faith by exterior obeisance to a holy image.

The misdeeds of the accused sometimes bordered on heresy, although bishops' registers typically do not use this word. In 1491 Thomas Langton, Bishop of Salisbury, found many people in his diocese espousing Lollard-like sentiments against images and pilgrimages. Alice Hignell of Newbury, for instance, admitted that she had called people fools for offering burning candles to the images of St. Leonard or the Virgin Mary. Only when St. Leonard would "ete a candell and blowe owte anodir" or when the Virgin could "blowe away the same copwebbis from her face" would Alice be prepared to offer candles to these images. She derided St. Martin as a fool and implicitly mocked the confusion of image and prototype by saying that if "he" were wise he would not stand so long in that high cold place, but would come down and sit by the fire. Finally, Alice underscored the impotence of images (and anticipated sixteenth-century iconoclastic bonfires) by comparing them to firewood: She wished all the holy images were in her yard at home where she would hew them with an ax, "to sethe my mete and to make my potte to boyle." As part of her penance, for the rest of her life Alice was to genuflect daily before the images of the crucifix and the Blessed Virgin, saying the Lord's prayer and the Hail Mary each five times and the Apostle's Creed once.[96]

Alice's opinions were shared by others who were required to make atonement as she did. Isabel Dorte of East Hendred confessed, among other errors, to protesting the worship of saints' images because no man should worship "no stokkis ne stonys ne nothing made or graven with mannnys hand." Her penance included public procession and daily genuflection and prayer before the image of the Virgin Mary, as well as pilgrimage to a Marian shrine. Bishop Langton also found William Carpenter, John Tanner, and other men guilty of speaking against images, disparaging the powers of priests, and questioning the sacraments of the Eucharist and of baptism; Thomas Tailour and Augustine Stere each had a book of commandments forbidding the worship of any graven thing; their penance was public abjuration and daily genuflection and prayer before the crucifix.[97] Similarly, the penance of John Fynche, a tiler from Colchester convicted of Lollardy in the early fifteenth century, included offering at the image of the Holy Trinity at the cathedral in Norwich.[98] Henry Knighton wrote a vivid description of two Lollards, Richard Waytestathe and William Smith, who lived in a chapel outside Leicester in the 1380s. In need of a fire to cook their cabbage one day, they seized upon an old statue that Knighton formally and curiously describes as "carved and painted in honour of St. Catherine" [*quondam in honore Sancte Katerine formatam et depicta*]. The heretics joked about the "new martyrdom" Catherine would suffer by their ax and fire, and "banishing shame" as Knighton says, they cut up the image. Some years later, in reparation for his heresy, Smith had to parade around the marketplace of Leicester in a shift, "bearing a cross with the figure of the Crucified in his right hand, and in his left an image of St. Catherine." Knighton explicitly connects this penance to Smith's previous desecration of St. Catherine's image.[99] Such punishments were intended to fit the crimes, forcing these detractors to reverence images in affirmation of their orthodoxy and spiritual value.

Honoring images, however, was not uncommon in penitential rituals and need not be punishment for Lollard sentiments. For instance, in 1409 William Holtham, vicar of Ramsbury in Salisbury diocese, was ordered to offer a candle weighing one pound at the image of the Virgin in Salisbury and to distribute money to the poor, in amends for a sin that was probably fornication.[100] A 1499 episcopal visitation in Suffolk resulted in several offenders being required to offer candles either to the mass celebrant or to the principal image of their parish church. This formal expiation sometimes included a public procession to the church first.[101] The episcopal court of Lincoln diocese sentenced one man to visit and offer a penny both to the image of the Virgin in Lincoln and to the head of St. Hugh.[102] In 1519 the rector of Mulbarton, Norwich diocese, was ordered to offer a candle to the image of the Virgin in his own church for his refusal to serve a summons.[103]

In these penitential rites holy images served multiple purposes. They symbolized first the authority of the church, since offering candles and genuflecting before images displayed the sinner's acceptance of the church that sanctioned them. Also, a crucifix, a statue of the Virgin, a relic like the head of St. Hugh, all referred to a supernatural reality and power to which the penitent submitted by her own visible and public actions. Further, a person's membership in the Christian Church constituted not only a spiritual condition, but a physical and localized situation as well. One belonged to a community that included the saints in heaven, but one was also a member of a specific parish and attended its church. For this reason, the image devotions required as penance also demonstrated outwardly a sinner's reintegration into an earthly fellowship. By repeating the prayers, bodily movements, and oblations commonly performed by other parishioners, the offender signaled her acceptance of this community's material artifacts, rituals, and beliefs. Just as iconoclastic utterances singled out the heretical Lollards, so the reverencing of images marked the reunion of the fallen with the saved.

Conclusion

The clergy in late medieval England often tried to control the veneration of popular images, but they rarely worried about the threat of idolatry. Archbishop Greenfield's allusion to the dangers of idolatry in the case of the Foston Virgin received some echo decades later when the Bishop of Lincoln attacked the worship of Jurdon Cross; the two cases could be cited as proof of the clergy's concern for the spiritual danger that images posed for the laity. Overwhelmingly, however, the evidence reveals clerical support and encouragement for pilgrimages and oblations to images, some reputedly miraculous. Furthermore, the details of the Foston case strongly suggest that idolatry, far from being the central issue, was adduced by Greenfield primarily as a device for resolution of a conflict about income and jurisdiction.

The desire to control images had roots more economic than spiritual. Even if disputes over their income at times veiled more ominous and older feuds, money and images were nonetheless inextricably welded together. With pilgrims' offerings supplementing parishioner bequests and gild donations, popular images attracted money that many a parish church, chapel, or monastery needed. In turn, a parish had to commit regular sums of money to the maintenance of its images. In fact, the statues of the saints could even be repositories for the wealth of the parish, which literally covered them in the form of gold. Churchwardens' accounts frequently mention gilding images (an expense that could be recouped by removing the gold if need be), an embellishment that increased the aesthetic power and visibility of a statue.[104]

Holy images clearly served at times as media for propaganda. People may have venerated statues of the supposedly saintly Henry VI to seek spiritual help, but the Archbishop of York perceived in this worship a misguided political sentiment and so tried to quash it. Although the Yorkists opposed the cult and the Tudors supported it, both in pursuit of royal legitimacy, the veneration of Henry VI also sprang from a timeless need to esteem rulers as more than mere mortals. Images of Henry VI placed in churches were visual proclamations of his sanctity and reproaches to the less godly characters of his successors.

Issues of identification also overlay the ritualistic uses of holy images. Images announced the activities of gilds, which had masses said before their patrons' statues, lit candles before them, and bore banners depicting the saints in procession on feast days.[105] A gild's economic responsibility for its patronal image and its rituals involving the image were among its defining characteristics. Membership in the Christian Church was likewise signified by the public veneration of holy images in penitential rites imposed by bishops.

The study of the public uses of holy images reveals a complex relationship between church authorities and laypeople. Indulgences may have stirred pilgrimages and donations to relics and images, but they also responded to existing cults. The papal grants of indulgence to those people who visited the miraculous image of the Virgin at Kersey, for example, rewarded an already established devotion. On the other hand, efforts to repress the worship of cult images met strong resistance: Jurdon Cross in Lincoln continued to attract worshippers after episcopal prohibition, as did the image of Henry VI and of course the Foston Virgin.

Should an image be associated with miracles, popular enthusiasm for it defied official efforts to dampen devotion. Images could designate the site where miracles occurred, as the gild return from Lynn suggested in noting that miracles took place before its image of the Holy Trinity. Such wonders symbolized and amplified the bond between image and place, illustrated as well by the denomination of an image by a place-name and by the donation of plots of land to image lights, reinterpreting within a Christian context the ancient pagan belief in holy places. In marking the location of miracles, images served as visual links between the supernatural and the terrestrial, buoys of an otherwise unseen sacred domain where God, the Virgin, and the saints reigned.

Very often people believed that certain images performed miracles, or rather that God chose to work miracles through some images. As Archbishop Greenfield put it, people thought there was more of the divine in one image than another. In this case, location appeared unimportant; when the Foston Virgin became the Fraisthorpe Virgin, her unabated powers continued to lure pilgrims. The plentiful tales of miraculous images in sermons and saints' lives likely helped to prompt such convictions, as did those images constructed to bow or roll their eyes to enhance their marvelousness.[106] Yet the faith in images' sacral power came equally from their traditional link to relics and their newer association—evidenced in gild regulations, religious literature, and finally in the behaviors of holy women and in prayer books, which are explored in the following chapters—with the consecrated Host.

CHAPTER 5

ART AND MORAL VISION:
JULIAN OF NORWICH AND MARGERY KEMPE

þis creatur sey a fayr ymage of owr Lady clepyd a pyte. And thorw þe beholdyng of
þat pete hir mende was al holy ocupyed in þe Passyon of owr Lord Ihesu Crist & in
þe compassyon of owr Lady, Seynt Mary, be whech sche was compellyd to cryyn ful
lowde & wepyn ful sor, as þei sche xulde a deyd.

When Margery Kempe began to sob noisily at the sight of a pietà in a church in Norwich, an astonished priest reminded her that Jesus was long since dead. Recovered from her outburst, Margery retorted that Christ's death "is as fresch to me as he had deyd þis same day," and so should it be all Christians, she pointedly added. We should always, she said, keep in mind his kindness and think about his "dolful deth."[1]

Margery Kempe's effusive and even violent reactions to holy images could astound her contemporaries, as did her frequent sobbing and cries on other occasions. Although this behavior has earned Margery the censure of some modern critics, others interpret Margery's insistent physicality or "corporeality" as an energetic expression of her spirituality originating in the social experience of medieval women.[2] Certainly Margery's markedly physical reactions to the crucifix or the pietà were not unique; they found echoes in those of other medieval holy women, such as Julian of Norwich and Angela of Foligno. Holy images served these women in several ways. Portrayals in art of Christ, the Virgin, and the saints shaped the forms of their visions; statues or paintings could eclipse historical time, moving beyond representation to make Jesus "present" to them; and holy images provided appropriate objects for the moral education of their senses.

Margery Kempe and Julian of Norwich make an uneasy pair in the history of medieval religion. Close contemporaries from Norfolk in the eastern part of England, females, and writers in the vernacular, their superficial similarities seem to link them together naturally. Yet Julian has received recognition as a serious mystic and theologian, while Margery's place in the history of late medieval religion and mysticism undergoes continuous revision.[3] She can seem as odd to modern readers as she did to her fellow pilgrims and others who knew her and tried unsuccessfully to quiet and restrain her. Margery's tumultuous modes of praying, worshipping, going on pilgrimage, and simply talking about her faith, contrast sharply with the anchoress Julian's life in her cell. Margery's *Book* recounts her marriage; sexual temptations; journeys to the Holy Land, Rome, and elsewhere; accusations of heresy launched against her; and her frequent, almost domestic, discussions with God. It is lively, boisterous, self-justifying, and often moving. Most of all, Margery's *Book* portrays her pious activities and hopes as worked out in the specific social circumstances she encountered, in the towns and cities she lived in and visited, in talking to clergy in the churches she attended, or in traveling with her fellow pilgrims. In contrast, Julian's *Revelations* describes and interprets the series of visions she received, her text an elaboration of her profound spiritual understanding. Both works, however, reveal their authors' intense and intimate relations with holy images.

Julian of Norwich and Bodily Vision

The circumstances of Julian of Norwich's life are obscure. Her book, known either as *Showings* or *Revelations of Divine Love,* exists in both a short and an expanded version, and is the primary source of information about her. It provides little concrete data about Julian, and scholars have pieced together only a bit more. Julian was probably born in 1343, and may or may not have become a nun. At some time she became an anchoress at the church of St. Julian, Conisford, near Norwich. When she reached the age of thirty, Julian became sick and thought she would die. Instead this illness culminated in a series of visions, or showings, which began in May 1373. Julian dedicated the following twenty years to reflection on these showings. She probably wrote the short text of her book soon after the visions occurred, and the revised longer text after her years of meditation. The brief prologue to the short version of *Showings* says that Julian is still alive and a recluse at Norwich in 1413.[4]

The *Showings* begins with Julian's memory that she had desired "thre graces" of God: "to have mynde" of Christ's Passion; "bodelye syeknes"; and the "thre wonndys" of contrition, compassion, and longing for God. Her elaboration of the first grace offers the key to her understanding of holy images. She writes that she had "grete felynge" for Christ's Passion, yet wanted this to be increased. Particularly, she wanted to be present in time with Christ so that with her own eyes she might see his Passion, which would have allowed her to suffer with Christ. Julian is careful to say that she believes in the Passion "as halye kyrke schewys and techys, and also the payntyngys of crucyfexes that er made be the grace of god aftere the techynge of haly kyrke to the lyknes of Crystes passyon, als farfurthe as man ys witte maye reche."[5] Julian fully accepts paintings of the Passion as pedagogic tools to teach the faithful and bring to mind what, to her regret, she never saw—Christ's Passion. She reaffirms holy images' status as curious *aides-mémoire* to those crucial episodes in Christian history that medieval Christians could not, strictly speaking, remember. At best, these images inspired the recollection of the written or spoken verbal renderings of these events. Julian wants more, desiring the "bodylye syght" that would transcend the shortcomings of a painting. Julian pointedly notes the orthodoxy of such paintings, which are made by God's grace and according to Holy Church's teaching, but also recognizes their limitations. They resemble Christ's Passion, insofar as humans can know it, but this understanding must fall short, as no one can fully penetrate such ineffable mysteries of Christianity as the nature of the Trinity and the Passion of Christ. As she later remarks, human beings can only have a "lytylle knowyng" of what will be revealed to them in heaven.[6] Paintings thus leave unsatisfied her hunger for the bodily sight of Christ and her desire to be present among the faithful at his death.

Julian's clear distinction between a holy image and a bodily sight of Christ was not self-evident in the late Middle Ages. The animate and speaking statues and bleeding crucifixes, for example, that proliferated in *exempla* and saints' legends blurred these categories, suggesting that a crucifix might become Christ himself, or that the Virgin Mary herself might replace her own statue. In addition, disagreement existed over whether laypeople could even distinguish an image from a vision, and medieval ideas about devotional images clouded the differences between material and mental images. Thomas à Kempis, for instance, urged readers to turn their thoughts to the image of the crucified Lord, a directive that could be obeyed with the help of either mental or physical images. One art historian has suggested that fifteenth-century Flemish oil paintings not only represented visions, but could also function as visions for their spectators, transcending their own materiality.[7]

This potential confusion of material and mental images and divine visions perhaps moved Julian to separate so explicitly her desire for a "bodylye syght" of Christ's Passion from paintings of it. She accepts holy images' orthodoxy yet firmly relegates them to a secondary role in her quest for the "thre graces." Human artifacts cannot substitute for divine visions. Despite this lucid discrimination, however, holy images played a key role in the fulfillment of Julian's desire to attain fuller understanding of and deeper feeling for Christ's Passion.

After describing her three desires, Julian tells of the nearly fatal malady that she perceived as an answer to her request; as she says, "god sent me a bodily sicknes. . . ." She lay ill for three days and three nights, received last rites, then lingered two days and nights longer. On the third night she and those watching over her thought she would die. The next morning her body felt dead from the middle downward. She asked to be lifted up so that her heart would be freer to be at God's will and so she could think of God while her life lasted. Her curate was summoned and, as was common for a deathbed, he set a cross before her and urged her to look upon "the image of thy sauiour" and take comfort from it. Although Julian's eyes were already directed toward heaven, she agreed to set her eyes on the face of the crucifix if she could. Then her sight began to fail and the room became dark, except "in the image of the crosse, wher in held a comon light. . . ." Around the cross everything was ugly, as though filled with devils.[8]

As Julian's death throes began, her pain suddenly left her and she became completely sound again, which she attributed to God's intervention. Immediately she thought that she should desire the second wound, that the Lord would fill her body with "mynd and feeling of his blessed passion," so that his pains would be her pains. She wanted to suffer with Christ in her "deadly bodie." She received a bodily vision of the crucified Christ that seemed almost to be projected through the priest's crucifix: "And in this sodenly I saw the reed bloud rynnyng downe from vnder the garlande, hote and freyshely, plentuously and liuely, right as it was in the tyme that the garland of thornes was pressed on his blessed head."[9] This "bodyly syght" (so the Short Text names it) began the series of showings by which Julian attained an understanding of certain spiritual truths. These truths became apparent to her in three ways: "by bodyly syght, and by worde formyde in my vnderstondyng, and by goostely syght." Scholars have linked these three modes of perception to the Christian tradition of distinguishing the physical and spiritual senses and their different objects. Spiritual (or ghostly) vision has purely spiritual objects, such as the relationship between the members of the Trinity, and so is divorced from physical sense experience. Bodily vision, on the contrary, focuses on corporeal entities, typically the humanity of Christ. Julian's own narrative implies that her vision of the blood flowing from the crown of thorns resulted from external sense perception, from her gazing at the crucifix.[10]

Most of Julian's bodily visions, like this blood flowing from Christ's head, were closely linked to the image of the crucifix. The strong tradition of affective meditation on the Passion encouraged visualizations in which the meditator "saw" herself present at the Crucifixion. Julian's bodily visions of the tortured Christ evoke the power and grisliness of reality, stimulated not only by the intensity of disciplined and habitual meditation, but also by the crucifix on which she gazed. Contemporary crucifixes and paintings of the Crucifixion typically emphasized Christ's bodily anguish and the flow of blood from his wounds, and this sacred art shaped Julian's visions and those of many other mystics.[11] Readers of the *Showings* may also think that in the hallucinations of fever, she "saw" the crucifix come alive, as it did in several of the Middle English stories described above (chapter 2). Julian's precise and detailed accounts stress the vividness of her bodily sights, as in this description of Christ's bleeding head:

> The grett droppes of blode felle downe fro vnder the garlonde lyke pelottes, semyng as it had comynn ouȝte of the veynes. And in the comyng ouȝte they were bro(wn)e rede, for the blode was full thycke; and in the spredyng abrode they were bryght rede.[12]

Julian emphasizes her external sense perceptions of the crucifix when she later describes how she saw "with bodely sight in the face of the crucifix that hyng before me" and saw Christ endure spitting, blows, contempt, and many pains.[13] In her eighth revelation, Julian concentrates again on the crucifix. She watches Christ dying, observing his face change from "deede pale" to blue to brown, and his body turn brown and finally black.[14] For five chapters she ponders this dying and drying of Christ's body. While she waits for death to take hold of him, "sodenly I beholdyng in the same cross he channgyd in blessydfulle chere."[15] The continuity of her physical gaze upon the crucifix—"the same cross"—is clear, as is the crucifix's function as the medium for her corporeal visions.

Julian openly acknowledges the link between the crucifix and her visions when she speaks to a cleric who came to her and asked how she did. Julian replied that she had been raving, at which he laughed. Then she told him that it had seemed to her that the cross in front of her face "bled fast," at which the cleric "waxsed all sad" and marveled at it.[16] The man's earnest response to Julian's suggestion that the crucifix itself had bled makes her ashamed. By suggesting that her visions were illusory, she denied her belief in their divine origin as well as their true spiritual significance. The gravity with which the cleric received her report of a bleeding crucifix, however, recalls the widespread tales of and belief in miraculous images. These precedents meant that he could not simply dismiss Julian's account, even if he thought it implausible.

The crucifix that the priest held up to the dying Julian initiated her bodily and then spiritual visions. She did not believe that she saw a bleeding crucifix, but the prototype of all crucifixes, the actual body of Christ undergoing the torments of the Passion. Julian presents her first revelation in a temporal framework that shows how bodily sight led to spiritual vision and understanding. Looking at the crucifix, Julian has a bodily vision of the Passion, seeing the red blood running down from the crown of thorns. From this follows her spiritual understanding of the Trinity: "And in the same shewing sodeinly the trinitie fulfilled my hart most of ioy. . . ." The sight of the Passion and the understanding of the Trinity bring her comfort. Julian explicitly connects the visions again: "In this same tyme that I saw this sight of the head bleidyng, our good lord shewed a gostly sight of his homely louyng." The bodily and spiritual sights work concurrently: "And in alle þat tyme that he schewd thys that I haue now seyde in gostely syght, I saw the bodely syght lastyng of the (plentuous) bledyng of the hede." Finally the bodily vision ceased, but the spiritual vision "dwellth in my vnderstondyng."[17]

Julian's explication of another of her bodily visions implies that she witnessed the crucifix undergo actual physical changes. In the second revelation, when she looked with "bodely sight in the face of the crucifixe," she observed Christ's face changing color. Each half of his face was alternately caked with dried blood, which then vanished. She is reminded of the Vernicle at Rome, the revered kerchief or veil on which Christ imprinted the image of his face as he carried the cross to Calvary. The Vernicle was also subject to changes. Like the face of Christ in her vision, the Vernicle "me(u)yth by dyverse channgyng of colour and (chere), somtyme more comfortable and lyuely, and some tyme more rewfull and deadly, as it may be seen." Julian believed that her bodily vision "was a fygur and a lyknes of our fowle blacke dede" that Christ "bare for our synne." Her desire to see more clearly was answered in her reason, leading her to understand that the soul's continual search pleased God. The vision ends, then, by offering a spiritual understanding of the soul's relation to God. Yet by the comparison of the crucifix's changes with those of another image, the Vernicle, she implied that the crucifix did indeed alter before her eyes. However strange this transformation might seem, the Vernicle's example shows it was not impossible. No image could more truly be Christ's likeness than the Vernicle, since he himself created it. This fusion of relic and image gave the Vernicle a powerful hold on the religious imagination, making it a popular component in late medieval piety: Depictions of the Vernicle commonly appear, for instance, in Books of Hours and other prayer books, small pictures of it were mass produced, and pilgrims visited Rome in order to see the original.[18] By identifying her crucifix with the Vernicle,

Julian both asserted the authority of her revelation and also implied the physical reality of the changes she observed in the crucifix.

Julian's defense of and experiences with images formed part of her conception of the place of the created universe in the process of the soul's ascent to God. In one of her best-known visions, God showed her "a little thing, the quantitie of an haselnott" lying in the palm of her hand, which was his creation. Astonished that so slight a thing could endure, she was given to understand "It lasteth and ever shall, for god loueth it." Still humans must know the littleness of the created universe, in order to love God, who is not created. No created thing should come between God and the human soul, and no soul can find rest until it rejects all created things. Nonetheless, God's love fills and overflows his creation, and everything made reveals God's goodness. The material world poses dangers if one is too much attached to it, yet God's benevolence is at work in it.[19]

Undeniably the spiritual wisdom she attained was of the highest significance for Julian. She believed God touched her through illness, image, and vision, yet these were only conduits for the message of God's love, Julian's primary subject. Historians recognize illness and vision as common media for experiencing the divine in the lives of many medieval holy people, and recent scholarship has begun to establish as well the crucial part played by sacred art in this respect.[20] Julian's perceptions of the crucifix and its forceful impact on her are better understood when placed in this broader context of medieval mystical experiences, and the rest of this chapter aims to sketch these connections.

Julian was also, of course, a woman of a particular time and place, specifically late medieval Norfolk. The temporal and geographic frame of her life may provide clues for interpreting her connections with images. The analysis of East Anglian wills (in chapter 3) suggests that women felt a closer attachment to the familiar church images than did men. Julian, of course, was not any parish wife, but an anchoress enclosed within the church walls. Further, she was lettered, again unlike most other women of her town and era. Julian's famous reference to herself as "a symple creature vnlettyrde" was not an admission of illiteracy. Although the sources of Julian's education are unknown, little doubt exists that she was literate in at least the modern sense; that is, she could read the vernacular language, if not Latin.[21] Images did not substitute for books for Julian, and their ancient and most repeated defense as *libri laicorum* was irrelevant for her as it was for many other mystics. Julian's strong emotional and spiritual response to the crucifix, however, shows the power of sacred art, and may illuminate the perceptions of her secular female contemporaries.

The standard defense of images as books for the illiterate might seem more applicable in the case of Julian's counterpart, Margery Kempe.

Margery could hardly present a greater contrast to Julian of Norwich. A wife and mother whose orthodoxy was questioned by ecclesiastical authorities, Margery was scorned by many who knew her for the loud and disruptive exhibitions of her spiritual yearnings. Margery fed her great appetite for religious intensity with all the late medieval accouterments of sermons, devotional meditations, chastity, holy conversations, and pilgrimages. For all the apparent differences between the two women, however, Julian's and Margery's uses of holy images bore strong similarities.

Margery Kempe and the Act of Beholding

Where Julian of Norwich's spiritual life centered on contemplating her showings in a solitary cell, Margery Kempe's often found expression in the public spaces of churches, processions, and sermon audiences. In this Margery was more typical of the late medieval laity for whom the social organism of the parish provided and organized most religious activities. Born around 1373 in Lynn in Norfolk, Margery married John Kempe when she was about twenty, and bore fourteen children over the following twenty years. After the birth of her first child, she fell into despair before a vision of Christ restored her to sanity. Margery then seems to have resumed the normal life of a town woman, running the household and embarking on small business ventures like brewing, in which she failed. She underwent a mystical conversion, began to fast and pray regularly, talked with God and the Virgin Mary, and finally persuaded her husband to agree to mutual celibacy, a condition Margery found essential to her new religious vocation. At about the age of forty she received the Church's consent to live apart from her family.[22]

Margery made pilgrimages to the Holy Land, Rome, Spain, Prussia, and to shrines in England such as Walsingham in her native Norfolk. In all these places her devotions were frequently marked by loud "crying and roaring." She also argued fearlessly with clergymen who tried to prevent her from fulfilling what she believed God required of her, such as dressing in white clothes. Not surprisingly, Margery annoyed people a great deal. She was arrested and examined for heresy, but never convicted; one preacher forbade her to attend his sermons as her noise disturbed the rest of the audience; fellow pilgrims abandoned her on the way to Jerusalem because they could no longer endure her crying and her unvarying conversation on religious topics.

Margery extended her capacity to irritate beyond her own lifetime by composing her spiritual autobiography, *The Book of Margery Kempe*. She dictated it to two scribes in the 1430s; she herself died some time after 1438. The *Book* was discovered in the 1930s, and since then Margery's claims as devout laywoman, as mystic, and as author have been the focus of much scholarly research and dispute. Margery's ability to annoy the present century as well as the fifteenth is clear: One scholar called her hysterical; another declared that she represents the decline of medieval feminine mysticism. More recent and more positive assessments of Margery's spirituality, however, point to her similarities with holy women from the Continent, contending that Margery remained within recognized boundaries of lay and female piety, despite her excesses.[23]

Like many other people in the late Middle Ages, Margery centered her devotions on the events of Christ's life. She prayed before crucifixes and pietàs and enjoyed lengthy meditations on the childhood of the Virgin Mary, the Nativity, and Christ's Passion. Her pious activities conformed to those recommended in written texts of the period; Middle English religious literature is replete with devotional treatises and poems demanding that their readers and auditors "behold," "see," or "look" at the scenes that the texts sketch in words, such as the Virgin sorrowing over her dead son, or the particular sufferings of Christ as he slowly died on the cross. These works have such strong graphic qualities that they seem designed to stimulate their audience's mental visualizations. In his *Meditations on the Passion,* for example, Richard Rolle repeatedly declares how he can "see" Christ's tortures, which he vividly portrays: "A, lord swete Ihesu, me þinkiþ I se þi reed blood renne doun bi þi chekis, stremynge aftir ech strook. . . ." "I se how þei leden þee forþ naked as a worm, turmentours aboute þee. . . ." Rolle's piece provides a model for how to imagine the scene and then to scan it slowly, pausing to look intently at each wound:

> Now, swete Ihesu, me þinkiþ I se þi bodi on þe rode, all bled, and streyned þat þe ioyntis twinnen; þi woundis now openen, þe skyn al to-drawen recciþ so brode þat merueile is it halt; þin heed crowned wiþ þornis, þi bodi al ful of woundis, nailis in þin hondis & feet so tendre. . . . þi bodi is streyned as a parchemynskyn upon þe harowe. . . . þou hongist and stondist on nailis; stremes of blood rennen doun bi þe rode. . . .

> ["Now, sweet Jesu, in my mind I can see your body on the cross, dehydrated from loss of blood, strained so that the joints pull apart: now your wounds open, the taut skin is completely ripped asunder and gapes so wide that it's a marvel it holds together; your head is crowned with thorns, your body one mass of injuries, nails in your soft hands and feet . . . your body is taut like a skin prepared for parchment on the stretching-frame. . . . you are hanging and standing on nails; torrents of blood gush down the cross. . . ."][24]

Rolle's vivid details of blood and tortured body place the reader before the cross. In a like manner *The Doctrinal of Sapience,* printed by Caxton in

1489, paints a precise picture of Christ's wounds pulled open by the weight of his body, his sinews and veins breaking, and urges its readers: "O thou sinnar, man or woman, byholde and see in thys myro[u]r of pacyence and lerne to suffre."[25] Poetry also implored readers to gaze at Christ on the cross; in one poem, for instance, the crucified Christ hanging on the cross addresses a passerby, ordering him to "behold" his broken body, torn hands and feet, crown of thorns, and his thousands of wounds.[26]

Perhaps the work best known for conjuring such mental pictures is Nicholas Love's *Mirror of the Blessed Life of Jesus Christ,* a popular English reworking of the Franciscan *Meditationes Vitae Christi.* Several scholars have noted the markedly visual quality of this work and related it to Margery Kempe's meditations, but this element is not uncommon in Middle English texts. Love's book recreates the life of Christ, interpolating non-biblical scenes and coaxing readers, "lewde men & women & hem þat bene of symple vndirstondyng," to join imaginatively in the events of the Incarnation, Passion, and Resurrection. With these images in mind, wrote Love, a "symple soule þat kan not þenke bot bodyes or bodily þinges mowe haue somwhat accordynge vnto is affecion where wiþ he maye fede & stire his deuocion. . . ." Love's intent was to melt the barriers between the outer and inner senses. Those who truly wanted to grasp the "fruyte of þis boke" had to make themselves present in their souls at those events of Christ's life described in his book as though they heard them with their "bodily eres" or saw them with their eyes. The reader or listener thus became an active participant in various scenes of Christ's life, exhorted to look at Jesus' actions and the critical moments of his life as though these scenes were living tableaux before her eyes. These meditations relied upon the reader's/listener's capacity for visual imagining, aiming to help her develop personal relationships with Christ and other holy people. Although Love's language directs the use of the mind's eye to see the holy scenes, its repeated exhortations to look, to see, to gaze, could be met with the eyes of the body as well.[27]

Margery's narration demonstrates how she often fused the body's senses with the inner or spiritual senses. Describing her visual imaginings of the scenes of Christ's life, Margery used the vocabulary of the inner senses; she wrote that she saw these scenes "in þe cite of hir sowle" or with "hir gostly eye." Yet there is no doubt that carved and painted holy images on which she looked with her bodily eyes also inspired her to imagine the Passion's details of blood and suffering flesh. Margery's spiritual and physical senses were closely linked, and she described their interplay with notable clarity. She claims, for example, that when she saw a crucifix or a wounded man or a man beating a child or whipping a horse, then she thought she saw "owyr Lord" being beaten or wounded.[28] In another instance, Margery tells how her mind became wholly concerned with spiritual matters when a priest showed the crucifix to the congregation on Palm Sunday. During that mass she wept and sobbed for "hir thowt þat sche saw owr Lord Crist Ihesu as verily in hir sowle wyth hir gostly eye as sche had seyn be-forn þe Crucifixe wyth hir bodily eye."[29] For Margery, crucifixes, human beings, and beaten beasts were all devotional images that recalled her to Christ. Seeing these tangible objects with her bodily eyes stimulated visions of her ghostly eye. This connection of the physical and spiritual led Margery to perceive the quotidian material world as suffused with supernatural meaning.

The dialogue between physical images and mental imaginings, and between her corporeal and spiritual or ghostly eyes, continues throughout Margery's book. Images inspired her to think of the Passion, and the specific depictions of the Passion in the art of late fourteenth- and fifteenth-century England and northern Europe supplied the visual details of her meditations. Clarissa Atkinson, for instance, points out the similarity of Margery's meditations to a retable given to Norwich Cathedral in 1381 depicting Christ's Passion, burial, and ascension.[30] Margaret Aston similarly connects Margery's vision of the crucified Christ's body as "more ful of wowndys" than was a dove-house of holes to late medieval pictures showing his body pocked with hundreds of bleeding cuts.[31]

While painting and statues could contour Margery's spiritual visualizations, her deeply felt affinity to these images was also shaped by written texts. Scholars usually consider Margery unable either to read or write, skills taught separately in the Middle Ages, because she had books read to her and hired scribes to write her story.[32] If she were indeed illiterate, Margery nonetheless belonged to a culture increasingly informed by the written word, as her own connections with several texts suggests. She mentions that a priest read to her several devotional works and saints' lives, which fed her desire for literature and learning and finally, no doubt, for creating her own work. Sermons were of the utmost importance to her for "sche hungryd ryth sor" for God's word.[33] She believed that by "heryng of holy bokys" and "holy sermownys" she increased in "contemplacyon & holy meditacyon."[34]

Because of her knowledge of the New Testament and of works by Walter Hilton, Bonaventure, St. Bridget, and others, it is misleading to think of Margery as cut off from all writing. On the contrary, Margery exemplifies the way in which a technical illiterate may participate in written culture by availing herself of others' skills.[35] She indicates the narrowness and even insignificance of the gap separating readers from nonreaders when she reports that the Lord said he was pleased with her "wheþyr þu redist er herist redyng. . . ."[36] The sermons, devotional works, and saints' lives that Margery heard likely fostered her meditations and the emotive behavior that she displayed when looking at holy images. Her comments on and reactions to images show both the influence of meditative manuals' references to sensory stimulation and also connections to religious literature like sermon *exempla*. Although we cannot know precisely all that Margery heard in her decades of devotional listening, the examples below cite parallels between Margery's experiences and various written texts in order to suggest how they might have interacted.

The sight of a holy image like a crucifix or pietà could leave Margery rapt in thoughts of the Passion and lead her to cry out uncontrollably. The bodily action of looking at the image led to mental absorption in and emotional identification with the scene or person depicted, resulting finally in the physical expression of tears or cries. More than once she clearly describes this dynamic interaction between image, mind, and body. On one occasion, upon entering a church in Leicester "sche behelde a crucyfyx was petowsly poyntyd & lamentabyl to be-heldyn, thorw whech beheldyng þe Passyon of owr Lord entryd hir mende, whe<r>thorw sche gan meltyn & al-to-relentyn be terys of pyte & compassyown."[37] Another time at a church in Norwich, she saw a pietà. Through "beholdyng" this pietà her mind became "al holy ocupyed" in Christ's Passion and in the "compassyon" of the Virgin Mary, and by this "sche was compellyd to cryyn ful lowde & wepyn ful sor, as þei sche xulde a deyd."[38]

Margery's multiple part reception of these images resembles those responses that various religious texts outlined and urged on their readers. The author of *The Pore Caitiff* wrote that when men see Christ on the cross in the church, they will "have mind" of his Passion and his pains, which he suffered for their salvation, and thank him for it.[39] A sermon from *Mirk's Festial* also says that crosses are set on high in holy church so that people "by syȝt þerof haue mynd of Cristis passion."[40] The devotional *Tretyse of Love* demanded a deeper emotional reaction. It encouraged the reader to gaze on the instruments of the Passion, known as the *Arma Christi,* in order to "haue his deth in remembraunce" and "wepe euery daye for this that our lorde & souerayn loue was dede for vs."[41] Whether the devotee should look with the mind's eye or the bodily eyes is not specified and in fact the distinction is lost. But another work that advises readers on the nine points needed to please God, underscores the importance of the body's vision, suggesting to readers that they have God present in the mind and heart "as þouȝ þou syȝe hym present wiþ þi bodyly yȝe, and so drede hym and reuerence hym and loue hym as he were euermore in þi syȝte. . . ." [as though you saw him present with your bodily eyes, and so dread him and reverence him and love him as if he were always in your sight]. Since we who are in the world cannot see God in his godhead, it goes on, we should often behold him in his manhood, hanging upon the cross.[42]

Medieval religious literature thus provides some context for Margery's electrifying responses to holy art, but the significance of her actions and desires can still be hedged with ambiguity. Soon after her conversion, for instance, Margery said she was smitten with the "dedly wownd of veynglory." She fasted easily, feared no devil, and felt no temptations of the flesh or the world. A curious sign of her pride was that she often wished that the crucifix might "losyn hys handys fro þe crosse" and embrace her "in tokyn of lofe."[43] Apparently Margery considered this desire proof of her sin, although her wish also shows the ease with which she transmuted the carved wooden Christ into the heavenly one. Margery may have visualized the crucifix coming to life, as it did in so many *exempla,* but other literary parallels to her desire had roots in a mysticism of the cross well developed by the fifteenth century. In an analogous passage from *Dives and Pauper,* Pauper encourages Dives to make an end of pride and other sins. The image, says Pauper, shows that the bowed head is ready to kiss you, the spread arms and hands ready to embrace you.[44] Similarly *The Tretyse of Love,* quoting St. Bernard, tells the reader to look at Jesus on the crucifix, "And se the inclinacyon of hys hed to kysse yow; se the spredyng of hys armys to clyppe yow. . . ."[45] These texts employ the physical attributes of the crucifix to point to spiritual truths, the fullness of Christ's forgiveness expressed in his desire to embrace his beloved. Margery uses the same language to show her presumption in expecting Christ's attention and mercy. Yet miraculous animated crucifixes that perform this action appear in sermon stories, such as the one in which the crucifix figure embraces the knight who forgives his son's killer (discussed in chapter 2). Whether the miraculous or metaphorical were foremost in Margery's mind we cannot know, and possibly the two fused so that her desire was for both physical touch and spiritual consolation.

Only once did Margery encounter image devotions as rapturous as her own. Returning from her pilgrimage to the Holy Land, she traveled for a time with a woman who had a chest that contained an image of Christ as an infant or child. When they came to cities, this woman took the image out and set it in women's laps like a baby. These women would dress the image and kiss it as though it were "God hym-selfe." When Margery observed how these women treated the image, she was "takyn wyth swet deuocyon & swet meditacyons" so that she wept loudly. Margery was moved because in England she had had high meditations on Christ's birth and childhood, and she was grateful to God for the "gret feyth" of these women "in þat sche sey wyth hir bodily eye lych as sche had be-forn wyth hir gostly eye." Whether it was the doll itself or the women's coddling of it that Margery recognized is not clear, but she insists here that this scene recreated her spiritual vision. Seeing Margery weep, sob, and cry so that she was almost overcome, these women put her in a "good soft bed" and comforted her.[46] Uncharacteristically, Margery did not participate in this image-caressing; her emotion seems to have been induced by witnessing the other women's behavior toward the Christ child image. This loving treatment of images of the Christ child was not unusual in late medieval Europe, and likely appealed to Margery for making concrete what she had heretofore only meditated upon. Perhaps Margery felt unusual reservations in this instance due to Lollard condemnations of such image worship, yet she herself clearly approved of it, as she emphasizes by comparing the scene to her spiritual visions.

Like most members of the late medieval laity, Margery made offerings to famous images near her home, in Norwich and Yarmouth, and prayed before images in churches, approved and conventional practices. Yet Margery moved beyond the everyday veneration of sacred art, using it to catalyze her imagination or, as she might say, her spiritual vision. A crucifix or a pietà worked on her with forceful immediacy, striking her so powerfully that other thoughts were eclipsed. Overcome by what she saw, Margery understood and expressed her vision physically and mentally. Crucifixes and pietàs led her to contemplate Christ's Passion in her mind, but in her body's lament of cries and sobs she voiced the pain of Christ or the Virgin Mary.

Margery's bodily reactions to holy images paralleled her responses to the consecrated Host, underscoring the close ties between the two in late medieval religious culture. On pilgrimage she received communion every possible Sunday with "gret wepyngys & boystows sobbyngys. . . ." In Rome she received weekly communion "wyth gret wepyng, boistows sobbyng, & lowde crying. . . ." When the Host was carried in procession around the town, it moved her as images did to "many holy thowtys & meditacyonys" as well as to crying and roaring "as þow sche xulde a brostyn. . . ."[47]

As a lay female and perhaps an illiterate, Margery Kempe belonged to the class for whom theologians defended images as *libri laicorum*. Despite occasional misunderstandings with church authorities, Margery was obedient to them and always remained an orthodox member of the church. She knew the tenets of her faith, most likely through sermons and the instruction of her confessors, as she proved when answering to heresy charges. Margery's employment of images, however, burst through the narrow confines envisioned and sanctioned by the phrase "books of the laity." Like Julian of Norwich, Margery used holy images depicting the suffering of Christ and the Virgin Mary to focus her thoughts on the events of the

Passion. Also like Julian's, Margery's meditations became more than visualizations of Christ's sufferings. Images convincingly recreated or reenacted these scenes for her, and this incarnational power formed their bond with the consecrated Host.

Although the crucifix held before her eyes formed a critical component in Julian's showings, she moved away from the material to a deeper understanding of the revelation of God's love. In contrast, Margery evidenced a continued connection to physicality, to whatever could be seen and touched by her body; she emphasized the truth or reality of a vision by saying it was as though she had seen or heard it with her bodily senses. In her soul's sight she once saw Christ standing over her, so near that she took his toes in her hand and they felt to her "very flesch & bon."[48] Julian did not confirm the truth of her visions by comparing them to her bodily sense experience, but Margery felt compelled to do so. Like holy images, relics and other parts of the sensory world fueled and inspired Margery's devotions. Margery wept, sobbed, and cried when she saw the Blessed Virgin's kerchief at Assisi. She wept again at the sight of male babies or a "semly man" or lepers because they reminded her of Christ's manhood;[49] she thus contradicted Lollard contentions that people sought Christ in images rather than in their fellow human beings. Margery's imagination was, as one scholar remarks, of a "concrete" quality that fastened on the tangible and visual as she sought for what was ineffable.[50] So while Margery insisted that her relations with God could not be put into words, her *Book* testifies to her urgent need and striking ability to describe and interpret the more mundane experiences of her life, including the people, places, and material conditions and objects that she encountered.

Neither Julian of Norwich nor Margery Kempe was unique in her reactions to holy images. Despite their profound differences the two women both valued the power of images to stimulate their onlookers' perception of and identification with their divine prototypes. This was not an untrodden path. Such uses of images were characteristic of the piety displayed by many late medieval saints or holy people. A sketch of this milieu provides a deeper context for Julian's and Margery's experiences, but this trail leads away from England, which was somewhat short of saints in this period, and turns toward the Continent.

Vision and Images on the Continent

In the thirteenth century the mystic Angela of Foligno declared herself so enrapt in love for God that if someone even spoke to her of God she would cry out. Her reaction to artistic renderings of Christ was even more violent. As she described it: "Also, whenever I saw the passion of Christ depicted, I could hardly bear it, and I would come down with a fever and fall sick. My companion, as a result, hid paintings of the passion or did her best to keep them out of my sight."[51] Angela's illness induced by seeing a picture of the crucified Christ was consistent with her absorption in Christ's Passion. Her ardent devotion to the crucified Christ stamped her life and her teachings. She meditated often on the Passion, identifying with St. John and the Blessed Virgin, who stood at the foot of the cross. She prayed to them to obtain for her the grace "of always feeling something of the sorrow of Christ's passion or at least something of their own sorrow" and believed this request was granted.[52] Like other medieval saints, Angela's preoccupation with the Passion often fixed on its material details, such as the flesh torn by nails or the blood flowing from the crown of thorns. She sought spiritual enlightenment through the corporeality of Christ's body.

During her life and after her death Angela was honored for her holiness and her teachings, which were known through her dictations to her confessor, Brother A.[53] In a manner probably not unusual for women of her class, Angela learned to read but may never have learned to write. Born in 1248 to a wealthy family, she married and bore children. Within a short period Angela lost her children, mother, and husband. She turned from the world, divested herself of her goods, and around 1290 made her profession as a third-order Franciscan. With a small group of companions she lived near the convent of the Franciscans in Foligno until her death. In her *Memorial* Angela detailed the steps of her spiritual ascension. Meditation on Christ's corporeality and physical suffering framed and inspired her struggles and was aided, at least in the early part of her spiritual journey, by religious art.[54]

Looking at sacred art affected Angela's entire being. The sight of a Passion painting could both provoke bodily fever and inflame her spiritually. Gazing at carved or painted images depicting holy people and events became one means by which Angela encountered God. An act of vision could join the material and spiritual universes for her. One time as she contemplated the cross, she received an illuminating knowledge of Christ's death that filled her with such fire that standing by the cross she took off all her clothes and offered herself to Christ.[55] Another time when she looked at a crucifix she felt Christ's embrace (as Margery Kempe had desired to when she wanted the crucifix to loosen its arms):

> Once I was at Vespers and was gazing at the cross. And while I was thus gazing at the cross with the eyes of the body, suddenly my soul was set ablaze with love; and every member of my body felt it with the greatest joy. I saw and felt that Christ was within me, embracing my soul with the very arm with which he was crucified.[56]

Angela then reemphasized the importance of her bodily vision in this sensation, saying, "This took place right at the moment when I was gazing at the cross or shortly afterward." The joy she received from this event reassured her of the divine origin of her mystical experiences.

While walking toward St. Francis's church in Assisi, Angela believed she heard the Holy Spirit's voice telling her of God's love for her. She heard these words of love until she entered the church and saw a stained-glass window depicting St. Francis held closely by Christ. The Holy Spirit used this image to reveal her own spiritual destiny, saying: "Thus I will hold you closely to me and much more closely than can be observed with the eyes of the body."[57] At first unwilling to believe that God would value such a sinful creature, Angela was finally reassured and consoled.

Eventually Angela realized the limitations of physical artifacts as signifiers of spiritual realities. She came to believe that her spiritual development and deeper understanding of supernatural mysteries made material images unnecessary, saying that she no longer looked at paintings of the Passion because their representation of Christ's suffering was "nothing in comparison with the extraordinary suffering which really took place and which had been shown to me and impressed in my heart." These paintings seemed to signify "almost nothing by comparison to what really happened."[58] Her spiritual vision's increased acuity and scope rendered her bodily eyes less crucial for accessing supernatural truths. Holy images were part of a material world that became increasingly insignificant. When Angela asked God for a "tangible sign," like a candle or stone, to help allay her doubts about her spiritual experiences, he indicated its limitations. A material sign could give her joy when she saw or touched it, but could not keep her from doubt and might deceive her. He promised Angela a better sign, a love for him that would always burn in her soul.[59]

The life of Jeanne-Marie de Maillé, born into a noble family in Touraine in 1331, provides several parallels with those of Margery Kempe, Julian of Norwich, and Angela of Foligno. Like Angela, Jeanne-Marie gave her wealth to the poor. She lived with her husband in mutual chastity, as Margery Kempe eventually convinced her husband to do. She listened avidly to preachers and made pilgrimages, but finally decided to live as an anchoress. Jeanne-Marie's *Vita* claims her piety was notable even as a child, when she collected flowers for images of the saints and the Virgin, and read holy books (in the vernacular) for solace. Reading and image devotions remained motifs in her life, although overall her holiness was defined by her chastity, alms-giving to the point of penury, incessant prayer, and prophecy. Like Angela of Foligno, Jeanne-Marie favored the Franciscans. Her confessor was a Franciscan, she had visions of St. Francis and other members of the order, and at death she was dressed in the habit of St. Clare and buried in the Franciscan church in Tours.[60]

Christ's Passion absorbed Jeanne-Marie de Maillé, and she used images to enhance her contemplation of his sufferings. To imprint [*infigeretur*] the memory of the Passion on her heart, she carried an image of the crucifix depicted on a piece of parchment hidden between her breast and her cloak. This proximity of the image to her heart makes the "imprinting" seem literal as well as metaphorical. Sometimes she held it up [*elevatam*] in her hands, recalling the action of the priest with the Host at the Consecration of the Mass.[61]

Jeanne-Marie's faith in images' mnemonic and inspirational value led her to share them with others, perhaps so they could participate in the kind of rapturous devotions that she enjoyed. She had the *Arma Christi*— the lance, vinegar and sponge, crown of thorns, nails, and all the instruments used in the torture of Christ—which "continuously rolled before the eyes of her mind" painted on parchment "in order to excite others to the memory of the Passion."[62] Similarly, she considered how she might "excite those near her to the praise and honor of the glorious virgin." She decided to have three sculpted images of the Virgin placed in churches: two in the choir of St. Martin of Tours and one in the hermitage of the Blessed Mary of la Planche-de-Vaux, near Ambillou. She called one of the choir statues "the Virgin of sweet consolation." Since it seems inconceivable that the church of St. Martin had no images of the Virgin, these statues must have expressed some of the Virgin's attributes to which Jeanne-Marie was particularly devoted and wished others to be as well.[63]

Jeanne-Marie employed images to stir the memory and excite devotion, but they also stimulated her visions. One priest testified that she told him that on the feast of the Annunciation she prayed before the Virgin's image. While prostrate in prayer, she saw the Annunciation enacted, with the Angel Gabriel greeting and the Virgin Mary answering.[64] Relics provided similar experiences: When she prayed at the tomb of St. Gatian (the first bishop of Tours who died ca. 301) in Tours, he and St. Martin appeared to her. Praying at the relic of Christ's foot, in the monastery in Poitiers founded centuries before by Radegunda, Jeanne-Marie had a vision of Christ and St. Radegunda.[65] Relics and images alike led her to a sensory, usually visual, contact with the supernatural.

Images did not replace books for Jeanne-Marie, as her *Vita* mentions her holy reading several times. Her reading of the lives of the saints allowed her to recite their lives and miracles to her husband on their wedding night and thereby convince him they should live chastely. She often read the lives of the saints, a Bible given her by Marie of Brittany, and other holy books.[66] Jeanne-Marie was no unlearned woman, and she had no need of images as visual substitutes for the written word. Instead images provided her a focus for meditation, stimuli for visions, and sensory contact with the spiritual.

Ecstatic reactions to images marked the piety of many holy women. Although, or perhaps because, meditation on Christ's suffering was paramount for them, confrontations with visual depictions of the Passion often proved more than they could bear. Ludolph of Saxony told of a nun who lost control of herself and fell to the ground every time she saw an image of Christ crucified.[67] Marie d'Oignies (d. 1213) wept copiously after a "visitation" by Christ, so that "she could neither gaze at an image of the cross" nor speak of the Passion or hear others speak of it "without falling into ecstasy through a defect of the heart."[68]

Sacred art allowed these holy people to escape the bounds of the finite physical world. Like the consecrated Host and like relics, images were sites where the spiritual and material fused. The *Vita* of Agnes of Montepulciano dramatized this union by describing how she levitated up to the crucifix on the altar, kissed and hugged it, so that all could see "the spiritual union of her internal unity with Christ through her embrace with a material image. . . ."[69] This junction gave images a power to which spiritually sensitive people like Margery Kempe and Angela of Foligno responded, appropriately, in both body and soul. Placed in the context of Continental holy women, Margery Kempe's reactions to images no longer appear extreme. Even her loud sobbings seem to subside in comparison to Henry Suso's famously devout mother who, at a cathedral during Lent, looked at a carving of the descent from the cross and identified with the Virgin Mary: "In front of this piece of art she somehow felt the intense pain that the gentle Mother had felt beneath the cross." This caused her to suffer "so much pain out of sympathy that her heart palpably burst. . . ." Carried home in a faint, she lay sick until Good Friday when, in an ultimate act of identification with Christ, she died at three o'clock as the Passion was being read.[70]

The significance of holy images in these women's devotions cannot be explained through a supposed incapacity of their viewers, such as the inability to read. In fact, Julian of Norwich, Angela of Foligno, and Jeanne-Marie of Maillé could read. The learned discourse defending sacred art above all as *libri laicorum* seems inapplicable and extraneous to the powerful experiences of these women, which are better understood by examining the effects of art on its viewers. These women responded to material objects with their bodies, with faints, cries, tears, fevers. Their own descriptions emphasize the act of looking: Margery Kempe, for example, says that it was *through the beholding* of a crucifix and *through the beholding* of a pietà that the Lord's Passion entered her mind. This deliberate viewing, with the eyes of the body fixed on the sacred scene, is a key for understanding the interactions between these devout women and images.

A Theory of Moral Vision

Writing about the physicality that marked medieval female mysticism, Laurie Finke has argued that the way we experience our bodies relies on "cultural representations of them" and that these are "not universal but have historical specificity."[71] Medieval theories and interpretations of the human body and the senses differed in many ways from modern ones. Most crucial for delineating the connection between viewer and artwork is the medieval understanding of the eye's anatomy and the mechanics of vision. Margery Kempe's frequent references to the communication between her "ghostly" and bodily eyes suggest that she understood physical vision to occur within a spiritual context. Julian of Norwich also spoke often of the "eye of the soul" or of the "spiritual eye." The five spiritual senses were a common theme in mystical writings, originating in the doctrine of Origen, who believed that humans possessed spiritual sense organs corresponding to their physical ones. St. Augustine had proposed ways by which looking with one's bodily eyes could lead to spiritual knowledge or vision.[72] In the thirteenth century, new hypotheses about the eyes and the mechanics of vision advanced by scientists promoted the bond between "ghostly" sight and physical sight. Their ideas about vision provide a valuable tool for interpreting the visual receptions and responses of Margery Kempe and the other holy women.

The influx of Arabic and Greek works into medieval universities inspired tremendous interest in the natural sciences. Several thirteenth-century scientists proposed theories of optical anatomy and physiology that were based on the work of the Arab scientist Alhazen (ca. 965–ca. 1039). Alhazen had advanced an intromission theory of vision that proposed that vision occurred when an object sent its rays to the viewer's eyes. The Franciscans Roger Bacon (d. ca. 1292) and John Pecham (d. 1292)—known as *perspectivists*—used Alhazen's idea of intromission as a basis for their own theories of vision, which became widely taught.[73] Pecham's *Perspectiva communis,* for example, became an elementary text in optics from the early fourteenth century to the end of the sixteenth century.[74] Either Pecham's or Bacon's work also served as the basis for a popularized and moralized version of optical theory set out in a thirteenth-century manual for preachers called *De Oculo Morali.* This manual was likely written by the Franciscan Peter of Limoges, master of arts and later dean of the faculty of medicine at the University of Paris in the 1260s. Over 100 fourteenth- and fifteenth-century manuscript copies of *De Oculo Morali* testify to its enthusiastic reception and enduring popularity. In fifteenth-century England, for example, copies existed in the libraries of the Archbishop of York and the Bishop of Norwich, among other places. It was first printed in 1496.[75]

De Oculo Morali turned the intromissionist theories of vision and the eye's anatomy into moral and spiritual arguments. According to *De Oculo,* the bodily eye [*oculo corporis*] and vision parallel the spiritual or mind's eye [*oculo mentis*], and also become metaphors for spiritual understanding. For example, Peter of Limoges described the three varieties of vision distinguished by perspectivists: "The first is through straight lines; the second through broken lines; the third through reflected lines. Of these, the first is more perfect than the other two; the second more certain than the third, and the third less certain." Similarly, he then says, the spiritual eye of man has a triple vision. The first and most perfect vision will come after the last resurrection, when one is in a state of glory. The less perfect second vision occurs after death, when the soul separates from the body. The third and weakest of the three spiritual modes of vision is what one has in this earthly life.[76]

These correspondences between the bodily eye and the spiritual eye occupy several chapters of *De Oculo.* In an anatomical comparison, for instance, Peter of Limoges describes the so-called seven guards protecting the physical pupil as two humors, a web, three skins, and an eyelid. Similarly, he says, our "spiritual pupil" requires the seven guards of the three theological and four cardinal virtues.[77]

The structure and placement of the bodily eyes also teach moral lessons that may appear farfetched. For example, the author explains that the eyes are "two in number," so that one may strengthen the other, as Alhazen proved. Peter of Limoges infers from this that the eye recommends a social mode of life. As the two eyes support each other, so too can people in a group or society [*in collegio*]. The lesson is emphasized by a biblical quotation from Ecclesiastes 4:9: "It is better therefore that two should be together, than one; for they have the advantage of their society."[78]

Preachers might easily incorporate such standard moral lessons in their sermons, but *De Oculo Morali* also details particular intersections between spiritual vision and bodily vision. In fact, Peter of Limoges implies that physical vision can itself be morally formative. He draws upon conventional and folkloric beliefs about the eyes and vision to impress their significance and potency upon readers and auditors, and so to caution them about where and how they looked. The eye, he says, is the index of the soul [*index animi*]. The eye's motion can reveal one's interior state: A very active eye signifies an unstable mind, a very slow one denotes stubbornness of will. A person's mind may be judged through the eye, which will reveal whatever lies hidden in that person. Also, the eye is easily attracted toward that to which emotion inclines. Therefore, he concludes, the eye of an honest man should be closed to indecent and immodest sights [*obscenis & impudicis spectaculis*], lest his eye reveal the lewdness of an incontinent mind. Like the hand or the tongue, the eye should be chaste.[79]

De Oculo Morali thus proposes that the object of sight influences one's moral development. The reason this is so may be found in the perspectivists' understanding of the mechanics of vision. According to intromissionist theory, as *De Oculo* outlines it, vision is not completed when species or rays from visible objects enter the eyes. Vision is achieved in the common nerve [*communis nervus*] behind the eyes, where the nerves from both eyes intersect. This arrangement protects us from double vision, a potential danger from receiving visual species in both eyes, and also benefits us morally. Rather than acting impulsively on something just seen with the external eyes and making rash judgments based on appearances, we may instead through deliberation have recourse to internal judgment. The author cites Isaiah 11:3: "He shall not judge according to the sight of the eyes" to warn against superficial decisions based on first sight. By helping to prevent this, the design of our visual anatomy works to better our characters and behavior.[80]

Physical vision therefore both parallels and shapes spiritual vision. What we see with the eyes of the body affects our moral formation and thus the degree of our spiritual sight or blindness. For this reason Peter of Limoges warns against looking at morally dangerous objects and also recommends appropriate ones. First he demonstrates that vision occurs when the species issued by visual objects contact the eye. Citing Alhazen's *Perspectiva,* he notes that after one looks at the sky in daylight through an aperture, then shuts the eyes or turns to a dark place, the eyes still perceive the form of that opening. This proves that the species have entered the eyes and are stored in the visual memory. The moral lesson derived from this is that we ought to gaze at Christ's side, which was pierced when Christ was on the cross: "Let each one . . . contemplate the wound of Christ with the mind's eye" so that he may conform to or imitate the suffering Christ.[81]

The specific connections between bodily and spiritual vision proposed by *De Oculo Morali* imply more profound linkages. Although Peter of Limoges recommends gazing at the wound in Christ's side with "the mind's eye," the side wound clearly formed a desirable object for the body's eyes as well. The wound could be viewed on innumerable crucifixes and depictions of the crucified Christ who was often portrayed pointing to the wound or otherwise calling the viewer's attention to it. The wound became a cult object, sometimes depicted by itself on woodcuts, or in conjunction with the wounds in Christ's hands and feet.[82] The wound was the object of numerous prayers and many mystics cultivated special devotion to it. Angela of Foligno for one wrote that Christ called her to place her mouth to the wound in his side, and it seemed to her that she saw and drank the blood that flowed from it.[83] Julian of Norwich describes her revelation in which Christ revealed through the wound in his side "a feyer and delectable place" for all who will be saved.[84] According to *De Oculo Morali*'s theory of vision, gazing at a depiction of the wound would implant the image's species in the visual memory, where they could be contemplated with the mind's eye, to the spiritual benefit of the viewer. The contemplation of sacred art thus becomes an act charged with the possibility of moral development and spiritual flowering.

The notion that what one perceived by the physical senses affected one's moral status was a common one. Margery Kempe and Julian of Norwich must have been familiar with references to the dangers of vision, which are scattered through the Middle English literature of religious instruction. Warnings against idle eyes as the "first arms of uncleanness" and "ravishers to sin" abound. Only careful guarding of the senses will protect the purity of the heart says *The Pore Caitiff*.[85] *De Oculo Morali,* however, provided an anatomical paradigm for the intersection of body and spirit in which the body's eyes could further moral improvement. This idea mirrored and perhaps—given their Franciscan connections—even influenced the experiences of women like Margery Kempe, Angela of Foligno, and Jeanne-Marie de Maillé. Margery often evidenced the link between knowledge gained through the spirit and knowledge acquired through the body, as when she declared the truth of a vision by saying it was as though she had seen it with her bodily eyes. She compares, for instance, the "gostly" or spiritual sights of the Passion to the physical vision of her bodily eyes, asserting that she saw them "as freschly & as verily" as if they had appeared to "hir bodily syght. . . ."[86] In fact, for Margery the physical and the spiritual lay so close together that she could confuse them: "For sumtyme þat sche vndirstod bodily it was to ben vndirstondyn gostly. . . ."[87]

Angela of Foligno reiterated *De Oculo's* urging for "chaste vision." "While looking at the cross" she was given a "greater perception" of how Christ had "died for our sins," and this produced in her a painful awareness of her own sins. She offered herself to Christ by vowing to maintain the purity of her limbs and senses:

> Although very fearful, I promised him then to maintain perpetual chastity and not offend him again with any of my bodily members, accusing each of these one by one. I prayed that he himself keep me faithful to this promise, namely, to observe chastity with all the members of my body and all my senses.[88]

De Oculo Morali insists that the body, and specifically the eye, is not morally neutral, and the holy women discussed here also recognized the senses' power to create or destroy virtue. For this reason they directed their vision toward spiritually potent objects like the crucifix, the pietà, paintings of the Passion, the *Arma Christi*. Further, the common element among the holy images that these women found most compelling was the incarnated Christ, who was the primary focus of their spiritual contemplations. They believed that by his Passion, Christ made his human flesh the source of human redemption. Five of Julian's visions centered on the Passion, as did many of Margery Kempe's and Angela of Foligno's. Their absorption with the "incarnational" union of spiritual and physical led them to react to holy images as though they bodied forth the divinity of their prototypes. The charged interaction between image and eye, and between spiritual and bodily vision, brought Christ to mind and to body, producing spiritual visions or "ghostly sights," and sometimes violent physical responses.[89] Gazing at, meditating on, or, in the medieval usage, "beholding" sacred art became for these women a deliberate and creative act by which the body nourished the spirit.

CHAPTER 6

STAYING THE SENSES:
IMAGE AND WORD IN PRAYER BOOKS

> *But if the persone be unlettered and moche encombred with wandryng cogitacions of theyr herte / than it is expediente for suche to have afore theyr eyes some deuoute remembraunce or obiecte / as some pycture of the passyon of Christe / or some other saynt / to whome they haue moste devocion. That whyle the sences be stayed and fyxed in that sensyble deuoute ymage / theyr spirite may more lyberally ascende to god / or to the saynt to whome they pray.[1]*

Of all the holy images in England—from the "fair images" in the thousands of parish churches like Roger Martin's to beloved pilgrimage statues such as Our Lady of Walsingham—none was more ubiquitous or more intimate than those in prayer books. These books provide the greatest number of privately owned holy images from the late Middle Ages. Driven by a passion for continual visual contact with sacred scenes, wealthy people possessed tabernacles, golden tablets engraved with scenes from Christ's life, alabaster carvings, and other richly made images, and poor people acquired cheap woodcuts depicting the pietà or Christ as the Man of Sorrows.[2] Yet pictures in prayer books must, as a group, have finally surpassed all of these in availability and also flexibility, as the ways in which laypeople used prayer books images were almost as many and varied as the books themselves.

Prayer books, especially Books of Hours, played a central role in the private devotions of the late medieval laity, whose demand for these books helped to stimulate the lively English book market of the fifteenth century. Even before the use of paper and the advent of print in the second half of the century combined to make books cheaper and more abundant and accessible, the desire for books of all kinds—service books, books for the professions, romances, devotional works—stimulated the making and selling of books. The commercial production of manuscript books in England flourished from the late fourteenth century to the end of the fifteenth century, with a gild of book artisans organized in 1403 in London, where book craftsmen—scribes, binders, illuminators—tended to cluster around St. Paul's Cathedral. Less is known about book production outside of London. Overall, though, it is clear that Books of Hours were a major part of this market; the demand for them was steady and perhaps overwhelming, requiring the importation from the Low Countries of Books of Hours of the use of Sarum, the distinctively English liturgy.[3]

Books of Hours, known as "primers" in England, had an audience perhaps more varied than that for any other book. In the fifteenth century, aristocrats, men and women of the merchant and professional classes, nuns, and clergymen owned primers. There is at least one account of a servant woman owning a primer in 1500.[4] The tremendous popularity primers achieved in this century owed much to the great increase in lay literacy. While most of the texts of English Books of Hours remained in Latin in the fifteenth century, some French prayers can also be found, and rubrics in both French and English often direct the reader's prayers. A large proportion of the English laity could read English in the fifteenth century, and many of course still read French. Many Latin prayers would have been familiar even if the particulars of the language were unknown.

The relatively high cost of all books in the manuscript era might prevent primers being considered, as one scholar claims, central to late medieval "popular culture."[5] The great variety that characterizes Books of Hours as a genre (for example, some were sumptuously illuminated while many had few decorations, and the number of texts also varied) makes it impossible to assign them an average price. We know that in 1447 the Pastons paid 2s. for a primer, not a great expense.[6] Also, many people received prayer books as bequests; late medieval wills commonly mention them, showing the esteem and affection in which their owners held them. In her 1399 will Eleanor, Duchess of Gloucester, left to her daughter Joan a book with the primer, Psalter, and other prayers, "which book I have often used," she said, given "with my blessing." At the end of the fifteenth century Lady Ann Scrope left to her goddaughter Ann Fitzwater "a premer clasped with silver and gylte, for a remembraunce, to pray for me." One might own several prayer books, like the Norwich widow Margaret Purdans, who in 1481 bequeathed the "English psalter" to a priest and a "small psalter" to her son. The Paston family owned psalters, primers, and prayer books, some of them passed down the generations.[7]

While people acquired prayer books through gifts, and might also buy secondhand copies from stationers,[8] a prospective purchaser could also order a primer to his or her own taste and purse—specifying prayers to be added to the regular offices and choosing to include particular images. Also, primer owners often added texts to the prayer book in their own hands. Manuscript Books of Hours can reflect quite individual devotional interests, but as a single type of book created for a large market, they also tend to include texts and images of general appeal.

The advent of printing expanded the audience for Books of Hours. Sometimes printed on vellum, but more often on the much cheaper paper, printed Books of Hours of Sarum use appeared in great numbers in the fifteenth and early sixteenth century, indicating the early printers' confidence in the continued strong demand for these books. William Caxton printed a Sarum hours in 1475, and thereafter published several more editions, as did other printers in England and also on the Continent. Mary C. Erler has found evidence for twenty-nine Sarum editions before 1500, and for ninety-eight editions between 1474 and 1527, and she suggests that a conservative number of copies per edition would be four to five hundred. In this period, then, tens of thousands of printed primers came on the market, while manuscript primers continued to be produced as well. The introduction of more English into the Sarum primer by François Regnault beginning in 1527 must have helped the primer to find an even wider readership.[9]

Although wills, inventories, and notations and marks in the prayer books themselves can testify to their ownership and regular use, the precise contours of their employment remain a topic of investigation. Their immense variety defies easy categorization and generalizations. While a Book of Hours, for example, allowed the owner to follow the canonical hours at home by reciting the small Office of the Virgin, prayers to be said at the consecration or after communion indicate that people also carried Books of Hours to Mass. The many accretions to the Books of Hours, ranging from the well-known prayers to the Virgin called the *Obsecro Te* and *O Intemerata,* to meditational images, songs on the Passion, and indulgenced prayers and pictures, confirm that these books went far beyond the simple task of providing pious invocations for the devout Christian. People bought books for their standard prayers and offices, but also for texts and images of borderline orthodoxy that supposedly allowed users to accrue centuries of pardon and offered magical guarantees of safety and help.[10] Additions by owners molded the prayer books to their particular spiritual interests. So, for example, a prayer asking Henry VI for his intercession added to a fifteenth-century Book of Hours declares the owner's pious and perhaps political interests.[11] Someone appended to another

Book of Hours a litany to the Blessed Virgin; beginning "Most wysest lady / Most chastest lady," the invocation ends with a lengthy notation of the pardon earned for reciting "thes x Avyes," which are "in worshype of hyr X v[ir]tues."[12] Variations like these made Books of Hours infinitely adaptable for use in public and private, at home and in church, for customary devotions and for more individualized ones, at the canonical hours but also whenever a spare moment could be snatched for earning indulgence by reading a special prayer.

An incident from the life of Margery Kempe highlights some of the difficulties in delineating just how the laity used their prayer books. Kempe recounts that one day she was kneeling in church and praying, "hir boke in hir hand," when she was hit by a stone that fell from the church vault.[13] If Kempe were illiterate, as many scholars insist, then the scene she describes here is puzzling: Why would an illiterate person even own or carry a book (here, presumably, a prayer book)? Was it a talisman of some kind, or simply a sign of her status? What could she do with a book besides reading its text?[14] The medieval view of images as crutches for the uneducated, combined with the large number of miniatures often found in late medieval prayer books, points to the conclusion that Margery Kempe—like other laywomen—might have looked at the book she held for its pictures, and not read its texts. This assumed opposition of text and image in prayer is clearly expressed by the sixteenth-century *Pomander of Prayer* (quoted above), which declared that the *unlettered* person might need a picture of Christ's Passion as a stabilizer or ballast for the senses, which otherwise introduce distractions and cause thoughts to wander.[15] It is possible, however, that a literate Kempe did indeed *read* the prayers, at times wanting—despite her frequent colloquies with God—the structure of an established, and perhaps Latin, prayer to shape her address to him.

Late medieval people clearly had a variety of options in how they could employ the rich diversity of images and texts in prayer books, so that this investigation can only touch on a few elements. Books of Hours alone offer innumerable variations on a basic structure.[16] Most of the prayers and images discussed below are "accessory" texts to the Book of Hours—supplements to the standard texts made by the fashions of piety and individual whim—because these provide the best examples of self-conscious and prescriptive bonds between word and picture. In fifteenth-century English primers most of this material reflects an overwhelming absorption with the humanity of Christ and his consequent sufferings in his Passion. This commonplace of late medieval religious culture, explicated at length by scholars of art, history, and literature, can still stun modern readers and viewers of Books of Hours. The particulars of Christ's physical torments are invoked again and again in the prayers to Christ crucified, in the images of Christ as the Man of Sorrows and of his wounds displayed heraldically, in the rubrics that guide the reader to gaze at his wounds and blood, and in the fascination with the Vernicle, the cloth on which Christ supposedly left the picture of his face.[17]

While the origins of many of these prayers and images can be found in earlier centuries, in England the fourteenth to early sixteenth centuries saw their fullest elaboration and greatest vogue, evidenced by their near-ubiquity in this era's prayer books. Devotion to the five wounds of Christ, for example, seems to have begun among monks in the eleventh or twelfth centuries, but was taken up enthusiastically by the fifteenth-century English laity. As the Man of Sorrows, Christ faced the viewer and displayed his wounds—a visual summoning of the beholder to think upon his pain and identify with it. In the fourteenth century, pilgrims returning from Rome brought to northern Europe the image of the Mass of St. Gregory, in which the pope says mass before an altar and Christ appears to him in a vision as the Man of Sorrows, typically surrounded by the *Arma Christi,* or the instruments of the Passion. Large indulgences became attached to this image, increasing its attractions so that its popularity peaked in the late fifteenth and early sixteenth centuries, when it can be found in tiny prayer books, large-scale oil paintings, statues, and reredos.[18]

Like those of the five wounds, late medieval representations of the Instruments of the Passion are often detached from the larger scene, so that the viewer can study each item independently. These *Arma Christi*—literally the arms by which Christ suffered and conquered Satan—appear in early medieval art, but were elaborated in the fourteenth and succeeding centuries as never before. Intense concentration on each stage, each moment, of Christ's agony led to the multiplication of the Instruments of the Passion so that no item involved in his torment would go unconsidered. Artists painted them in devotional rolls and in prayer books, and carved them in churches, so that anyone might be able to ponder the physical pain and symbolic meaning of the lance, crown of thorns, whip, column, the nails and the forceps used to withdraw them from Christ's body, and so on.[19]

This focus on Christ's Passion led naturally to concern with the Virgin Mary's sufferings as well, most clearly evidenced in the popularity of the pietà. This rendering of the Virgin holding in her lap the broken body of her son became known in England in the fourteenth century as Our Lady of Pity; in the fifteenth century it was eagerly taken up and produced in wood and alabaster sculptures found in parish churches throughout the country. It also appeared as painted miniatures and woodcuts in manuscript and then printed prayer books. Our Lady of Pity summoned the viewer to a deeper emotional identification with the Virgin's pain and grief, emphasizing her humanity.[20]

Many of these pictures gave viewers access to objects that were considered relics and only one step removed from physical contact with Christ. Relics from the East had flowed into the West in the thirteenth century, and St. Louis himself had brought to France what was believed to be Christ's crown of thorns, as well as the lance, sponge, and other instruments of the Passion. Pictures of these relics in prayer books, as of the Vernicle in Rome, witness people's interest in physical closeness with the originals, which had of course touched the very body of Christ. This absorption in the corporeal reality of the Passion led to such minutiae as the enumeration of the number of Christ's wounds and drops of blood.[21] It was an obsession demanding the saturation of the senses so that the realization of Christ's every pain could be brought home to the body and mind. For the many thousands of women and men who used primers made from the late fourteenth to early sixteenth centuries, the accessory prayers and images gave entrée to this knowledge by demanding that the user both read about and look at Christ's suffering. The wide availability of these books combined with the particularly late medieval emphasis on the suffering and bloodied Christ to produce a new experience. Late medieval prayer books effected a fusion of the two acts that had for so long been considered separate and antithetical: reading and—in the medieval usage—beholding.

Images as Teachers

> For, as Ion Bellet tellet, ymages and payntours ben lewde menys bokys, and I say bo[l]dly þer ben mony þousand of pepul þat couþ not ymagen in her hert how Crist was don on þe rood, but as þei lerne hit be syȝt of ymages and payntours.[22]

This passage from the fifteenth-century preaching manual *Mirk's Festial* was directed against Lollards, and it reiterates in elementary terms the major orthodox argument put forth by Roger Dymmok and others—that images teach simple people about their faith. Unintentionally, the author also indicates the limitations of images' instruction: The crucifix can show viewers how Christ was nailed onto the cross, but it cannot teach the deeper significance of this event. Fuller tutoring must rely on language. Avril Henry has argued this point in connection with the *Biblia Pauperum*, sometimes known as the "bible" for illiterates because they supposedly learned from its lavish array of depictions. Henry contends, on the contrary, that the *Biblia Pauperum* can be understood only with "receptive sensitivity to image and word," and that no one could master the basic tenets of faith or even the biblical stories simply by looking at an image.[23]

Verbal accompaniments to pictures are common in late medieval prayer books. These book images often mimicked the subject matter of church images—both groups included representations of the pietà, the Crucifixion, the saints and their attributes, and so on—but the books also offered texts that explained images and guided the reader in how to regard them. In their Suffrages (or Memorials) of the saints, many manuscript and early printed primers, for example, offer individual portraits of the saints to embellish the prayers addressed to each one. Typically the pictures display each saint's best-known attribute: St. George kills a dragon, Thomas Becket is slain at an altar, St. Christopher carries Christ across a river, St. Katherine holds the wheel on which she was tortured.[24] The book user then reads the appropriate prayer for that saint, a guide not usually available in churches;[25] once the prayer is learned, however, the reader might easily associate it with that saint's image wherever it appeared, on the page or in the parish church. In thus linking images to texts, prayer books could direct people's responses to images beyond the book.

Another instructional function of prayer book images was more utilitarian; pictures could help the initiate locate a particular text in the book. Primers and prayer books often contained so many prayers intended for different occasions and purposes that a book could swell to a few hundred folios. Finding one's place could be made easier by decorated capitals and rubrics that mark the beginnings of many prayers, and miniatures that emphatically divide one office from another, or separate the different hours within an office, acting in effect as permanent bookmarks.[26] The Hours of the Blessed Virgin often begin with a picture of the Annunciation; a miniature of a church interior with people singing the Office of the Dead frequently introduces the text of that office; a crucifixion opens the Hours of the Cross.[27] Like images that partitioned the space within a church, marking personal devotions and gild allegiances, these book images signal the spatial and devotional divisions between prayers.

In these teaching capacities prayer book images do not act as *libri laicorum,* or replacements for texts, and such an appellation is patently ridiculous. These pictures combine with texts to comprise books, not to substitute for them.[28] Images made biblical scenes and saintly attributes visible and concrete for the book user. Miniatures that illustrate a text, like a crucifixion scene introducing the Hours of the Cross, also reminded the reader of whom to think while praying. Like their counterparts in churches and shrines, however, book images never remained solely instructional but served many other purposes—meditational, devotional, even quasi-magical.

Reading, Viewing, and Praying

*After, caste thine eye on something, and hold it thereon while thou makest thy
prayers, for this helps much to stabling of the heart: and paint there thy Lord
as he was on the Cross: think on his feet and hands that were nailed to the
tree, and on the wide wound in his side, through the which way is made to
thee to win to his heart. . . .*[29]

This passage prescribes images as a focus for meditational prayer; like *The
Pomander of Prayer,* it assumes that a visual target for the eye steadies the
heart and makes prayer easier. Both works consign to second place the object of the eye's focus—the visual artifact stills the carnal body so that the
spirit can move freely. This traditional hierarchy of spirit above body or of
mind above material is, however, subverted by those prayer books in which
images are integral components in the dynamics of reading and praying.

Prayer books commonly use rubrics to direct their readers' actions and
dispositions in regard to images, most often the crucifix or the statue of the
Virgin Mary. One Book of Hours in Latin, French, and English evokes
Bishop Hilary of Poitiers (d. 368) as the source of a directive to genuflect
devoutly before the cross while saying two psalms. A later rubric recommends that the reader in mortal sin or anguish should kneel before the
cross and gaze upon Christ's feet while praying for mercy. A third rubric
suggests that the prayer on Christ's five wounds, *Adoramus te Christe et
benedicamus tibi quia per sanctam crucem,* be said each day before the figure of
Christ on the cross for the remission of sin.[30] Clearly physical proximity to
the crucifix is thought to encourage prayer; the rubrics requiring the sup-
plicant's body to genuflect, kneel, and gaze presume that these actions also
shape his spiritual posture.

A more immediate and practical result is promised by a miscellany of
Latin and English prayers, compiled or owned by a monk. A lengthy Latin
rubric pledges that whoever recites a series of prayers in front of the crucifix will receive whatever justice he seeks; the reader is then directed to
look at Christ's feet, side, and hands while saying the *Pater noster, Ave Maria,*
and other prayers.[31] This book does not contain a crucifixion picture, but
assumes the reader has a crucifix available, as the promised reward could
not be earned without it nor the devotions properly completed.

Prayer books also prompted devotees to greet the image of the Virgin
Mary in order to obtain her favor. A rubric that appears in many English
prayer books warns that if the reader wishes to venerate the Virgin, he should
not pass silently by her figure without saying "ave." The following prayer,
Salve virgo virginum stella matutina, provides the words for a fuller greeting.[32]
A picture of the Virgin sometimes, but not always, accompanies this rubric

6.1   A Prayer "Ad imaginem crucifixi." British Library Stowe MS. 16, f. 128 verso.
By permission of the British Library.

and prayer. A French Book of Hours elaborates the greeting by prompting the reader to genuflect before the Virgin's image fifteen times in honor of her fifteen joys.[33] A fifteenth-century book of Latin prayers counsels the reader to recite devoutly before the image of the Virgin the names bestowed on her by the Holy Ghost, along with forty *Ave Maria's*—with the promise that before death the Virgin would "visibly appear" to the believer.[34] Many late medieval prayer books promise that the Virgin Mary would appear at the hour of death to those who prayed before her image, suggesting that physical closeness to the image during prayer ultimately won the reward of real contact with the image's prototype, the Virgin herself.

Prayer books often include the images that their rubrics require for devotions. A fifteenth-century English primer, now B. L. Stowe MS. 16, contains a fairly common ensemble of an image and texts. A large picture of the crucifix with the simple rubric *Ad ymaginem crucifixi* introduces the popular prayer on Christ's wounds, *Omnibus consideratis.*[35] [plate 6.1] Following this crucifix are four pages of rubrics paired with stanzas addressed to Christ's wounds. The rubrics direct the reader's gaze to each significant part of the picture, saying "To the wood of the holy cross" [*Ad lignum sancte crucis*], "To the head and crown of thorns of Christ" [*Ad caput et coronam spineam christi*], "To the wound in the right hand" [*Ad vulnu dextera manus*], and so on.

This multipage cluster of the picture of the crucifix and its allied texts obviously encouraged and supervised the reader in meditating on the crucifixion, and specifically on the five wounds. An unlearned person might, of course, simply gaze at the picture while praying, just as a more learned user could disregard the image of the crucifix and say the prayers. But the devotion is meant to contain both verbal and visual components, as the physical layout of the three elements—image, rubrics, prayer—steered the user in reading and looking. Although reading is, as Roger Chartier has described it, an ephemeral act that "only rarely leaves traces" and "is scattered in an infinity of singular acts," he also reminds us that readers do not encounter texts that are abstracted from the artifacts that carry them. The act of reading is structured by the material composition of the book.[36] In this case, Stowe 16's construction—the particular arrangement of texts and images on the pages—worked to guide the reader's physical activity in the mechanics of her reading and viewing, and from these to shape her frame of mind.

First, the image of the crucifix visually dominates the top of the page; when the eye leaves the crucifix, it is immediately redirected toward it by the words, "*Ad ymaginem crucifixi.*" The subsequent rubrics address stanzas to the cross, crown of thorns, and the wounds, each visible in the image. The combination of text and image captures the attention of the reader/viewer more fully than either could do alone, keeping both mind

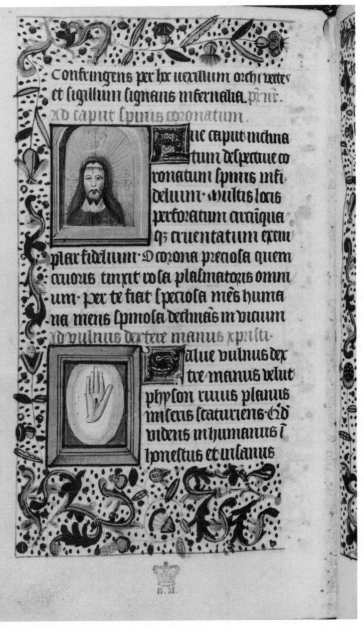

Confringens per hoc uexillum orchi uedes
et figillum fignans infernalia. p̄r nr.
Ad caput fpinis coronatum.

ue caput inclina
tum despectiue co
ronatum fpinis infi
delium · uultas lotis
perforatum ciuique
qz cruentatum exem
plar fidelium · O corona preciosa quem
auoris timpit cola plasmatoris omni
um · per te fiat speciosa mea huma
na mens fpinosa declinas in diuum
Ad uulnus dextere manus xpristi.

alue uulnus dex
tre manus uelut
phyfon riuus planus
miscris scaturiens · Oŏ
uidens in humanus i
honestus et insanus

6.2   Prayers and images of the wounds of Christ. British Library Arundel MS. 318,
f. 82 verso. By permission of the British Library.

and eye absorbed in the piteousness of Christ's suffering, his agony dramatized by the slowly shifting focus from one bodily wound to another.

This sequence in Stowe 16 continues for five pages.[37] To use the image
in union with the prayers as the rubrics instruct, the reader must flip back
and forth through the pages, moving from reading the rubric, gazing at a
wound in the image, and turning pages forward to read the prayer. This
seems clumsy, and alternatives suggest themselves: that the reader used a
crucifix in church or at home to gaze at, or that the reader gradually mem-
orized the stanza for each wound and repeated it at the rubric's prompt,
turning to the image in the book to pray from memory. Either possibility
(there are doubtless others) sketches a process of frequent stops and starts
in the reading, as the user moves physically—eyes advancing forward to the
next rubric then pushed back to the image, and hands turning pages—
from the rubric to the image to the prayer. The devotion as a whole summons the book's user to a merging of visual and verbal devotion, as the
physical and temporal movements of reading intertwine the discrete spaces
of image and text.

This devotion appeared in several prayer books,[38] part of the increasingly popular reverence paid to Christ's wounds in the late Middle Ages.[39]
Prayer books sometimes highlight the separate wounds with individual depictions of the left and right hands, the feet, the side, the head crowned
with thorns, each of these images matched with its own rubric and prayer.
Modern viewers may find the detachment of the limbs from Christ's body
somewhat bizarre, but the series provides a visually dramatic enticement to
the viewer to scrutinize the particularities of Christ's sufferings. Such a layout occurs in one English primer (B. L. Arundel MS. 318), heightening the
focus on the wounds, and making the devotion physically easier for the
user, who need not search the pages for the crucifix. [plate 6.2] Both visual and verbal elements are immediately accessible. Still, the reading
process consists of a series of distinct moments, each introduced by a rubric
that draws the eye toward a new image and a new text (again, *Omnibus consideratis*). These couplings of images and prayers demand that the eye move
constantly between them, as each text requires an image for its fulfillment.

Similar prayers or variations on those above abound in late medieval
prayer books. Two examples here can sketch some of the additional interactions between word and image. One English primer contains a series of
rubrics introducing prayers to be said while looking at the crucifix. The
reader should "beholde þe wound on þe syde," "þan beholde the ry3th
hand," "þan beholde þe lyfte hand," and so on. Each wound receives its
prayer; however, despite the repeated command to "beholde," no picture
adjoins this sequence. Unless she wished to rely on mental images, the
devotee had to find a crucifix to look at in order to fulfill this devotion

"unto þe passyone of ihesu christ."[40] The rubrics thus position her body
before a crucifix and order her relation to it in this union of written and
oral prayer with visual meditation.

The second example diverges slightly from the image and prayer in
Stowe 16 that began this discussion, the crucifix and *Omnibus consideratis*. In
this book [B.L. Harley MS. 1251], a crucifixion scene includes the Blessed
Virgin and St. John. The subsequent rubrics again guide the reader/viewer's
attention to each of Christ's wounds while she says a verse of the prayer.
After the prayer to the wound in the left foot, two additional rubric—"Ad
ymaginem beate marie" and "de sancto iohanne"—introduce the stanzas of
Omnibus consideratis dedicated to the Virgin and St. John.[41] This crucifixion
scene reproduces the roodloft group found in many a parish church, and so
was perfectly comprehensible without the text. The rubrics binding picture
to prayer presume that the image completes the text; for the reader/viewer,
the pious words layered the familiar roodloft group with added significance
by making it an object of meditation.

While many prayers thus explicitly call for an image, prayer book images could also require a text for their explication. Certainly the proper
understanding of any image demanded at least basic instruction, but some
visual representations in prayer books are more opaque than the common
run of crucifixion scenes or pietàs would suggest. In an unusually dramatic instance, several of B. L. Egerton MS. 1821's first eight leaves are
covered by blood drops on solid black or red backgrounds. Folio nine displays a woodcut of a lanced heart on a cross; two hands and two feet, each
nailed and gushing blood, occupy the four corners.[42] This woodcut belongs to the cult of the five wounds of Christ, but the drops of blood on
the preceding pages are more unusual. Their graphic forcefulness commands attention without the urging of any rubric or prayer; nonetheless,
their impact depended on the viewer's familiarity with texts that termed
the torn body of Christ the "charter" on which the promise of heaven
was written. Some Middle English poems name the whips as the "pens"
that wrote this charter: "þe pennes þat þe letter was with wryten / was of
skourges þat I was with smyten." The "letters" of the charter's words were
Christ's wounds: "How many lettres þare-on bene / Rede & þou may
wyten & sene / ffyue thowsand four hundreth fyfty & ten / woundes on
me bath blak & wen." *The Pore Caitiff* declared "þer weren vpon þe
blessed bodi of crist opun woundes bi noumbre fyue þousand foure hun-
drid seuenti & fyue / þis is þe noumbre of lettris with which oure chartre
was writun."[43] This metaphor prompts the reader of Egerton 1821 to interpret its blood drops picturing the outpourings from Christ's wounds,
as letters of the spiritual charter, thus dissolving the distinction between
image and word.

These late medieval prayer books joined *The Pore Caitiff* and the *Pomander of Prayer* in promoting prayer with the aid of images, making the book user both reader and viewer. In contrast to the *Pomander's* recommendation, however, image and text may coalesce into a single prayer that unites spirit and senses. The prayer books also drew on the literary tradition of devotional treatises and poems that encouraged the imaginative recreation of holy scenes (discussed in chapter 5). Such visually oriented contemplations are common in late Middle English devotional works. Like the prayer book rubrics, Nicholas Love's *Mirror* exhorts his readers to "behold" or "see" Christ and the Virgin Mary as they enacted the Gospel drama. Richard Rolle's meditation on the Passion also urges the reader to visualize Christ's pains and to participate in the scene at Calvary. Rolle "watches" as the soldiers kicked Christ as they marched him toward crucifixion, exclaiming, "A, þis is a ruful siȝt!" Similarly the *Tretyse of Love* urged readers to "see" how Christ's head bends to kiss her, "see" his arms spread to embrace her, and "behold" the opening in his side. The *Speculum Devotorum,* another extended meditation on Christ's life, repeatedly encourages readers to "beholdyth" or "beholdyth gostly" the events of Christ's life from the Annunciation to the Resurrection, and its detailed descriptions aid the process.[44] Sermons incorporated these graphic elements of the crucifixion as well, pressing auditors to behold with the eye of the soul "þe blody swetynge, þe greves strokes of þe scourgus, þe boffettes, þe crown of þorne, þe spittynge in þe face" and other familiar scenes of the Passion.[45] Poetry on the Passion also solicited visual engagement in Christ's pain; John Lydgate's verse, for instance, urged readers to look on Christ's "bloody woundis, set here in picture / Hath hem in mynde knelyng on your kne."[46]

This visual participation in holy scenes was a commonplace in late medieval religious texts, and the devotions of Margery Kempe display its powerful influence. Readers and/or auditors became spectators and even actors. Linked to a textual milieu that advocated a mental imaging of holy people and events, primers and other prayer books also shared in the marked tendency in late medieval art to focus on the humanity and sufferings of Christ, the Virgin, and the saints.[47] These books combined texts and images in a new way. The exhortations of Richard Rolle and Nicholas Love to contemplate an image of the suffering Christ were paralleled and augmented by prayer book rubrics instructing readers to pray in front of painted or carved images. The textual and visual cultures of the laity did not contest for primacy here but worked synergistically, with text and image demanding mutual support. Furthermore, these rubric/image/prayer combinations not only directed book users to meditate and pray using images, but also assumed they could read. Book owners perhaps knew the Latin prayers well enough to recite them at the familiar prompt of the opening words, but the rubrics had to be read to carry out the full devotion, one reason why many rubrics were written in English or French. Some degree of literacy in one language or another was essential for contemplating these images and integrating them with one's prayers in the manner that the books proposed.

Images and Indulgences

Further integration of images and texts can be found in the devotions offering indulgences. Many rubrics promised benefits for particular prayers: The Virgin Mary would appear to one before death; the devotee would peacefully resolve personal conflict for reciting "with good devotion" the *Gloria in excelsis deo;* a general pardon was obtained on the authority of "holy wryt" for the prayer *Omnis virtus te decorat.*[48] More notorious are the often spurious indulgences that cite dubious authorities for days, years, and even centuries of pardon first granted to unnamed or unknown kings. Many rubrics credit the obscure Pope Boniface VI (r. April–May 896), for example, with bestowing an indulgence at the request of one King Philip of France for reciting the prayer *Domine Iesu Christi qui hanc sacratissimam carnem* between the elevation of the Host at Mass and the third *Agnus Dei.*[49] Despite their questionable origins, such indulgences appear in simple and elegant prayer books alike, attesting to their broad appeal to and acceptance by many levels of medieval society. In the fifteenth century, for instance, Richard III owned a prayer book containing several indulgences, as did Anne of Brittany, twice Queen of France.[50]

One could earn indulgences by looking at holy images as well as by saying prayers. The best-known indulgenced images are those associated with the legendary Mass of Pope Gregory and his vision of Christ as the Man of Sorrows, which often introduce the Hours of the Cross or the Penitential Psalms in fifteenth-century Books of Hours. Some pictures capture the entire scene of Gregory celebrating mass beneath the Man of Sorrows, who appears in place of the Host above the altar. [plate 6.3] The prayer book user sees, in this instance, an image of the vision of Christ within the picture of Gregory saying mass. Variations show only the vision itself, placing the book user in the position of Gregory, so that her view mimics his: Christ held by angels, arising out of the tomb and surrounded by the instruments of the Passion; or simply Christ as the Man of Sorrows, or Image of Pity, displaying his wounds. [Plate 6.4]. A standard rubric explains the image, asserting the value of gazing at it in two ways. First, the Lord appeared to blessed Gregory "in such a likeness" [*in tali effigie*], suggesting that this vision sanctioned representations of the Man of Sorrows. In looking at

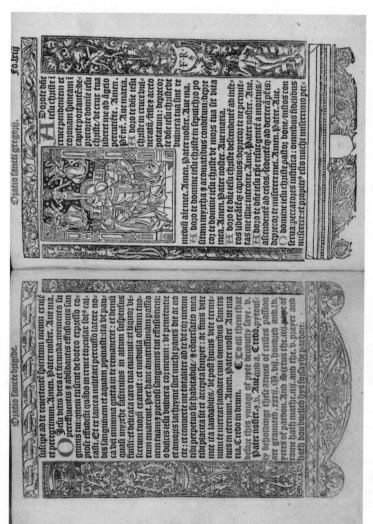

6.3 St. Gregory's vision of the Man of Sorrows. British Library C 35. H.2, f. lxii verso-lxiii recto. By permission of the British Library.

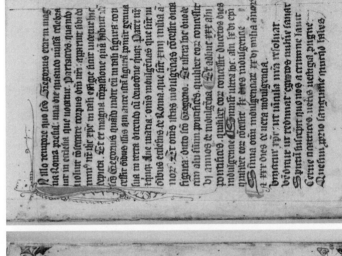

6.4 The Man of Sorrows and the indulgence of St. Gregory. British Library Additional MS. 33381, ff. 89 verso–90 recto. By permission of the British Library.

the picture, the devotee reenacts Gregory's experience—the image now stands in for the "real" vision of Christ that appeared to the pope. Second, this image so moved Gregory, as one rubric explains, that he granted 14,000 years of indulgence to all who "devoutly look at" the Man of Sorrows while kneeling and saying five *Pater nosters* and *Ave Marias*. Later popes added to the indulgence, so the rubric says, and an early printed version affirms a total of 32,755 years of pardon.[51]

These indulgenced images stemming from the Mass of St. Gregory exemplify the merging of devotional image and text. Although the devotee could earn the indulgence by gazing at the image and repeating the familiar prayers, he must read the rubric to discover this. The rubric also contains several lures for the reader: the extraordinary number of years of pardon, the description of Gregory's vision, the additional grants made by later popes—verbal persuasions of the image's antiquity, authority, and value. The great popularity enjoyed by this indulgenced image is affirmed by its reproduction in many early printed books. Printed primers tend to be more replete with pictures than even their most lavish manuscript counterparts, but the placement of the Mass of St. Gregory on the page usually distinguishes it from the often complex and potentially distracting marginal images. Also, the rubric of indulgence in these books is usually in English, which sets the devotion off from the surrounding Latin. In a 1534 printed primer, for example, the depiction of the Mass in the upper left-hand corner dominates that page and the entire opening. [Plate 6.3] It is clearly distinct from the decorative borders, and draws the eye's attention immediately, so in fact one must look to the previous page for the English indulgence.

An indulgence was also granted for gazing at the *Arma Christi* or instruments of the Passion by themselves. Sermons claimed that Christ would come at the end of the world, bearing these "tokenes of his passion" as a sign of his mercy, so that these tools reminded beholders both of Christ's suffering and their own final end.[52] The variety of the instruments seemed to fascinate artists, and pictures can include the nails, the hammer used to drive the nails in and the forceps to extract them, the lance, the crown of thorns, the pillar to which Christ was tied, the whips, the sponge soaked in vinegar, the ladder to take Christ down from the cross, and more. Manuscript prayer book rubrics promised 6,000 or 11,000 days of indulgence to their contrite onlooker, but early printed prayer books expanded the pardon to thousands of years.[53]

Curiously, some early printed primers included a much shortened form of the *Arma Christi* rubric, but no image at all. A 1497 book prints the pardon in English, again to ensure that the reader understood the value of the devotion: "To them that before thys ymage of pyte deuoutly say .v. Pater noster .v. Aves & a Credo pythously beholdyng these armes of cristes passion are graunted .xxxii.m vii hondred & lv. yers of pardon."[54] An unknowing user might have puzzled over this indulgence dependent on beholding "thys ymage" where none exists. Perhaps the book's makers assumed the Image of Pity and the *Arma Christi* were so common that any reader might easily refer to one at home or in church. In fact, cheap woodcuts combine these elements, with the *Arma Christi* bordering either the Man of Sorrows or the pietà. [Plate 6.5] Prayer rolls, which were likely displayed in churches but were privately owned as well, show the symbols of the Passion and the five wounds, and some also guarantee years of indulgence for looking at these images and reciting the *Pater Noster, Ave Maria,* and a *Credo.*[55] Parish churches exhibit the *Arma Christi* in various formats: They are carried by angels floating on the roof beams in Mildenhall, Suffolk, and carved on the pews in Fressingfield, Suffolk.[56] Nonetheless, it seems more likely that the printer paid little attention to the relation between this text and the image that existed in manuscripts, and freely using one and dispensing with the other made nonsense of this devotion. Another printed primer highlights this neglect with an English rubric that requires "beholdyng these armes of cristes passion," but with an accompanying woodcut that pictures only the Man of Sorrows without the tools of his torture.[57]

Like the five wounds, the instruments of the Passion could be separated so that each received its own space on a page or roll and its own time within the devotion, extending visually and verbally the reader/viewer's contemplation of them. Some texts specify the moral relation of each instrument to the viewer's life, reminding her that humanity's sins both caused and were redeemed by Christ's suffering. Coupled to a picture of the nails that pierced Christ's hands and feet, for example, this verse prods the reader to consider the possible offenses of her own limbs: "The naylys throwe fete and handys also / Lord, kepe me owt of synne and woo / That I haue in myn lyffe doo / With handys handyld or on fote goo." Similarly, the vinegar-soaked sponge reminded the devotee of his own gluttony, and the hands that tore Christ's hair and hit him under the ear recall the sins of "pride of here" and those one has "herkynd to" with ears.[58] This layout of pictures and verses conducts the user in reading and viewing, the eye moving from image to text and then back to the image. This arrangement firmly binds each picture to a verse, and also leads the reader to pause and consider the image and the verse before moving on. The familiar images receive new meaning, as rubrics and verses not only promise rewards for looking at them, but also describe and insist upon their surprisingly direct relevance to the beholder's spiritual life. Also, in deepening the significance of the *Arma Christi,* the texts reach beyond the artifact of the book or roll,

6.5 The *Pietà* with a border of the *Arma Christi* and indulgence. Folio 1 verso from MS Rawlinson D 403. By permission of the Bodleian Library, University of Oxford.

shaping a new relationship between the reader and the images wherever they appear.

Few prayer book devotions interweave image and text so tightly as those connected with the Mass of St. Gregory. Others worth noting are the prayers to the Veronica, or Vernicle, and a few associated with the Virgin Mary. As the veil on which Christ imprinted his face while carrying the cross to Calvary, the Veronica was revered in the Middle Ages as both image and relic, perhaps the only authentic depiction of Christ's face that existed. Moreover, Christ himself was the artist, as he had caused his features to be stamped on the cloth offered to him by the woman. Just as his appearance in a vision to Pope Gregory authorized pictorial renderings of the Man of Sorrows, so Christ's creation of the Veronica seemed to legitimate reproductions of it as an image worthy of indulgence and veneration. Ten days' indulgence accrued for reciting a prayer composed by Innocent III honoring the Vernicle. Later an indulgence was supposedly granted for seeing an image of the Veronica as well as saying the prayer, although the promised number of days of pardon varied widely.[59] One prayer to the Veronica states the case for considering it a true representation of Christ: "O vernacule i honoure him and the / þat þe made þorow his preuité / þo cloth he set to his face / þe prent laft þere þorow his grace / his moth, his nose, his ine to, / his berd, his here dide al so. . . ." It concludes with a plea stressing the intercessory and redemptive power of looking at the image: "Of sinnus þat i haue do / Lord of heuen, for-ȝeve it me / þorow syht of þe figur þat i here se."[60] A book of Latin prayers credits Pope Gregory with granting a 100-day indulgence for gazing at the Veronica while saying the prayer *Omnis terra adoret te deus;*[61] early-sixteenth-century English primers declare that Pope John XXII granted 10,000 days of pardon to those who devoutly say the prayer *Salve sancta facies* while "beholdyng the gloryous vysage or vernakell of our lorde," and provide a picture of the image of Christ's face on the cloth as well.[62]

Prayer books also contain indulgenced invocations for recital before images of the Virgin Mary. An early-fifteenth-century miscellany of prayers recommends saying the *Ave Maria* in honor of the feet, womb, heart, breasts, hands, mouth, tongue, lips, nostrils, eyes, ears, body, and soul of the Virgin while kneeling before her image or altar. The rubric helpfully, although inaccurately, calculates the yearly indulgence earned by this daily piety, so that the persistent devotee could reckon on annually banking this amount of time. A second rubric promises one hundred and forty days' indulgence and a vision of the Virgin before death for praying the *Ave regina celorum ave domina angelorum* before her image.[63]

Because no tradition or biblical pronouncement prohibited depictions of the Virgin Mary, the prayer books show no concern for justifying her

6.6 Pope Sixtus prays before an image of Maria "in sole." British Library Additional MS. 35313, f. 237 recto. By permission of the British Library.

Aue maria fons et pulchritudo confessorum
Aue maria decus et corona virginum . Aue
maria salus et consolatrix viuorum et mor-
tuorum. Mecū sis in oibus tēptatiōibus/tri-
bulatiōibus/necessitatibus/angustijs/ ¿isir
mitatibus meis . Et ipetra michi veniā oim
delictorum meorū: et maxime in hora exitus
mei non desis michi o pijssima virgo maria .
Amē. Pater noster. Aue maria. ℂ Our holy
father Bonifaci⁹ pope of rome hath graunted vnto all them that say deuoutly thys pra-
ers. ℂ dais of pardon.   Oratio.

Ue maria alta stirps lilij
castitatis. Aue pfundabio
la ballis humilitatis. Aue lataro
sa cāpi diuie charitatis. Aue abys-
salis fons ois gratie ¿ mie celi ros
fructifer omīs diuine suauitatis ¿
deuotiōis. Amē. Pat nē. ℂ Our holy father
Sixtus the iiij. pope hath graūted all thēm
that deuoutly say this prayer befo
re the ymage of our lady in the sō-
ne. xj. thousande yeres of pardon.
Ue sanctissima maria ma
ter dei/regia celi/ porta pa
radisi:domina mundi:tu es singu

6.7   The image of Our Lady in the Sun, with indulgence. Folio 44 verso from
Douce BB 141 (1). By permission of the Bodleian Library, University of Oxford.

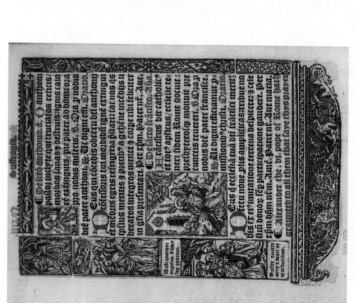

6.8 The Image of St. Anne, Mary, and Jesus with indulgences *Hore beatissime virginis Marie.* Paris, 1527. ff. xcii verso–xciii recto. This item is reproduced by permission of The Huntington Library, San Marino, California.

representations as they do for those of Christ. Nor do these books always provide an image of the Virgin required by the rubrics or indulgenced prayers. Some readers had to bring text and image together by kneeling before a statue or picture of the Virgin in church or at home. A striking example of this activity comes from a Flemish Book of Hours, now at the British Library, in which a miniature depicts a pope kneeling before a table holding an open book, and raising his hands in prayer while he gazes at a picture of the Virgin. [Plate 6.6] The rubric reads, "Pope Sixtus grants eleven thousand years of indulgence to those saying this prayer before the image of the Virgin Mary in the sun," and is followed by the prayer *Ave sanctissima virgo maria mater dei.* This miniature shows the reader how to be-have toward a holy image, what reward may be gained from it, and whose authority sanctioned it.[64] This rubric also appears in a 1506 primer, printed in Paris for William Bretton of London, and in a 1519 English primer that includes a small woodcut of the Virgin holding the Christ child, encircled by the sun's flames.[65] [Plate 6.7]

A final indulgenced image joins the focus on Christ's humanity with adoration of the Virgin and her mother, St. Anne. The rubric promises 100 days of pardon on the authority of a cardinal and legate named "Ray-mundus" for saying the prayer *Quotquot maris sunt gutte et arene terre grane et gramine* "before the ymage of saynt Anna Maria and Jesus." The prayer cel-ebrates the mystery of Mary's fertility and chastity [*Ave castissima mater dei fecundissimaque virgo maria*], and one primer's woodcut emphasizes the bod-ily connection of the generations by picturing Mary holding Jesus, the two of them placed in an oval of rays in front of St. Anne.[66] [Plate 6.8]

Indulgenced prayer book images bring together two tendencies in late medieval piety: the emphasis on vision and the amassing of earned rewards in a kind of spiritual treasure chest. I noted above the link between prayer book images and devotional literature's insistence on visual participation in sacred events, especially Christ's Passion. In addition, prayer books fre-quently highlight the potential holiness of deliberate and purposeful acts of vision. Although one could also earn indulgence through the other senses—saying prayers is crucial, and devoutly listening to the Gospel of St. John merits some years of pardon—these books articulate the primacy of vision. The consecrated Host was, as the body of Christ, considered the holiest of objects, and in the late Middle Ages seeing it was a vital part of attending mass.[67] Prayers to be said at the elevation of the Host during mass, such as the *Anima christi sanctifica me,* are sometimes indulgenced.[68] One fifteenth-century Latin prayer book includes two indulgenced prayers (*Ave verum corpus domini nostri ihesu christi, Ave principium nostre creacionis*) to be said at the elevation and a third in view of the body and blood of Christ (*in visione corpus & sanguinis christi*).[69] This directed viewing of a sacred object—the consecrated Host—while simultaneously reciting a specific prayer, duplicated the actions recommended by rubrics for winning indulgences attached to images. The equal treatment of Host and image imparts some of the Host's indisputably greater authority to images; gazing at both objects verged on a "sacramental viewing" that bestowed spiritual benefits. Eagerness to see the consecrated Host could easily transfer to the image of the Man of Sorrows, which represented what believers considered the Host to be—the sacrificed yet living body of Christ. Further, the legend of the Mass of St. Gregory plainly shows the desire (echoed in many similar visions experienced by saints) to see beyond the simple disc of the Host to Christ's bloodied body—a wish that the popular image of the Man of Sorrows fulfilled.

A rubric that appears in some early printed primers reinforced this bond between Host and image by linking both to indulgences earned for the prayer *Precor te amantissime domine iesu christe.* Pope Sixtus IV, it is said, granted to those that "be yn the estate of grace sayenge thys prayer folowyng ymmedeatly after the eleuation of the body of our lorde" remission of all their sins "perpetually enduryng." The unlikely Pope John III (r. 561–574) is then credited with granting "at the requeste of the quene of englonde" to those that say the prayer devoutly "before the image of our lord crucyfyed" an indulgence worth as many days of pardon as Christ had wounds in his body, numbered at 5465.[70] In its excessive pardons and questionable origins and authority, this rubric exemplifies the corruption of late medieval indulgences; but its coupling of Host and crucifix underscores the spiritual power that was attributed to images.

Images and Charms

In 1375 Bishop Brinton of Exeter preached that those who saw the Host were protected from sudden death, failing eyesight, aging, and the need for food.[71] Similarly, some prayer books promise that viewing particular images or saying certain prayers raised a magical shield against misfortune. Like indulgences, these charms could defend the soul, keeping it safe from the devil and hell. More often, though, their power wards off temporal dangers like flood, fire, sickness, and difficult childbirth. Rubrics tend to ignore distinctions between indulgences—which despite their wilder manifestations had their origins in church doctrine—and the simply magical charms, sometimes cheerfully combining the two into a sturdy armor of defense against any threat to the devout Christian. A lengthy English rubric in a Book of Hours, for example, promises that a prayer will grant remission of sin, protection from sudden death or danger in battle, safety in travel and freedom from robbers; saying it over water and then drinking will keep a woman safe in childbirth; throwing such water in the sea will quiet a tempest; reciting the prayer over "clene whete brede" and then eating will cure illness. Bearing the prayer on one's person will bring one the love, worship, and honor of "prynce emperor or kyng erle barowne or oþire lordyng." Almost as an afterthought, the rubric concludes by noting that "the holy man Innocent" granted 300 days of pardon for saying the prayer.[72]

Rubrics invoking the efficacy of prayers against worldly and otherworldly evils find almost exact parallels in charms summoning the power of images. Holy images offering such protections are typically associated with Christ's Passion. A printed primer promises that to those in a state of grace who say the *Obsecro te* "before owre blessid lady of pitye" the Virgin will show her "blessid vysage" and warn them of the day and hour of death; also "in there laste ende the angelles of god shalle yelde there sowles to heuen," and the devotee will obtain in pardon 500 years and "soo manie lenttis of pardon grawnted by holy fathers popes of Rome."[73]

The hour of death is a persistent concern of the image charms, especially those associated with the *Arma Christi*. A Latin rubric in a prayer miscellany lists several indulgences earned by "anyone who gazes at these arms of our lord Jesus Christ" and then adds

> Moreover, whoever devoutly looks at these arms of the Lord, recalling the passion of our Lord Jesus Christ, that day he will not die a sudden death, nor die in war, nor in fire, nor in water, nor by deadly poison, nor will he be vexed by the devil, nor by any other malicious spirit. And if any woman, tormented in childbirth, looks devoutly at these arms, she will be freed quickly nor will the infant perish.[74]

A Middle English version of this charm, rhymed for easier memorization, lists several indulgences to the one who "þis armes ouer se," and then promises:

> And also who þat eueri day
> þis armus of crist be hold may
> þat day he ne sal dee no wiked ded
> Ne be cumbert with þe kued;
> And also to wymen hit is meke and mild
> When þey trauelne of her chi[l]d[75]

Evidence for medieval readers' response to these pledges of magical help can be deduced from their frequent appearance in both Latin and English in late medieval prayer books; people took them in earnest. As Eamon

Duffy argues, these legends and charms belong not to the "devotional underground" but the "devotional mainstream."[76] Margery Kempe offers direct testimony, once again, for the power and pervasive influence of these texts. Such charms are clearly related to the promise Kempe believed God made to her when she fearfully imagined a martyr's death for herself. Commending her willingness to die for him, the Lord assured her "& ӡet schal no man sle the, ne fyer bren þe, ne watyr drynch þe, ne wynd deryn þe. . . ." His next words link this promise to his Passion: "for I may not forӡetyn þe how þow art wretyn in myn handys & my fete; it lyken me wel þe peynes þat I haue sufferyd for þe."[77]

Representations of the individual elements of the *Arma Christi* were also believed to fend off dangers. To anyone who carried on his person an image showing the exact length of the nails that fastened Christ to the cross, one Pope Innocent was said to grant several gifts—protections against the familiar hazards of sudden death, fire, water, travel, storm, and childbirth. The cult of Christ's five wounds promoted images on woodcuts and in prayer books that purportedly duplicated the exact dimensions of the wound in Christ's side. Kissing, wearing, and gazing at this image won indulgence and earned magical protections.[78]

This metamorphosis of holy images into magical amulets sprang from several sources. Indulgenced images clearly contributed to the process, as they offered—on the supposed or real authority of various popes—supernatural rewards. This power shifted easily from the spiritual to the temporal world; fear of purgatory and fear of sudden and unshriven death by storm or fire could not seem unrelated. Second, long-held belief in the miraculous qualities of three-dimensional holy images—their ability to move, speak, and change location, for instance—reinforced the powers of their two-dimensional counterparts. Statues and pictures often depicted the same subject and, as many rubrics cited above suggest, the two kinds of images could be used interchangeably to study Christ's wounds or to direct a prayer to the Virgin Mary. Third, the treatment of other holy objects also blended piety and magic: the consecrated Host appears in a Middle English charm for curing fevers;[79] the chemise believed to be worn by the Virgin at the Annunciation was used to ensure the safe delivery of French royal babies; Elizabeth of York paid for a girdle from a cult statue of the Virgin to protect her in childbirth.[80] Medieval sorcery and medicine also used astrological and waxen images for protection and cures. These belonged to the world of simple and great folk alike, as learned doctors, popes, and kings trusted in such images.[81] Holy images used as amulets drew credibility from this tradition as well as from devotional cults. Finally, the written (or printed) word guaranteed the magical properties of these images; one rubric affirms the genuineness of the *Arma Christi*'s magical uses by saying that these were passed on or taught in writing [*in scriptis tradidit*].[82] The extended prose explanations and rhymed couplets not only attract and teach the reader how to use images, they are also certificates of authenticity, and their detailed enumeration of the precise benefits to be gained by devoutly looking at images lends them authority.

As portable material objects, prayer book images could be seen and studied, touched or stroked, and carried on one's person; they belonged to the sensible world. As representations of holy bodies and events, however, they linked their viewers to the spiritual universe. These combined attributes promoted holy images' simultaneous use as bearers of indulgence and charms, guards against supernatural and natural terrors alike. Their dual nature perhaps also contributed to the anxieties of contemporary Decalogue treatises (discussed in chapter 2), which insisted that the First Commandment's prohibition of images warned against witchcraft, astrology, and charming, but allowed representations of pious subjects. The clerical authors of these texts adhered to a distinction between religion and magic that was erased in popular practice.

The Clergy and the Laity

Some clerics, however, must have shared the laity's appreciation for prayer book images as meditative objects, conveyors of indulgences, and charms. Primers are usually and rightly associated with the laity, but clerics also owned prayer books that used images in all of these ways. Much is known about the content of the pious reading material of the late medieval laity, and recent research has begun to show the inclusiveness and fluidity of a book culture that in the late Middle Ages increasingly encompassed clerics and laypeople alike.[83] Both clerics and laymen and -women, for example, owned Love's *Mirror of the Blessed Life of Jesus Christ,* and works by Walter Hilton and Richard Rolle.[84] Middle English copies of a Franciscan manual for novices were addressed to laywomen, to laymen, to the nuns of Syon, and also to clerics.[85] Even Books of Hours, the hallmark of lay piety, were owned by men of the church: When he died in 1409 the monk William Appelby left to Durham College an Hours of the Virgin that he may have written himself; at his death in 1433 John Curlew, a Benedictine monk and Bishop of Dromore, Ireland, left his new primer to one John Hunt; Augustine Hawkins, citizen and grocer of London, left his primer and Bible to his chaplain in 1449. A fifteenth-century Dominican friar and anchorite, John Lacy, even wrote out a Book of Hours for his own use, as he states in his will, and afterwards for the use of others in order to excite them to "deuotion and preyers to God."[86]

Not only did laypeople and clerics read the same pious texts, they also shared the physical artifacts that bore them. Wills show that the laity commonly bequeathed books to clerics, as was only natural since they were bound together by ties of family, affection, patronage, and duty. In 1494 Lord John Scrope, for example, left his "Portose" [breviary] to the "parson of Weston" and a "Masse book, inprented" to the parson of Barnhambrone. Sir Thomas Lyttelton in 1481 bequeathed his "gloset-saulter" to the priory of Worcester, and a variety of other books to chapels and convents. Many testators referred to their blood relationship with the clerical beneficiaries: In 1397 the Duke of Lancaster left a missal and breviary to his son, the Bishop of Lincoln; one Thomas Ryhale bequeathed his breviary to his relative and chaplain, another Thomas Ryhalle; John Baret of Bury left the distinctly secular book "with the sege of Thebes in englysh" to "sere John Cleye my cosyn, and preest." Alice Thwaites passed on to Jake of Thwaites her "Messe-buke" if "he shalbe preste, or els nott."[87] This movement of books between lay and clerical hands included Books of Hours and other prayer books. In 1420 John Brykkisworth of Kent left a primer to a canon of the monastery of Langdon; Margery Maureward left her psalter to the cleric Richard Holt in her 1425 will; in 1429 Simon Northew, canon of Chichester, bequeathed to Lady Eve Seynt John a book with the Matins of the Blessed Mary and other devotions; in 1446 a chaplain in York left his goddaughter a primer "with images."[88]

The movement of books among laypeople and clerics allowed the transmission of prayers, images, indulgences, and charms in both directions. In the course of a century or so, a single manuscript book could easily pass between priest, laywoman or layman, and monk or nun, linking them by the devotions that each used in turn. One example of this diffusion is the late-fourteenth-century collection of Latin and English religious prose and verse compiled by the Cistercian monk John Northwood at Bordesley Abbey. This book contains numerous indulgences; one precedes English prayers for the Hours of the Cross, another is attached to a Latin prayer following the elevation of the Host. One rubric promises that a prayer before the Virgin Mary's image will result in a vision of her before death; another announces the pardon associated with the Mass of Pope Gregory for those who kneel before the figure of the Man of Sorrows and say five *Pater noster*s and five *Ave Maria*s. The *Arma Christi* indulgence is included, along with its declared protection against death in fire, war, water, and so on. Although, so far as we know, this book was produced in a monastery for a monk, it also suited the preferences of a lay audience. In fact, in the fifteenth century Northwood's book passed into the hands of Goditha Peyto, wife of Sir Edward Peyto, and she herself gave it to another woman. Notes in the manuscript show female ownership of the volume in the sixteenth century as well.[89]

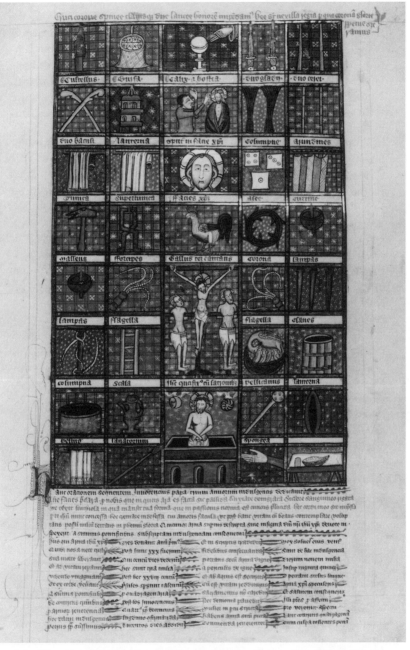

6.9 The *Arma Christi* with indulgence and prayer of protection. British Library, Royal MS. 6 E VI, f. 15 recto. By permission of the British Library.

Another prayer miscellany, associated with the priory of Ely in the thirteenth century, includes offices and meditations to which indulgences for saying prayers and looking at images were added in the fifteenth century. Among these is one lengthy rubric that explains the Mass of Pope Gregory and promises pardon, accompanied by a full-page miniature of a bloody Christ standing in the tomb. Another rubric declares the reward for looking at the *Arma Christi,* and guarantees safety from various dangers for carrying a depiction of them.[90] Whether a layperson or a monk made the additions is unknown, although either case argues for increasing affinity between their devotions in the late Middle Ages.

A final example, although not from a prayer book, focuses once more on the *Arma Christi,* the most popular indulgenced image in late medieval English books. The fourteenth-century encyclopedia, the *Omne Bonum,* depicts a complete array of the Passion instruments in thirty-eight small pictures. [Plate 6.9] These illustrations are accompanied by verses declaring the indulgences granted on papal authority for looking at them, and their familiar protection against fire, water, demons, and the difficulties of childbirth.[91] While the entry may be informational, it is also unquestionably intended for devotion as the comprehensiveness of the pictures and the repeated verbal insistence on indulgences indicate.

These books point to a culture shared by clerics and laity, in which the magical element of charms and the suspicious promises of indulgences join sanctioned cults like that of the five wounds to pattern the beliefs of priest and parishioner alike. Nor are the two groups consistently separated by language, as both Latin and the vernacular can be found in books belonging to each. While historians of Books of Hours have emphasized their origins in the laity's desire to emulate clerical piety, this influence was not unidirectional. Both the transmission of books between laypeople and clergy, and the similar contents of many of their books, argue that even suspect devotions moved freely and found adherents in both groups.

Books of the Laity

Their sometimes profound integration of pictures and texts, as well as their large audience, made prayer books a natural site for the ongoing debates over images in the fifteenth and sixteenth centuries; printed editions especially became part of the propaganda wars over points of doctrine between traditionalists and reformers.[92] Protesting the allures of "dead" images, one fifteenth-century English primer evinces Lollard-like sentiments in its explanation of the First Commandment:

And as it is a cursed auoutry a man to drawe awey some of his loue from his trewe wif and sette it on his concubynes so it is gostlich a cursed auoutri bifore god a man to drawe awei eny part of his loue ouþ of his trust and sette it on oþir dede ymages or in dremes or in oþer fantasyes. For god wol noȝt þus be worschuped in dede ymages bote in queke men þe whiche ben only godes ymages and liknes of the trinite. þis is the treuthe.[93]

On the opposite side, another fifteenth-century manuscript that teaches the method for saying the rosary insists that some moments of prayer require an image to replace a book. While reciting the first fifty *Aves*, it directs: "Here, in place of any book, you shall keep before your eyes the sweet image of the Blessed Mary, and say every *Ave Maria* in honour of her chief members." This point is soon reiterated; the devotee should meditate upon Christ's life while saying the *Aves*:

Here the child Jesus in the arms of His Mother will be thy book, and His members and powers will be, as it were, the leaves. For images are, according to the opinion of the holy doctors of the Church, the books of the faithful. Therefore let the beautiful image of Mary be before you, since an evil image is not a true but a false image of Mary, because of Her is sung "*Tota pulchra es.*"

Similarly, at the beginning of the second round of fifty *Aves*, the book demands that "Here, in place of a book, thou shalt have the image of Christ suffering and crucified." Curiously however, and in apparent self-contradiction, these injunctions to use an image instead of a book are controverted by the detailed written meditation provided for each of the 150 *Aves* of the rosary.[94] While these texts appear essential for the devotion, the instructions seem to demand that they be set aside. Only if we understand the order to put an image in place of a book not as a dismissal of written texts but as an encouragement to a certain kind of learning, does this all make sense. Rather than teaching basic points of theology to the laity, in the style of the manuals of religious instruction, this rosary book aims at another kind of knowledge. The instructions lead the reader in a meditative process that demands an "image" and that includes both reading and gazing in order to inspire a direct and empathetic apprehension of Christ and Mary. "Book" and "image" become here, not writings and statues or pictures, but epistemological methods that seek different ends.

Sixteenth-century prayer books show increasing tension over images. A 1535 English primer seems to challenge any representation of the deity, as its thorough explication of the Creed decrees that confidence should be placed in nothing but God, "whiche can not be sene with mannes iye, whiche can not be comprehended with mannes witte." In its form for confession, the sinner acknowledges violations of the commandments, admitting that he has given God's honor and worship to his creatures "& deade things, ymagined of myn owne fonde fantasie. I meane in the mysusynge of ymages." Finally, in a "frutefull remembraunce of Christes passion" the author scorns the use of holy images as charms. Some people who meditate on Christ's passion do not profit from it:

> Neyther sought they any thyng therin, but theyr owne priuate welth. For some caryed aboute them ymages / paynted papers / carued crosses / and suche other. Yea and some fell to suche madde ignoraunce, that they thought themselues thrughe suche thynges to be safe from fyre, water, and all other perylous jeopardies: as though this crosse of Christ shulde delyuer them from such outwarde troubles, and not rather the contrary.[95]

The author mocks those who ignore the transformative power and meaning of Christ's Passion and instead "haue thoughte it sufficient to beholde the storye of the passion, paynted upon the walles."

The assault on images was even more ferocious in the primer printed by John Bydell for the reformer William Marshall in 1535, which warned its readers against "pernicious" prayer books filled with "infinite errours and peryllous prayers." These books were "garnyshed" with "redde letters, promysyng moche grace" and pardon, "to þe great decepte of the people." Perhaps worse than indulgences were rubrics directing prayers to be said before images: "But what blyndnes is that to appoynte the prayer to be sayde before the ymage of our lady of Pitie. . . ." Suppose that a man instead said the prayer before the "ymage (as they call it) of our lady of grace. Shall he than lese þe inestimable priuileges before promysed." Echoing the Lollards, he asks, "why myghte not a man smell a lytle Idolatrie here," since all images are made of the same materials, and cannot see, hear, or walk. These prayers, appointed by rubrics as signs of a "peculier honour and reverence to be done to þe same ymage or picture" were, he concluded, blasphemous.[96]

Perhaps responding to these accusations, an English and Latin primer from the early 1540s voiced a moderate defense of images. It cautioned readers against "goodly paynted prefaces" that promised "Many thynges both folyshe and false as the delyveraunce of XV soules out of purgatorye, with other lyke vanyties" for saying the popular fifteen prayers of St. Bridget. The prayers themselves, however, are "ryght good and vertuous, yf they be sayde with out any such superstitious trust or blynde confydence." Indeed, St. Bridget herself said them daily "before the ymage of the Crosse, in Saynt Paules church at Rome." With proper devotion thus neatly distinguished from superstition, the primer later reaffirmed the apparent fixity of holy images in English prayer books, labeling and directing a prayer begging Christ for forgiveness of sins, "A prayer unto the ymage of the body of Christ."[97]

Conclusion

Many prayer book devotions required a combination of deliberate and prolonged gazing at images and reading of texts. One need not do as the rubrics direct, of course, but in the absence of personal testimony we must rely on the evidence presented by the books themselves to understand how their owners employed them. This limited survey suggests that image and text, rather than being treated as separate components, were instead often blended into a single pious supplication for spiritual and physical succor. Reading prayers and viewing pictures or statues were mutually sustaining acts, and both insisted that the devotee approach God and the saints through sight.

The idea that images substituted for texts confuses and obscures their meanings and functions in late medieval prayer books. Far from replacing texts, many of these prayer book images demanded reading literacy in English or French, or sometimes Latin, for their proper or designated use. Owners who could not read Latin are presumed to read English, as in an early sixteenth-century Sarum primer, in which a rubric prefacing the Latin prayer to the Vernicle, *Salve sancta facies,* advises those "that kan not saye thys prayer lette them say v *Pater noster* and v *Ave*s and v *Credo.*"[98] If the owner could read only English, she could still understand the rubric, look at the Vernicle image as directed, and say these basic prayers. Rubrics named images, linked them to prayers, described their indulgences, established their histories, legitimated them, and told readers how to use them. Sometimes the layout of text and image on the page could also encourage reading as an aid to contemplating the image, and images as a fulfillment of the text.

Although this chapter surveys only a few of the large number of images, prayers, and rubrics in English prayer books, their dynamic interplay and mutual reliance indicates that book producers, at least, considered their clientele to be literate. Careful analysis of rubrics and prayers in late medieval prayer books would tell us more about the shape of that literacy, which perhaps most often combined an easy fluency in reading English with a more glancing ability in Latin. In any case, the devotions examined here demanded that book users read, and this challenges assumptions especially about high female illiteracy, since legacies in wills and ownership marks in books show that women often owned primers and other prayer books.[99] Thus, to the question of what Margery Kempe was doing with her book in church, the most likely answer is that she was reading its words and "beholding" its images, in an act of prayer.

Just as these prayers and images cannot be abstracted from the books that carry them, so too the books themselves cannot be isolated. The joined workings of their texts and pictures could shape the devotee's physical environment and her responses to it: the first by demanding that the reader find an image in front of which to pray; the second by reproducing on the page those holy images commonly found in churches or shrines, and tying them to indulgences, moral verses, or specific prayers. The associations with the image that became habitual with repeated use of the prayer book might naturally extend to the image of the crucifix, the *Arma Christi,* or the Virgin Mary, in more public arenas.

Finally, the most suggestive but also intangible evidence yielded by the interplay of word and image is for the intimate and elusive act of reading. In the examples cited above, the layout of text and picture on a page influenced the rhythm of the reader's devotions. Reading these parts of the prayer book consisted of a series of grouped actions, each a complex of activities that might involve reading a rubric, viewing an image, contemplating its meaning, and saying a prayer. The prayers were not simply read in a linear fashion, nor would the user have engaged in that rote and mechanical repetition that has sometimes been used to characterize late medieval prayer.[100] These devotions demand concentration, careful observation, and deliberation, not mindless recitation. The material artifact of the book and its component parts can thus lead us to the heart of the devotional lives of book users—or as close as we are likely to get—by tracing for us the shifting attention to words and pictures and statues, the eye's movements and also its lingering gazes, and the physical motions of hands and genuflecting knees that together composed the reading of these books of the laity.

CONCLUSION

"THINGS TENDING TO IDOLATRY"

The orthodox polemic concerning holy images flowed into the turbulent religious arena of the sixteenth century partly through the writings of Thomas More. In *A Dialogue Concerning Heresies,* More wrote at length about images and pilgrimages, defending them against reformers who echoed Lollard criticisms of them. In making a case for why holy images should remain part of religious practice, More leaned heavily on the arguments, examples, and terminology of his medieval predecessors. Like them, More regarded the Decalogue prohibition of images as necessary to curb the Jews' inclination to idolatry; its intent was to banish pagan idols, not the statues of the saints.[1] To prove the divine sanction of images, More summoned up the ancient story that Roger Dymmok and Walter Hilton had also used, of Jesus sending a cloth bearing the picture of his face to King Abgar. He also cited the Holy Vernicle as proof of Christ's approval of images, as well as the tale of St. Luke as the portraitist of the Virgin Mary.[2] More repeated Dymmok's assertion that images might "more effectually represent the thynge then shall the name eyther spoken or wrytten" and that they are also "good bokes bothe for lay men and for the lerned to."[3] Aware of the distinction between *latria* and *dulia,* More stated that no one should offer to any image the honor that belonged only to God, but one may "do some reuerence to an ymage / not fyxynge his fynall intente in the ymage / but referrynge it further to the honour of the person that the ymage representeth."[4]

More's debating opponent in the *Dialogue,* the Messenger, raises the issue of idolatry several times. Although he finally accepts More's contention that the church cannot err in the faith, he proposes that some within the church could indeed err, suggesting that "the good men" who are "vndeceyued" are those who believe the "worshyp of ymagys and prayeng to sayntys to be ydolatry." Those who accept image-worship are "mysbyleuers and foule deceyued." More convinces him that the Holy

Ghost would never allow the church "so hole & so long in so damnable ydolatry / as this were / if it were supersticyon / & not a part of very fayth & true deuout relygyon."[5]

More lost the battle to keep images and pilgrimages as indispensable elements of religion in England. His conventional and hoary arguments—that images were mere representations that pointed to the saints and could be "read" as laymen's books—seemed powerless to protect holy images from the increasing denunciations of idolatry. The weakness of More's position stemmed partly from its incomplete understanding of holy images. As this study has attempted to show, the pervasiveness of holy images in religious culture meant, inevitably, that they moved beyond the confines of pure representation and challenged their narrow definition as "books of the laity." Indeed, the characterization of images as *libri laicorum* endured into the late Middle Ages more on account of sheer repetition than because it was an accurate rendering of real practice. Gregory the Great's description of images as books for illiterates was so powerful that it lived on even when the conditions that shaped it were fading. Images no doubt remained the tools of pedagogues. A sixteenth-century sermon insisted that they helped those people "whiche haue noo learnyng in the stede of bowkes" because from them they could "learne the example of pacience, mekenes, chastite, cherite, and of all other vertewes."[6] Yet as literacy spread, people did not reject images. Despite the traditional dichotomy that opposed images and illiteracy against books and literacy, images held a central position in the religious practice of literates and illiterates alike.

The multifaceted relationship between texts and holy images in the late Middle Ages makes it simplistic to consider one a replacement for another. People who could read often found sacred art a compelling and necessary component of their devotions, as the lives of Julian of Norwich, Angela of Foligno, and Jeanne-Marie de Maillé demonstrate. Late medieval vernacular texts, from *The Pore Caitiff* to prayer book rubrics, encouraged readers to respond in a heartfelt way to crucifixes and statues of the Virgin Mary and the saints. In a different vein, saints' lives and *exempla,* whether read or heard, worked to shape their audiences' perceptions of images by conveying stories of statues and pictures as miracle-workers that spoke, moved, bled, and inspired belief. These tales credited especially crucifixes and carvings of the Virgin with supernatural powers, as though they were, indeed, the holy people they represented.

This extraordinary potency of images was reinforced through their multiple ties to the consecrated Host, the holiest of objects. Walter Hilton called holy images the "milk of corporeal signs" upon which the weak children of the church could feed, as they could, literally, on the Host. The *bonus tractatus de decem mandatis* and *The Pore Caitiff* outline a hierarchy for viewing the objects in a church in which one looks first at the Host, then the cross, then statues and paintings of the saints. The kinship of Host and images is clear in their sharing of the beholder's attention, although the Host, of course, claims precedence. Host, cross, and saint's statue all move the viewer's thoughts closer to heaven. Gild provisions of lights for their patron saints' images and at the elevation of the Host reasserted this functional parallel; these were material objects that must be seen. Providing candles or torches permitted and encouraged this all important viewing. Prayer books, too, treated image and Host analogously. Readers could, for instance, earn indulgences for saying prayers at the elevation of the Host or for looking at the body of Christ, just as they could for gazing at and reciting prayers before the *Arma Christi* and the Man of Sorrows. The theological status of images as material objects that pointed their viewers toward supernatural truths prevented them from attaining the sublimity of the Host, which was held to be Christ's body. The Host's higher status was aptly demonstrated by a court case in which parishioners of Grayingham, Lincolnshire, sued their rector for setting up in the church an image that blocked their view of the Host at the elevation.[7] Still, the affinity of the two holy artifacts allowed images to share in the indisputably greater sanctity and power of the Host.

Some people responded to crucifixes and pietàs as though they made Christ and the Virgin present. Angela of Foligno and Margery Kempe could not have reacted more strongly to Christ's suffering had they seen it in the flesh than they did to its depictions in wood and paint. Sacred art offered them a medium for "seeing" Christ's Passion as though it were happening before them, a visual reincarnation that invoked their tears, sorrow, and pain. These images fulfilled the common desire so clearly expressed by Julian of Norwich to be present at the crucifixion and to suffer along with Christ's mother and friends.

While Margery Kempe and Julian of Norwich cannot be held as typical or representative of East Anglian women in general, it seems that women may have had a special attachment to images. In their wills women paid more attention to images than did men, although why this was so is not clear. Research into women's activities in the parish may enable us to sift the significance of these bequests more finely. A keener understanding of how men and women compared as parishioners—as patrons, donors, gild officers, churchwardens, participants in liturgical activities, and so on—will provide a more meaningful context for their legacies. Still, it seems likely that women found in images appropriate and even beautiful objects for their devotional affections, rather than amendment and compensation for the supposed defect of their illiteracy.

Despite their centrality in late medieval religious culture, holy images were never free from the blemish or suspicion of idolatry, and this was due in part to their multifarious and sometimes unorthodox functions. No one objected to their use as devotional aids, but the line between this and magical talismans was so thin that it often simply dissolved. Breaking the barrier of mere representation, holy images were also used as magical amulets or charms, with their users commanding rather than beseeching supernatural aid. The *Arma Christi* pictures and rubrics in prayer books exemplify this blending. First, the Passion instruments were to remind viewers of Christ's sufferings. Then indulgences, promising release from punishment in purgatory, became attached to them. Finally, the *Arma Christi* images became charms that guaranteed protection against the terrors of sudden death, diabolic torment, and death in childbirth. This magical use of images was yet another tie to the Host, the sight of which also guaranteed the viewer numerous benefits: sufficient meat and drink for the day, forgiveness for idle words and oaths, and freedom from sudden death and blindness.[8]

Surprisingly, however, such magical possibilities of holy images drew less fire than did the way people behaved toward statues of the saints. The three-dimensionality of statues seemed to express an animate quality that gave rise to fears that people mistook them for real saints, thereby committing idolatry. Lollards had expressed this apprehension, and so too had Bishop Fitzralph and later Alexander Carpenter, who worried that the custom of naming statues indicated a belief that they were, in fact, individuals. This fear resurfaced in the 1520s in the character of Thomas More's Messenger, who says:

> But ouer this it semeth to smell of ydolatry / whan we go on pylgrymage to this place and that place / As thoughe god were not lyke stronge or not lyke present in euery place. But as ye deuylles were of old / vnder ye false name of goddes / present and assystent in the ydolles and mammettes of the paganes / so wolde we make it seme / that god and his sayntes stode in this place / and that place / bounde to this post & that post cut out & carued in ymages.

The Messenger charges that the custom of attending more to one statue than another means that people cast their "affeccyons to the ymages selfe" because they believe these images were indeed the "very sayntes selfe . . ." He underscores the danger of this regard for statues by comparing it to the black magic of necromancers who "put theyr trust in theyr cercles / wythin whyche they thynke themselfe sure agaynst all the deuyls in hell."[9] With a slighting phrase More tries to demolish this accusation; "there is no dogge so madde," he says, "but he knoweth a very cony from a cony carued & paynted."[10] More and his Messenger continue their debate, and More later on even admits that some people might misuse images, but this is no reason to get rid of them. In refuting the Messenger's gravest charge against images—that people mistaking them for the saints commit idolatry—More replies that though some might err in this way, "yet were it not as ye call it the people." For, as More explains, "a fewe dotynge dames make not the people."[11] Like his predecessors, More insists that images direct their viewers to the unseen, the spiritual. But the Messenger contends, as had the Lollards before him, that the material nature of images mattered.

The physical properties of images undoubtedly concerned the people who prayed to them, or before them. Parishioners commissioned the creation of images for their churches, paid for their painting and gilding, left clothes, jewelry, money, and lands to them, and made them the visual focus of rituals. As objects, images were the nexus of multiple economic interactions involved not only in their production and maintenance, but also in the expression of fondness for them. Although distinctions between medieval people's devotion to the saint and the saint's representation should not be overstated, we can still hear the whisper of their affection for the specific lines, carvings, and colors that shaped a beloved image. Roger Martin's wistful remembrance of the parish church at Long Melford was not a lament for the loss of the saints or the Virgin Mary, whom he still believed in and worshipped. Of course he bemoaned the change in religion, but he expressed it by mourning the disappearance of the *things* that had adorned his church.

In the sixteenth century the tide turned against holy images. As early as 1538 Cromwell issued a set of Injunctions condemning pilgrimages and offerings to relics and images "as things tending to idolatry and superstition" and thus detested by God.[12] A series of anti-image injunctions culminated under Edward VI with a 1547 order to destroy shrines, pictures, and paintings, and then with the 1550 statute fining anyone possessing "anye Images of Stone Tymbre Alleblaster or Earthe graven carved or paynted. . . ."[13] While these orders were not undisputed, many churchwardens' records nonetheless voice their compliance with them, as parishes whitewashed their wall paintings, removed their statues and paintings, and replaced windows. In East Anglia wardens of St. Lawrence in Ipswich substituted plain glass for nine windows containing "ffanyd storyse."[14] In Long Melford the parish church accounts show money paid "for the havyng downe of the imagys & tabernacles."[15] Wardens of the church of St. John of Bearestrete, Norwich, paid nineteen shillings and eight pence "for makinge of a glasse wyndow wherein Thomas Beckett was."[16] Still, parish churches were not completely stripped of their art. Disapproving descriptions written in the later sixteenth and seventeenth centuries prove that stained-glass windows and even carvings of religious subjects had survived, at least for a while.[17] Following Edward VI's death, Mary Tudor attempted to restore holy images as part of traditional Catholicism, but the religious culture to which they had been integral could never again be wholly recreated. The tattered and mutilated remains of medieval wall paintings, rood screens, stained glass, and alabaster and wooden carvings testify to the fear, finally hardened into conviction, that these holy images were indeed the cause of idolatry.

ABBREVIATIONS

BRUC	Emden, A. B. *A Biographical Register of the University of Cambridge to 1500.* Cambridge: CUP, 1963.
BRUO	Emden, A. B. *A Biographical Register of the University of Oxford to A. D. 1500.* 3 vols. Oxford: Clarendon Press, 1957–1959.
CPL	*Calendar of Entries in the Papal Registers relating to Great Britain and Ireland: Papal Letters.* 18 vols. London: H. M. S. O., 1893–1994.
CUP	Cambridge University Press
CYS	Canterbury and York Society
DNB	*Dictionary of National Biography.* 22 vols. London: Oxford University Press, reprint ed., 1967–68
DS	*Dictionnaire de Spiritualité Ascétique et Mystique, Doctrine et Histoire.* 17 vols. Paris: Beauchesne, 1932–1995.
EETS	Early English Text Society
JBS	*Journal of British Studies*
JEH	*Journal of Ecclesiastical History*
MWME	*A Manual of the Writings in Middle English 1050–1500.* 10 vols. Vols. 1–2 ed. J. Burke Severs; vols. 3–10 ed. Albert E. Hartung. New Haven: The Connecticut Academy of Arts and Sciences, 1967–1998.
NA	*Norfolk Archaeology*
NRO	Norfolk Record Office
PG	*Patrologiae cursus completus: series graeca.* 162 vols. Ed. J.-P. Migne. Paris, 1857–1866.
PL	*Patrologiae cursus completus: series latina.* 221 vols. Ed. J.-P. Migne. Paris, 1841–1864.
PSIA	*Proceedings of the Suffolk Institute of Archaeology and History*
RS	Rolls Series
RSTC	*A Short-title Catalogue of Books Printed in England, Scotland & Ireland and of English Books Printed Abroad 1475–1640.* 3 vols. 2nd ed., rev. & enlarged. Ed. W. A. Jackson, F. S.

Ferguson, and Katharine F. Pantzer. London: The Bibliographical Society, 1976–1991.

SROB   Suffolk Record Office, Bury St. Edmunds

SROI   Suffolk Record Office, Ipswich

VHC Norfolk   *The Victoria History of the County of Norfolk.* 2 vols. Vol. 1 ed. H. Arthur Doubleday; vol. 2 ed. William Page. Westminster: Constable, 1901 & 1906.

VHC Suffolk   *The Victoria History of the County of Suffolk.* 2 vols. Ed. William Page. London: Constable, 1907.

NOTES

Introduction

1. Gregory the Great, "Epistola XIII ad Serenum Massiliensem Episcopum," *PL*, vol. 77, col. 1128: "Nam quod legentibus scriptura, hoc idiotis praestat pictura cernentibus, quia in ipsa etiam ignorantes vident quid sequi debeant, in ipsa legunt qui litteras nesciunt. Unde et praecipue gentibus pro lectione pictura est." See also cols. 1027–8. On the history of Gregory's defense of art, see Lawrence G. Duggan, "Was art really the 'book of the illiterate'?" *Word & Image* 5:3 (1989): 227–51. On early hostility to Christian art, see Ernst Kitzinger, "The Cult of Images in the Age Before Iconoclasm," *Dumbarton Oaks Papers* 8 (1954): 129–34.

2. Copenhagen, Det Kongelige Bibliotek MS. Gl. Kgl. S. 1605, f. 20r-v. The text reads: "Unum cole deum. In hoc Precepto potest quis peccare de fide male sentiendo ydolatrando demones invocando divinando dies vel cerimonias supersticiosas observando." For a description of this fifteenth-century Flemish prayer book, see Ellen Jørgensen, *Catalogus Codicum Latinorum medii aevi Bibliothecae Regiae Hafniensis* (Copenhagen, 1926), 213. The medieval Western Church considered the command against graven images part of the First Commandment until the sixteenth century; see Margaret Aston, *England's Iconoclasts* vol. 1 *Laws Against Images* (Oxford: Clarendon Press, 1988), 371–92.

3. W. R. Jones, "Lollards and Images: the Defense of Religious Art in Later Medieval England," *Journal of the History of Ideas* XXXIV (1973): 27–50, reviews the arguments of many of the anti-Lollard writers. For Lollard criticisms of images, see Margaret Aston, "Lollards and Images," in *Lollards and Reformers: Images and Literacy in Late Medieval Religion* (London: Hambledon Press, 1984), 135–92; and Anne Hudson, *Premature Reformation: Wycliffite Texts and Lollard History* (Oxford: Clarendon Press, 1988), 301–309.

4. Margaret Aston, *Faith and Fire: Popular and Unpopular Religion 1350–1600* (London: Hambledon Press, 1993), 1. See also Miri Rubin's comments on the problem of the "fragmentary nature" of medieval evidence, in *Corpus Christi: The Eucharist in Late Medieval Culture* (Cambridge: CUP, 1991), 9–10.

5. On iconoclasm in early modern England, see Aston, *England's Iconoclasts,* 62–95; and John Phillips, *The Reformation of Images: Destruction of Art in England 1535–1660* (Berkeley: University of California Press, 1973).

6. See Hans Belting, *Likeness and Presence: A History of the Image before the Era of Art,* trans. E. Jephcott (Chicago: University of Chicago Press, 1994), 1–9. David Freedberg, *The Power of Images* (Chicago: University of Chicago Press, 1989), contains many examples of how people treated images in the fifteenth and sixteenth centuries.

7. *Dives and Pauper,* vol. 1, ed. P. H. Barnum (London: EETS 275, 1976), 93.

8. Jonathan Sumption, *Pilgrimage: an Image of Mediaeval Religion* (Totowa, N. J.: Rowman & Littlefield, 1975), 273; William R. Jones, "Art and Christian Piety: Iconoclasm in Medieval Europe," in *The Image and the Word: Confrontations in Judaism, Christianity and Islam,* ed. Joseph Gutman (Missoula, Mont.: Scholars Press, 1977), 90–91.

9. See, for example, the late medieval compilation called *The Pore Caitif,* ed. Mary T. Brady (Ph.D. dissertation, Fordham University, 1954), 30–31. Thomas Aquinas, among other theologians, also commented on the tendency of the Old Testament Jews to commit idolatry; see *Summa Theologica* Ia. Q 61. art.1.

10. Numerous examples appear in late medieval sermon collections. See, for example, the legends of St. Simon and St. Jude in the *Speculum Sacerdotale,* ed. Edward H. Weatherly (London: EETS 200, 1936), 217, and of St. Bartholomew in *Mirk's Festial,* ed. T. Erbe (London: EETS e.s. 96, 1905), 235–39.

11. A vast scholarly literature is dedicated to pilgrimage; works with information on English shrines include Sumption, *Pilgrimage;* J. C. Dickinson, *The Shrine of Our Lady of Walsingham* (Cambridge: CUP, 1956); Donald J. Hall, *English Mediaeval Pilgrimage* (London: Routledge & K. Paul, 1965); Ronald C. Finucane, *Miracles and Pilgrims: Popular Beliefs in Medieval England* (Totowa, N. J.: Rowman and Littlefield, 1977).

12. Eamon Duffy, *The Stripping of the Altars: Traditional Religion in England c. 1400–c.1580* (New Haven: Yale University Press, 1992); Rubin, *Corpus Christi;* Gail McMurray Gibson, *The Theater of Devotion: East Anglian Drama and Society in the Late Middle Ages* (Chicago: University of Chicago Press, 1989); Jeremy Catto, "Religious Change Under Henry V," in *Henry V: the Practice of Kingship,* ed. G. L. Harriss (Oxford: Oxford University Press, 1985), 97–115.

13. On the shifting position and definition of the medieval laity, see André Vauchez, *The Laity in the Middle Ages,* ed. Daniel E. Bornstein, trans. Margery J. Schneider (Notre Dame: University of Notre Dame Press, 1993); and Ann W. Astell, "Introduction" to *Lay Sanctity, Medieval and Modern: A Search for Models,* ed. Ann W. Astell (Notre Dame: University of Notre Dame Press, 2000), 1–26.

14. On lay literacy in medieval England, see M. B. Parkes, "The Literacy of the Laity," in *Literature and Western Civilization: the Mediaeval World,* ed. D. Daiches and A. Thorlby (London: Aldus, 1973), 555–77; J. B. Trapp, "Literacy, Books and Readers," in *Cambridge History of the Book in Britain,* vol. III, ed. Lotte Hellinga and J. B. Trapp (Cambridge: CUP, 1999); 31–43;

Carol M. Meale and Julia Boffey, "Gentlewomen's Reading," in *ibid.*, 526–40; George R. Keiser, "Practical Books for the Gentleman," in *ibid.*, 470–94. Several recent studies suggest that women's literacy of the period has been underestimated; see Julia Boffey, "Women authors and women's literacy in fourteenth- and fifteenth-century England," in *Women and Literature in Britain 1150–1500*, 2nd ed., ed. Carol M. Meale (Cambridge: CUP, 1996), 159–82; and Carol M. Meale, "' . . . alle the bokes that I haue of latyn, englisch, and frensch': laywomen and their books in late medieval England," in *ibid.*, 128–58. For definitions of literacy and illiteracy in the Middle Ages, see Michael Clanchy, *From Memory to Written Record: England 1066–1317* 2nd ed. (Oxford: Blackwell, 1993), 224–52; and D. H. Green, "Orality and Reading: the State of Research in Medieval Studies," *Speculum* 65 (1990): 267–80.

15. Mary C. Erler, "Devotional Literature," in *Cambridge History of the Book*, vol. III, 495–525.

16. In the third century, for example, the pagan Porphyry wrote about reading from statues "as from books the things there written concerning the gods"; see Paul J. Alexander, *The Patriarch Nicephorus of Constantinople* (Oxford: Clarendon Press, 1958), 29.

17. Katherine L. French, *The People of the Parish: Community Life in a Late Medieval English Diocese* (Philadelphia: University of Pennsylvania Press, 2001), examines the ways in which laypeople contributed to the parish; see also Gervase Rosser, "Communities of Parish and Guild in the Late Middle Ags," in *Parish, Church and People: Local Studies in Lay Religion 1350–1750*, ed. S. J. Wright (London: Hutchinson, 1988), 29–55.

18. N. J. G. Pounds, *A History of the English Parish* (Cambridge: CUP, 2000), 38–9, 182–86; French, *People of the Parish*, 68–72.

19. On parish church patronage, see Katherine L. French, "'To Free Them from Binding': Women in the Late Medieval English Parish," *Journal of Interdisciplinary History* 27:3 (Winter 1997): 387–412; Judy Ann Ford, "Art and Identity in the Parish Communities of Late Medieval Kent," in *The Church and the Arts*, ed. Diana Wood (Oxford: Blackwell, 1992), 225–37; R. N. Swanson, *Church and Society in Late Medieval England* (Oxford: Blackwell, 1989), 256–60; Paul Binski, "The English Parish Church and Its Art in the Later Middle Ages: a Review of the Problem," *Studies in Iconography* 20 (1999): 1–25.

20. See Kitzinger, "Cult," 115–19; Freedberg, *Power of Images*, 93–98; Jeffrey Denton, "Image and History," in *Age of Chivalry: Art in Plantagenet England 1200–1400*, ed. Jonathan Alexander and Paul Binski (London: Royal Academy of Arts, 1987), 20.

Chapter 1

1. All biblical quotations and citations, unless otherwise noted, are from the Douay-Rheims Bible, the sixteenth- and seventeenth-century English

translation of the Latin Vulgate, revised by Bishop Challoner in the eighteenth century.

2. Christina Von Nolcken, *The Middle English Translation of the Rosarium Theologie* (Heidelberg: Winter, 1979), 97.

3. Norman P. Tanner, ed., *Heresy Trials in the Diocese of Norwich 1428–31,* Camden Fourth Series, vol. 20 (London: Royal Historical Society, 1977), 43–51.

4. Von Nolcken, *Rosarium Theologie,* 100.

5. *An Apology for Lollard Doctrines, attributed to Wicliffe* (London: Camden Society vol. 20, 1842), 87.

6. See also Wisdom 14:21, 14:27, 15:13, and 15:15–18; and J. Wilhelm, "Idolatry," in *The Catholic Encyclopedia,* vol. 7 (New York: Robert Appleton Co., 1910), 636–38.

7. See Edwyn Bevan, *Holy Images* (London: Allen & Unwin, 1940), 90–95, on early Christian beliefs about devils in images.

8. Minucius Felix, *Octavius,* trans. Gerald H. Rendall (Cambridge: Harvard University Press, 1931, reprt. 1977), 397.

9. Quoted in Elaine Pagels, *The Origin of Satan* (New York: Random House, 1995), 119. On Justin Martyr's life, works, and the centrality of evil angels or daemons to his thought, see L. W. Barnard, *Justin Martyr: His Life and Thought* (Cambridge: CUP, 1967), especially 106–10. For the explanation of why Christians cannot worship idols, see St. Justin Martyr, *The First and Second Apologies,* trans. L. W. Barnard (New York: Paulist Press, 1997), 27–28.

10. Tertullianus, *De Idololatria,* with critical text, translation, and commentary by J. H. Waszink and J. C. M. Van Winden (Leiden: Brill, 1987), sections 1.1–1.5; see also sections 3.2 and 4.2 for the association of the devil and demons with images.

11. Augustine, *The City of God,* trans. Henry Bettenson (Harmondsworth: Penguin, 1972), 329–37. For an introduction to the mythical Hermes Trismegistus and the *Asclepius,* see Brian P. Copenhaver, *Hermetica: The Greek Corpus Hermeticum and the Latin Asclepius in a new English translation* (Cambridge: CUP, 1992). Pagels, *Origin of Satan,* 48–50, discusses the idea found in first-century and later Jewish and Christian texts that demons were the offspring of fallen angels and human females.

12. John T. McNeill and Helena M. Gamer, *Medieval Handbooks of Penance* (New York: Columbia University Press, ca. 1938), 256 and 306.

13. *The Tripartite Life of Patrick,* ed. and trans. Whitley Stokes, RS (London, 1887), 90–93.

14. David Freedberg, *Power of Images* (Chicago: University of Chicago Press, 1989), 370.

15. Thomas Aquinas, *Summa Theologiae,* 2a2ae, Qu. 94, art.1 & 4.

16. For the St. Bartholomew legend, see Jacobus de Voragine, *The Golden Legend,* trans. William Granger Ryan (Princeton: Princeton University Press, 1993), vol. 2, 109–16; St. Thomas's life is in vol. 1, 29–35.

17. About New York, Morgan Library, MS. H. 8, see *Description of the Great Book of Hours of Henry the Eighth, illuminated by Jean Bourdichon of Tours* (n.p., privately printed, 1923).

18. Reginald Pecock, *The Repressor of Over Much Blaming of the Clergy,* ed. Churchill Babington, RS (London, 1860), 244–45. Pecock was convicted of heresy in 1457, but in the past century historians have defended his orthodoxy; see Roy Haines, "Reginald Pecock: A Tolerant Man in an Age of Intolerance," in *Persecution and Toleration,* ed. W. J. Sheils (Oxford: Blackwell, 1984), 125–37, and the classic study by V. H. H. Green, *Bishop Reginald Pecock: A Study in Ecclesiastical History and Thought* (Cambridge: CUP, 1945).

19. H. L. D. Ward, *Catalogue of Romances in the Department of Manuscripts in the British Museum,* vol. II (London, 1893), 668, # 21.

20. The *Omne Bonum* exists in London, B. L. Royal MSS. 6 E VI and 6 E VII; the discussion of astronomical and necromantic images is in Royal 6 E VII, f. 531r.; on its author, sources, and illustrations see Lucy Freeman Sandler, *Omne Bonum: A Fourteenth-Century Encyclopedia of Universal Knowledge,* 2 vols. (London: Harvey Miller, 1996). See also Alexander Carpenter, *Destructorium Viciorum* (Paris, 1521), Pars VI, cap. 52, on astrological figures.

21. *Walter Hilton's Latin Writings,* vol. 1, ed. John P. H. Clark and Cheryl Taylor (Salzburg: Institut für Anglistik und Amerikanistik, Universität Salzburg, 1987), 201; my translation. Hilton goes on to argue that sensible images, far from being idolatrous, attract people's minds to the spiritual.

22. Carpenter, *Destructorium Viciorum,* Pars VI, cap. 45. On Carpenter and this treatise, see *DNB,* vol. 3, 1062–3; *BRUO,* vol. 1, 360; and G. R. Owst, *The Destructorium Viciorum of Alexander Carpenter: A Fifteenth-Century Sequel to Literature and Pulpit in Medieval England* (London: S.P.C.K., 1952).

23. Carpenter, *Destructorium Viciorum,* Pars IV, cap. 36. Carpenter quotes from the Books of Wisdom and Baruch against idols, declaring that people who believe they are aided by images are deceived.

24. In the Middle Ages the clause against graven images was considered part of the First Commandment, a tradition followed by Luther and Zwingli; other sixteenth-century reformers regarded it as part of the Second Commandment; see Aston, *England's Iconoclasts,* vol. 1, 371–92, and also Jaroslav Pelikan, *The Christian Tradition* vol. 4 *Reformation of Church and Dogma (1300–1700)* (Chicago: University of Chicago Press, 1984), 216.

25. London, B.L. Royal MS. 6 E VII, f. 227v.

26. Norman H. Baynes, "Idolatry and the Early Church," in *Byzantine Studies and Other Essays* (London: Athlone Press, 1955), 117–25.

27. On early Christian and later Orthodox attitudes toward art, see Kitzinger, "Cult of Images;" Leonid Ouspensky, "Icon and Art," in *Christian Spirituality: Origins to the Twelfth Century,* ed. B. McGinn and J. Meyendorff (New York: Crossroad, 1985), 382–93; and Jaroslav Pelikan, *Imago Dei: the Byzantine Apologia for Icons* (Princeton: Princeton University Press, 1990.)

28. Gregory the Great, "Epistola XIII ad Serenum Massiliensem Episcopum." For interpretations of Gregory's meaning, see Mary J. Carruthers, *The Book of Memory; A Study of Memory in Medieval Culture* (Cambridge: CUP, 1990), 222–23; and Duggan, "Was art really the 'book of the illiterate'?" 227. On the history of the idea of images as "books of the laity" see Duggan; L. Gougaud, "Muta Praedicatio," in *Revue Bénédictine* 42 (1930): 168–71; and

Ann E. Nichols, "Books-for-Laymen: the Demise of a Commonplace," *Church History* 56:4 (December 1987): 457–73.

29. Alain Boureau, "Les Théologiens Carolingiens devant les Images Religieuses. La Conjoncture de 825," in *Nicée II, 787–1987: Douze Siècles d'Images Religieuses,* ed. F. Boespflug and N. Lossky (Paris: Les Éditions du Cerf, 1987), 247–62.

30. For the Latin text and an English translation of St. Bernard of Clairvaux, "Apologia ad Guillelmum Abbatem," see Conrad Rudolph, *The "Things of Greater Importance": Bernard of Clairvaux's* Apologia *and the Medieval Attitude Toward Art* (Philadelphia: University of Pennsylvania Press, 1990), 227–87; for the protest against saints' images, see 280f. On the Christian tradition of considering support for art in opposition to the care of the poor, see Rudolph's discussion, 80–103.

31. See Denton, "Image and History," 20–25, for a survey of the position of religious art in England. A basic guide to the period is Joan Evans, *English Art 1307–1462* (Oxford: Clarendon Press, 1949). Specific studies on carving, stained glass, wall paintings, and illuminated prayer books are cited in the following chapters.

32. Aston, "Lollards and Images," 135–92; see also Anne Hudson, *The Premature Reformation: Wycliffite Texts and Lollard History* (Oxford: Clarendon Press, 1988), 301–309.

33. See *Fasciculi Zizaniorum Magistri Johannis Wyclif Cum Tritico,* ed. W. W. Shirley, RS (London: 1858), 370–71. On Wyche's ideas and career, see Christina von Nolken, "Rychard Wyche, a Certain Knight, and the Beginning of the End," *Lollardy and the Gentry in the Later Middle Ages,* eds. M. Aston and C. Richmond (New York: St. Martin's, 1997), 127–54. On Lollard biblical scholarship, see Hudson, *Premature Reformation,* 229–77.

34. Tanner, *Heresy Trials,* 73.

35. *Register of Thomas Langton, Bishop of Salisbury 1485–93,* ed. D. P. Wright (CYS, pt. 147, 1985), 81 and 72.

36. Leslie Barnard, "The Theology of Images," in *Iconoclasm,* ed. A. Bryer and J. Herrin (Birmingham: Center for Byzantine Studies, University of Birmingham, 1977), 10.

37. *Register of Bishop Philip Repingdom 1405–19,* vol. III, ed. Margaret Archer (Lincoln Record Society, 1982), 11.

38. Aston, *England's Iconoclasts,* vol. 1, 98–104. See Wycliffe's *Tractatus De Mandatis Divinis,* ed. Johann Loserth and F. D. Matthew (London: Wyclif Society, 1922; reprt. New York & London: Johnson Reprint Corp., 1966), cap. xv, especially 156–60. In his sermons on the commandments, Wycliffe warned that image adoration violates the First Commandment, but reluctantly acknowledged: "Scio tamen quod populus plene instructus per curatos idoneos, qui nimis deficiunt, posset facere quod tales sculpture sint libri utiles laicorum;" see *Sermones,* vol. 1, ed. Johann Loserth (London: Wyclif Society, 1887), 92. Wycliffe's view that images could be good or evil, depending on their use, is reiterated by the *Rosarium Theologie's* entry

under "ymage," 99, and is cited in the discussion of the First Command-ment in the Wycliffite treatise in London, B. L. Harley MS. 2398, f. 81v: "Ffor a gret clerk seyþ þat ymages mowe be maked wel and eke ylle. . . ."

39. Baynes, "Idolatry," 118–20.

40. Tanner, *Heresy Trials,* 95. For William White's view of images, see *Fasciculi Zizaniorum,* 429–30.

41. A. K. McHardy, "Bishop Buckingham and the Lollards of Lincoln Dio-cese," in *Schism, Heresy and Religious Protest,* ed. D. Baker (Cambridge: CUP, 1972), 144.

42. *Apology for Lollard Doctrines,* 86. The author cites the "prophet Baruc," or Baruch, believed to be the author of the Book of Baruch and Jeremiah's friend and secretary; in the Vulgate, the anti-idolatry polemic known as the Epistle of Jeremiah formed Chapter Six of the Book of Baruch, a very popular text among image critics.

43. *Selections from English Wycliffite Writings,* ed. Anne Hudson (Cambridge: CUP, 1978), 87.

44. These objections to idols are found in Psalms 113 and 134; in Wisdom 13:10 and 15:15; and in The Apocalypse 9:20.

45. Tanner, *Heresy Trials,* 142, 148, 154.

46. Tanner, *Heresy Trials,* 71. Hudson, *English Wycliffite Writings,* 181, n.17, iden-tifies pseudoChrysostom as the origin of the idea of poor men as the true images of Christ. Clement of Alexandria, Origen, and others argued that the true image of God was the just or virtuous man; see Alexander, *Patri-arch Nicephorus,* 40–41.

47. *Apology for Lollard Doctrines,* 89.

48. *Register Langton,* 79; *Apology,* 90.

49. For a Latin version of the *Twelve Conclusions,* see *Fasciculi Zizaniorum,* 360–69. Hudson, *English Wycliffite Writings,* prints an English Version, 24–29. H. S. Cronin, "The Twelve Conclusions of the Lollards," *English Historical Review* 22 (1907): 292–304, provides both English and Latin texts.

50. Aquinas cites as authority John of Damascus, who cited St. Basil; his dis-cussion of *latria* and *dulia* are in the *Summa Theologiae,* 3a. Qu. 25, art. 3, 4, 5. On the distinctions between *dulia, latria,* and the third form of venera-tion reserved to the Virgin Mary, *hyperdulia,* see the article by A. Chollet, "Culte en Général," in *Dictionnaire de Théologie Catholique* vol. 3 (Paris: Letouzey et Ané, 1908), cols. 2404–2427.

51. Aquinas, *Summa Theologiae,* 3a. Qu. 25, art.3.

52. Aston, "Lollard and Images," 156–58, discusses Holcot's views. On Holcot's life and work, see *DNB,* vol. IX, 1007–1009, which lists a 1480 printed edition of his Wisdom commentary, followed by many later editions; see also Emden, *BRUO,* vol. 2, 946–47. On the popularity of Holcot's Wisdom commentaries, see Janet Coleman, *Medieval Readers and Writers 1350–1400* (New York: Columbia University Press, 1981), 263.

53. *The Lanterne of Liȝt,* ed. Lilian M. Swinburn (London: EETS 151, 1917), 84.

54. For Dymmok, or Dymock, see *DNB*, vol. 6, 293–94; and *BRUO*, vol. 1, 617. His treatise is published in *Rogeri Dymmok liber contra xii errores et hereses Lollardorum*, ed. H. S. Cronin (London: Wyclif Society, 1922). For the context of the anti-Lollard literature and a review of its arguments, see Jones, "Lollards and Images." On Dymmok's audience and the dissemination of his treatise, see Fiona Somerset, "Answering the *Twelve Conclusions:* Dymmok's Halfhearted Gestures Towards Publication," in *Lollardy and the Gentry*, 52–76. John Carpenter, a prominent citizen and town clerk of London, received a copy of Dymmok's work from one John Wilok and in 1442 bequeathed it to Master William Byngham; see Susan H. Cavanaugh, "A Study of Books Privately Owned in England 1300–1450," (Ph.D. dissertation, University of Pennsylvania, 1980), 167.

55. The discussion of images is in Part 8 of Dymmok's *Liber contra xii errores,* and answers the eighth conclusion of the Lollards, which is given in English and then Latin. Dymmok, 182: "quia usus ecclesie in factura ymaginum fuit utilis et a Deo institutus."

56. Dymmok, 183. The apocryphal story of Abgar was told by John of Damascus, whose defense of images was one of Dymmok's major sources; see his *De Imaginibus PG,* vol. 94, cols. 1261 & 1262. An English translation is St. John of Damascus, *On the Divine Images,* trans. David Anderson (Crestwood, N.Y.: St. Vladimir's Seminary Press, 1980). On the history of this ancient legend, see "Abgar (La Légende D')," *Dictionnaire d'Archéologie Chrétienne et de Liturgie* (Paris: Letouzey et Ané, 1924), vol. 1, cols. 87–97. On the histories and relationship of the Abgar image and the Veronica, see also Belting, *Likeness and Presence,* 208–24. St. Luke was often depicted in medieval art as an artist painting a portrait of the Virgin Mary; see Belting, 57–59, and the poem by John Lydgate, "The Image of Our Lady," ll. 1–8, in Henry Noble MacCracken, ed., *The Minor Poems of John Lydgate* (London: EETS e.s. 107, 1911 (for 1910)), 290.

57. Dymmok, 187. He also cites the Gospel of St. John (20:30), that Jesus did many other things "not written in this book."

58. Dymmok, 184. The reference to the cherubim comes from Exodus 25:18–20. John of Damascus used this example repeatedly in *De Imaginibus, PG,* vol. 94, cols. 1243–44, 1275–76, 1291–92.

59. Dymmok, 186, cites Aquinas as the source of this response, but this argument is much older as it was used by Byzantine image defenders against iconoclasts; see Edward James Martin, *A History of the Iconoclastic Controversy* (London: S.P.C. K., 1930), 117–29.

60. Dymmok's defense of the Trinity, 200, addressed the repeated Lollard complaint against representations of the Trinity. Wycliffe, for example, protested the common representation of God the Father as an old man holding the crucified Jesus on his knees, with the Holy Spirit shown as a dove; see his *Tractatus De Mandatis Divinis,* 156. The *Twelve Conclusions of the Lollards,* 27, also singles out the image of the Trinity as particularly "abhominable."

61. Ambrosios Giakalis, *Images of the Divine: the Theology of Icons at the Seventh Ecumenical Council* (Leiden: Brill, 1994), 33–34; St. Basil's defense of unwritten tradition was included in Gratian's *Decretum* and regularly cited thereafter; see Pelikan, *Imago Dei,* 62–65.

62. Norman H. Baynes, "The Icons Before Iconoclasm," in *Byzantine Studies,* 231; Leonid Ouspensky, *Theology of the Icon,* vol. 1, trans. Anthony Gythiel (Crestwood, N.Y.: St.Vladimir's Seminary Press, 1992), 133.

63. Kenneth Parry, *Depicting the Word: Byzantine Iconophile Thought of the Eighth and Ninth Centuries* (Leiden: Brill, 1996), 70–80.

64. Dymmok, 199–200.These two stories are found in "The Exaltation of the Holy Cross" in *The Golden Legend,* vol. 2, 170–71.

65. Dymmok, 182. See Chrysostom's Homily XIV on Hebrews viii 1, 2 in P. Schaff, ed., *A Select Library of the Nicene and Post-Nicene Fathers of the Christian Church,* vol. 14 (New York: Scribner's, 1889), 434; Latin and Greek texts of this work are in *PG,* vol. 63, cols. 109–16.

66. Cited in Pelikan, *Imago Dei,* 103.

67. Cicero, *De Oratore,* II.lxxxvii, trans. E. W. Sutton (Cambridge: Harvard University Press, 1942), 469. See Frances A. Yates, *The Art of Memory* (Chicago: University of Chicago Press, 1966), 1–49, on memory in the ancient world.

68. Yates, *Art of Memory,* 51.

69. Pelikan, *Imago Dei,* 113; Giakalis, *Images of the Divine,* 78–83.

70. Duggan, 232.

71. Dymmok, 182.

72. Dymmok, 183.

73. Dymmok, 185. See Pelikan, *Imago Dei,* 116–17, for iconodule arguments that icons took the place of witnessing sacred events for Christians born too late to see the historical Christ. St. Bonaventure and Peter Lombard, among others, comment on the efficacy of images as mnemonic aids; see Duggan, 232.

74. Mistrust solidified into prohibition in 1407 when Archbishop Arundel forbade people to own vernacular biblical texts without episcopal permission; see D. Wilkins, ed. *Concilia Magnae Britanniae et Hiberniae* vol. 3 (London, 1737), 317. On heresy and reading, see Anne Hudson, "'Laicus litteratus': the Paradox of Lollardy," in *Heresy and Literacy, 1000–1530,* ed. Peter Biller and Anne Hudson (Cambridge: CUP, 1994), 222–36.

75. See Ouspensky, *Theology of the Icon,* 138–39, on the Seventh Ecumenical Council's insistence that icons were equivalent to scripture.

76. There also existed a medieval tradition of regarding art as a valid spiritual aid for clerics; see Rudolph, *The "Things of Greater Importance,"* 107–10, and especially the comments of Hugh of St-Victor, 109.

77. Dymmok, 183–85.

78. Dymmok, 187–88.

79. The discussion of the saints is in Dymmok, 191–98. Dymmok makes no distinction between relics and images, as can be seen in several statements;

for example, 193: "cum sanctis Dei merito affici debeamus et eos debitis honoribus uenerari, quia personas ipsas in presenti habere non possumus, saltem ad eorum reliquias uel ymagines adorandas accedere monemur."

80. *Selections from English Wycliffite Writings,* 84.

81. Dymmok, 193.

82. Dymmok, 194–97. In discussing the sacraments, for instance, Aquinas in *Summa Theologiae* 3a. Qu. 60, art. 4, argues that it is "connatural to man to arrive at a knowledge of intelligible realities through sensible ones, and a sign is something through which a person arrives at knowledge of some further thing beyond itself." E. Ruth Harvey details the connections between Aquinas's theory that humans acquire knowledge through the five senses of the body and his theology of holy images in "The Image of Love," in *The Complete Works of St. Thomas More,* vol. 6, pt. II, eds. Thomas M. C. Lawler, et al. (New Haven: Yale University Press, 1981), 745–48.

83. Parry, *Depicting the Word,* 166; Augustine, *City of God,* 371–77.

84. Parry, *Depicting,* 25; Gervais Dumeige, *Nicée II* (Paris, Éditions de L'Orante, 1978), 69–72. See the English translation of St. Theodore the Studite's comments on the relation of image and prototype in Cyril Mango, *Art of the Byzantine Empire 312–1453* (Englewood Cliffs, N.J.: Prentice-Hall, 1972), 173.

85. For the transmission of Greek image defenses to the West, see Jean-Claude Schmitt, "L'Occident, Nicée II et les Images du VIIIe au XIIIe Siècle," in *Nicée II, 787–1987,* 271–301.

86. Gilbert Dagron, "Le culte des images dans le monde byzantin," in *La romanité en Orient* (London: Variorum Reprints, 1984), 153; Giakalis, *Images,* 46–49; Bevan, *Holy Images,* 143.

87. Dymmok, 199.

88. The treatise is published in *Walter Hilton's Latin Writings,* vol. 1, 179–214. On the date of the work and its attribution to Hilton, see Joy M. Russell-Smith, "Walter Hilton and a Tract in Defence of the Veneration of Images," *Dominican Studies* 7 (1954): 180–214. J. P. H. Clark, "Walter Hilton in Defence of the Religious Life and of the Veneration of Images," *Downside Review* 103 (1985): 1–25, provides further evidence for Hilton as the author and summarizes some of the treatise's arguments. See also G. R. Owst, *Literature and Pulpit in Medieval England,* 2nd ed. (Oxford: Blackwell, 1961), 137–39. On Hilton's life and work, see the *Introduction* by John P. H. Clark and Rosemary Dorward to *The Scale of Perfection* (New York: Paulist Press, 1991), 13–68.

89. Like Dymmok, Hilton cites arguments derived from John Damascene, Basil, Gregory the Great, the legend of King Abgar, and instances of valid images from the Old Testament, such as the carved cherubim on the Ark of the Covenant. These were standard elements in all defenses of images in this period.

90. Hilton, 187.

91. Hilton, 187–88. See Clark, "Walter Hilton," 11, for a similar passage in another work by Hilton.

92. Hilton, 189. The allusion is to 1 Corinthians 3:1–2: "And I, brethren, could not speak unto you as unto spiritual, but as unto carnal. As unto little ones in Christ. I gave you milk to drink, not meat. . . ."

93. Hilton, 202: "ibi per crucem altare, per ymaginem vero sacrificium quod super altare [f]it designamus."

94. Hilton, 189–90. See Luke 14:12–24.

95. Hilton, 191–92. See Jones, "Lollard and Images," 40–41, for a similar argument made by the Franciscan William Woodford.

96. Hilton, 205. Hilton here draws upon the Bernardine ideal of imageless devotion; St. Bernard urged that one should "by the purity of the mind, raise yourself above the phantasms of corporeal likenesses rushing in from every direction"; cited in Sixten Ringbom, *Icon to Narrative* 2nd ed. (Doornspijk: Davaco, 1984), 16.

97. Hilton, 205–6. Like St. Bernard, Hilton refers to those capable only of a lesser "carnal" love, making this a justification for images. Russell-Smith, "Walter Hilton," 191, links this discussion to a similar one in Hilton's *Scale of Perfection;* Clark, "Walter Hilton in Defence of the Religious Life," 14, points to the Thomist emphasis on "virtual intention." See Dagron, "Le culte des images," 142, on views of early Christian writers who consider the cult of images on the lowest level, but still acceptable: "l'image est tolérée dans la mesure où sa beauté peut être le reflet ou le relais de la sainteté. . . ."

98. Hilton, 207. This argument reiterates the words of the early-eighth-century patriarch Germanos, who insisted that his bishops take into account the intention of the person performing the act when considering the veneration of images; see Parry, *Depicting,* 167.

99. Hilton, 213.

100. For a survey of several contributions to this debate, including works by the Carmelite Thomas Netter and the Franciscan William Woodford, see Jones, "Lollard and Images"; James Crompton, "Lollard Doctrine with special reference to the controversy over Image-worship and Pilgrimage," (B. Litt. thesis, Oxford, 1950), especially 130f. identifies several manuscripts relevant to this debate; Aston, "Lollards and Images," 177–187, discusses Bishop Reginald Pecock's views; J. I. Catto, "William Woodford O.F.M. (c.1330-c.1397)," (D. Phil. thesis, Oxford, 1969), 150–55, details Woodford's defense of images in his *Postilla Super Matthaeum.*

101. Carpenter, *Destructorium Viciorum,* Pars VI, cap. 45, "ideo dicitur large loquendo quod ymaginem adoramus. Unde videtur michi dicendum quod non adoro ymaginem christi: qui lignum: nec quia ymago christi: sed adoro christum coram ymagine christi et quia est ymago christi: excitat me ad adorandum christum."

102. London, B. L. Harley MS. 2398, ff. 81v–82v. Aston, "Lollards and Images," 153–56, and 153 n. 64, calls the treatise's view of images "ambiguous," but considers the work overall as sympathetic to Lollardy; see also Hudson, *Premature Reformation,* 425, n. 151.

103. "To Sir John Oldcastle," ll. 409–424 in *Hoccleve's Works*, vol. 1 *The Minor Poems*, ed. Frederick J. Furnivall (London: EETS e.s. 61, 1892), 21. On Hoccleve's life and work, see William A. Matthews, "Thomas Hoccleve," in *MWME*, vol. 3, 746–56; and J. A. Burrow, *Thomas Hoccleve* (Brookfield, Vermont: Ashgate, 1994).

104. *Minor Poems of John Lydgate*, 297–99. Derek A. Pearsall, *John Lydgate (1371–1449): a bio-bibliography* (Victoria, B.C.: English Literary Studies, University of Victoria, 1997) provides an overview of work on the poet.

Chapter 2

1. K. Horstmann, "Orologium Sapientiae or The Seven Poyntes of Trewe Wisdom aus MS. Douce 114," *Anglia* 10 (1888): 328.

2. For the flourishing of pastoral literature after 1215, see Leonard E. Boyle, "The Fourth Lateran Council and Manuals of Popular Theology," in *The Popular Literature of Medieval England*, ed. Thomas J. Heffernan (Knoxville: University of Tennessee Press, 1985), 30–43; Judith Shaw, "The Influence of Canonical and Episcopal Reform on Popular Books of Instruction," in *ibid.*, 44–60; G. H. Russell, "Vernacular Instruction of the Laity in the Later Middle Ages in England: Some Texts and Notes," *Journal of Religious History* 2 (1962): 98–119. Robert R. Raymo describes many of these works in "Works of Religious and Philosophical Instruction," in *MWME*, vol. 7, 2255–2378. See also Norman F. Blake, "Varieties of Middle English Religious Prose," in *Chaucer and Middle English Studies in honour of Rossell Hope Robbins*, ed. Beryl Rowland (London: Allen & Unwin, 1974), 348–56, and Vincent Gillespie, "Vernacular Books of Religion," in *Book Production and Publishing in Britain 1375–1475*, ed. Jeremy Griffiths and Derek Pearsall (Cambridge: CUP, 1989), 317–44.

3. Richard Rolle, "A notabill Tretys off the ten Comandementys," in *Yorkshire Writers* vol. 1, ed. C. Horstmann (London: Swan Sonnenschein, 1895), 195.

4. *Jacob's Well*, ed. Arthur Brandeis (London: EETS 115, 1900), 94; see also its condemnation of those who break crosses, altars, and images, 16. For its sources and composition, see Joan Young Gregg, "The Exempla of 'Jacob's Well': A Study in the Transmission of Medieval Sermon Stories," *Traditio* 33 (1977): 359–80. For views on church rituals and magic, see R. N. Swanson, *Religion and Devotion in Europe, c. 1215-c. 1515* (Cambridge: CUP, 1995), 186–7; and Keith Thomas, *Religion and the Decline of Magic* (New York: Scribners', 1971), 25–50.

5. *Speculum Christiani*, ed. Gustaf Holmstedt (London: EETS 182, 1933). The description is Vincent Gillespie's, "The Evolution of the *Speculum Christiani*," in *Latin and Vernacular: Studies in Late-Medieval Texts and Manuscripts*, ed. A. J. Minnis (Cambridge: D. S. Brewer, 1989), 39–60. Holmstedt's *Introduction*, clxxx–cxcv, discusses the structure of the work and the addition of later material to the original composition, although Gillespie disputes this at points.

6. *Speculum Christiani,* 186.

7. *Book of Vices and Virtues,* ed. W. N. Francis (London: EETS 217, 1942), 1, 317–19. On Middle English versions of the *Somme le Roi,* see Francis' discussion, ix-x & xxxii-xl; and Alexandra Barratt, "Works of Religious Instruction," in A. S. G. Edwards, ed., *Middle English Prose: a Critical Guide to Major Authors and Genres* (New Brunswick, N. J.: Rutgers University Press, 1984), 416. On idolatry, see also *Middle English Sermons,* ed. W. O. Ross (London: EETS 209, 1940), 22, 106–8; *A Myrour to Lewde Men and Wymmen: a prose version of the Speculum Vitae,* ed. Venetia Nelson (Heidelberg: Winter, 1981), 138–9; and Robert Mannyng of Brunne's *Handlyng Synne,* ed. Idelle Sullens (Binghamton, N.Y.: Medieval and Renaissance Texts and Studies 14, 1983), 154.

8. *Speculum Christiani,* 186–88.

9. Aquinas, *Summa Theologiae,* 3a Qu. 25. art. 3 & 4; on images of the saints, see 2a2ae Q. 94. art. 2. Roger Dymmock repeats this argument in *Liber contra xii errores,* 183.

10. *Speculum Sacerdotale,* 1–2. See Thomas J. Heffernan, "Sermon Literature" in *Middle English Prose,* 191–92, on this work's audience.

11. *Dives and Pauper,* 81–220. Once contested, *Dives and Pauper's* orthodoxy is asserted by Anne Hudson in "Wycliffite Prose," in *Middle English Prose,* 263; and Raymo, "Works of Religious and Philosophical Instruction," 2287.

12. *Dives and Pauper,* 81–83.

13. *Dives and Pauper,* 86.

14. *Dives and Pauper,* 107–108.

15. *Quattuor Sermones: Printed by William Caxton,* ed. N. F. Blake (Heidelberg: Winter, 1975), 26–7.

16. *Dives and Pauper,* 83–85.

17. On Lollardy and *The Pore Caitif,* see Brady's comments in the Introduction to *The Pore Caitif,* cxxxvi-cxlvii; and also her "Lollard Interpolations and Omissions in Manuscripts of *The Pore Caitif,*" in *De Cella in Seculum,* ed. Michael G. Sargent (Cambridge: Brewer, 1989), 183–203. On Lollard interpolations in orthodox texts, see Coleman, *Medieval Readers and Writers,* 211.

18. *Pore Caitif,* 30–31.

19. Aquinas, *Summa Theologiae,* 1a. Q 67. art. 4 and 1a2ae. Q101. art. 3. John of Damascus had also declared the Jews prone to idolatry; see Alexander, *Patriarch Nicephorus,* 46. For interpretations of the Old Law by medieval Christian theologians, see Beryl Smalley, "William of Auvergne, John of La Rochelle and St. Thomas Aquinas on the Old Law," in *St. Thomas Aquinas 1274–1974 Commemorative Studies,* vol. 2 (Toronto: Pontifical Institute of Mediaeval Studies, 1974), 11–71. For Aquinas's views on the Jews, idolatry, and the Mosaic Law, see John Y. B. Hood, *Aquinas and the Jews* (Philadelphia: University of Pennsylvania Press, 1995), 38–61. Medieval Hebrew chronicles often classified Christianity as idolatry; see Mark R. Cohen,

Under Crescent and Cross: the Jews in the Middle Ages (Princeton: Princeton University Press, 1994), 141.

20. *Pore Caitif,* 31–32.

21. *Pore Caitif,* 32.

22. Michael Camille, *The Gothic Idol: Ideology and Image-making in Medieval Art* (Cambridge: CUP, 1989), 217. Caroline Walker Bynum, *Holy Feast and Holy Fast: the Religious Significance of Food to Medieval Women* (Berkeley: University of California Press, 1987), 59–69. See also Rubin, *Corpus Christi,* 120–122.

23. The Introduction to *The Pore Caitif,* lix, prints this variant from Hunterian MS. 520. See Brady's discussion on the variations among image discussions in *Pore Caitif* manuscripts in "Lollard Interpolations," 185–90.

24. Introduction to *The Pore Caitif,* lix-lx. For Lollard criticism of images as false depictions, see Hudson, *Selections from English Wycliffite Writings,* 84. For orthodox critics who also worried about an excessive focus on images, see Archbishop Fitzralph's comments in G. R. Owst, *Literature and Pulpit in Medieval England* 2nd ed. (Oxford: Blackwell, 1961), 140–41; and Jean Gerson's cautions in Sixten Ringbom, *Icon to Narrative* 2nd ed. (Doornspijk: Davaco, 1984), 19–20.

25. This chapter focuses on tales from late medieval English works that have been printed. This is, of course, highly selective, as many collections are only in manuscript. For example, in his *Catalogue of Romances,* vol. 2, Ward lists over thirty manuscripts in the British Library alone containing "Miracles of the Virgin." See H. Leith Spencer, *English Preaching in the Late Middle Ages* (Oxford: Clarendon Press, 1993), 88–91, who cautions against using sermons as evidence for popular belief in the Middle Ages, but also maintains that sermons "indicate certain habitual modes of expression and thought; they disseminate the commonplaces of their time, great as well as trivial." On the history and variety of *exempla,* see J.-Th. Welter, *L'Exemplum dans la littérature religieuse et didactique du moyen age* (Paris, 1927), especially Part 3 for the fifteenth century; Claude Bremond, Jacques le Goff and Jean-Claude-Schmitt, *L'Exemplum* (Turnhout: Brepols, 1982); and *Les* Exempla *médiévaux: Introduction à la recherche* (Carcassonne: Garae/Hesiode, 1992). On English sources for sermon tales, see H. G. Pfander, "The Mediaeval Friars and Some Alphabetical Reference-Books for Sermons," *Medium Aevum* 3 (1934): 19–29. Jacques Berlioz, "*Exempla* as a Source for the History of Women," in *Medieval Women and the Sources of Medieval History,* ed. Joel T. Rosenthal (Athens: University of Georgia Press, 1990), 37–50, considers *exempla* a valuable source for women's history. For analyses of *exempla,* see Ruth Mazo Karras, "The Virgin and the Pregnant Abbess: Miracles and Gender in the Middle Ages," *Medieval Perspectives* 3 (1988): 112–32; Jacques Le Goff, "Le juif dans les *exempla* médiévaux: le cas de l'*Alphabetum Narrationum,*" in *Mélanges Léon Poliakov. Le racisme, mythes et sciences* (Paris, 1981), 209–20; Ivan G. Marcus, "Images of the Jews in the *Exempla* of Caesarius of Heisterbach," in *From Witness to Witchcraft: Jews and Judaism in Medieval Christian Thought,* ed. Jeremy

Cohen (Wiesbaden: Harrassowitz, 1996), 247–56. Joan Young Gregg, *Devils, Women, and Jews: Reflections of the Other in Medieval Sermon Stories* (Albany: State University of New York Press, 1997), makes available many *exempla* in modern English.

26. See M. R. James, *The Bohun Manuscripts: A Group of Five Manuscripts Executed in England about 1370 for Members of the Bohun Family* (Oxford: Roxburghe Club, 1936). James identifies the *exempla* in Copenhagen, K.B. MS. Thotts Saml. 547, and in Oxford, Bodleian Lib., MS. Auct. D. 4. 4., and lists other manuscripts that include illuminations of miracles of the Virgin.

27. On Host desecration narratives, see Miri Rubin, *Gentile Tales: The Narrative Assault on Late Medieval Jews* (New Haven: Yale University Press, 1999). See also Jean-Pierre Myette, "L'image du Juif dans la *Lègende dorée,*" in *Legenda aurea—la Lègende dorèe (XIIIᵉ–XVᵉ s.), Le Moyen français* vol. 32 (1993), 111–23. These views were predicated on the belief that Christ's crucifixion was the fault of the Jews; on this, see Hood, *Aquinas and the Jews,* 62–76.

28. Beverly Boyd, *The Middle English Miracles of the Virgin* (San Marino, Cal.: The Huntington Library, 1964), 126.

29. *Mirk's Festial,* 252. On lay readers of the *Festial,* see Aston, *Lollards and Reformers,* 127. *Speculum Sacerdotale,* 206–8. For these stories, see *The Golden Legend,* vol. 2, 168–73. Jeremy Cohen, "The Jews as the Killers of Christ in the Latin Tradition, From Augustine to the Friars," *Traditio* 39 (1983): 1–27, traces the development of the notion that Jews killed Christ out of envy and hatred, not through ignorance of his status as God.

30. *Mirk's Festial,* 145–6. This version is also in *The Golden Legend,* but connecting this miraculous blood with the shrine at Hailes seems to have been an English invention. For similar tales of crucifixes and paintings of Christ that bleed when pierced by Jews, see J. A. Herbert, *Catalogue of Romances in the Department of Manuscripts in the British Museum,* vol. III (London, 1910), 517, 537, 605, 664; and see Frederic C. Tubach, *Index Exemplorum, Folklore Fellows Communications No. 204* (Helsinki, 1969), 110, #1373.

31. See Karras's comments in "The Virgin and the Pregnant Abbess," 113.

32. Hans Belting, *Likeness and Presence: A History of the Image Before the Era of Art,* trans. Edmund Jephcott (Chicago: University of Chicago Press, 1994), 197, 304–5.

33. Rubin, *Gentile Tales,* 108.

34. Richard Trexler, *Public Life in Renaissance Florence* (New York: Academic, 1980), 69.

35. *Mirk's Festial,* 123–24; see variants in *Jacob's Well,* 252–53; and *An Alphabet of Tales: An English 15th Century Translation of the Alphabetum Narrationum,* ed. M. M. Banks (London: EETS 126 & 127, 1904–5), 337. Ward, *Catalogue of Romances,* vol. II, 665, lists a thirteenth-century Latin version of this story, and identifies its immediate source as the *Dialogus* of Cesarius, who derived it from earlier writings.

36. *Middle English Sermons,* 160–62. Another version is in *Minor Poems of the Vernon MS.,* pt. 1, ed. C. Horstmann (London: EETS 98, 1892), 145–49. See also Tubach, *Index,* 194 #2456.

37. Boyd, *Middle English Miracles*, 125. For other versions, see the *Speculum Sacerdotale*, 210–12; and *An Alphabet of Tales*, 438–39. For sources and variants see P. F. Baum, "The Young Man Betrothed to a Statue," *PMLA* 34:4 (1919): 523–79.

38. *Mirk's Festial*, 301–303. A related story appears in *Jacob's Well*, 277–79.

39. Boyd, *Middle English Miracles*, 38–43, 117–18. First written in the sixth century, this ancient tale has many analogues in several languages; see the study of it by Eugene Wolter, *Der Judenknabe* (Halle, 1879); and R. W. Southern, "The English Origins of the 'Miracles of the Virgin,'" *Mediaeval and Renaissance Studies* 4 (1958): 191–92. *The Golden Legend*, vol. 2, 87–88, includes the story on the feast of the Assumption. For the ill-made statue of the Virgin, see Ward, *Catalogue*, vol. II, 676, #61.

40. *Speculum Sacerdotale*, 45–46.

41. *Speculum Sacerdotale*, 202–203. See also *Alphabet of Tales*, 319–20; *Jacob's Well*, 271–72. A thorough study is R. Guiette, *La Légende de la Sacristine: Étude de littérature comparée* (Paris: H. Champion, 1927).

42. *The Myracles of Oure Lady*, ed. from Wynken de Worde's edition by Peter Whiteford (Heidelberg: Winter, 1990), 42–45; see the catalogue of Middle English miracles of the Virgin, 97–133.

43. *Speculum Sacerdotale*, 25–26; a similar tale is in *Alphabet of Tales*, 321–22.

44. Boyd, *Middle English Miracles*, 44–49. This tale can be traced to the ninth century; see the bibliography in Thomas D. Cooke, "Tales," *MWME* vol. 9, 3532.

45. Sherry L. Reames, *The Legenda Aurea: a Reexamination of Its Paradoxical History* (Madison: University of Wisconsin Press, 1985), 101 & 197, says the *Legenda* was intended as a sourcebook for clerics, but was widely read in both Latin and the vernacular. For surveys of Middle English versions of materials from *The Golden Legend* and other saints' legends, see Charlotte D'Evelyn and Frances A. Foster, "Saints Legends," in *MWME* vol. 2, 410–57; and also the more complete work by M. Görlach, "Middle English Legends, 1220–1530," in *Hagiographies*, vol. 1 (Turnhout: Brepols, 1994), 429–85.

46. Jo Ann Hoeppner Moran, *The Growth of English Schooling 1340–1548: Learning, Literacy, and Laicization in Pre-Reformation York Diocese* (Princeton: Princeton University Press, 1985), 204. Cavanaugh, "Study of Books," lists many books of saints lives; for example, 65, 78, 92, 98, 120, 151, 154, 163, 197, 274, 324, 361, 477, 748.

47. Annie Samson, "The South English Legendary: Constructing a Context," in *Thirteenth Century England I*, ed. P. R. Coss and S. D. Lloyd (Woodbridge: Boydell,1986), 185–95; *The South English Legendary: A Critical Assessment*, ed. Klaus P. Jankofsky (Tübingen: Franke, 1992); see the useful bibliography on 177–82.

48. Many of these saints' legends may be found in numerous works; the following citations are minimal. For St. Andrew, St. Laurence, and St. John, see *Mirk's Festial*, 8–9, 219, 147. For St. Eustace and Mary Magdalen, see *The*

Early South English Legendary, ed. Carl Horstmann (London: EETS 87, 1887), 400, 468. For St. George, see Speculum Sacerdotale, 129–30.

49. Life of St. Anne, ed. R. E. Parker (London: EETS 174, 1928), 44–45. The Mirour of Mans Saluacioun: a Middle English translation of Speculum Humanae Salvationis, ed. Avril Henry (Aldershot: Scolar Press, 1986), 83–85, tells how the infant Jesus, escaping from Herod, enters Egypt and overthrows all the idols there.

50. For Simon and Jude, see the Speculum Sacerdotale, 217, and Mirk's Festial, 265. For St. Bartholomew, see Mirk's Festial, 236–37.

51. Speculum Sacerdotale, 218–19; Mirk's Festial, 266.

52. Mirk's Festial, 139; The Early South English Legendary, 364.

53. Thomas J. Heffernan, Sacred Biography: Saints and Their Biographers in the Middle Ages (Oxford: Oxford University Press, 1988), 275f., discusses the sexual abuse of female virgin martyrs and the erotic overtones of their legends in Middle English versions of their lives.

54. Osbern Bokenham, Legendys of Hooly Wummen, ed. Mary S. Serjeantson (London: EETS 206, 1938). A modern English translation is A Legend of Holy Women: A Translation of Osbern Bokenham's Legends of Holy Women, trans. and ed. by Sheila Delany (Notre Dame: University of Notre Dame Press, 1992). In Virgin Martyrs (Ithaca, N.Y.: Cornell University Press, 1997), 119, Karen A. Winstead describes the audience for Bokenham's work as "local aristocrats, landowners, and members of religious houses." A. S. G. Edwards notes the number of Bokenham's female patrons in "The Transmission and Audience of Osbern Bokenham's Legendys of Hooly Wummen," in Late-Medieval Religious Texts and Their Transmission: Essays in Honour of A.I. Doyle, ed. A. J. Minnis (Cambridge: Brewer, 1994), 157–67.

55. Legendys of Hooly Wummen, 17, 59, 100, 117.

56. Legendys, 119, 76, 132.

57. Legendys, 175, 69, 62, 102, 228. The bond between idolatry and lust appears elsewhere; Chaucer's Merchant's Tale calls Solomon "a lecchour and an ydolastre [idolator]" [l.2298]; Fasciculus Morum: A Fourteenth-Century Preacher's Handbook, ed. and trans. Siegfried Wenzel (University Park: Pennsylvania State University Press, 1989), 696–97, couples fornication and idolatry as two sins especially pleasing to demons because they stain both "body and soul."

58. Legendys, 64.

59. John Capgrave, The Life of St. Katharine of Alexandria, ed. Carl Horstmann (London: EETS 100, 1893). Karen A. Winstead places this work in specific social and political contexts in "Piety, Politics, and Social Commitment in Capgrave's Life of St. Katherine," Medievalia et Humanistica n.s. 17 (1991): 59–80; and "Capgrave's Saint Katherine and the Perils of Gynecocracy," Viator 25 (1994): 361–76.

60. On Capgrave's life and works, see Peter J. Lucas, From Author to Audience: John Capgrave and Medieval Publication (Dublin: University College Dublin Press, 1997); and J. C. Fredeman, "The Life of John Capgrave O.E.S.A.

(1393–1464)," *Augustiniana* 20 (1979): 197–237. On Lollard activity in eastern England in the fifteenth century, see John A. F. Thomson, *The Later Lollards 1414–1520* (Oxford: Oxford University Press, 1965), 117–38; and Tanner, *Heresy Trials.*

61. John Capgrave, *Abbreuiacion of Cronicles,* Intro. by Peter J. Lucas (London: EETS 285, 1983), 191.

62. *Abbreuiacion of Cronicles,* 204; 220; 205; 216; 239.

63. Winstead, *Virgin Martyrs,* 175–77. I agree with her that Capgrave was not promoting Lollardy, but used the safety of hagiography to raise questions that were too dangerous to bring up for open debate in the troubled atmosphere of England in the 1440s.

64. *St. Katharine,* 279–80.

65. *St. Katharine,* 309–10.

66. *St. Katharine,* 313.

67. *St. Katharine,* 354.

68. Freedberg, *Power of Images,* 28, calls this "the slip from representation to presentation"; see also his chapter on "Live Images: The Worth of Visions and Tales," 283–316.

69. *Lollard Sermons,* ed. Gloria Cigman (London: EETS 294, 1989), 114.

Chapter 3

1. Roger Martin's brief memoir, "The State of Melford Church . . . as I did know it," is printed in David Dymond and Clive Paine, *The Spoil of Melford Church: The Reformation in a Suffolk Parish* (Ipswich: Salient Press, 1989), 1–9; on Martin's life, see vi–vii.

2. Chapter 5 discusses Kempe's reactions to images.

3. Gail McMurray Gibson, *Theater of Devotion* (Chicago: University of Chicago Press, 1989), 21–22; John A. F. Thomson, *The Later Lollards 1414–1520* (Oxford: Oxford University Press, 1965), 117–38. *VHC Norfolk,* vol. II, and *VHC Suffolk* vols. I–II, provide useful surveys of the histories of these counties and their religious institutions. On Norwich, the episcopal seat, see Norman P. Tanner, *The Church in Late Medieval Norwich 1370–1532* (Toronto: Pontifical Institute of Mediaeval Studies, 1984).

4. All population figures for the period are uncertain. J. C. Russell, *British Medieval Population* (Albuquerque: University of New Mexico Press, 1948), 142, estimates Great Yarmouth's at over 2900 and Ipswich's at 2260 based on the 1377 poll tax returns. Alan R. H. Baker, "Changes in the Later Middle Ages," in *A New Historical Geography of England,* ed. H. C. Darby (Cambridge: CUP, 1973), 186–247, suggests the 1377 poll tax figures are a better guide to relative densities of populations rather than absolute numbers; these figures show Norfolk as one of the most densely populated counties.

5. J. C. Dickinson, *The Shrine of Our Lady of Walsingham* (Cambridge: CUP, 1956).

6. David Knowles and R. Neville Hadcock, *Medieval Religious Houses* (London: Longmans, Green, 1953); see the index of religious houses, 367–87.

7. J. L. Bolton *The Medieval English Economy 1150–1500* (London: Dent, 1980), 153–59, 290–301; David Dymond and Roger Virgoe, "The Reduced Population and Wealth of Early Fifteenth-Century Suffolk," *PSIA* 36 (1986): 73–100.

8. Susan Reynolds, *An Introduction to the History of English Medieval Towns* (Oxford: Clarendon Press, 1977), 141–59; Robert S. Gottfried, *Bury St. Edmunds and the Urban Crisis: 1290–1539* (Princeton: Princeton University Press, 1982), 94–107; R. S. Schofield, "The Geographical Distribution of Wealth in England, 1334–1649," *Economic History Review* 2nd ser., vol. XVIII (1965): 483–510.

9. Reynolds, *English Medieval Towns,* 145.

10. John Harvey, *The Perpendicular Style 1330–1485* (London: Batsford, 1978); see the "Table of Dated Buildings of the Perpendicular Style," 275–81. See also H. Munro Cautley, *Suffolk Churches and Their Treasures,* 4th rev. ed. (Ipswich: Boydell, 1975), 4–26, on fourteenth- and fifteenth-century changes; and on roodlofts, 137–42.

11. Christopher Brooke, "Religious Sentiment and Church Design in the Late Middle Ages," in *Medieval Church and Society* (London: Sidgwick & Jackson, 1971), 162–82; Miri Rubin, *Corpus Christi: the Eucharist in Late Medieval Culture* (Cambridge: CUP, 1991), 293.

12. Arthur Gardner, *English Medieval Sculpture* (Cambridge: CUP, 1951), 269–75; Christopher Woodforde, *The Norwich School of Glass-Painting in the Fifteenth Century* (London: Oxford University Press, 1950).

13. Francis Cheetham, *English Medieval Alabasters* (Oxford: Phaidon-Christie's Ltd., 1984), 11–54.

14. Cheetham, *Alabasters,* 61, n. 78.

15. Recent works stressing the centrality of the parish to the late medieval laity include Katherine L. French, *The People of the Parish* (Philadelphia: University of Pennsylvania Press, 2001); Beat A. Kümin, *The Shaping of a Community: the Rise and Reformation of the English Parish, c. 1400–1560* (Aldershot: Scolar Press, 1996); Katherine L. French, et al., ed., *The Parish in English Life 1400–1600* (Manchester: Manchester University Press, 1997); and S. J. Wright, ed., *Parish, Church and People: Local Studies in Lay Religion 1350–1750* (London: Hutchinson, 1988).

16. Martin, "The State of Melford Church," 1.

17. H. Munro Cautley, *Norfolk Churches* (Ipswich: Adlard, 1949), 1, claims that Norfolk and Suffolk have a greater density of churches than any other county. He counted 659 pre-1700 churches in Norfolk.

18. For the description of this composite parish church, I rely heavily on Cautley's *Norfolk Churches* and *Suffolk Churches and Their Treasures;* on the works by Nikolaus Pevsner in the *Buildings of England* series: *North-west and South Norfolk* (Harmondsworth: Penguin, 1962), *Suffolk* (Harmondsworth: Penguin, 1961), with Bill Wilson, *Norfolk 1: Norwich and North-East,* 2nd

ed. (London: Penguin, 1997), as well as on my own observations of churches in Ipswich, Lavenham, Norwich, Blyburgh, and several other localities. Medieval inventories exist for many churches, but these rarely enumerate statues or paintings, probably because they were permanent fixtures; see *Archdeaconry of Norwich. Inventory of Church Goods* temp. *Edward III,* transcribed by Aelred Watkin (Norfolk Record Society vol. 19, pt. 2, 1948), xcviii.

19. On these fonts, see Ann Eljenholm Nichols, *Seeable Signs: The Iconography of the Seven Sacraments 1350–1544* (Woodbridge: Boydell, 1994); a font gazateer is on 325–53. Among the churches in my will study, St. Mary's in Little Walsingham has a fifteenth-century Seven Sacrament font; see Cautley, *Norfolk Churches,* 261. Roy Tricker, *Ipswich Churches Ancient and Modern* 2nd ed. (Ipswich: Brechinset Pub., 1983), 4, describes the font of St. Matthew's.

20. John Salmon, *Saints in Suffolk Churches* (Suffolk Historic Churches Trust, 1981), 13–14, 29–30; Cautley, *Suffolk Churches,* 194; Ernest A. Kent, "The Mural Painting of St. George in St. Gregory's Church, Norwich," *NA* 25 (1935): 167–69.

21. For the angel roofs of the Swaffham and Mildenhall churches, see M. R. James, *Suffolk and Norfolk* (1930; reprint, Bury St. Edmunds: Alastair Press, 1987), 188 & 64; Cautley, *Suffolk Churches,* 332; Pevsner, *North-west and South Norfolk,* 331; H.G. St. M. Rees, *An Illustrated History of Mildenhall, Suffolk and Its Parish Church of the Blessed Virgin Mary* (Gloucester, n. d.).

22. On wall paintings, see Cautley, *Suffolk Churches,* 193–96; the essay "Medieval Painting," in *VHC Norfolk,* vol. II, 529–54; Pevsner, *Suffolk,* 38.

23. Little of the glorious stained glass from the period escaped being smashed by iconoclasts in later centuries. The best preserved, at Long Melford, depicts the Clopton family as well as saints; see Cautley, *Suffolk Churches,* Plate V, 197. On workshops producing stained glass in East Anglia, see Woodforde, *Norwich School,* and Richard Marks, *Stained Glass in England during the Middle Ages* (Toronto: University of Toronto Press, 1993), 198; see also Marks's bibliography for the voluminous literature on stained glass, 280–86. Brian Coe, *Stained Glass in England: 1150–1550* (London: W. H. Allen, 1981), provides a useful (although incomplete) listing of stained glass by county; see Norfolk, 108–11, and Suffolk, 119–20. Coe, 51, lists the window of St. Luke as a painter in Stratton Strawless, Norfolk. A reproduction of a pietà from Long Melford, Suffolk, is in John Baker, *English Stained Glass of the Medieval Period* (London: Thames and Hudson, 1978), Plate 66, and in Woodforde, plate XXVII.

24. Martin, 1–3. Eamon Duffy, "The Parish, piety, and patronage in late medieval East Anglia: the evidence of rood screens," in *The Parish in English Life,* 134, counts eighty screens in Norfolk and thirty-nine in Suffolk that still have paintings; this essay offers the fullest account of the endowment and construction of roodscreens and their significance as a "crucial focus of ritual activity and piety." On East Anglian roodscreens, see also W. W.

Williamson, "Saints on Norfolk Rood-Screens and Pulpits," *NA* 31 (1955–57): 299–346, and Bede Camm, "Some Norfolk rood screens," 239–95, in *A Supplement to Blomefield's Norfolk,* ed. C. Ingleby (London, 1929). On Etheldreda and other East Anglian saints' cults, see D. H. Farmer, "Some Saints of East Anglia," *Reading Medieval Studies* XI (1985): 31–49.

25. G. H. Cook, *Mediaeval Chantries and Chantry Chapels* (London: Phoenix House, 1963), 214.

26. Alabaster images survived partly because they were shipped to the Continent after sixteenth-century injunctions against holy images in England; see Cheetham, *English Medieval Alabasters,* for their history and over 250 examples of extant pieces. Rare survivals of wooden figures are depicted in Paul Williamson, *Northern Gothic Sculpture 1200–1450* (Victoria and Albert Museum, 1988), no. 40; Lawrence Stone, *Sculpture in Britain: the Middle Ages,* 2nd ed. (Harmondsworth: Penguin, 1972), 172, plate B; and listed by Gardner, *English Medieval Sculpture,* 269, n. 1.

27. Stone, *Sculpture,* 191–92.

28. Gardner, *English Medieval Scultpure,* 273. See *Medieval Art in East Anglia 1300–1520,* ed. P. Lasko and N. J. Morgan (London: Thames & Hudson, 1974), #108 & #109, for examples of possible Flemish influence on sculptors in eastern England in the late fifteenth century.

29. Cheetham, *Alabasters,* 19.

30. Cheetham, *Alabasters,* 26–27, discusses the usual methods of painting alabasters. On representations of the Trinity, see 296, and for the description of this figure, 302.

31. On Sebastian's cult in the Middle Ages, see Farmer, *Oxford Dictionary of Saints,* 380–81. He was invoked against the plague in Europe and in England. Flemish influence in the late Middle Ages may have been the reason Sebastian appeared on one or two rood screens in East Anglia; see James, *Suffolk and Norfolk,* 20. St. Catherine's wild popularity in East Anglia is attested by her appearance in alabaster, glass, rood screens, wall paintings, bosses, and other media; see the index entry under her name in James, *ibid.,* 235; and W. W. Williamson, "Saints on Norfolk Rood-Screens and Pulpits," 31 *NA* (1955–57): 310–11.

32. Although I follow modern usage that makes "will" synonymous with "testament," the two were distinct in the Middle Ages; "wills" dealt with real property and "testaments" were concerned with moveable goods. See Michael L. Zell, "Fifteenth- and Sixteenth-Century Wills as Historical Sources," *Archives* 14:62 (1979): 67–74. On the processes of making and administering wills, see Michael M. Sheehan, *The Will in Medieval England* (Toronto: Pontifical Institute of Mediaeval Studies, 1963), and "English Wills and the records of the ecclesiastical and civil jurisdictions," *Journal of Medieval History* 14:1 (1988): 3–12. Problems in interpreting fifteenth- and sixteenth-century wills are discussed by M. G. A. Vale, *Piety, Charity, and Literacy among the Yorkshire Gentry, 1370–1480* (York: Borthwick Institute of Historical Research, 1976); and Clive Burgess, "Late medieval wills and

pious convention: testamentary evidence reconsidered," in *Profit, Piety and the Professions in Later Medieval England,* ed. Michael Hicks (Gloucester: Sutton, 1990), 14–33.

33. P. J. P. Goldberg, "Women," in *Fifteenth-Century Attitudes: Perceptions of Society in Late Medieval England,* ed. Rosemary Horrox (Cambridge: CUP, 1994), 115; he notes that the number of wills from married women declined over the course of the century.

34. Clive Burgess, "The Benefactions of Mortality: the Lay Response in the Late Medieval Urban Parish," in *Studies in Clergy and Ministry in Medieval England,* ed. David M. Smith (University of York, 1991), 66–7. Other scholars who have used wills to study late medieval religion include Tanner, *Church in Late Medieval Norwich;* Peter Heath, "Urban Piety in the Later Middle Ages: the Evidence of Hull Wills," in *The Church, Politics and Patronage in the Fifteenth Century,* ed. Barrie Dobson (Gloucester: Sutton, 1984), 209–29; P. H. Cullum and P. J. P. Goldberg, "Charitable Provisions in Late Medieval York: 'To the Praise of God and the Use of the Poor,'" *Northern History* XXIX (1993), 24–39.

35. Philippa Maddern, "Friends of the Dead: Executors, Wills and Family Strategy in Fifteenth-Century Norfolk," in *Rulers and Ruled in Late Medieval England: Essays Presented to Gerald Harris,* ed. Rowena E. Archer and Simon Walker (London: Hambledon, 1995), 155–74.

36. This study includes 10 women's wills dated before 1441, and 154 dated between 1441 and 1500.

37. Aston, *England's Iconoclasts,* vol. 1, 107. J. Giles Milhaven, "A Medieval Lesson on Bodily Knowing: Women's Experience and Men's Thought," *Journal of the American Academy of Religion* 57:2 (1989): 341–72, discusses theologians' disparagement of medieval women's physical responses to sculpture.

38. Andrew D. Brown, *Popular Piety in Late Medieval England: the Diocese of Salisbury 1250–1550* (Oxford: Clarendon Press, 1995), 214–15.

39. Tanner, *Church in Late Medieval Norwich,* 118.

40. On female literacy, see the Introduction, n. 14. There are no precise figures for women's reading or writing literacy in the late Middle Ages and historians' estimates vary widely. For instance, G. L. Barnes, "Laity Formation: The Role of Early English Printed Primers," *Journal of Religious History* 18: 2 (1994): 141, suggests a very low 1 percent literacy rate for English women in 1500, and a 10 percent literacy rate for men. In contrast, Sylvia Thrupp, *Merchant Class of Medieval London,* (Ann Arbor: University of Michigan Press, 1948), 158–61, estimates that 50 percent of lay male Londoners could read English in the late Middle Ages, and that all the men and "most of the intelligent women" of the merchant class could. Discussions of female literacy in the Middle Ages typically rely on evidence of activities such as book reading and bequeathing and literary patronage; in general these point to increasing female literacy. Sandra Penketh, "Women and Books of Hours," in *Women and the Book: Assessing the Visual Evidence,* ed. Jane H. M. Taylor and Lesley Smith (London and Toronto: The British Li-

brary and the University of Toronto Press, 1997), 266–81, discusses visual evidence for women's literacy.

41. Christiane Klapisch-Zuber, "Holy Dolls: Play and Piety in Florence in the Quattrocento," in *Women, Family and Ritual in Renaissance Italy*, trans. Lydia Cochrane (Chicago: University of Chicago Press, 1985), 310–29.

42. Margaret Miles, *Image as Insight: Visual Understanding in Western Christianity and Secular Culture* (Boston: Beacon, 1985), 66–73, 88–89.

43. Joanna E. Ziegler, *Sculpture of Compassion: the Pietà and the Beguines in the Southern Low Countries c. 1300-c. 1600* (Bruxelles: Brepols, 1992), see especially 103–06; 143–49; 169–72.

44. See Ruth Mazo Karras, "Gendered Sin and Misogyny in John of Bromyard's 'Summa Predicantium,'" *Traditio* 47 (1992): 233–57.

45. David Wallace, "Mystics and Followers in Siena and East Anglia: A Study in Taxonomy, Class and Cultural Mediation," in *The Medieval Mystical Tradition in England*, ed. Marion Glasscoe (Cambridge: Brewer, 1984), 184, argues that for most medieval people paintings were "the only texts that could be read without direct clerical intervention." While his assumption of mass illiteracy and of Margery Kempe's in particular is questionable, his insistence on the "malleable" nature of images points out a major reason why women might be drawn to them. Ziegler, *Sculpture of Compassion*, 42, argues that "viewers endow images with their own meanings. . . ." See also Belting, *Likeness and Presence*, 1, on the difficulty of controlling the meaning or interpretation of images.

46. The 1389 gild certificates show women's membership in parish gilds; see H. F. Westlake, *The Parish Gilds of Mediaeval England* (London: S. P. C. K., 1919), especially 137–238, for a summary of the gild returns. French, *People of the Parish*, 77–78, 87–88, discusses female churchwardens.

47. See Cheetham, *Alabasters, Appendix I: Saints*, 55; Salmon, *Saints*, 11 and 37.

48. Eamon Duffy, "Holy Maydens, Holy Wyfes: The Cult of Women Saints in Fifteenth- and Sixteenth-Century England," in *Women in the Church*, ed. W. J. Sheils and Diana Wood (Oxford: Blackwell, 1990), 175–96.

49. For bequests to female saints other than the Virgin Mary, see, for example: NRO, Reg. Fuller, f. 13r; NRO Reg. Grey, f. 163v; NRO, Reg. Hyrnyng, f. 106r; NRO, Reg. Jekkys, f. 7v. Geoffrey of Monmouth claimed Helen was British, and there were many dedications to her in England; see Farmer, *Oxford Dictionary of Saints*, 201–2.

50. See the descriptions of Mildenhall Church in Cautley, *Suffolk Churches*, 330–32; Pevsner, *Suffolk*, 335–37.

51. See Edmund Waterton, *Pietas Mariana Britannica* (London: St. Joseph's Catholic Library, 1879), Book 2, 257–58; A. W. Morant, "Notices of the Church of St. Nicholas, Great Yarmouth" *NA* 7 (1872): 223; W. M. Ormrod, "The Personal Religion of Edward III," *Speculum* 64 (1989): 861.

52. Sumption, *Pilgrimage*, 269; Tanner, *Church in Late Medieval Norwich*, 85–86.

53. K. L. Wood-Legh, *Perpetual Chantries in Britain* (Cambridge: CUP, 1965), 37–39; R. B. Dobson, "Citizens and Chantries in Late Medieval York," in

Church and Society in the Medieval North of England (London: Hambledon, 1996), 268–69.

54. Gibson, *Theater of Devotion,* 97. John Walsyngham of Swaffham requested a pilgrimage to Walsingham in his will; NRO, Reg. Caston, ff. 57v–58r; as did Alice Grenehood of Ipswich, who also asked for pilgrimages to several other East Anglian shrines; NRO, Reg. Aleyn, f. 18v.

55. *The Commonplace Book of Robert Reynes,* ed. Cameron Louis (New York: Garland, 1980), 323.

56. *VHC Norfolk,* vol. II, 399, describes the pilgrimage routes in Norfolk; see also David Dymond, *Norfolk Landscape* (London: Hodder and Stoughton, 1985), 130. Pevsner, *North-west and South Norfolk,* 229, describes a fifteenth-century chapel in King's Lynn that served as a wayside chapel for pilgrims traveling to Walsingham. On the shrine itself, see Dickinson, *Shrine.*

57. Colin Richmond, *John Hopton: A Fifteenth Century Suffolk Gentleman* (Cambridge: CUP, 1981), 175. See also C. Pamela Graves, "Social Space in the English Medieval Parish Church," *Economy and Society* 18:3 (August 1989): 306–7, on how the physical arrangement of altars and chapels in a church shaped its rituals.

58. Sumption, *Pilgrimage,* 164–65, claims Becket's cult declined based on the evidence of offerings at the Canterbury shrine.

59. Bequests for the chapel, gild, and lights of St. Guthlac appear in the wills of Thomas Styward, NRO, Reg. Surflete, f. 127r; James Norman, NRO, Reg. Grey, f. 121v; Agnes Serjant, NRO, Reg. Grey, f. 60v; Katherine Serjant, NRO, Reg. Grey, f. 52r; Margaret Brystotte, NRO, Reg. Jekkys, f. 7v; and others. *Nova Legenda Anglie* vol. II, ed. Carl Horstmann (Oxford: Clarendon Press, 1901), 1–13 and 698–727, prints two late medieval versions of Guthlac's life.

60. John atte Fen of Great Yarmouth, NRO, Reg. Hyrnyng, f. 49r, left money to several houses of friars, as did Bartholomew Elys of Yarmouth, NRO, Reg. Hyrnyng, f. 133v; Roger Hoddys, NRO, Reg. Aleyn, f. 56v; Margaret Parker, NRO, Reg. Hyrnyng, f. 116v; Simon Gardener of Mildenhall, SROB, Reg. 2, f. 518r; and many others.

61. NRO, Reg. Hyrnyng, f. 106r. Many people who left money to more than one image did not name them all, making it difficult to assess the significance of these bequests. In 1404 Christina Wombe of Swaffham, for example, after naming lights for St. Peter and another (illegible) image, left 4d. to every other light in the church [*ad quodlibet aliud lumen*]; NRO, Reg. Harsyk, f. 308r. Bequests to one or two image lights were, however, more common.

62. NRO, Reg. Grey, f. 279v: "Item communi lumini quatuor Gildarum in quibus ego sum ffratrus vjs. viijd. equalibus porcionibus dispositur."

63. NRO, Reg. Sayve, ff. 36v–37r: "Item lego lumini beate marie ibidem iijd. sub condicione quod confratres eiusdem gylde recipiant me in sororem eiusdem gylde."

64. NRO, Reg. Liber 1, f. 123r–123v.

65. NRO, Reg. Cage, f. 5v.

66. NRO, Reg. Fuller, f. 143v.

67. NRO PD52/473:"quae pertinent ad Gildam S. Marie, non ad lumini." For a summary and history of the Black Book, see J. F. Williams, "The Black Book of Swaffham," *NA* 33 (1965): 243–53.

68. NRO, Reg. Gelour, ff. 125v–126r. Blomefield notes several gifts of annual rent to support candles before images in Great Yarmouth's church from as early as 1280; see Francis Blomefield and Charles Parkin, *An Essay Towards a Topographical History of the County of Norfolk,* vol. 11 (London, 1810), 373–74.

69. NRO, Reg. Caston, f. 162v. The Black Book of Swaffham, NRO PD52/473, 2. See Chapter 4 on "lamplands" and images. D. R. Dendy, *The Use of Lights in Christian Worship* (London: S.P.C.K., 1959), 108–19, discusses the history of votive lights in the cult of the saints and the custom of granting land to lights.

70. NRO, Reg. Typpes, ff. 89v–90r. On the sepulcher, see Ronald Hutton, *The Rise and Fall of Merry England: the Ritual Year 1400–1700* (Oxford: Oxford University Press, 1994), 23–25.

71. Tanner, *Church in Late Medieval Norwich,* 118.

72. I found this prayer printed on a sheet of paper placed before the statue of the Virgin Mary in the church of Loguivy-les-Lannion, France, in June, 1997:"Je te salve marie, vierge de clarté modèle de vie, lumineuse pour tous, consomée pour dieu. La flamme de ce cierge témoin de mon passage, signe de ma présence continuera ma prière près de toi, comme la lumiére devant le tabernácle redit la présence et rappel de ton fils Jésus, lumiére de vie."

73. NRO Phi/580. This document is a later copy of an original. On bequests to the church as part of a spiritual economy of gift giving, see Joel T. Rosenthal, *The Purchase of Paradise: Gift Giving and the Aristocracy, 1307–1485* (London: Routledge & Kegan Paul, 1972), 9–10; and Clive Burgess, "'A Fond Thing Vainly Invented': an Essay on Purgatory and Pious Motive in Later Medieval England," in *Parish, Church and People,* 56–84.

74. Philippe Ariès, *The Hour of Our Death,* trans. Helen Weaver (New York: Knopf, 1981), 49. In his survey of seventeenth-century French parishes, Ariès also notes that social position was a key factor in determining whether one would be buried in the church or cemetery, 82–90. On burial in church and cemetery, see also R. C. Finucane, "Sacred Corpse, Profane Carrion: Social Ideals and Death Rituals in the Later Middle Ages," in *Mirrors of Mortality: Studies in the Social History of Death,* ed. Joachim Whaley (New York: St. Martin's, 1981), 40–60.

75. In 1292 the Statutes of Chichester, for example, allowed church patrons and their wives to be buried in the church; F. M. Powicke and C. R. Cheney, *Councils and Synods with other Documents Relating to the English Church,* part II (Oxford: Clarendon Press, 1964), 1117.

76. Vanessa Harding, "'And one more to be laid there': the Location of Burials in Early Modern London," *The London Journal* 14:2 (1989): 120.

Christopher Daniell, *Death and Burial in Medieval England 1066–1550* (London: Routledge, 1997), 58–60.

77. NRO, Reg. Multon, f. 76r.

78. NRO, Reg. Cage, f. 52r. On the hierarchy of burial locations and their costs, see Vanessa Harding, "Burial Choice and Burial Location in Later Medieval London," in *Death in Towns: Urban Responses to the Dying and the Dead, 100–1600,* ed. Steven Bassett (London: Leicester University Press, 1992), 131–32. Alec Clifton-Taylor, *English Parish Churches as Works of Art* (London: Batsford, 1974), 212, cites a poem that ridicules the hierarchy of grave sites by insisting on the democracy of death: "Here lie I at the chancel door / Here lie I because I'm poor / The further in the more you pay / Here lie I as warm as they."

79. NRO, Reg. Grey, f. 89r.

80. About 3 percent of clerics and 3 percent of women asked for burial before or near a holy image; fewer than 2 percent of laymen did so. An analysis of 4,700 late medieval wills from Yorkshire and Nottinghamshire reveals somewhat lower figures for burials near images, with 66 such requests out of the total; see Daniell, *Death and Burial,* 97–100.

81. Will of Alice Langcroft of Ipswich, 1486, NRO Reg. Awbreye, f. 104r; will of Cecilia Bukke, 1483, of Walberswick, SROI, Reg. 3, f. 12v.

82. Margaret Fastolf of Ipswich, SROI, Reg. 1, f. 178v; William Coote of Mildenhall, SROB, Reg. 3, f. 238v.

83. NRO, Reg. Hyrnyng, f. 133v; SROI, Reg. 2, f. 5v.

84. John Bossy, *Christianity in the West 1400–1700* (Oxford: Oxford University Press, 1985), 30. On burial near the bodies of saints, see Caroline Walker Bynum, *The Resurrection of the Body in Western Christianity, 200–1336* (New York: Columbia University Press, 1995), 203; Ariès, *Hour of Our Death,* 40–42; Peter Brown, *The Cult of the Saints: Its Rise and Function in Latin Christianity* (Chicago: University of Chicago Press, 1981), 23–35.

85. Margaret Aston, "Death," in *Fifteenth-Century Attitudes,* 208–09.

86. NRO, Reg. Cage, f. 52r.

87. Will of Robert Peteman, SROI, Reg. 3, f. 65r; will of Sibyl Cruse, SROI, Reg. 4, f. 85v.

88. Robert Dinn, "Death and Rebirth in Late Medieval Bury St Edmunds," in *Death in Towns,* 151–69, argues that the "ritual of reintegration" of the dead and the affirmation of the "cohesiveness of the community" were essential features of the approach to death in the late Middle Ages. On relations between the living and the dead, see Burgess, "'A fond thing,'" and Jacques Le Goff, *The Birth of Purgatory,* trans. Arthur Goldhammer (Chicago: University of Chicago Press, 1981), 293–94, 319–20, 326–28, 350–52.

89. NRO, Reg. Sayve, ff. 17v–18r.

90. Ariès, *Hour of Our Death,* 76.

91. In his dialogue *On Pleasure,* the fifteenth-century humanist Lorenzo Valla expressed the hope that kinship ties would continue in the afterlife; his character Antonio is tormented by his desire to see the dead members of

his family, over whom he has wept himself "nearly blind"; see Colleen Mc-
Dannell and Bernhard Lang, *Heaven: A History* (New Haven: Yale University Press, 1988), 127.

92. SROI, Reg. 1, f. 148v.

93. Will of Isabel Sextayn, SROI, Reg. 3, f. 88r; will of Cecilia Bukke, SROI, Reg. 3, f. 12v; will of Thomas Chyldyrston, SROB, Reg. 3, f. 235r; will of Henry Bencrost, SROI, Reg. 2, f. 317r.

94. SROI, Reg. 2, f. 308r: "Item volo habere unam ymaginem in ecclesia predicta de sancte Marie pety peyntyd cum auro et hoc secundum forma ymagine beate marie pet<y> de Sewold."

95. SROI, Reg. 3, f. 82v.

96. Dymond and Paine, *The Spoil of Melford Church*, 1, n. 3.

97. NRO, Reg. Grey, f. 193v; NRO, Reg. Fuller, f. 249v.

98. SROI, Reg. 3, f. 212v.

99. On the custom of robing statues of the Virgin, see Waterton, *Pietas Mariana Britannica*, 250–53. For Our Lady of Halberton, see Robert Whiting, *The Blind Devotion of the People* (Cambridge: CUP, 1989), 49.

100. Gibson, *Theater of Devotion*, 71.

101. See, for example, Marina Warner, *Alone of All Her Sex: the Myth and the Cult of the Virgin Mary* (New York: Knopf, 1976), 117, on the jewels, capes, robes, and crowns given to the Virgin of the Pillar in Saragossa.

102. Boyd, *Middle English Miracles*, 125.

103. Whiting, *Blind Devotion*, 53.

104. Christopher Harper-Bill, "A Late Medieval Visitation—the Diocese of Norwich in 1499," *PSIA* 34 (1977): 38.

105. Maddern, "Friends of the Dead," 164–65; she stresses the importance of the will as the document that named the executors.

106. *CPL*, letter dated 1398, vol. 5, 91.

107. NRO, Reg. Hubert, f. 64r.

108. NRO, Register Caston, f. 195r-v.

109. NRO, MS9712 / 8F2. See also Aston, "Death," 213–15, on the mistrust of executors.

110. Blomefield, *Norfolk*, vol. 11, 365–66.

111. Cautley, *Suffolk Churches*, 194.

112. SROI, Reg. 1, f. 181r-v; Great and Little Blakenham are northwest of Ipswich. Many testators left money to parish churches other than the one where they would be buried; gifts of money or other goods to holy images located in churches other than the testator's parish church are much rarer.

Chapter 4

1. Greenfield's order is printed in Wilkins, *Concilia*, vol. 2, 423–4; and in *Register of William Greenfield 1306–15*, part III, eds. W. Brown and A. Hamilton Thompson (London: Surtees Society, vol. 151, 1936), 209–10. A summary of these events is in *A History of the County of York East Riding,*

ed. K. J. Allison, vol. II (published for the Institute of Historical Research by Oxford University Press, 1974), 187–88, 207.

2. See the *Introduction* to *Register Greenfield,* pt. III, xxvi.

3. Jonathan Sumption, *Pilgrimage: an Image of Mediaeval Religion* (Totowa, N. J.: Rowman & Littlefield, 1975), 278.

4. *Calendar of Inquisitions Miscellaneous (Chancery)* (London, 1916), vol. 1, 358–9. This document is incorrectly dated as 1280; Thomas de Poynton died in 1299; see *History of the County of York East Riding,* vol. II, 207, n. 43.

5. W. T. Lancaster, *Abstracts of the Charters and Other Documents Contained in the Chartulary of the Priory of Bridlington* (Leeds, 1912), 448–49.

6. *Calendar of Patent Rolls 1313–1317* (London, 1898), 60–61.

7. *Reg. Greenfield,* pt. III, 215–17.

8. Gerard's successor was elected in March 1315; see *Reg. Greenfield,* pt. III, xxvi. The summons by the bishop was issued in January 1315–16; see *Reg. Greenfield,* pt. V, ed. W. Brown and A. Hamilton Thompson (London: Surtees Society vol. 153, 1940), 266.

9. *Reg. Greenfield,* pt. III, 265–66.

10. *CPL 1305–1342,* vol. 2, 186–87.

11. *Calendar of Patent Rolls 1330–34* (London, 1893), 203.

12. *Chartulary of the Priory of Bridlington,* 440.

13. *CPL 1417–1431,* vol. 7, 379. See also Emma Mason, "The Role of the English Parishioner, 1100–1500," *JEH* 27:1 (January 1976): 17–29.

14. *CPL 1396–1404,* vol. 5, 591. Terrington St. Clement and the smaller Terrington St. John lie about three miles apart in the sparsely populated area between King's Lynn and Wisbech. *The Book of Margery Kempe,* ed. Sanford Brown Meech (Oxford: EETS 212, 1940), 58–60, recounts a dispute between a parson and his parishioners who wanted to upgrade the status and responsibilities of their chapel, showing the determination of parishioners to control their own churches.

15. Extant churchwardens' account prior to 1540 are rare. The following evidence relies only on those from Norwich diocese. On churchwardens' accounts and duties, see Katherine L. French, *The People of the Parish* (Philadelphia: University of Pennsylvania Press, 2001), 44–98, and J. Charles Cox, *Churchwardens' Accounts from the Fourteenth Century to the Close of the Seventeenth Century* (London: Methuen, 1913), and for expenditures on images, 142–48. See Robert Whiting, *The Blind Devotion of the People* (Cambridge: CUP, 1989), 48–55, for records of images in late medieval churchwardens' accounts in Devon and Cornwall. Ronald Hutton, *The Rise and Fall of Merry England: the Ritual Year 1400–1700* (Oxford: Oxford University Press, 1994), 263–93, includes an appendix listing churchwardens' accounts prior to 1690.

16. *Walberswick Churchwardens' Accounts A.D. 1450–1499.* Transcribed by R. W. M. Lewis (London, 1947), 14, 15, 22.

17. *Walberswick Accounts,* 29, 45–47, 50, 58, 66, 67–68. A noble was worth 6s. 8d.

18. *Walberswick Accounts,* 65.

19. *Walberswick Accounts,* 80, 77.

20. *Walberswick Accounts,* 261. Colin Richmond, *John Hopton: A Fifteenth Century Suffolk Gentleman* (Cambridge: CUP, 1981), 178, also discusses the maintenance of Walberswick church. "Tabyll" probably refers to a retable.

21. A. D. Stallard, *The Transcript of the Churchwardens' Accounts of the Parish of Tilney All Saints, Norfolk 1443–1589* (London: Mitchell Hughes and Clarke, 1922), 43.

22. William Holland, *Cratfield: A Transcript of the Accounts of the Parish,* ed. J. J. Raven (London: Jarrold & Sons, 1895), 22, 24, 25, 29.

23. Mildenhall churchwardens' accounts, SROB EL 110/5/3, ff. 2v, 4v, 5v.

24. Shipdam churchwardens' accounts, NRO PD 337/85, ff. 33v–34r.

25. Swaffham churchwardens' accounts, NRO PD 52/71, f. 52r

26. See, for example, *Tilney All Saints* for expenditures on wax, 61, 62, 68; for repair of a veil, 47. Mildenhall accounts, SROB EL 110/5/3, record payments for painting the roodloft, f.2v; setting up and taking down the Easter sepulcher, ff. 16r and 18r. The Brundish, Suffolk, Town Book, SROI FC/89/A2/1, shows various expenditures on the candlebeam, ff. 9v, 10v, 13v. East Dereham, Norfolk, churchwardens' accounts, NRO Phi/461/2, include payments for having images painted. Snettisham churchwardens' accounts, NRO PD 24/2, 6, show expenditures for "makynge of owre ladyse kandelstekys."

27. See Gervase Rosser, "Communities of Parish and Gild," in *Parish, Church And People: Local Studies in Lay Religion 1350–1750,* ed. S. J. Wright (London: Hutchinson), 31–2, who stresses the voluntary nature of the laity's involvement in parish affairs.

28. The number of gilds in any one place at a given time in the fourteenth and fifteenth centuries is uncertain. For example, Lawrence S. Snell, "London Chantries and Chantry Chapels," in *Collectanea Londiniensia,* ed. J. Bird, et al. (London: London and Middlesex Archaeological Society, 1978), 220, claims that about 70 gilds and fraternities were attached to London churches; Caroline M. Barron says 150 parish gilds existed in London; see her "The Parish Fraternities of Medieval London," in *The Church in Pre-Reformation Society,* ed. Caroline M. Barron and C. Harper-Bill (Woodbridge, Suffolk: Boydell, 1985), 18. J. F. Williams, "The Gild of St. John the Baptist at Swaffham," *NA* 33 (1965): 2, lists only 7 gilds for Swaffham, although my evidence shows that were several more. Gervase Rosser, "Going to the Fraternity Feast: Commensality and Social Relations in Late Medieval England," *JBS* 33 (October 1994): 430–31, estimates that there were 30,000 gilds in fifteenth-century England.

29. Historians have paid most attention to this function of gilds; see Westlake, *Parish Gilds,* 9–10; Barron, "Parish Fraternities," 24; Snell, "London Chantries," 220.

30. Barbara A. Hanawalt, "Keepers of the Lights: Late Medieval English Parish Gilds," *Journal of Medieval and Renaissance Studies* 4 (1984): 21–37. Ben R.

McRee discusses the changing nature of gilds and their relationship to city politics in "Religious Gilds and Civic Order: The Case of Norwich in the Late Middle Ages," *Speculum* 67 (1992): 69–97, and assesses their charitable activities in "Charity and Gild Solidarity in Late Medieval England," *JBS* 32 (July 1993): 195–225. See Virginia R. Bainbridge, *Gilds in the Medieval Countryside* (Woodbridge: Boydell, 1996), for the historiography of gilds and their mingled social, economic, and religious roles.

31. For the political context of Parliament's demand, see David J. F. Crouch, *Piety, Fraternity and Power: Religious Gilds in Late Medieval Yorkshire 1389–1547* (University of York: York Medieval Press, 2000), 13–16. See also Westlake, *Parish Gilds,* 36–38. Westlake provides summaries of the 1389 gild certificates in an appendix, but these are not always complete. Toulmin Smith and Lucy Toulmin Smith, *English Gilds* (London: EETS 40, 1870, reprt. 1963), print the 1389 certificates written in English.

32. PRO C47/45/377, "Societas Sutorum beate marie de Arneburgh de magna Jernemuch non est gilda, eo quod nullas habente constituciones, or-dinaciones, aut provisiones, nec aliquod iuramentum est inter eos praesti-tum, sed per illorum communem concensum inveniunt per totum annum unum cereum ardentem coram ymagine beate marie antedicte in eadem Jernemuch. . . ." The return of the society of St. John, PRO C47/45/376, is very similar.

33. Bainbridge, *Gilds,* 46, argues that gild membership was limited to wealthy peasants in rural areas, but that artisans and craftsmen joined "less prestigious" ones in towns. This group and some of the others discussed here seem in-deed to have been more limited in services and rituals than many gilds.

34. PRO C47/46/410; the regulations were "quod fratres et sorores dicte Gilde invenient xiii cereos ardentes coram ymagine sancti Jacobi omnibus diebus dominicis ac aliis festivis per totum annum. Alias consuetudines non habent. . . ." Summaries of Norfolk and Suffolk gild provisions on lights and other matters are in Catherine B. Firth. "Village Gilds of Norfolk in the Fifteenth Century," *NA* 18 (1914): 161–203; and V. B. Redstone, "Chapels, Chantries and Gilds in Suffolk," *PSIA* 12 (1904–06): 1–87.

35. PRO C47/45/400; the brothers and sisters of the gild were to provide "xxvi cereos ardentes coram imagine beate marie omnibus diebus do-minicas(?) <et> festivis in eadem ecclesia per totum annum. . . ."

36. PRO C47/46/432.

37. Westlake, *Parish Gilds,* 29–30 & 175; for a similar example, see the entry for the gild of the Invention of the Holy Cross, 162–63.

38. Barron, "Parish Fraternities," 28, says the provision of lights for images dis-appeared in fifteenth- and sixteenth-century London gild ordinances; how-ever, at least some Norfolk and Suffolk gilds continued to provide lights. See F. E. Warren, "Gild of S. Peter in Bardwell," *PSIA* 11 (1901–03): 142–3; and G. A. Carthew, "Wymondham Gilds," *NA* 9 (1884): 248, 252, 266.

39. For example, the gild of All Saints, Swaffham, ordered all its members to gather at vespers on the vigil of All Saints under penalty of a half pound

of wax, unless excused; PRO C47/44/329. Members of the gild of St. John the Baptist in Lynn, Norfolk, paid a halfpenny for a candle lit before St. John's image during services on Sundays and other holy days; see Smith, *English Gilds,* 79.

40. Smith, *English Gilds,* 214–15.

41. Rosser, "Communities of Parish and Gild," 37–38, argues that one structural purpose of the gild was to set its members apart from others. Barron, "Parish Fraternities," 28, speculates that in large London parishes some parishioners wanted a smaller unit with which they might identify, although this might apply to smaller village parishes as well. Trexler discusses how the "patchwork of ritual spaces" within a church was marked by holy objects in *Public Life in Renaissance Florence,* 53–54.

42. PRO C47/45/397.

43. PRO C47/46/430.

44. The Tilney gild returns were submitted together, now in PRO C47/44/333.

45. PRO C47/43/275, "ubi frequens in dies ad est populi multitudo propter miracula que exp<er>i<mur>(?) coram dicto ymagine fuerunt atque vere plurimi frequenter a suis infirmitatibus et lang<u>oribus sanantur. . . ."

46. See Redstone's summary of the 1546 Suffolk chantry certificates in "Chapels, Chantries and Gilds in Suffolk," 30–69. The certificates' most common provision is the endowment of a light in the church.

47. *Visitations of Religious Houses in the Diocese of Lincoln,* vol. III: *Records of Visitations held by William Alnwick Bishop of Lincoln 1436–1449,* Part II, ed. A. Hamilton Thompson (Lincoln Record Society, 1929), 304, 316–317.

48. PRO E301/45, no. 189.

49. The Suffolk certificates are in PRO E301/45. Among the endowed lights are: no. 76, Akenham, a light before the image of St. Nicholas; no. 111, Wyrlingworth, a taper before the image of our lady; no. 150, Lyvermere Magna, a light before "our Lady of pyttie;" no. 86, Brantham, a light before the roodloft; no. 169, Asheffelde, 3 tapers "aboute the Sepulcure;" no. 232, Burgh, "our Ladys light."

50. PRO DL38/6: endowed parish lights existed in Gressenhall, Grimston, Taverham, Croxton, Brampton, and several other localities. In East Bilney and Frettenham, profits from an acre of land were given to gilds.

51. See Ken Farnhill, "The Religious Gilds of Wymondham, c. 1470–1550," *NA* 42 (1996): 321–31, for examples of parishioners who paid for images and their gilding and tabernacles.

52. For gifts to Walsingham made by English queens, see Anne Crawford, "The Piety of Late Medieval English Queens," in *The Church in Pre-Reformation Society,* 50, 52. J. C. Dickinson, *The Shrine of Our Lady of Walsingham* (Cambridge: CUP), 26, 29, 37, 60.

53. J. John Parker, *Our Lady of Ipswich* (Ipswich, n.d.), 1–9. In his early sixteenth-century will, the clerk Thomas Chamber requested a pilgrimage to Our Lady of Ipswich; see *Norwich Consistory Court Depositions, 1499–1512*

and 1518–1530, calendared by E. D. Stone (Norfolk Record Society, vol. 10, 1938), case 204. Anne Harling of East Harling, Norfolk, had her rosary divided into four strands for Our Lady of Walsingham, Our Lady of Pity at Ipswich, St. Edmund of Bury, and St. Thomas of Canterbury; see Gibson, *Theater of Devotion,* 97. See Francis Haslewood, "Our Lady of Ipswich," *PSIA* 10 (1900): 53–5, for evidence of the cult. Edward Hall, *Hall's Chronicle* (London, 1809), 826, says the Ipswich image was burned with the images of Walsingham, Worcester, the lady of Wilsdon, "and many other."

54. Cited in G. R. Owst, *Literature and Pulpit in Medieval England* 2nd ed. (Oxford: Blackwell, 1961), 140–41.

55. Carpenter, *Destructorium Viciorum,* pars VI, cap. xlv.

56. Thomas More addressed this complaint in *A Dialogue Concerning Heresies,* pt. 1, vol. 6 of *Complete Works of Thomas More,* 99 & 231–2. See also the perceptive discussion by Victor Turner and Edith Turner in *Image and Pilgrimage in Christian Culture* (New York: Columbia University Press, 1978), 142–4, on the process whereby such images develop meanings apart from their original purpose as signifiers of sacred persons.

57. See Francis Wormald, "The Rood of Bromholm," *Journal of the Warburg Institute* 1 (1937–38): 31–45. On Bromholm's sixteenth-century claims, see David Knowles, *The Religious Orders in England,* vol. 3 (Cambridge: CUP, 1959), 288. The papal bulls, both dated 1401, are in *CPL,* vol. 5, 384 and 432.

58. *CPL 1404–1415,* vol. 6, 301. Indulgences' economic importance for churches is noted by Béatrice Matray, "Les Indulgences au XIVe Siècle: Etude des Lettres de Jean XXII (1316–1334) et D'Urbain V (1363–1370)," *Cahiers d'histoire* 33:2 (1988): 141.

59. *CPL 1431–1447,* vol. 9, 109. For additional examples in the Norwich diocese, see *CPL 1396–1404,* vol. 5, 281, 586; vol. 8, 79, 529. See also Andrew D. Brown, *Popular Piety in Late Medieval England: The Diocese of Salisbury 1250–1550* (Oxford: Clarendon Press, 1995), 39.

60. *CPL 1427–1447,* vol. 8, 171.

61. *CPL 1404–1415,* vol. 6, 376; vol. 9, 38. On the history of the Blood of Hailes, see Peter Marshall, "The Rood of Boxley, the Blood of Hailes and the Defence of the Henrician Church," *JEH* 46: 4 (Oct. 1995): 689–96. On Hailes in the late Middle Ages, see Christopher Harper-Bill, "Cistercian Visitation in the Late Middle Ages: the Case of Hailes Abbey," *Bulletin of the Institute of Historical Research* 53:127 (May 1980): 103–14.

62. *CPL 1396–1404,* vol. 5, 168. Boniface IX granted the Portiuncula, an indulgence associated with St. Francis' chapel, to several churches; see Henry Charles Lea, *History of Auricular Confession and Indulgences* vol. 3 (Philadelphia: Lea Bros., 1896), 236–52.

63. *CPL 1396–1404,* vol. 5, 415.

64. *CPL 1396–1404,* vol. 5, 589.

65. *CPL 1455–1464,* vol. 11, 146.

66. *CPL 1305–1342,* vol. 2, 256. William A. Christian, *Apparitions in Late Medieval and Renaissance Spain* (Princeton: Princeton University Press, 1981),

21, comments that statues of Mary found underground support "Mary's role as successor to mother goddesses dealing with fertility." For the Kersey image, see *CPL 1458–1471,* vol. 12, 419–20; for the Tintern statue, see *CPL 1404–1415,* vol. 6, 452; for the Stayner picture, *CPL 1431–1447,* vol. 9, 253.

67. *CPL 1427–1447,* vol. 8, 117.

68. *CPL 1396–1404,* vol. 5, 207; *1471–1484,* vol. 13, part 1, 219.

69. *Visitations of Religious Houses in the Diocese of Lincoln,* vol. III, 348. An example from Ireland was an image of St. Radegund in an Augustinian priory church in Limerick that was linked to miracles; see *CPL 1427–1447,* vol. 8, 603.

70. *VHC Suffolk,* vol. 2, 77.

71. Among the few remains of the Virgin Mary was a vial of her breast milk at Walsingham; Hailes, of course, claimed to have some of Christ's blood. On Marian image cults, see Sumption, *Pilgrimage,* 277–78, and Steven D. Sargent, "Miracle Books and Pilgrimage Shrines in Late Medieval Bavaria," *Historical Reflections* 13 (1986): 466–69.

72. Dorothy M. Owen, "Bacon and Eggs: Bishop Buckingham and Superstition in Lincolnshire," in *Popular Belief and Practice,* eds. G. J. Cuming and D. Baker (Cambridge: CUP, 1972), 141. It is not clear from Owen's account that the bishop's condemnation of this cult was based solely on disapproval of suspect practices; money was also involved in the dispute.

73. *CPL 1417–1431,* vol. 7, 86–87.

74. *CPL 1484–1492,* vol. 15, 498–99. The church of St. Magnus the Martyr stood at the end of London Bridge; see *Victoria History of London* vol. 1, ed. William Page (London: Constable, 1909), Ecclesiastical Map II.

75. *Knighton's Chronicle 1337–1396,* ed. and tran. G. H. Martin (Oxford: Clarendon Press, 1995), 191.

76. *CPL 1471–1484,* vol. 13, part 2, 590–91.

77. *Chronica Monasterii de Melsa,* vol. 3, ed. Edward A. Bond, RS (London, 1868), 35–6; the English translation is by Rosemary Horrox, printed in *The Black Death* (Manchester: Manchester University Press, 1994), 67.

78. Aston, *Lollards and Reformers,* 159–62. F. A. Gasquet, *Eve of the Reformation* 3rd ed. (London: Bell, 1905), 373, cites a sixteenth-century tract in which the author, Lancelot Ridley, complains of money extorted "by images, by pardons, by pilgrimages, by indulgences. . . ."

79. John A. F. Thomson, "Tithe Disputes in Later Medieval London," *English Historical Review* 78 (1963): 1–17; Peter Heath, *English Parish Clergy on the Eve of the Reformation* (London: Routledge & Kegan Paul, 1969), 150–56; R. N. Swanson, *Church and Society in Late Medieval England* (Oxford: Blackwell, 1989), 211–16.

80. Brown, *Popular Piety,* 70–80; Heath, *English Parish Clergy,* 107–111.

81. Swanson, *Church and Society,* 17; Norman P. Tanner, *The Church in Late Medieval Norwich 1370–1532* (Toronto: Pontifical Institute of Mediaeval Studies, 1984), 11–12.

82. R. N. Swanson, "Parochialism and Particularism: the Dispute Over the Status of Ditchford Frary, Warwickshire, in the Early Fifteenth Century," in *Medieval Ecclesiastical Studies in Honour of Dorothy M. Owen,* ed. M. J. Franklin and C. Harper-Bill (Woodbridge: Boydell, 1995), 241–57; John A. F. Thomson, *Early Tudor Church 1485–1529* (New York: Longman, 1993), 285–87.

83. Brown, *Popular Piety,* 80; Tanner, *Norwich,* 141–62; Swanson, *Church and Society,* 15–24.

84. For the image of St. Edmund, see *VHC Suffolk,* vol. 2, 77. For St. Walstan and the Virgin at Thetford and at Lynn, see *VHC Norfolk,* vol. 2, 256, n.1. Thomas Fuller of Mildenhall requested pilgrimage on his behalf to the rood of Northacre, the Rood of Grace, Canterbury, Walsingham, the "vicary" of St. Stephen of Norwich, St. Nicholas of Thebenham, and St. Walstan; SROB, Reg. 3, f. 349r. Similarly, Alice Grenehood of Ipswich asked for pilgrimages to Walsingham and Hoxne, the monastery of St. Etheldreda in Eye, the churches of Laxfield, Stanton, and St. Peter of Thorp; NRO, Reg. Aleyn, f. 18v. For the images of the Virgin at Stoke, which received yearly offerings of 40 s., and Chipley, see the *Valor Ecclesiasticus Temp. Henr. VIII,* vol. 3 (London, 1817), 470. See also R. Hart, "The Shrines and Pilgrimages of the County of Norfolk," *NA* 6 (1864): 277–94.

85. Greenfield's concern was later echoed by Lollards; see Aston, "Lollards and Images," 151. The Messenger in Thomas More's *Dialogue Concerning Heresies,* pt. 1, 99, also makes this complaint.

86. Dickinson, *Shrine of Our Lady,* 110–14. See Benedicta Ward, *Miracles and the Medieval Mind* rev. ed. (Philadelphia: University of Pennsylvania Press, 1987), 145, on the localization of the Virgin Mary's cult.

87. For other accounts of holy images that refused to be moved from a particular spot, see especially Christian, *Apparitions,* 16–21; René Basset, "Les Statues qu'on ne peut déplacer," *Revue des Traditions Populaires* 26 (1911): 22–23; Stith Thompson and Jonas Balys, *The Oral Tales of India* (Bloomington: Indiana University Press, 1958), 144. Edward Muir comments that lay devouts believed images indicated the presence of a saint, and thus of a sacred place; see "The Virgin on the Street Corner: the Place of the Sacred in Italian Cities," in *Religion and Culture in the Renaissance and Reformation,* ed. Steven Ozment (Kirksville, Mo.: Sixteenth Century Journal Publications, 1989), 30.

88. See, for example, Turner and Turner, *Image and Pilgrimage,* 62–103, on the intense political associations of cult images of the Virgin in Mexico.

89. Salmon, *Saints,* 25; see the entry under her name in the index to James, *Norfolk and Suffolk,* 234; Williamson, "Saints," 307. Bainbridge, *Gilds,* 61, lists gilds named for St. Etheldreda, and other evidence of her cult. See Farmer, *Oxford Dictionary of Saints,* 148–49, for a summary of her life.

90. M. R. James, "Lives of St. Walstan," *NA* 19 (1917): 238–67.

91. On royal saints, see Michael Goodich, *Vita Perfecta: the Ideal of Sainthood in the Thirteenth Century* (Stuttgart: Hiersemann, 1982), 186–91. For the po-

litical and religious implications of the cult of Henry VI, see John W. McKenna, "Piety and Propaganda: the Cult of Henry VI," in *Chaucer and Middle English Studies,* ed. Beryl Rowland (London: Allen & Unwin, 1974), 72–88; Brian Spencer, "King Henry of Windsor and the London Pilgrim," in *Collectanea Londiniensia,* 235–64; John M. Theilmann, "The Miracles of King Henry VI of England," *The Historian* 42 (1980): 456–71, and "Communitas among Fifteenth-Century Pilgrims," *Historical Reflections* 11 (1984): 253–70. The miracles of Henry VI are edited by Paulus Grosjean, *Henrici VI Angliae Regis Miracula Postuma* (Bruxelles: Société des Bollandistes, 1935); for an English translation of some of the miracles, see *The Miracles of King Henry VI,* ed. Ronald Knox and Shane Leslie (Cambridge: CUP, 1923). See also Theilmann, "Political Canonization and Political Symbolism in Medieval England," *JBS* 29 (July 1990): 241–266, on saints as political symbols.

92. Knox and Leslie, *Miracles,* 3.

93. James, *Suffolk and Norfolk,* 20; F. A. Gasquet, *The Religious Life of King Henry VI* (London: Bell, 1923), 119–34, discusses the posthumous cult; *VHC Norfolk* vol. 2, 329; Blomefield, *Norfolk,* vol. 11, 366.

94. Blomefield, *Norfolk,* vol. 10, 445; Westlake, *Parish Gilds,* 125.

95. Oxford, Bodleian Lib., Jones MS. 46, described in *Medieval Art in East Anglia 1300–1520,* 35–36; Fitzwilliam Museum (Cambridge) MS. 55, f. 141v, described by M. R. James, *A Descriptive Catalogue of the Manuscripts in the Fitzwilliam Museum* (Cambridge: CUP, 1895), 138–40.

96. *Reg. Langton,* 78–79. On Lollardy in Salisbury Diocese, see Brown, *Popular Piety,* 202–22. Margaret Aston discusses reasons for destroying images by fire in "Iconoclasm in England: Rites of Destruction by Fire," in *Bilder und Bildersturm im Spätmittelalter und in der frühen Neuzeit,* ed. Bob Scribner (Wiesbaden: Harrassowitz, 1990), 175–99.

97. *Reg. Langton,* 70–75, 79, 81–82.

98. Norman P. Tanner, ed., *Heresy Trials in the Diocese of Norwich, 1428–31,* Camden Fourth Series, vol. 20 (London: Royal Historical Society, 1977), 188.

99. *Knighton's Chronicle,* 297, 535.

100. *Register of Robert Hallum, Bishop of Salisbury 1407–17,* ed. Joyce M. Horn (CYS vol. 72, 1982), 215.

101. See Harper-Bill, "A Late Medieval Visitation," 39. See also *Norwich Consistory Court Depositions,* case 339.

102. *An Episcopal Court Book for the Diocese of Lincoln 1514–1520,* ed. Margaret Bowker (Lincoln Record Society, 1967), 32.

103. *Norwich Consistory Court Depositions,* case 194.

104. Margaret Aston, "Gold and Images," in *The Church and Wealth,* ed. W. J. Sheils and D. Wood (Oxford: Blackwell, 1987), 189–207.

105. See, for example, *Records of the Gild of St. George in Norwich, 1389–1547: a Transcription with an Introduction,* by Mary Grace (Norfolk Record Society, vol. 9, 1937), 17. The processional banners of the gild bore the arms and image of St. George.

106. Aston, *England's Iconoclasts,* vol. 1, 235–6; Sumption, *Pilgrimage,* 270.

Chapter 5

1. Margery Kempe, *The Book of Margery Kempe,* ed. Sanford Brown Meech (Oxford: EETS 212, 1940), 148.

2. On negative receptions of *The Book of Margery Kempe,* see Clarissa Atkinson, *Mystic and Pilgrim: the Book and the World of Margery Kempe* (Ithaca: Cornell University Press, 1983), 195–220. For a more recent positive assessment of the physical nature of Kempe's spirituality, see Wendy Harding, "Body into Text: *The Book of Margery Kempe,*" in *Feminist Approaches to the Body in Medieval Literature,* ed. Linda Lomperis and Sarah Stanbury (Philadelphia: University of Pennsylvania Press, 1993), 168–87. David Wallace, "Mystics and Followers in Siena and East Anglia: A Study in Taxonomy, Class and Cultural Mediation" in *The Medieval Mystical Tradition in England,* ed. Marion Glasscoe (Cambridge: Brewer, 1984), 184, argues that images were texts that Kempe could read without clerical intervention, thus linking Kempe's responses to images to her illiteracy and to gender.

3. No consensus of opinion exists about Kempe, and the modern critical reception of Kempe and her *Book* has itself become a subject of scholarly discussion. The following citations suggest the wide variety of responses to her and her work: Ute Stargardt, "The Beguines of Belgium, the Dominican Nuns of Germany, and Margery Kempe" in *The Popular Literature of Medieval England,* ed. Thomas J. Heffernan (Knoxville: University of Tennessee Press, 1985), 277–313, sees Kempe as part of the "decay of feminine mysticism." W. A. Pantin, *The English Church in The Fourteenth Century* (reprt. ed., Toronto: University of Toronto Press, 1980), 258–59, placed her image worship within the normal bounds of late medieval popular piety, as does Richard Kieckhefer, *Unquiet Souls: Fourteenth-Century Saints and Their Religious Milieu* (Chicago: University of Chicago Press, 1984), 185–88. Susan Dickman, "Margery Kempe and the Continental Tradition of the Pious Woman" in *The Medieval Mystical Tradition in England,* ed. Marion Glasscoe (Cambridge: Brewer, 1984), 150–68, locates Margery within the tradition of "pious wives." Karma Lochrie, *Margery Kempe and Translations of the Flesh* (Philadelphia: University of Pennsylvania Press, 1991), 5, critiques attempts to show influences on Kempe for "marginalizing" rather than "contextualizing" her. For a positive and feminist interpretation of Kempe's spirituality, see Sandra J. McEntire, "The Journey into Selfhood: Margery Kempe and Feminine Spirituality," in *Margery Kempe: A Book of Essays,* ed. Sandra J. McEntire (New York: Garland, 1992), 51–69. Nancy F. Partner, "Reading the Book of Margery Kempe," *Exemplaria* 3:1 (1991): 29–66, offers a psychoanalytic interpretation of Kempe, and Mary Hardiman Farley, "Her Own Creature: Religion, Feminist Criticism, and the Functional Eccentricity of Margery Kempe," *Exemplaria* 11:1 (1999): 1–21, argues that Margery had what modern psychology terms a "Personality Disorder."

4. For biographical information on Julian, see *A Book of Showings to the Anchoress Julian of Norwich,* ed. Edmund Colledge and James Walsh (Toronto: Pontifical Institute of Mediaeval Studies, 1978), 33–39; and Brant Pelphrey, *Love Was His Meaning: the Theology and Mysticism of Julian of Norwich* (Salzburg: Institut für Anglistik und Amerikanistik, Universität Salzburg, 1982), 8–18. In the *Introduction* to *A Book of Showings,* 43–44, Colledge and Walsh say Julian became an anchoress only after she wrote the long text; other scholars disagree. Nicholas Watson, "The Composition of Julian of Norwich's *Revelation of Love,*" *Speculum* 68 (July 1993): 637–83, challenges the traditional dating of both the long and short texts, placing both much later than do Colledge and Walsh. Frederick Christian Bauerschmidt, *Julian of Norwich and the Mystical Body Politic of Christ* (Notre Dame: University of Notre Dame Press, 1999), 203–12, reviews arguments about Julian's life, education, and the dates of her writings.

5. The Short Text, *A Book of Showings,* 201–2. The statement about paintings of crucifixes was omitted from the Long Text. Watson, "Composition," 657–66, interprets this passage as Julian's response to the contemporary debate on images.

6. *Book of Showings,* 708.

7. On the conceptual blurring of mental and corporeal images, see Sixten Ringbom, *Icon to Narrative: the Rise of the Dramatic Close-up in Fifteenth-Century Devotional Painting* 2nd ed. (Doornspijk: Davaco, 1984), 15–22; and "Devotional Images and Imaginative Devotions," *Gazette des Beaux-Arts* 73 (1969): 159–70. Craig Harbison, "Visions and Meditations in Early Flemish Painting," *Simiolus* 15:2 (1985): 117–18, comments that qualities of oil allowed paintings to stand as visions and not simply as "limited" material artifacts.

8. *Book of Showings,* 289–91.

9. *Book of Showings,* 294.

10. *Book of Showings,* 323. Paul Molinari, *Julian of Norwich* (London: Longmans, Green, 1958), 62–63, argues that Julian's bodily visions did not include external sense perception, but belonged to the sphere of the imaginative vision. Andrew Ryder, "A Note on Julian's Visions," *Downside Review* 96 (1978): 303, disagrees. Roland Maisonneuve, *L'Univers Visionnaire de Julian of Norwich* (L'Université de Paris IV thesis, 1979), 56f., says the bodily sights "correspond à une perception par l'oeil humain" and that Julian describes them as if they were actual sights before her eyes. Bauerschmidt, *Julian of Norwich,* 42–50, considers Julian's classification of three kinds of vision an attempt to connect her visions to a recognized visionary tradition. He thinks her "bodily sights" "are closely related to the material object of the crucifix," but argues that Julian's concern was not with the experience of "bodily seeing" itself but in understanding its object, the crucified Christ.

11. J. A. W. Bennett, *Poetry of the Passion* (Oxford: Clarendon Press, 1982), 32–61, discusses Passion meditations in medieval English literature. On the influence of art on Julian, see B. A. Windeatt, "The Art of Mystical Loving:

Julian of Norwich," in *Medieval Mystical Tradition*, 66–67; and especially Denise Nowakowski Baker, *Julian of Norwich's* Showings: *From Vision to Book* (Princeton: Princeton University Press, 1994), 40–62. Jeffrey Hamburger discusses the importance of images in late medieval mysticism in *The Rothschild Canticles* (New Haven: Yale University Press, 1990), 1–7, 162–67.

12. *Book of Showings,* 311. This description from the Long Text is more elaborate and detailed than that in the Short Text. Susan K. Hagen, "St. Cecilia and St. John of Beverly: Julian of Norwich's Early Model and Late Affirmation," in *Julian of Norwich: a Book of Essays,* ed. Sandra J. McEntire (New York: Garland, 1998), 91–114, argues that the Long Text's elaboration of visual detail serves a pedagogic function in making the visions more memorable.

13. *Book of Showings,* 324.

14. *Book of Showings,* 357.

15. *Book of Showings,* 379.

16. *Book of Showings,* 632–33.

17. *Book of Showings,* 294–318. Julian's constant movement from bodily sight to spiritual understanding underscores her refusal to focus purely on the physicality of Christ's sufferings, as Passion meditations like Rolle's tend to do. David Aers argues that Julian resists and finally "supersedes" the late medieval commonplace devotion to Christ's tortured body; see his "The Humanity of Christ: Reflections on Julian of Norwich's *Revelation of Love,*" in David Aers and Lynn Staley, *The Powers of the Holy: Religion, Politics, and Gender in Late Medieval English Culture* (University Park: The Pennsylvania State University Press, 1996), 77–194.

18. *Book of Showings,* 324–35. For the history of the Vernicle, see Hans Belting, *Likeness and Presence: A History of the Image Before the Era of Art,* trans. Edmund Jephcott (Chicago: University of Chicago Press, 1994), 215–24; and for a study of the Vernicle in England, see Flora Lewis, "The Veronica: Image, Legend and Viewer," in *England in the Thirteenth Century,* ed. W. M. Ormrod (Woodbridge, Suffolk: Boydell, 1986), 100–106. Chapter 6 discusses the Vernicle in late medieval prayer books.

19. *Book of Showings,* 299–303. On the meaning of this passage, see A. M. Allchin, "Julian of Norwich and the Continuity of Tradition," in *The Medieval Mystical Tradition in England,* ed. Marion Glasscoe ([Exeter]: University of Exeter, 1980), 79–80, and Joan M. Nuth, *Wisdom's Daughter: the Theology of Julian of Norwich* (New York: Crossroad, 1991), 99–100.

20. Investigations of medieval women's responses to art include Hamburger, *The Rothschild Canticles;* "The Visual and the Visionary: The Image in Late Medieval Monastic Devotions," *Viator* 20 (1989): 161–82; Joanna E. Ziegler, *Sculpture of Compassion: the Pietà and the Beguines in the Southern Low Countries c. 1300–c. 1600* (Bruxelles: Brepols, 1992); Margaret Miles, *Image as Insight: Visual Understanding in Western Christianity and Secular Culture* (Boston: Beacon, 1985).

21. Julian's education is a much debated topic. Colledge and Walsh argue for her literacy and wide reading in their *Introduction* to *A Book of Showings*. Pelphrey, *Love Was His Meaning*, 18–28, reviews the historical evidence for both lay- and religious women's education, concluding that Julian had "the simplest kind" of education, if any. Baker, *Julian of Norwich's* Showings, 8–11, shows that Julian's phrase "a symple creature vnlettyrde" could have various meanings unconnected to reading literacy. Felicity Riddy, "'Women talking about the things of God': a late medieval sub-culture," in *Women and Literature in Britain 1150–1500* 2nd ed., ed. Carol M. Meale (Cambridge: CUP, 1996), 112, believes that Julian was influenced by vernacular texts that were "vividly pictorial."

22. Atkinson, *Mystic and Pilgrim,* 14–18, provides a lucid summary of Kempe's life.

23. See notes 2 and 3, this chapter.

24. "Richard Rolle's Meditations on the Passion," *Yorkshire Writers,* vol. 1, 83–103. The modern English translation is from Richard Rolle, *The English Writings,* trans. & ed. Rosamund S. Allen (New York: Paulist Press, 1988), 118. See Thomas H. Bestul, *Texts of the Passion: Latin Devotional Literature and Medieval Society* (Philadelphia: University of Pennsylvania Press, 1996), 64–68; 145f., for other vernacular examples of this genre.

25. *The Doctrinal of Sapience, ed. from Caxton's printed edition, 1489,* ed. by Joseph Gallagher (Heidelberg: Winter, 1993), 68. The *Doctrinal* is a translation of the French manual of religious instruction known as *Le Doctrinal de Sapience* or *Le Doctrinal aux Simples Gens.*

26. "Thou Sinful Man that by Me Goes," in *Religious Lyrics of the XVth Century,* ed. Carleton Brown (Oxford: Clarendon Press, 1939), 151–56. See also #95, "Behold Jesus on the Cross"; #103, "Woefully Arrayed"; and #104, "Unkind Man, Take Heed of Me."

27. *Nicholas Love's* Mirror of the Blessed Life of Jesus Christ: *a Critical Edition,* ed. Michael G. Sargent (New York: Garland, 1992). For the popularity of Love's work, see Sargent's *Introduction,* lxiii, and M. Deanesly, "Vernacular Books in England in the Fourteenth and Fifteenth Centuries," *Modern Language Review* XV (1920): 353. On the origins of Love's work and its relation to other texts, see Sargent's *Introduction,* ix–xliv; Elizabeth Zeeman, "Nicholas Love—a Fifteenth-Century Translator," *Review of English Studies* 6 (1955): 113–127; and Michael G. Sargent, "Bonaventura English: a Survey of the Middle English Prose Translations of Early Franciscan Literature," in *Spätmittelalterliche Geistliche Literatur,* Band 2, 148f. Shearle Furnish, "The *Ordinatio* of Huntington Library, MS. HM 149: an East Anglian Manuscript of Nicholas Love's *Mirrour,*" *Manuscripta* 34 (1990): 50–65, discusses a copy of Love intended for private meditation. Scholars who have connected the *Mirrour* to Kempe include Wallace, "Mystics and Followers," 180–81; Lynn Staley, *Margery Kempe's Dissenting Fictions* (University Park: The Pennsylvania State University Press, 1994), 141–46. See Denise Despres, *Ghostly Sights: Visual Meditation in Late-Medieval Literature* (Norman,

Okla.: Pilgrim Books, 1989), 19–54, on the Franciscan influence in visual meditation. On participatory visions, see also Elizabeth Alvilda Petroff, *Medieval Women's Visionary Literature* (New York: Oxford University Press, 1986) 6, 11–14.

28. *Book of Margery Kempe,* 69.

29. *Book of Margery Kempe,* 187.

30. Atkinson, *Mystic and Pilgrim,* 93–94. On the connections between late medieval Northern art and religious sensibility, see Douglas Gray, *Themes and Images in the Medieval English Religious Lyric* (London: Routledge & Kegan Paul, 1972), 27–28. See also Ringbom, *Icon to Narrative,* 17–19, and Henk van Os, et al., *The Art of Devotion in the Late Middle Ages in Europe 1300–1500* (Princeton: Princeton University Press, 1994).

31. *Book of Margery Kempe,* 70; Aston, *Lollards and Reformers,* 121 and Figure 6.

32. See Meech's *Introduction* to *The Book of Margery Kempe,* ix; Atkinson, *Mystic and Pilgrim,* 91, assumes Kempe had no education from books until she got a priest to read to her; Lochrie, *Margery Kempe,* 101–03, places Kempe as an illiterate author in the context of a manuscript culture in which oral and written texts were closely linked. In opposition to the generally accepted notion of Kempe's illiteracy, Josephine K. Tarvers, "The Alleged Illiteracy of Margery Kempe: A Reconsideration of the Evidence," *Medieval Perspectives* 11 (1996): 113–24, argues that Kempe was literate in English.

33. *Book of Margery Kempe,* 142.

34. *Book of Margery Kempe,* 144.

35. Brian Stock, *The Implications of Literacy* (Princeton: Princeton University Press, 1983), 88–92, argues for the importance of texts to illiterates by his concept of textual communities composed of illiterate people whose activities center on texts or a literate interpreter of them. Anthony Goodman comments on Kempe's "oral learning" in "The Piety of John Brunham's Daughter, of Lynn," in *Medieval Women,* ed. Derek Baker (Oxford: Blackwell, 1978), 349.

36. *Book of Margery Kempe,* 218. Lochrie, *Margery Kempe,* 126, suggests this statement implies Margery's ability to read, but I interpret this statement as Christ reassuring Margery that the inability to read was unimportant.

37. *Book of Margery Kempe,* 111.

38. *Book of Margery Kempe,* 148.

39. *The Pore Caitif,* ed. Mary Teresa Brady (Ph.D. dissertantion, Fordham University, 1954), 31–32.

40. John Myrc, *Mirk's Festial,* ed. T. Erbe (London: EETS e.s. 96, 1905), 171.

41. *The Tretyse of Love,* ed. John H. Fisher (London: EETS 223, 1951), 113–14.

42. *Yorkshire Writers,* vol. 2, 376–77.

43. *Book of Margery Kempe,* 14.

44. *Dives and Pauper,* vol. 1, part 1, ed. Priscilla Heath Barnum (London: EETS 275, 1976), 84–85.

45. *Tretyse of Love,* 15–16. There are earlier English versions of this theme; for example, the poem quoted in Bennett, *Poetry of the Passion,* 48. Wolfgang

Riehle, *The Middle English Mystics,* trans. B. Standring (London: Routledge & Kegan Paul, 1981), 39–40, notes the similarity of Margery's desire to the development of this theme in standard "Bernardian-Franciscan mysticism of the cross."

46. *Book of Margery Kempe,* 77–78. On women's use of images of the Christ child in Italy, see Klapisch-Zuber, "Holy Dolls," 310–29. These women bathed, dressed, and made clothes for the dolls, activities Savonarola condemned as idolatrous. On the use of infant Jesus dolls in northern Europe, see Ulinka Rublank, "Female Spirituality and the Infant Jesus in Late Medieval Dominican Convents," *Gender & History* 6:1 (April 1994): 37–57.

47. *Book of Margery Kempe,* 61, 80, 172.

48. *Book of Margery Kempe,* 208.

49. *Book of Margery Kempe,* 86, 176.

50. Susan Dickman, "Margery Kempe and the English Devotional Tradition," in *The Medieval Mystical Tradition in England,* ed. Marion Glasscoe ([Exeter]: University of Exeter, 1980), 156–72. See also Caroline Walker Bynum's comments on Kempe's "literalism" in "Women's Stories, Women's Symbols: A Critique of Victor Turner's Theory of Limnality," in *Anthropology and the Study of Religion* ed. Robert L. Moore and Frank E. Reynolds (Chicago: Center for the Scientific Study of Religion, 1984), 113. Riehle, *Middle English Mystics,* 11, goes so far as to say that Kempe could not distinguish the sensual from the spiritual.

51. *Angela of Foligno: Complete Works,* trans. Paul Lachance (New York: Paulist Press, 1993), 131. The critical edition in Italian and Latin is *Il Libro della Beata Angela da Foligno,* 2nd ed., ed. L. Thier and A. Calufetti (Grottaferrata [Rome]: Editiones Collegii S. Bonaventurae ad Claras Aquas, 1985).

52. *Angela of Foligno: Complete Works,* 128.

53. Catherine M. Mooney, "The Authorial Role of Brother A. in the Composition of Angela of Foligno's Revelations," in *Creative Women in Medieval and Early Modern Italy: A Religious and Artistic Renaissance,* ed. E. Ann Matter and John Coakley (Philadelphia: University of Pennsylvania Press, 1994), 34–63, argues for Brother A. as an "active and energetic collaborator" in creating the *Memorial.*

54. On Angela's life, see Paul Lachance, *The Spiritual Journey of the Blessed Angela of Foligno According to the Memorial of Frater A.* (Rome: Pontificium Athenaeum Antonianum, 1984), 79–122; Clément Schmitt, ed., *Vita e spiritualità della Beata Angela da Foligno* (Pérugia Serafica Provincia di San Francesco, 1987); an admiring biography is Martin Jean Ferré, *Sainte Angèle de Foligno, sa vie—ses oeuvres* (Paris: Libraire Plon, 1936). Angela's reading literacy is clearly documented; her writing literacy is less certain; see Paul Lachance's comments in the *Introduction* to *Complete Works,* 16. See also the *Préface* to Sainte Angèle de Foligno, *Le Livre de L'Expérience des Vrais Fidèles,* ed. M.-J. Ferré and L. Baudry (Paris: E. Droz, 1927), xiii.

55. *Angela of Foligno: Complete Works,* 125–26. Lachance, 366–67, n. 9, relates this act to practices of contemporary heretical groups who prayed nude.

Other scholars have interpreted Angela's action as an imitation of St. Francis; see, for example, Ann Stafford, "Angela of Foligno," in *Spirituality through the Centuries: Ascetics and Mystics of the Western Church,* ed. J. Walsh (New York: Kennedy & Sons, 1964), 183.

56. *Angela of Foligno: Complete Works,* 175.

57. *Angela of Foligno: Complete Works,* 141. On this window, see Jerome Poulenc, "Saint François dans le vitrail des anges de l'église supérieure de la basilique d'Assise," *Archivum Franciscanum Historicum* 76 (1983): 701–13.

58. *Angela of Foligno: Complete Works,* 162.

59. *Angela of Foligno: Complete Works,* 149–50.

60. The *Vita* and *Processus Canonizationis* of Jeanne-Marie de Maillé are in the *Acta Sanctorum,* March, t. 3, 735–65. Vauchez, *Laity,* 205–15, discusses the importance of these documents for shedding light on Franciscan activity in central France in the fourteenth century. See also Père Lèon, *Lives of the Saints and Blessed of the Three Orders of Saint Francis,* trans. from *Aureole Seraphique* (Taunton, 1885–87), vol. 2, 106–30, who claims Jeanne-Marie was a third-order Franciscan.

61. *Vita* of Jeanne-Marie de Maillé, 737.

62. *Vita* of Jeanne-Marie de Maillé, 744. Gertrud Schiller, *Iconography of Christian Art,* trans. Janet Seligman vol. 2 (Greenwich, Conn.: New York Graphic Society, 1971), 191, says the *Arma Christi* were meant to provide an aid for meditation. Margaret of Faenza saw the *Arma Christi* in a vision; see her *Vita* in *Acta Sanctorum,* August, t. 5, 849. Lydwina of Schiedam saw angels carrying the symbols and standing around her bed holding them; see her *Vita* in *Acta Sanctorum,* April, t. 2, 331.

63. *Vita* of Jeanne-Marie de Maillé, 740.

64. *Processus Canonizationis* of Jeanne-Marie de Maillé, 757.

65. *Processus Canonizationis* of Jeanne-Marie de Maillé, 758.

66. *Vita* of Jeanne-Marie de Maillé, 738 & 740.

67. Cited by Kieckhefer, *Unquiet Souls,* 90.

68. Jacques de Vitry, *The Life of Marie D'Oignies,* trans. Margot H. King (Toronto: Peregrina, 1993), 50.

69. Quoted by Klapisch-Zuber, "Holy Dolls," 327.

70. Henry Suso, *The Exemplar with Two German Sermons,* trans. and ed. Frank Tobin (New York: Paulist Press, 1989), 167.

71. Laurie A. Finke, "Mystical Bodies and the Dialogics of Vision," in *Maps of Flesh and Light: The Religious Experience of Medieval Women Mystics,* ed. Ulrike Wiethaus (Syracuse: Syracuse University Press, 1993), 36.

72. On the spiritual senses in English mystical writings, see Riehle, *Middle English Mystics,* 104–27. Margaret Miles, "Vision: The Eye of the Body and the Eye of the Mind in Saint Augustine's *De trinitate* and *Confessions,*" *The Journal of Religion* 63 (April 1983): 125–42, argues for the intersection of physical and spiritual vision in Augustine's thought. See "Sens Spirituel," *DS,* vol. 14, cols. 599–617, for an overview and bibliography of the history of the doctrine of the spiritual senses.

73. David Lindberg, *Theories of Vision from Al-Kindi to Kepler* (Chicago: University of Chicago Press, 1976), 107–21. Lindberg explains intromissionist theory in lucid detail; my description is a simplified summary.

74. David Lindberg, ed. and trans., *John Pecham and the Science of Optics:* Perspectiva Communis (Madison: University of Wisconsin Press, 1970), 32.

75. For a partial list of manuscripts and printed versions of the *De Oculo Morali,* see Hieronymus Spettman, "Das Schriftchen 'De Oculo Morali' und Sein Verfasser," *Archivum Franciscanum Historicum* 16 (1923): 314–17; and David C. Lindberg, *A Catalog of Medieval and Renaissance Optical Manuscripts* (Toronto: Pontifical Institute of Mediaeval Studies, 1975), 72–3. On the attribution of the *De Oculo Morali* to Peter of Limoges, see Spettman and also David C. Clark, "Optics for Preachers: the *De Oculo Morali* by Peter of Limoges," *Michigan Academician* 9:3 (Winter 1977), 330. I cite from an edition printed in Viterbo in 1655. Cavanaugh, "A Study of Books," 118, 823, 899, 927, lists several copies owned in medieval England.

76. *De Oculo Morali,* 9–10.

77. *De Oculo Morali,* 4.

78. *De Oculo Morali,* 46–47.

79. *De Oculo Morali,* 82–83.

80. *De Oculo Morali,* 13–14.

81. *De Oculo Morali,* 67.

82. Caroline Bynum discusses the blood from Christ's wound as nourishment and provides several visual images of it in "The Female Body and Religious Practice in the Later Middle Ages," in *Fragmentation and Redemption: Essays on Gender and the Human Body in Medieval Religion* (New York: Zone Books, 1991), 181–238. On the cult of the image of the wound, see W. Sparrow Simpson, "On the Measure of the Wound in the Side of the Redeemer," *Journal of the British Archaeological Association* 30 (1874): 357–74; and Flora Lewis, "The Wound in Christ's Side and the Instruments of the Passion: Gendered Experience and Response," in *Women and the Book: Assessing the Visual Evidence,* ed. Jane H. M. Taylor and Lesley Smith (London and Toronto: The British Library and University of Toronto Press, 1997), 204–29.

83. *Angela of Foligno: Complete Works,* 128.

84. *Book of Showings,* 394.

85. *The Tretyse of Love,* 121, places idle eyes among the sins of the flesh. Warning against the danger of vision, *The Pore Caitif,* 179, blames the eyes for Eve's sin. Each of the five senses or "wits" was associated with particular sins in late medieval literature. Sight, for example, was often linked to lust as in this warning, "Thynne yȝen ben þe fyrste dartys of luste, syȝyte ys desyer of woman, and woman of man; mynde ys cauȝte by þe yȝen;" *Yorkshire Writers,* vol. 2, 368. The senses were not only tied to sins, however, as various works also acknowledged their potential for good. One late Middle English treatise emphasized how easily the eyes were deceived, and then explains how sight should be used for moral betterment; see *The Fyve*

Wittes: A Late Middle English Devotional Treatise, ed. R. H. Bremmer (Amsterdam: Rodopie, 1987), 2–14. For a history of the five senses in medieval English devotional and penitential literature, see Bremmer, xxxiv–xlviii.

86. *Book of Margery Kempe,* 190.
87. *Book of Margery Kempe,* 220.
88. *Angela of Foligno: Complete Works,* 125–26.
89. Maria R. Lichtmann argues for the centrality of bodily experience in Julian's thought in "'God fulfylled my bodye': Body, Self, and God in Julian of Norwich," in *Gender and Text in the Later Middle Ages,* ed. Jane Chance (Gainesville: University Press of Florida, 1996), 263–78. Bauerschmidt, *Julian of Norwich,* 45–46, says Julian's bodily sights involve a "participative model of knowing," so that she "sees" with her eyes and "her entire body." See also Susan Dickman, "Julian of Norwich and Margery Kempe: Two Images of Fourteenth-Century Spirituality," and Marion Glasscoe, "Means of Showing," both in *Spätmittelalterliche Geistliche Literatur,* Band 1, 178–193 and 155–77. On the significance of the body, or the carnal, in redemption and communication with God, see Caroline Walker Bynum "The Female Body and Religious Practice;" Sarah Beckwith, "A Very Material Mysticism: The Medieval Mysticism of Margery Kempe," in *Medieval Literature: Criticism, Ideology and History,* ed. David Aers (Brighton: Harvester Press, 1986), 48, and *Christ's Body: Identity, Culture and Society in Late Medieval Writings* (London and New York: Routledge, 1993), especially 78–111 on Margery Kempe.

Chapter 6

1. [Richard Whiteford], *The Pomander of Prayer* (London: Robert Redman, 1531), cap. viii. *RSTC* 25421.5.
2. These artifacts dot the wills of the wealthy: In 1356 Elizabeth Bohun, Countess of Northhampton, bequeathed to the Earl of Hereford "a tablet of gold with the form of a crucifix thereon"; *Testamenta Vetusta,* ed. N. H. Nicolas (London: Nichols & Son, 1826), 60. The infamous Alice Perrers, mistress of Edward III, owned "a pair of small 'trussyngcoffres' with an image of the Blessed [Virgin] . . .]" and "an image of St. Mary in a tabernacle worth 100 s." *Calendar of Inquisitions Miscellaneous (Chancery)* vol. IV *1377–1388* (London, 1957), 14–15. In 1487, Elizabeth Poyninges (born a Paston) left to her daughter "a tablet with the Salutacion of Our Lady and the iii kingis of Collayn"; Gail McMurray Gibson, *The Theater of Devotion: East Anglian Drama and Society in the Late Middle Ages,* (Chicago: University of Chicago Press, 1989), 61. The Norfolk knight Sir John Fastolf owned several images of Christ, the Virgin, and other saints; see *Paston Letters and Papers of the Fifteenth Century,* vol. 1, ed. Norman Davis (Oxford: Clarendon Press, 1971), 159. On late medieval woodcuts, see Campbell Dodgson, "English Devotional Woodcuts of the Late Fifteenth Century, with Special Reference to Those in the Bodleian Library," *The Walpole Society* 17 (1928–29): 95–108.

3. On the commercial trade in manuscripts and the growth of the London book trade, see Graham Pollard, "The Company of Stationers Before 1557," *The Library* 4th ser. 18 (1937–38): 1–38; H. S. Bennett, "The Production and Dissemination of Vernacular Manuscripts in the Fifteenth Century," *The Library* 5th ser. 1 (1946–47): 167–78; and C. Paul Christianson, "The rise of London's book-trade," in *Cambridge History of the Book in Britain,* vol. III, ed. Lotte Hellinga and J. B. Trapp (Cambridge: CUP, 1999) 128–147, and "Evidence for the Study of London's Late Medieval Manuscript-Book Trade," in *Book Production and Publishing in Britain,* 87–108; Carol M. Meale, "Patrons, Buyers and Owners: Book Production and Social Status," in *Book Production and Publishing in Britain,* 201–38.

4. Mary C. Erler, "Devotional Literature," in *The Cambridge History of the Book in Britain,* vol. III, ed. Lotte Hellinga and J. B. Trapp (Cambridge: CUP, 1999), 497.

5. Erler, "Devotional Literature," 495.

6. Edwyn Birchenough, "The Prymer in English," *The Library* 4th ser. 18 (1937–38): 179. On the cost of medieval books, see H. E. Bell, "The Price of Books in Medieval England," *The Library* 4th ser. 17 (1936–37): 312–32; and H. S. Bennett, "Notes on English Retail Book-prices, 1480–1560," *The Library* 5th ser. 5 (1950–51): 172–78.

7. *Testamenta Vetusta,* 148; *Testaments Eboracensia,* vol. IV (London: Surtees Society, 1869), 153; Norman P. Tanner, *The Church in Late Medieval Norwich 1370–1532* (Toronto: Pontifical Institute of Mediaeval Studies, 1984), 112. For the Pastons see the fifteenth-century inventory that includes a "sawtere" and a "premere" in *Paston Letters and Papers,* vol. 2, 360; and Agnes Paston's 1510 will in which she left a "grete booke of prayers" and another "book of prayers keuered with redde and having a siluer clasp;" *Paston Letters,* vol. 2, 616.

8. On the trade in secondhand books, see Derek Pearsall, "Introduction," *Book Production and Publishing,* 6; and Kate Harris, "Patrons, Buyers, and Owners: the evidence for ownership and the rôle of book owners in book production and the book trade," *Book Production and Publishing,* 171–77.

9. Erler, "Devotional Literature," 499–505; and "*The Maner to Lyue Well* and the Coming of English in François Regnault's Primers of the 1520s and 1530s," *The Library* 6th ser. 6 (1984): 229–43.

10. Edgar Hoskins, *Horae Beatae Mariae Virginis or Sarum and York Primers* (London: Longmans, Green, 1901), xvi, notes the use of primers in church and at home; Eamon Duffy, *The Stripping of the Altars: Traditional Religion in England c. 1400–c. 1580* (New Haven: Yale University Press, 1992), 266–98, discusses charms and pardons in the primers; Paul Saenger, "Books of Hours and the Reading Habits of the Later Middle Ages," *Scrittura e Civiltà* 9 (1985): 239–69, argues that Books of Hours promoted "private silent reading" and thus new relations between reader and book.

11. London, B. L. Stowe MS. 16, f. 151r.

12. London, B. L. Harley MS. 1251, ff. 182r–183r.

13. Margery Kempe, *The Book of Margery Kempe,* ed. Sanford Brown Meech (Oxford: EETS 212, 1940), 21.

14. John Harthan, *The Book of Hours* (New York: Crowell, 1977), 31, claims that even illiterates wanted to own Books of Hours; but see Penketh, "Women and Books of Hours," who claims Books of Hours were often made for women who had sufficient Latin to read the prayers.

15. See note 1 above, and Robert A. Horsfield, "*The Pomander of Prayer:* Aspects of Late Medieval English Carthusian Spirituality and Its Lay Audience," in *De Cella in Seculum,* 205–13.

16. A basic guide to Books of Hours is V. Leroquais, *Les Livres d'Heures* 3 vols. (Paris, 1927), and *Supplément (Acquisitions récentes et donations Smith-Lesouef)* (Mâcon, 1943), whose Introduction discusses the history, development, and forms of Books of Hours. He defines what he calls the essential, secondary, and accessory elements of Books of Hours, vol. 1, xiv-xxxii. An excellent guide in English is Roger S. Wieck, *Time Sanctified: The Book of Hours in Medieval Art and Life* (New York: Braziller, 1988). A useful survey is Harthan, *Book of Hours,* 11–39. See also Edmund Bishop, "On the Origin of the Prymer," in *The Prymer or Lay Folks' Prayer Book,* ed. Henry Little-hales, Part II (London: EETS 109, 1897), xi-xxxviii. Duffy, *Stripping,* 209–98, asserts primers' centrality in the devotional life of the laity and investigates many of their prayers.

17. Emile Mâle, *Religious Art in France: the Late Middle Ages,* trans. M. Mathews (Princeton: Princeton University Press, 1986) 81–135; Henk van Os, et al., *The Art of Devotion in the Late Middle Ages in Europe 1300–1500,* trans. Michael Hoyle (Princeton: Princeton University Press, 1994); Miri Rubin, *Corpus Christi: the Eucharist in Late Medieval Culture* (Cambridge: CUP, 1991), 302–316; Duffy, *Stripping,* 234–56. On these images in late medieval English books, see Kathleen L. Scott, *Later Gothic Manuscripts 1390–1490* pt. 1 (London: Harvey Miller, 1996), 56–7.

18. Rosemary Woolf, *The English Religious Lyric in the Middle Ages* (Oxford: Clarendon Press, 1968), 389–91.

19. Gertrud Schiller, *Iconography of Christian Art,* vol. 2, trans. Janet Seligman (Greenwich, Conn.: New York Graphic Society, 1971), 184–97.

20. Nigel Morgan, "Text and Images of Marian Devotion in Fourteenth-Century England," in *England in the Fourteenth Century,* ed. Nicholas Rogers (Stamford: Paul Watkins, 1993), 53–57.

21. Giles Constable, "The Ideal of the Imitation of Christ," in *Three Studies in Medieval Religious and Social Thought* (Cambridge: CUP, 1995), 218–48; and see Flora Lewis, "Rewarding Devotion: Indulgences and the Promotion of Images," in *The Church and the Arts,* 179–94, on the transmission of these images in late medieval English manuscripts.

22. *Mirk's Festial,*171; see also Alan J. Fletcher, "John Mirk and the Lollards," *Medium Aevum* 56 (1987): 217–24.

23. Avril Henry, *Biblia Pauperum: a facsimile and edition* (Ithaca, N.Y.: Cornell University Press, 1987), 17–18.

24. See Wieck, *Time Sanctified,* 111–23. Examples of these depictions of the saints can be found in a great many prayer books. Among those I have examined, London B. L. Arundel MS. 318, ff. 15v–33v includes pictures of and prayers to Sts. John the Evangelist, Thomas Becket, George, Christopher, Anne, Katherine, Barbara, Mary Magdalene, and Margaret—all saints that were frequently depicted in wall paintings, stained glass, rood screens, and statues; London B. L. Harley MS. 2846, ff. 28v–49r includes a very similar group of texts and portraits, as does Harley MS. 1251 ff. 33v–54r.

25. A spectacular exception is John Clopton's fifteenth-century chantry chapel in Long Melford, Suffolk, where verses by the East Anglian monk and poet John Lydgate at places implore the beholder to gaze at and remember certain images. See Gibson, *Theater of Devotion,* 86–89; and J. B. Trapp, "Verses by Lydgate at Long Melford," *Review of English Studies* ns VI (1955): 1–11.

26. See Kathleen L. Scott, "Design, Decoration, and Illustration," in *Book Production and Publishing in Britain,* 31. Martha Driver, "Pictures in Print: Late Fifteenth- and Early Sixteenth-Century English Religious Books for Lay Readers," in *De Cella in Seculum,* 236, calls miniatures in primers "text markers," noting that images added to the standard picture cycles in printed primers helped to organize the text.

27. No generality can encompass the diversity of the illuminations in these books; one of the most interesting aspects of primers is their variation. For the decoration of Books of Hours, see Leroquais, vol. 1, xl–l; Wieck, *Time Sanctified,* Chapters IV–XII, and also his *Painted Prayers: The Book of Hours in Medieval and Renaissance Art* (New York: Braziller, 1997).

28. On medieval religious books of images for laypeople, see L. Delisle, "Livres d'Images," 213–85 in *Histoire Littéraire de la France,* t. XXXI (Paris, 1893). *The Pomander of Prayer* alludes to books filled with pictures of Christ's life and Passion; see Horsfield, "*The Pomander of Prayer,*" 212.

29. *Coasts of the Country: An Anthology of Prayer drawn from the Early English Spiritual Writers,* ed. Claire Kirchberger (Chicago: Henry Regnery, n.d.), 36.

30. London, B. L. Harley MS. 1260, f. 103r: "Seint Hillerie Evesque de Poyters, ordina cestes Psalmes qe sont cy escripte en ordre, et grant Remedie trovera chescon bone Cristiene de ferme Foi, qe les dirra en bone Devocion, quant il avera mestiere de Grace et de Eide. Qui voudra Dieu priere de Eide & de Grace, dirra en genulant devoutement ceux deux Psalmes devaunt la Croice; si trouvera Grace de Dieu." F. 163r: "Si vous soiez en mortiel Pecche, ou en Anguisse, alez à monstier, et illoques genulez devant le Croice, et priez a Dieu q'il et Mercy de nous; et qil vous delivere de nostre Anguisse. Et ne priez nul reni qe soit contre le Foi. Et regardez bien les piez Ihesu." F. 173v: "Ici comence les v. peyns que noster seignour suffrit en la crois. Et si sunt eus bons a dire chescoun iour qe poit devaunt le figur de nostre seignour en la croice pur remission de pecche & salvacion de alme."

31. London, B. L. Additional MS. 37787, ff. 95v–96r: "Si quis in dies dixerit istam salutacionem ante crucifixum quicquid iustum pecierit dabitur ei."

The rubrics read "Primo respiciens pede ihesu in cruce dicens . . ." "Deinde respicias costam dicens . . ." and so on.

32. The rubric in B. L. Harley MS. 2846, f. 106r., reads: "Has videas laudes qui sacre virgine gaudes. Et venerando piam studeas laudare mariam. Virginis intacte cum veneris ante figuram. Pretereundo cave ne taceatur ave. Invenies veniam sic salutando mariam." The same rubric, with very slight differences, is found in B. L. Stowe MS. 16, ff. 119v–120r, and B. L. Additional MS. 27948, f. 50r.

33. "Belle tres doulce dame, et ie megenoillerais XV foix devant vostre doulce ymage en lonneur des XV ioie que vous eustes de vostre chier filz en terre." Paris, B. N. MS. Lat. 1361, cited by Leroquais, *Les Livres d'Heures* vol. 1, 172.

34. London, B. L. Additional MS. 22720, f. 45r.: "Hec sunt nomina domine nostre beatissime et gloriose virginis que sibi per spiritum sanctum ut fertur in eius miraculus imposita fuerit sicuti ipsa virgo gloriosa uni clerico sibi devoto semel apparuit que dilexit que erit episcopus unius civitatis que sclavonia vocat et dedit ei ista nomina sancta et dixit sibi quod quicumque homo ea devote recitaverit qualibet die cum quadraginta ave maria in ecclesia coram ymagine sua vel extra existens in via penitencie quos ipsa sibi ante mortem suam visibiliter appareret et in exitu vite sue eum confortaret et in regno filii sui heredem faceret. Ideo percepit episcopus quod ea nomina sancta clericis et plebi ostenderet. Et tu dic ad nomen quodlibet ave hoc modo . . ."

35. B. L. Stowe MS. 16, f. 128v. The full ten stanzas of *Omnibus consideratis* are printed in C. Blume and G. M. Dreves, *Analecta Hymnica Medii Aevi,* vol. 31 (Leipzig: Reisland, 1898), 87–88. Leroquais, *Livres d'Heures,* vol. 1, 247, lists this prayer in a fifteenth-century horae of Rouen usage; and in a late-fourteenth-century prayer book, vol. 1, 321. Neither book contains a rubric directing this prayer to an image.

36. Roger Chartier, *The Order of Books: Readers, Authors, and Libraries in Europe between the Fourteenth and Eighteenth Centuries,* trans. Lydia G. Cochrane (Stanford, Calif.: Stanford University Press, 1994), 1–3.

37. B. L. Stowe MS. 16, ff. 128v–130v.

38. Similar combinations of image and text can be found, for example, in B. L. Harley MS. 1251, ff. 23r–27v; B. L. Harley MS. 2982, f. 53r–54r; B. L. Arundel MS. 318, ff. 82r–85r.

39. On the cult of the five wounds, see Louis Gougaud, *Dévotions et Pratiques Ascétiques du Moyen Age* (Paris, 1925), 78–90; Simpson, "On the Measure of the Wound"; Douglas Gray, "The Five Wounds of Our Lord," *Notes and Queries* 208 (1963): 50–51; 82–89; 127–34; 163–68; R. W. Pfaff, *New Liturgical Feasts in Later Medieval England* (Oxford: Clarendon Press, 1970), 84–91; Duffy, *Stripping,* 238–48. Dodgson, "English Devotional Woodcuts," reproduces two woodcuts from Sheen Priory in which the bleeding feet, hands, and heart are heraldically displayed on a shield. John B. Friedman, *Northern English Books, Owners, and Makers in the Late Middle Ages* (Syracuse,

N.Y.: Syracuse University Press, 1995), 160–62, discusses the cult of the five wounds in northern English manuscripts.

40. London, B. L. Harley MS. 2869, ff. 217v–218v.

41. B. L. Harley MS. 1251, ff. 23r–27v.

42. London, B. L. Egerton MS. 1821. F. A. Gasquet discusses this book and translates some of its texts in "An English Rosary Book of the 15th Century," *Downside Review* XII (1893): 215–28.

43. Quoted in Mary C. Spalding, *The Middle English Charters of Christ* (Bryn Mawr, Penn.: Bryn Mawr College Monographs vol. 15, 1914), 26; and see also her comments on the metaphor of Christ's body as a legal deed and his wounds as the letters of the document; *The Pore Caitif*, 129. The late medieval fascination with Christ's wounds and the number of drops of blood he shed can be found in a variety of texts and images; see, for example, Thomas W. Ross's comments on the drops of blood in "Five Fifteenth-Century 'Emblem' Verses from Brit. Mus. Addit. MS. 37049," *Speculum* 32 (1957): 275; and also Vincent Gillespie, "Strange Images of Death: the Passion in Later Medieval English Devotional and Mystical Writing," in *Zeit, Tod und Ewigkeit in der Renaissance Literatur* Band 3, ed. J. Hogg (Salzburg: Institut für Anglistik und Amerikanistik, Universität Salzburg, 1987), 111–59.

44. *The Speculum Devotorum of an Anonymous Carthusian of Sheen*, edited from the Manuscripts Cambridge University Library Gg.I.6 and Foyle, with an Introduction and a glossary by James Hogg, 3 vols. (Salzburg: Institut für Englische Sprache und Literatur, Universität Salzburg, 1973–74).

45. *Middle English Sermons*, 94.

46. "The Dolerous Pyte of Crystes Passioun," in *Minor Poems of John Lydgate*, 250; and see Woolf, *English Religious Lyric*, 198–99.

47. See James H. Marrow, *Passion Iconography in Northern European Art of the Late Middle Ages and Early Renaissance* (Kortrijk:Van Ghemmert, 1979); and Ellen M. Ross, *The Grief of God: Images of the Suffering Jesus in Late Medieval England* (New York: Oxford University Press, 1997), 41–66.

48. The promise about the Gloria in B. L. Stowe MS. 16, f. 136r, says "Si discordia fuerit inter te et aliquem hominem dic istam orationem bona devocione et habebis pacem bonam et racionabilem." The preface to *Omnis virtus* in B. L. Harley MS. 2869, f. 203v, says, "Hyt is þer(?) founde in holy wrytThat þe dede seyde to þe quikTher nis noon so foul a holur Ne noon so gret a lechour ȝif he ofte sey þis orisoun of his synnis he schal have pardon." For identification of this prayer, see Ulysse Chevalier, *Repertorium Hymnologicum*, vol. 3 (Louvain, 1904), 461, #31302.

49. Books that contain this indulgence include B. L. Harley MS. 2869, f. 88v; B. L. Additional MS. 22720, f. 34v; B. L. Harley MS. 2846, f. 131r; B. L. Arundel MS. 318, ff. 88r-v; B. L. Additional MS. 33381, f. 98r; B. L. Harley MS. 2982, ff. 57v–58r. On the prayer see André Wilmart, *Auteurs Spirituels et Textes Dévots du Moyen Age Latin* (Paris: Études Augustiniennes, 1971), 378, n.10. Charles the Simple was king of the west Franks

during Boniface's VI's reign. More likely the indulgences refer to Boniface VIII and Philip IV, although Philip V of France (r.1316–1322), who received eleven letters of personal indulgence from Pope John XXII, could also be the source of the rubrics' "King Philip." See Matray, "Les Indulgences au XIVe Siècle," 138.

50. On indulgences, see Lea, *History of Auriculur Confession and Indulgences* vol. 3. Anne F. Sutton and Livia Visser-Fuchs, *The Hours of Richard III* (Wolfboro Falls: Alan Sutton, 1990), 52, includes the indulgence granted by Boniface VI. Chicago, Newberry Library MS. 83, a prayer book made for Anne of Brittany, contains several indulgenced prayers. Lewis, "Rewarding Devotion," discusses the origins and transmission of three indulgenced images in English manuscripts: the Veronica, the *Arma Christi,* and the Man of Sorrows in the Mass of St. Gregory.

51. One example is in B. L. Harley MS. 2869, f. 201r-v, which reads: "Beato gregorio missam celebrante dominus noster ihesus xpristus apparuit ei in tali effigie unde concessit omnibus qui talem figuram devote aspexerit ubicumque fuerit et genu flectando cum devocione dixerunt quinquies *Pater noster* et tociens *Ave Maria* quatuordecim milia annorum indulgencie. Et duodecim alii pape successores eius cuilibet eorum quingentos annos concesserunt. Et istud registratum in roma. Insuper Innocencius papa composuit subsequentem orationem et concessit omnibus eam devote dicentibus in honore tali effigiei xl dies indulgencie ubi hanc scripturam legis inspiciendo figuram."Variations of this rubric appear in B. L. Additional MS. 37787, f. 64v; B. L. Additional MS. 33381, f. 90r; a shortened English form is in B. L. Additional MS. 62105, f. 63r. Robert G. Calkins prints the rubric and illumination from B. L. Additional MS. 29433, f. 107v, in *Illuminated Books of the Middle Ages,* (Ithaca, N.Y.: Cornell University Press, 1983), plate 148, 269. The early printed primer here is *Hore beate marie secundum usum Sarum* (pro W. de Worde [in Westminster], 1497) *RSTC* 15884, f. 25r.

52. *Speculum Sacerdotale,* 112, and *Mirk's Festial,* 3. See also Mâle, *Religious Art in France: the Late Middle Ages,* 99–101.

53. B. L. Additional MS. 37787, f. 62v: "Quicumque intuetur hec arma domini nostri ihesu christi hic homo contritus et confessus haberet undecim milia dies indulgencie auctoritate beati petri apostoli primi." Later popes are said to grant further indulgences. Another example is in B. L. Additional MS. 33381, f. 177v. For this indulgence in two York Books of Hours, see T. F. Simmons, *The Lay Folks Mass Book* (London: EETS 71, 1879), 159–60. It appears in French books as well: Leroquais, *Livres d'Heures,* vol. 1, 322, lists a French horae promising 6,060 days of pardon "de par les papes de Rome." On the history of devotion to the *Arma Christi,* see Schiller, *Iconography,* vol. 2, 184–196.

54. *Hore beate marie, RSTC* 15884, f. 25r.

55. See Barbara A. Shailor, *The Medieval Book: Catalogue of an Exhibition at the Beinecke Rare Book & Manuscript Library Yale University* (New Haven, 1988), 85–87, for a picture of one such roll. Text and pictures of another, B. L. Addi-

tional MS. 22029 are printed in *Legends of the Holy Rood,* ed. Richard Morris (London: EETS 46, 1871), 171–193. See R. H. Robbins, "The 'Arma Christi' Rolls," *Modern Language Review* 34 (1939): 415–21. Friedman discusses a northern English roll in *Northern English Books,* 167. Beatrice Milreth, widow of a London mercer, left to her sister in 1448 "a roll of the passion of Our Lord Jesus Christ and of the letters of Nichodemus in French" and a "roll of fifteen 'Gaudes beate Marie'"; see Cavanaugh, "A Study of Books," 585–86.

56. H. G. St. M. Rees, *An Illustrated History of Mildenhall, Suffolk and Its Parish Church of the Blessed Virgin Mary* (Gloucester, n.d.); John Agate, *Benches and Stalls in Suffolk Churches* ([Suffolk]: Suffolk Historic Churches Trust, 1980), figure 27. Photographs of the carved symbols at Fressingfield and at other churches are in Edward G. Tasker, *Encyclopedia of Medieval Church Art,* ed. John Beaumont (London: Batsford, 1993), 187–89.

57. *Hore intemerate beatissime virginis secundum usum Sarum* (Paris?: P. Pigouchet, 1495) *RSTC* 15880, 74r.

58. *Legends of the Holy Rood,* 171–93.

59. On the Veronica tradition, see Freedberg, *Power of Images,* 207–209, and Lewis, "The Veronica: Image, Legend and Viewer." The English book London, B. L. Royal MS. 17 A. XXVII, f. 80v, promises 40 days of pardon "for syʒt of þe vernacul." A French Book of Hours, Paris, B. N. MS. Lat. 10528, ff. 238v–239r, claims that it was St. Gregory who granted 300 days of pardon for seeing "la Véronique" and 100 days for saying the prayer; see Leroquais, *Les Livres d'Heures,* vol. 1, 323.

60. *Legends of the Holy Rood,* 170–72; a depiction of the Veronica precedes this prayer.

61. B. L. Additional MS. 22720, f. 31r–v.

62. *Hore beatissime Virginis Marie* ([P. Pigouchet?], imp. F. bryckman, 1519) *RSTC* 15923, f. lxxi verso; and *Hore beate marie virginis ad vsum Sarum* (Antwerp: C. Endouien [Ruremund], 1525) *RSTC* 15939, f. lxxxiiii. For the prayer, see Guido M. Dreves, *Ein Jahrtausend Lateinischer Hymnendichtung,* vol. 2 (Leipzig: O. R. Reisland, 1909), 74; and for an English translation, Friedman, *Northern English Books,* 157–58.

63. The prayer to the parts of the Virgin's body is in B. L. Additional MS. 37787, ff. 80r–81r. The second indulgenced prayer to say before the image of the Virgin is on f. 170v. Ringbom, *Icon to Narrative,* 21 & 48–49, discusses the history of the devotion to the Virgin's limbs. For *Ave regina celorum,* see Chevalier, *Repertorium Hymnologicum,* vol. 1, 122, #2070.

64. London, B. L. Additional MS. 35313, f. 237r. The Latin rubric reads "Papa Sixtus concessit dicentibus hanc orationem ante ymaginem marie virginis in sole xi milia annorum indulgenciam." See Sixten Ringbom, "*Maria in Sole* and the Virgin of the Rosary," *Journal of the Warburg and Courtauld Institutes* 25:3–4 (1962): 326–30, on the connection of this image to the propagation of the doctrine of the Immaculate Conception. On fifteenth-century Flemish books in England, see J. J. G. Alexander, "Foreign illuminators and illuminated manuscripts," in *Cambridge History of the Book,* 47–64.

65. For the 1506 primer see Hoskins, *Horae,* 123; the 1519 primer is *Hore beatissime virginis Marie, RSTC* 15923, f. xliv verso. The rubric is also in *Hore beate marie virginis secundum vsum Sarum* (Antwerp: C. Ruremund for P. Kaetz in London, 1523) *RSTC* 15935, f. G.v.

66. *Hore beatissime virginis Marie* (Paris: F. Regnault, 1527), *RSTC* 15952, f. xciii. This rubric also occurs in a 1519 primer, *RSTC* 15923, f. lxxxiiii; and in the 1525 primer *RSTC* 15939, ff. xcvi–xcvii. A similar image from a French Book of Hours is printed in *Interpreting Cultural Symbols: Saint Anne in Late Medieval Society,* ed. Kathleen Ashley and Pamela Sheingorn (Athens, Georgia: University of Georgia Press, 1990), 79.

67. Francis Oakley, *The Western Church in the Later Middle Ages* (Ithaca: Cornell University Press, 1979), 88–89. On the development of the ritual of the elevation of the Host and the subsequent emphasis on seeing it, see Rubin, *Corpus Christi,* 55–64.

68. B. L. Additional MS. 33381, f. 151r–v.

69. B. L. Additional MS. 22720, ff. 28v–29r & 20r; a similar indulgence is in B. L. Additional MS. 37787, f. 67v. For the prayer *Ave principium nostre creacionis,* see Chevalier, *Repertorium Hymnologicum,* vol. 1, 121–22, # 2059.

70. *RSTC* 15923, ff. lxv verso–lxvi; *RSTC* 15939, ff. lxxviii verso–lxxix.

71. Rubin, *Corpus Christ,* 63.

72. B. L. Harley MS. 2869, ff. 95v–97v. Duffy, *Stripping,* 272–73, discusses similar rubrics in early printed primers.

73. *RSTC* 15923, ff. xl verso–xli.

74. B. L. Additional MS. 37787, f. 62v; my translation. This rubric is unfinished as the following page has been ripped out.

75. *Legends of the Holy Rood,* 195–96.

76. Duffy, *Stripping,* 278.

77. *Book of Margery Kempe,* 30.

78. Curt F. Bühler, "Prayers and Charms in Certain Middle English Scrolls," *Speculum* 39 (1964): 270–78; Simpson, "On the Measure of the Wound," 357–59; Louis Gougaud, "La Prière dite le Charlemagne," *Revue d'histoire ecclésiastique* XX (1924): 223–27; Gray, "Five Wounds," 88; "Images et Imagerie de Piété," *DS,* vol. 7, pt. 2, col. 1533, prints some of these indulgences.

79. Douglas Gray, "Notes on Some Middle English Charms," in *Chaucer and Middle English Studies in Honour of Rossell Hope Robbins,* ed. Beryl Rowland (London: Allen & Unwin), 59.

80. Gibson, *Theater of Devotion,* 64.

81. Lynn Thorndike, *A History of Magic and Experimental Science,* vol. 3 (New York: Columbia University Press, 1934), gives several examples: on wax images in sorcery, see 18–21; on various images in healing, 86, 588–89. See also "Image/Picture" in *A Dictionary of Superstitions,* ed. Iona Opie and Moira Tatem (Oxford: Oxford University Press, 1989), 207–8; and Richard Kieckhefer, *Magic in the Middle Ages* (Cambridge: CUP, 1989), 60. Hilary Carey "Astrology at the English Court in the Later Middle Ages," in *As-*

trology, Science and Society, ed. Patrick Curry (Woodbridge: Boydell, 1987), 41–56, provides a thoughtful analysis of attitudes toward astrology in the fifteenth century and quotes a contemporary description of the notorious Roger Bolingbroke with the "vestments and waxen images" of his magic.

82. London, B. L. Royal MS. 6 E VI, f. 15r.

83. See Gillespie, "Vernacular Books of Religion." Hilary M. Carey, "Devout Literate Laypeople and the Pursuit of the Mixed Life in Later Medieval England," *Journal of Religious History* 14:4 (1987): 361–81, discusses religious works read by the laity. Moran, *Growth of English Schooling,* 185–220, cites examples of several kinds of liturgical, devotional, and other books that passed between clerics and laity.

84. Deanesly, "Vernacular Books," 352–56, shows ownership of works by Love, Hilton, and Rolle, among others. See also Vincent Gillespie, "*Lukynge in haly bukes: Lectio* in Some Late Medieval Spiritual Miscellanies," in *Spätmittelalterliche Geistliche Literatur,* Band 2, 16–17.

85. Sargent, "Bonaventura English," 164–167.

86. Cavanaugh, "A Study of Books," 49, 226, 404, 491–2.

87. *Testamenta Eboracensia,* vol. 4, 96–97; *Testamenta Vetusta,* 367, 142; *Wills and Inventories of the Northern Counties of England,* Part I (London: Surtees Society, 1835), 76; *Wills and Inventories from the Registers of the Commissary of Bury St. Edmund's and the Archdeacon of Sudbury,* ed. Samuel Tymms (London: Camden Society, vol. 49, 1850) 35; *Testamenta Eboracensia,* vol. 4, 11.

88. Cavanaugh, "Study of Books," 138, 578, 618, 723–24.

89. B. L. Additional MS 37787; *A Worcestershire Miscellany compiled by John Northwood, c. 1400,* ed. Nita Scudder Baugh (Philadelphia, 1956), prints the English texts, and discusses the evidence for ownership, 15–16; for the Hours of the Cross, see 98–100. Rubrics on the vision of the Virgin are on f.170v; on the Man of Sorrows on f. 64v; the *Arma Christi* on f. 62v.

90. B. L. Additional MS. 33381. See Wilmart, *Auteurs Spirituels,* 553. Evidence for the Ely association includes a list of anniversaries of bishops and priors to be observed at Ely, f. 12. The picture of the bloody Christ is on f. 89v; the rubric faces it on 90r; the *Arma Christi* rubric is on f. 177v.

91. B. L. Royal MS. 6 E.VI, f. 15r.

92. Helen C. White, *The Tudor Books of Private Devotion* (Madison: University of Wisconsin Press, 1951); see especially, "The Primer as an Instrument of Religious Change," 87–102.

93. London, B. L. Additional MS. 27592, f. 42v.

94. The directions and most of the meditations are printed in Gasquet, "An English Rosary Book."

95. *The prymer with the pystles and gospels in Englysshe* (London: John Byddell 1535) *RSTC* 15997.5 (formerly 15990), 97–98.

96. *A goodly prymer in englyshe, newly corrected* (London: John Byddell, 1535) *RSTC* 15988 Ai. William Marshall was a reformer whose version of the primer was printed by Bydell three times; see Birchenough, "Prymer in English," 182–85; and Charles C. Butterworth, *The English Primers (1529–1545)*

(Philadelphia: University of Pennsylvania Press, 1953), 104–17. Rubrics that tell the reader to pray before "our lady of pity" are in MS. Magdalen Cam. 13, discussed by Woolf, *English Religious Lyric,* 394; and a 1494 Wynkyn de Worde primer, listed by Hoskins, *Horae,* 111.

97. *The primer in English and Latin* (London, ca. 1541) *RSTC* 16021.5 The St. Bridget rubric is on f. lvii; the image rubric is on f. cxxxvi verso. The Latin rubric "oratio ad imaginem corporis christi" introducing the prayer *Conditor celi & terre rex regum et dominus dominantium* is also in two books printed by F. Regnault in Paris with the same title, *This Prymer of Salysbury vse* (1527) *RSTC* 15955, f. cxxxvi verso and (1531) *RSTC* 15970, f. cxcix verso.

98. *RSTC* 15923, f. Lxxi verso.

99. On women's literacy, see above, introduction, n. 14, and chapter 3, n. 40.

100. Paul Saenger, for instance, discusses the objections of early Protestants to what they perceived as "rote vocal repetition of Latin prayer," in "Books of Hours," 260.

Conclusion

1. Thomas More, *A Dialogue Concerning Heresies,* vol. 6, pt. 1 of *The Complete Works of Thomas More,* ed. Thomas M. C. Lawler, et al. (New Haven: Yale University Press, 1981), 38, 45, 141–42.

2. More, *Dialogue,* 39.

3. More, *Dialogue,* 46–47; and on images as books of the laity, 359.

4. More, *Dialogue,* 45; and see also 357–59.

5. More, *Dialogue,* 207–10.

6. Oxford, Bodleian Library, MS. Bodley 119, f. 1v.

7. R. L. Storey, "Ecclesiastical Causes in Chancery," in *The Study of Medieval Records: Essays in Honour of Kathleen Major,* ed. D. A. Bullough and R. L. Storey (Oxford: Clarendon Press, 1971), 242.

8. John Myrc, *Instructions for Parish Priests,* ed. Edward Peacock (London: EETS 31, 1868), 10–11.

9. More, *Dialogue,* 52.

10. More, *Dialogue,* 56.

11. More, *Dialogue,* 237.

12. *Visitation Articles and Injunctions of the Period of the Reformation,* ed. W. H. Frere and W. M. Kennedy, vol. II (London: Longmans, Green, & Co., 1910), 34–43. Eamon Duffy, *The Stripping of the Altars: Traditional Religion in England c.1400–c.1580* (New Haven: Yale University Press, 1992), 406–07; Margaret Aston, *England's Iconoclasts* vol. 1 *Laws Against Images* (Oxford: Clarendon Press, 1988), 227–30.

13. *Statutes of the Realm* vol. IV, pt. 1 (London, 1819; reprint ed., Dawsons, 1963), 111. On the iconoclastic policy of Edward VI, see Aston, *England's Iconoclasts,* vol. 1, 246–77; and John Phillips, *The Reformation of Images: De-*

struction of Art in England 1535–1660 (Berkeley: University of California Press, 1973), 82–100.

14. H. Munro Cautley, *Suffolk Churches and Their Treasures* 4th rev. ed. (Ipswich: Boydell, 1975), 28.

15. David Dymond and Clive Paine, *The Spoil of Melford Church* (Ipswich: Salient Press, 1989), 40.

16. John P. Boileau, "Returns of Church Goods in the Churches of the City of Norwich," *NA* 4 (1864): 364, 373. See also Elaine M. Sheppard, "The Reformation and the Citizens of Norwich," 38 *NA* (1981): 46, on the removal of images.

17. Tessa Watt, *Cheap Print and Popular Piety 1550–1640* (Cambridge: CUP, 1991), 131–77, argues that not all medieval religious images disappeared under the impact of sixteenth-century iconoclasm.

PLATE INFORMATION

I.1   Worship of the Golden Calf   2
Det Kongelige Bibliotek, Gl. Kgl. S. 1605, f. 20 recto
By permission of the Manuscript Department,
The Royal Library, Copenhagen

1.1   Demon flees idol at the approach of St. Philip   18
The Pierpont Morgan Library, New York, H. 8, f. 177
By permission of The Pierpont Morgan Library

3.1   Alabaster of St. Eloy   79
Victoria & Albert Museum
Courtesy of the V&A Picture Library

3.2   Alabaster of St. Michael the Archangel   80
Victoria & Albert Museum
Courtesy of the V&A Picture Library

3.3   Alabaster of the Trinity   82
Victoria & Albert Museum
Courtesy of the V&A Picture Library

3.4   Statue of St. Catherine   83
Meester van Koudewater, ca. 1470
Courtesy of the Rijksmuseum Amsterdam

3.5   Statue of St. Sebastian   85
Mechelen, ca. 1520–1525
Courtesy of the Rijksmuseum Amsterdam

6.1   A Prayer "Ad imaginem crucifixi"   163
British Library Stowe MS. 16, f. 128 verso
By permission of the British Library

6.2   Prayers and images of the wounds of Christ   165
British Library Arundel MS. 318, f. 82 verso
By permission of the British Library

6.3   St. Gregory's vision of the Man of Sorrows   170
British Library C 35. h.2, f. lxii verso-lxiii recto
By permission of the British Library

6.4   The Man of Sorrows and the indulgence of St. Gregory   171
British Library Additional MS. 33381, ff. 89 verso–90 recto
By permission of the British Library

6.5   The *Pietà* with a border of the *Arma Christi* and indulgence   174
      Folio 1 verso from MS. Rawlinson D 403
      By permission of the Bodleian Library, University of Oxford

6.6   Pope Sixtus prays before an image of Maria "in sole"   176
      British Library Additional MS. 35313, f. 237 recto
      By permission of the British Library

6.7   The image of Our Lady in the Sun, with indulgence   177
      Folio 44 verso from Douce BB 141 (1)
      By permission of the Bodleian Library, University of Oxford

6.8   The Image of St. Anne, Mary, and Jesus with indulgences   178
      Hore beatissime virginis Marie. Paris, 1527. ff. xcii verso–xciii recto
      This item is reproduced by permission of
      The Huntington Library, San Marino, California.

6.9   The *Arma Christi* with indulgence and prayer of protection   185
      British Library Royal MS. 6 E VI, f. 15 recto
      By permission of the British Library

BIBLIOGRAPHY

Manuscript Sources

Bury St. Edmunds, Suffolk Record Office
    IC 500/2/9–13   Archdeaconry of Sudbury Will Registers
    EL 110/5/1–3   Mildenhall Churchwardens' Accounts
Chicago, Newberry Library
    MS. 83
Copenhagen, Kongelige Bibliotek
    Gl. Kgl. S. 1605
Ipswich, Suffolk Record Office
    IC/AA2/1–3   Archdeaconry of Suffolk Will Registers 1–3
    FC 89/A2/1   Brundish Town Book and Churchwardens' Accounts
London, British Library
    Additional MS. 22720
    Additional MS. 27592
    Additional MS. 27948
    Additional MS. 33381
    Additional MS. 35313
    Additional MS. 37787
    Additional MS. 62105
    Arundel MS. 318
    Egerton MS. 1821
    Harley MS. 1251
    Harley MS. 1260
    Harley MS. 2398
    Harley MS. 2846
    Harley MS. 2869
    Harley MS. 2982
    Royal MS. 6 E VI
    Royal MS. 6 E VII
    Royal MS. 17 A XXVII
    Stowe MS. 16
London, Public Record Office
    C 47/42–46   Suffolk and Norfolk gild certificates

DL 38/6   Certificates of Colleges and Chantries *temp.* Henry VIII
                     and Edward VI
E. 301/45 & 55   Certificates of Colleges and Chantries in Norfolk and
                     Suffolk, *temp.* Henry VIII and Edward VI
New York, Pierpont Morgan Library
    MS. H. 8
Norwich, Norfolk Record Office
    Archdeaconry of Norfolk Will Registers Grey, Liber 1, Shaw
    Archdeaconry of Norwich Will Register Fuller or Roper
    MS 9712, 8F2   Agreement concerning Cachecrost estate
Norwich Consistory Court Will Registers Heydon (1370–83) to Jekkys
    PD 24/2   Snettisham Churchwardens' Accounts
    PD 52/71   Swaffham Churchwardens' Accounts
    PD 52/233   Records of Gild of St. John, Swaffham
    PD 52/473   The Black Book of Swaffham (photocopy)
    PD 136/56   Denton Churchwardens' Accounts
    PD 337/85   Shipdam Churchwardens' Accounts
    Phi 461/1–9   East Dereham Churchwardens' Accounts
    Phi 580   Declaration by Henry Playford
    Phi 607/1–7   East Dereham Churchwardens' Accounts
Oxford, Bodleian Library
    MS. Bodley 119

Published Primary Sources

Acta Sanctorum quotquot toto orbe coluntur. Begun by Joannes Bollandus. Vol. 1-
    Antwerp, 1643-; Reprint ed. Bruxelles, 1965-

An Alphabet of Tales. Ed. Mary M. Banks. 2 vols. London: EETS 126–127,
    1904–1905.

Angela of Foligno. *Le Livre de l'expérience des vrais fidèles.* Eds. and trans. M.-J. Ferré
    and L. Baudry. Paris: Editions E. Droz, 1927.

———. *Angela of Foligno: Complete Works.* Trans. Paul Lachance. New York: Paulist
    Press, 1993.

An Apology for Lollard Doctrines, attributed to Wicliffe. London: Camden Society vol.
    20, 1842.

Aquinas, Thomas. *Summa Theologiae.* 61 vols. New York: Blackfriars in conjunction
    with McGraw-Hill, 1964–1981.

Archdeaconry of Norwich. Inventory of Church Goods. temp. *Edward III.* Transcribed
    by Aelred Watkin. Norfolk Record Society, vol. 19, part 2, 1948.

Augustine. *The City of God.* Trans. Henry Bettenson. Harmondsworth: Penguin, 1972.

Bokenham, Osbern. *Legendys of Hooly Wummen.* Ed. Mary S. Serjeantson. London:
    EETS 206, 1938.

Book of Vices and Virtues. Ed. W. N. Francis. London: EETS 217, 1942.

Brown, Carleton, ed. *Religious Lyrics of the XVth Century.* Oxford: Clarendon Press,
    1939.

Calendar of Inquisitions Miscellaneous (Chancery). 7 vols. London: HMSO, 1916–1968.

Calendar of the Patent Rolls. Edward II, 5 vols.; Edward III, 16 vols. London, HMSO, 1893–1916.

Capgrave, John. *Abbreuiacion of Cronicles.* Ed. Peter J. Lucas. London: EETS 285, 1983.

———. *The Life of St. Katharine of Alexandria.* Ed. Carl Horstmann. London: EETS 100, 1893.

Carpenter, Alexander. *Destructorium Viciorum.* Paris, 1521.

Chaucer's Major Poetry. Ed. Albert C. Baugh. New York: Meredith, 1963.

Chronica Monasterii de Melsa. Ed. Edward A. Bond. 3 vols. Rolls Series. London, 1866–68.

Cicero. *De Oratore.* Trans. E. W. Sutton. Cambridge: Harvard University Press, 1942.

The Coasts of the Country: an Anthology of Prayer drawn from the Early English Spiritual Writers. Ed. Claire Kirchberger. Chicago: Henry Regnery, n.d.

The Commonplace Book of Robert Reynes of Acle: An Edition of Tanner MS 407. Ed. Cameron Louis. New York: Garland, 1980.

Dives and Pauper. Vol. 1, part 1. Ed. Priscilla Heath Barnum. London: EETS 275, 1976.

The Doctrinal of Sapience, ed. from Caxton's printed edition, 1489. Ed. Joseph Gallagher. Heidelberg: Winter, 1993.

Dymmok, Roger. *Rogeri Dymmock liber contra xii errores et hereses lollardum.* Ed. H. S. Cronin. London: Wyclif Society, 1922.

Early South English Legendary. Ed. Carl Horstmann. London: EETS 87, 1887.

English Gilds. Ed. Toulmin Smith. Introduction and glossary by Lucy Toulmin Smith; essay by Lujo Brentano. London: EETS 40, 1870; Reprint, 1963.

An Episcopal Court Book for the Diocese of Lincoln 1514–1520. Ed. Margaret Bowker. Lincoln Record Society, 1967.

Fasciculi Zizaniorum Magistri Johannis Wyclif Cum Tritico. Ed. W. W. Shirley. Rolls Series. London: Longman, 1858.

Fasciculus Morum: A Fourteenth-Century Preacher's Handbook. Ed. and trans. Siegfried Wenzel. University Park: Pennsylvania State University Press, 1989.

The Fyve Wittes: A Late Middle English Devotional Treatise. Ed. R. H. Bremmer. Amsterdam: Rodopi, 1987.

A Goodly prymer in englyshe, newly corrected and printed. London: John Byddell for William Marshall, 1535. *RSTC* 15988

Gregory the Great. "Epistola XIII ad Serenum Massiliensem Episcopum." *PL* vol. 77, col. 1128.

Hall, Edward. *Hall's Chronicle.* London, 1809.

Henrici VI Angliae Regis Miracula Postuma. Ed. Paulus Grosjean. Bruxelles: Société des Bollandistes, 1935.

Henry, Avril. *Biblia Pauperum: a facsimile and edition.* Ithaca, N.Y.: Cornell University Press, 1987.

Hilton, Walter. *Walter Hilton's Latin Writings.* 2 vols. Eds. John P. H. Clark and Cheryl Taylor. Salzburg: Institut für Anglistik und Amerikanistk, Universität Salzburg, 1987.

Hoccleve, Thomas. *Hoccleve's Works,* vol. 1 *The Minor Poems.* Ed. Frederick J. Furnivall. London: EETS e.s. 61, 1892.

Holland, William. *Cratfield: A Transcript of the Accounts of the Parish.* Ed. J. J. Raven. London: Jarrold & Sons, [1895?].

Hore beate marie secundum usum Sarum. Pro W. de Worde [Westminster] 1497. *RSTC* 15884.

Hore beate marie virginis ad vsum Sarum. Antwerp: C. Endouien [Ruremund], 1525. *RSTC* 15939.

Hore beate marie virginis secundum vsum Sarum. Antwerp, C. Ruremund for P. Kaetz in London, 1523. *RSTC* 15935.

Hore beatissime Virginis marie. Paris: F. Regnault, 1534. *RSTC* 15984.

Hore beatissime virginis Marie. Paris: F. Regnault, 1527. *RSTC* 15952.

Hore beatissime Virginis Marie. [P. Pigouchet?] imp. F. bryckman, 1519. *RSTC* 15923.

Hore intemerate beatissime virginis secundum vsum Sarum. Paris?: P. Pigouchet 1495. *RSTC* 15880.

Horrox, Rosemary, ed. and trans. *The Black Death.* Manchester: Manchester University Press, 1994.

Horstman, C., ed. *Yorkshire Writers.* 2 vols. London: Swan Sonnenschein & Co., 1895–96.

Horstmann, K. "Orologium Sapientiae or The Seven Poyntes of Trewe Wisdom aus MS. Douce 114." *Anglia* 10 (1888): 323–89.

Hudson, Anne, ed. *Selections from English Wycliffite Writings.* Cambridge: CUP, 1978.

Jacob's Well. Ed. Arthur Brandeis. London: EETS 115, 1900.

Jacobus de Voragine. *The Golden Legend.* Trans. William Granger Ryan. 2 vols. Princeton, N. J.: Princeton University Press, 1993.

Jacques de Vitry. *Life of Marie D'Oignies.* Trans. Margot H. King. Toronto: Peregrina, 1993.

John of Damascus. *On the Divine Images.* Trans. David Anderson. Crestwood, N.Y.: St. Vladimir's Seminary Press, 1980.

Julian of Norwich. *A Book of Showings to the Anchoress Julian of Norwich.* 2 vols. Eds. Edmund Colledge and James Walsh. Toronto: Pontifical Institute of Mediaeval Studies, 1978.

Justin Martyr. *The First and Second Apologies.* Trans. L. W. Barnard. New York: Paulist Press, 1997.

Kempe, Margery. *The Book of Margery Kempe.* Ed. Sanford Brown Meech. Oxford: EETS 212, 1940.

Knighton's Chronicle 1337–1396. Ed. and trans. G. H. Martin. Oxford: Clarendon Press, 1995.

Lancaster, W. T. *Abstracts of the Charters and Other Documents contained in the Chartulary of the Priory of Bridlington.* Leeds, 1912.

Lanterne of Liȝt. Ed. Lilian M. Swinburn. London: EETS 151, 1917.

The Lay Folks Mass Book. Ed. Thomas F. Simmons. London: EETS 71, 1879.

A Legend of Holy Women: A Translation of Osbern Bokenham's Legends of Holy Women. Trans. and ed. Sheila Delany. Notre Dame, Ind.: University of Notre Dame Press, 1992.

Legends of the Holy Rood. Ed. Richard Morris. London: EETS 46, 1871.

Il Libro della Beata Angela da Foligno. 2nd ed. Ed. L. Thier and A. Calufetti. Grottaferrata, Rome: Collegii S. Bonaventurae ad Claras Aquas, 1985.

Life of St. Anne. Ed. R. E. Parker. London: EETS 174, 1928.

Lollard Sermons. Ed. Gloria Cigman. London: EETS 294, 1989.

Lydgate, John. *The Minor Poems of John Lydgate.* Ed. Henry Noble MacCracken.
London: EETS e.s. 107, 1911 (for 1910).

Mango, Cyril. *Art of the Byzantine Empire 312–1453: Sources and Documents.* Englewood Cliffs, N. J.: Prentice-Hall, 1972.

Mannyng, Robert, of Brunne. *Handlyng Synne.* Ed. Idelle Sullens. Binghamton, N.
Y.: Medieval and Renaissance Texts and Studies 14, 1983.

Marshall, William. *A Goodly prymer in englyshe, newly corrected.* J. Byddell, 1535.
RSTC 15988.

McNeill, John T. and Helena M. Gamer. *Medieval Handbooks of Penance.* New York:
Columbia University Press, c. 1938.

Middle English Sermons. Ed. W. O. Ross. London: EETS 209, 1940.

Minor Poems of the Vernon Ms. Ed. Carl Horstmann. London: EETS 98, 1892.

Minucius Felix. *Octavius.* Trans. Gerald H. Rendall.1931. Reprint, Cambridge:
Harvard University Press, 1977.

The Miracles of King Henry VI. Eds. Ronald Knox and Shane Leslie. Cambridge:
CUP, 1923.

The Mirour of Mans Saluacioun: a Middle English translation of Speculum Humanae
Salvationis. Ed. Avril Henry. Aldershot: Scolar Press, 1986.

More, Thomas. *A Dialogue Concerning Heresies,* vol. 6 in *The Complete Works of St.
Thomas More.* Eds. Thomas M. C. Lawler, Germain Marc'hadour, Richard C.
Marius. New Haven: Yale University Press, 1981.

The Myracles of Oure Lady. Ed. Peter Whiteford. Heidelberg: Winter, 1990.

Myrc, John. *Instructions for Parish Priests.* Ed. Edward Peacock. London: EETS 31, 1868.
———. *Mirk's Festial.* Ed. T. Erbe. London: EETS e.s. 96, 1905.

A Myrour to Lewde Men and Wymmen: a prose version of the Speculum Vitae. Ed. Venetia Nelson. Heidelberg: Winter, 1981.

Nicholas Love's Mirror of the Blessed Life of Jesus Christ. Ed. with introduction by
Michael G. Sargent. New York: Garland, 1992.

Nicolas, N. H. *Testamenta Vetusta.* London: Nichols & Son, 1826.

Norwich Consistory Court Depositions, 1499–1512 and 1518–1530. Calendared by
E. D. Stone, rev. by B. Cozens-Hardy. Norfolk Record Society vol. 10, 1938.

Nova Legenda Anglie. Ed. Carl Horstmann. 2 vols. Oxford: Clarendon Press, 1901.

Paston Letters and Papers of the Fifteenth Century. Ed. Norman Davies. 2 vols. Oxford:
Clarendon Press, 1971 & 1976.

Pecock, Reginald. *The Repressor of Over Much Blaming of the Clergy.* 2 vols. Ed.
Churchill Babington. Rolls Series. London, 1860.

Peter of Limoges. *De Oculo Morali.* Viterbo, 1655.

The Pomander of Prayer. London: Robert Redman, 1531. *RSTC* 25421.5.

The Pore Caitif. Ed. Mary Teresa Brady. Ph.D. Dissertation, Fordham University,
1954.

Powicke, F. M. and C. R. Cheney. *Councils and Synods with other Documents Relating to the English Church*. vol. 2. Oxford: Clarendon Press, 1964.

The Primer in English and Latin. London, ca. 1541. *RSTC* 16021.5.

The Prymer or Lay Folks' Prayer Book. Ed. Henry Littlehales. Part II London: EETS 109, 1897.

The prymer with the pystles and gospels in Englysshe. London: John Byddell, 1535. *RSTC* 15997.5. (formerly 15990)

Quattuor Sermones: Printed by William Caxton. Ed. N. F. Blake. Heidelberg: Winter, 1975.

Records of the Gild of St. George in Norwich, 1389–1547. Transcript with an introduction by Mary Grace. London: Norfolk Record Society, vol. 9, 1937.

Register of Bishop Philip Repingdom 1405–19. 3 vols. Ed. Margaret Archer. Hereford: Lincoln Record Society, 1963–82.

Register of Robert Hallum, Bishop of Salisbury 1407–17. Ed. Joyce M. Horn. CYS, vol. 72. Torquay: Devonshire Press, 1982.

Register of Thomas Langton, Bishop of Salisbury 1485–93. Ed. D. P. Wright. CYS, vol. 74. [Privately printed], 1985.

Register of William Greenfield, parts III and V. Ed. W. Brown and A. Hamilton Thompson. London: Surtees Society, vols. 151 and 153, 1936, 1940.

Rolle, Richard. *Richard Rolle: The English Writings*. Trans. and ed. R. S. Allen. New York: Paulist Press, 1988.

A Select Library of the Nicene and Post-Nicene Fathers of the Christian Church. Vol. 14. Ed. P. Schaff. New York: Scribner's, 1889.

Speculum Christiani. Ed. Gustaf Holmstedt. London: EETS 182, 1933.

The Speculum Devotorum of an Anonymous Carthusian of Sheen. 3 vols. Ed. with Intro. by James Hogg. Salzburg: Institut für Englische Sprache und Literatur, Universität Salzburg, 1973–74.

Speculum Sacerdotale. Ed. Edward H. Weatherly. London: EETS 200, 1936.

Stallard, A. D. *The Transcript of the Churchwardens' Accounts of the Parish of Tilney All Saints, Norfolk 1443–1589*. London: Mitchell Hughes and Clarke, 1922.

Statutes of the Realm. 11 vols. London, 1819; reprint by Dawsons of Pall Mall, 1963.

Suso, Henry. *The Exemplar, with Two German Sermons*. Trans. and ed. Frank Tobin. New York: Paulist Press, 1989.

Tanner, Norman P., ed. *Heresy Trials in the Diocese of Norwich, 1428–31*. Camden Fourth Series vol. 20. London: Royal Historical Society, 1977.

Tertullianus. *De Idololatria*. Critical text, translation and commentary by J. H. Waszink and J. C. M. Van Winden. Leiden: Brill, 1987.

Testamenta Eboracensia. Vol. IV. London: Surtees Society, 1869.

This prymer of Salysbury vse. Paris: F. Regnault, 1527. *RSTC* 15955.

This Prymer of Salysbury vse. Paris: F. Regnault, 1531. *RSTC* 15970.

The Tretyse of Love. Ed. John H. Fisher. London: EETS 223, 1951.

The Tripartite Life of Patrick. Ed. and trans. Whitley Stokes. Rolls Series. London, 1887.

Valor Ecclesiasticus Temp. Henr. VIII. 6 vols. London, 1810–34.

Visitation Articles and Injunctions of the Period of the Reformation. Eds. W. H. Frere and W. M. Kennedy. London: Longmans, Green, 1908–10.

Visitations of Religious Houses in the Diocese of Lincoln. vol. III. *Records of Visitations held by William Alnwick Bishop of Lincoln 1436–1449,* part II. Ed. A. Hamilton Thompson. Lincoln Record Society, 1929.

Von Nolken, Christina. *The Middle English Translation of the Rosarium Theologie.* Heidelberg: Winter 1979.

Walberswick Churchwardens' Accounts A. D. 1450–1499. Transcribed by R. W. M. Lewis. London, 1947.

Wilkins, David, ed. *Concilia Magnae Britanniae et Hiberniae.* 4 vols. London: Gosling, 1737.

Wills and Inventories from the Registers of the Commissary of Bury St. Edmund's and the Archdeacon of Sudbury. Ed. Samuel Tymms. London: Camden Society, vol. 49, 1850.

Wills and Inventories of the Northern Counties of England. Part I. London: Surtees Society, 1835.

A Worcestershire Miscellany compiled by John Northwood, c. 1400. Ed. Nita Scudder Baugh. Philadelphia, 1956.

Wycliffe, John. *Tractatus De Mandatis Divinis.* Ed. Johann Loserth and F. D. Matthew. London: Wyclif Society, 1922; reprint New York & London: Johnson Reprint, 1966.

———. *Sermones.* Vol. 1 Ed. Johann Loserth. London: Wyclif Society, 1887.

Secondary Works

Aers, David and Lynn Staley. *The Powers of the Holy: Religion, Politics, and Gender in Late Medieval English Culture.* University Park: The Pennsylvania State University Press, 1996.

Agate, John. *Benches and Stalls in Suffolk Churches.* [Suffolk]: Suffolk Historic Churches Trust, 1980.

Alexander, J. J. G. "Foreign Illuminators and Illuminated Manuscripts." In *The Cambridge History of the Book in Britain,* vol. III, eds. Lotte Hellinga and J. B. Trapp, 47–64. Cambridge: CUP, 1999.

Alexander, Paul J. *The Patriarch Nicephorus of Constantinople.* Oxford: Clarendon Press, 1958.

Allchin, A.M. "Julian of Norwich and the Continuity of Tradition." In *The Medieval Mystical Tradition in England,* ed. Marion Glasscoe, 72–85. [Exeter]: University of Exeter, 1980.

André-Vincent, Ignace. "Pour une théologie de l'image." *Revue Thomiste* 59 (1959): 320–338.

Ariès, Philippe. *The Hour of Our Death.* Trans. Helen Weaver. New York: Knopf, 1981.

Ashley, Kathleen and Pamela Sheingorn, eds. *Interpreting Cultural Symbols: Saint Anne in Late Medieval Society.* Athens, Georgia.: University of Georgia Press, 1990.

Astell, Ann W. "Introduction" to *Lay Sanctity, Medieval and Modern: A Search for Models,* ed. Ann W. Astell, 1–26. Notre Dame, Ind.: University of Notre Dame Press, 2000.

Aston, Margaret. "Death." In *Fifteenth-Century Attitudes: Perceptions of Society in Late Medieval England,* ed. Rosemary Horrox, 202–28. Cambridge: CUP, 1994.

———. *England's Iconoclasts.* Volume 1: *Laws Against Images.* Oxford: Clarendon Press, 1988.

———. *Faith and Fire: Popular and Unpopular Religion 1350–1600.* London: Hambledon Press, 1993.

———. "Gold and Images." In *The Church and Wealth,* eds. W. J. Sheils and Diana Wood, 189–207. Oxford: Blackwell, 1987.

———. "Iconoclasm in England: Rites of Destruction by Fire." In *Bilder und Bildersturm im Spätmittelalter und in der frühen Neuzeit,* ed. Bob Scribner, 175–99. Wiesbaden: Harrassowitz, 1990.

———. *Lollards and Reformers: Images and Literacy in Late Medieval Religion.* London: Hambledon Press, 1984.

Atkinson, Clarissa. *Mystic and Reformer: the Book and the World of Margery Kempe.* Ithaca, N.Y.: Cornell University Press, 1983.

Bainbridge, Virginia R. *Gilds in the Medieval Countryside: Social and Religious Change in Cambridgeshire c. 1350–1558.* Woodbridge: Boydell, 1996.

Baker, Alan R. H. "Changes in the Later Middle Ages." In *A New Historical Geography of England,* ed. H. C. Darby, 186–247. Cambridge: CUP, 1973.

Baker, Denise Nowakowski. *Julian of Norwich's Showings: From Vision to Book.* Princeton, N.J.: Princeton University Press, 1994.

Baker, John. *English Stained Glass of the Medieval Period.* London: Thames and Hudson, 1978.

Barnard, L. W. *Justin Martyr: His Life and Thought.* Cambridge: CUP, 1967.

Barnard, Leslie. "The Theology of Images." In *Iconoclasm,* eds. Anthony Bryer and Judith Herrin, 7–13. Birmingham: Center for Byzantine Studies, University of Birmingham, 1977.

Barnes, G. L. "Laity Formation: The Role of Early English Printed Primers." *Journal of Religious History* 18: 2 (1994): 139–58.

Barratt, Alexandra. "Works of Religious Instruction." In *Middle English Prose: a Critical Guide to Major Authors and Genres,* ed. A. S. G. Edwards, 413–32. New Brunswick, N. J.: Rutgers University Press, 1984.

Barron, Caroline M. "The Parish Fraternities of Medieval London." In *The Church in Pre-Reformation Society: Essays in Honour of F. R. H. Du Boulay,* eds. Caroline M. Barron and Christopher Harper-Bill, 13–37. Woodbridge, Suffolk: Boydell, 1985.

Basset, René. "Les Statues qu'on ne peut déplacer." *Revue des Traditions Populaires* 26 (1911): 22–23.

Bauerschmidt, Frederick Christian. *Julian of Norwich and the Mystical Body Politic of Christ.* Notre Dame, Ind.: University of Notre Dame Press, 1999.

Baum, P. F. "The Young Man Betrothed to a Statue." *PMLA* 34:4 (1919): 523–79.

Baynes, Norman H. *Byzantine Studies and Other Essays.* London: Athlone, 1955.

Beckwith, Sarah. *Christ's Body: Identity, Culture and Society in Late Medieval Writings.* London and New York: Routledge, 1993.

————."A Very Material Mysticism: the Medieval Mysticism of Margery Kempe." In *Medieval Literature: Criticism, Ideology and History,* ed. David Aers, 34–57. Brighton: Harvester, 1986.

Bell, H. E. "The Price of Books in Medieval England." *The Library* 4th ser. 17 (1936–37): 312–32.

Bell, Susan Groag. "Medieval Women Book Owners: Arbiters of Lay Piety and Ambassadors of Culture. *Signs* 7:4 (1982): 742–68.

Belting, Hans. *Likeness and Presence: A History of the Image Before the Era of Art.* Trans. Edmund Jephcott. Chicago: University of Chicago Press, 1994.

Bennett, H. S. "Notes on English Retail Book-prices, 1480–1560." *The Library* 5th ser. 5 (1951): 172–78.

————. "The Production and Dissemination of Vernacular Manuscripts in the Fifteenth Century." *The Library* 5th ser. 1 (1946–47): 167–78.

Bennett, J. A. W. *Poetry of the Passion.* Oxford: Clarendon Press, 1982.

Berlioz, Jacques. "*Exempla* as a Source for the History of Women." In *Medieval Women and the Sources of Medieval History,* ed. Joel T. Rosenthal, 37–50. Athens, Georgia: University of Georgia Press, 1990.

Bestul, Thomas H. *Texts of the Passion: Latin Devotional Literature and Medieval Society.* Philadelphia: University of Pennsylvania Press, 1996.

Bevan, Edwyn. *Holy Images: an Inquiry into Idolatry and Image-Worship in Ancient Paganism and in Christianity.* London: Allen & Unwin, 1940.

Binski, Paul. "The English Parish Church and Its Art in the Later Middle Ages: a Review of the Problem." *Studies in Iconography* 20 (1999): 1–25.

Birchenough, Edwyn. "The Prymer in English." *The Library* 4th ser. 18 (1937–38): 177–94.

Blake, Norman F. "Varieties of Middle English Religious Prose." In *Chaucer and Middle English Studies in honour of Rossell Hope Robbins,* ed. Beryl Rowland, 348–56. London: Allen & Unwin, 1974.

Blomefield, Francis and Charles Parkin. *An Essay Towards a Topographical History of the County of Norfolk.* 11 vols. London: Miller, 1805–10.

Blume, Clemens and Guido M. Dreves. *Analecta Hymnica Medii Aevi.* 55 vols. Leipzig: Reisland, 1886–1922.

Boffey, Julia. "Women authors and women's literacy in fourteenth- and fifteenth-century England." In *Women and Literature in Britain 1150–1500* 2nd ed., ed. Carol M. Meale, 159–82. Cambridge: CUP, 1996.

Boileau, John P. "Returns of Church Goods in the Churches of the City of Norwich." *NA* 4 (1864): 360–78.

Bolton, J. L. *The Medieval English Economy 1150–1500.* London: Dent, 1980.

Bossy, John. *Christianity in the West 1400–1700.* Oxford: Oxford University Press, 1985.

Boureau, Alain. "Les Théologiens Carolingiens devant les Images Religieuses. La Conjoncture de 825." In *Nicée II, 787–1987: Douze Siècles d'Images Religieuses,* eds. F. Boespflug and N. Lossky, 247–62. Paris: Les Éditions du Cerf, 1987.

Boyd, Beverly. *The Middle English Miracles of the Virgin.* San Marino, Calif.: The Huntington Library, 1964.

Boyle, Leonard E. "The Fourth Lateran Council and Manuals of Popular Theology. In *The Popular Literature of Medieval England,* ed. Thomas J. Heffernan, 30–43. Knoxville: University of Tennessee Press, 1985.

Brady, Mary T. "Lollard Interpolations and Omissions in Manuscripts of *The Pore Catif.*" In *De Cella in Seculum,* ed. Michael G. Sargent, 183–203. Cambridge: Brewer, 1989.

Bremond, Claude, Jacques le Goff, and Jean-Claude Schmitt. *L'Exemplum.* Vol 40, *Typologie des sources du moyen âge occidental.* Turnhout: Brepols. 1982.

Brooke, Christopher. "Religious Sentiment and Church Design in the Later Middle Ages." In *Medieval Church and Society,* 162–82. London: Sidgwick & Jackson, 1971.

Brown, Andrew D. *Popular Piety in Late Medieval England: The Diocese of Salisbury 1250–1550.* Oxford: Clarendon Press, 1995.

Brown, Peter. *The Cult of the Saints: Its Rise and Function in Latin Christianity.* Chicago: University of Chicago Press, 1981.

Bühler, Curt F. "Prayers and Charms in Certain Middle English Scrolls." *Speculum* 39 (1964): 270–78.

Burgess, Clive. "The Benefactions of Mortality: the Lay Response in the Late Medieval Urban Parish." In *Studies in Clergy and Ministry in Medieval England,* ed. David M. Smith, 65–86. University of York, Borthwick Institute of Historical Research, 1991.

———. "'A Fond Thing Vainly Invented': an Essay on Purgatory and Pious Motive in Later Medieval England." In *Parish, Church, and People: Local Studies in Lay Religion,* ed. S. J. Wright, 56–84. London: Hutchinson, 1988.

———. "Late Medieval Wills and Pious Convention: testamentary evidence reconsidered." In *Profit, Piety and the Professions in Later Medieval England,* ed. M. A. Hicks, 14–33. Gloucester: Sutton, 1990.

Burrow, J. A. *Thomas Hoccleve.* Brookfield, Vermont: Ashgate, 1994.

Butterworth, Charles C. *The English Primers (1529–1545).* Philadelphia: University of Pennsylvania Press, 1953.

Bynum, Caroline Walker. *Fragmentation and Redemption: Essays on Gender and the Human Body in Medieval Religion.* New York: Zone Books, 1991.

———. *Holy Feast and Holy Fast: the Religious Significance of Food to Medieval Women.* Berkeley: University of California Press, 1987.

———. *The Resurrection of the Body in Western Christianity, 200–1336.* New York: Columbia University Press, 1995.

———. "Women's Stories, Women's Symbols: A Critique of Victor Turner's Theory of Limnality." In *Anthropology and the Study of Religion,* eds. Robert L. Moore and Frank E. Reynolds, 105–25. Chicago: Center for the Scientific Study of Religion, 1984.

Calkins, Robert G. *Illuminated Books of the Middle Ages.* Ithaca, N.Y.: Cornell University Press, 1983.

Camille, Michael. *The Gothic Idol: Ideology and Image-making in Medieval Art.* Cambridge: CUP, 1989.

———. "Seeing and Reading: Some Visual Implications of Medieval Literacy and Illiteracy." *Art History* 8 (1985): 26–49.

Carey, Hilary M. "Astrology at the English Court in the Later Middle Ages." In *Astrology, Science and Society: Historical Essays,* ed. Patrick Curry, 41–56. Woodbridge, Suffolk: Boydell, 1987.

———. "Devout Literate Laypeople and the Pursuit of the Mixed Life in Later Medieval England." *Journal of Religious History* 14:4 (1987): 361–81.

Carruthers, Mary J. *The Book of Memory: A Study of Memory in Medieval Culture.* Cambridge: CUP, 1990.

Carthew, G. A. "Wymondham Guilds." *NA* 9 (1884): 240–74.

The Catholic Encyclopedia. 15 vols. New York: Appleton, 1907–12.

Catto, Jeremy. "Religious Change Under Henry V." In *Henry V: the Practice of Kingship,* ed. G. L. Harriss, 97–115. Oxford: Oxford University Press, 1985.

———. "William Woodford O. F. M. (c. 1330–c. 1397)." D. Phil. thesis, Oxford University, 1969.

Cautley, H. Munro. *Norfolk Churches.* Ipswich: Adlard, 1949.

———. *Suffolk Churches and Their Treasures.* 4th rev. edition. Ipswich: Boydell, 1975.

Cavanaugh, Susan H. "A Study of Books Privately Owned in England 1300–1450." Ph.D. Dissertation, University of Pennsylvania, 1980

Chartier, Roger. *The Order of Books: Readers, Authors, and Libraries in Europe between the Fourteenth and Eighteenth Centuries.* Trans. Lydia G. Cochrane. Stanford, Calif.: Stanford University Press, 1994.

Cheetham, Francis. *English Medieval Alabasters.* Oxford: Phaidon-Christie's Ltd., 1984.

Chevalier, Ulysse. *Repertorium Hymnologicum.* 6 vols. Louvain, 1892–1912; Bruxelles, 1920–21.

Christian, William A., Jr. *Apparitions in Late Medieval and Renaissance Spain.* Princeton, N. J.: Princeton University Press, 1981.

Christian Spirituality: Origins to the Twelfth Century. Eds. Bernard McGinn and John Meyendorff. New York: Crossroad, 1985.

Christianson, C. Paul. "The Rise of London's Book-trade." In *The Cambridge History of the Book in Britain,* vol. III, eds. Lotte Hellinga and J. B. Trapp, 128–47. Cambridge: CUP, 1999.

———. "Evidence for the Study of London's Late Medieval Manuscript-Book Trade." In *Book Production and Publishing in Britain 1375–1475,* eds. Jeremy Griffiths and Derek Pearsall, 87–108. Cambridge: CUP, 1989.

Clanchy, M. T. *From Memory to Written Record: England 1066–1307.* 2nd ed. Oxford: Blackwell, 1993.

Clark, David C. "Optics for Preachers: the *De Oculo Morali* by Peter of Limoges." *Michigan Academician* 9:3 (Winter 1977): 329–43.

Clark, John P. H. and Rosemary Dorward. *Introduction* to *The Scale of Perfection.* New York: Paulist Press, 1991.

Clark, John P. H. "Walter Hilton in Defence of the Religious Life and of the Veneration of Images." *Downside Review* 103 (1985): 1–25.

Clifton-Taylor, Alec. *English Parish Churches as Works of Art.* London: Batsford, 1974.

Coe, Brian. *Stained Glass in England: 1150–1550.* London: W. H. Allen, 1981.

Cohen, Jeremy. "The Jews as the Killers of Christ in the Latin Tradition, From Augustine to the Friars." *Traditio* 39 (1983): 1–27.

Cohen, Mark R. *Under Crescent and Cross: the Jews in the Middle Ages.* Princeton, N.J.: Princeton University Press, 1994.

Coleman, Janet. *Medieval Readers and Writers 1350–1400.* New York: Columbia University Press, 1981.

Constable, Giles. *Three Studies in Medieval Religious and Social Thought.* Cambridge: CUP, 1995.

Cook, G. H. *Mediaeval Chantries and Chantry Chapels.* London: Phoenix House, 1963.

Cooke, Thomas D. "Tales." In *MWME,* vol. 9, 3138–3328.

Copenhaver, Brian P. *Hermetica: The Greek* Corpus Hermeticum *and the Latin* Asclepius *in a New English Translation.* Cambridge: CUP, 1992.

Cox, J. Charles. *Churchwardens' Accounts from the Fourteenth Century to the Close of the Seventeenth Century.* London: Methuen, 1913.

Crawford, Anne. "The Piety of Late Medieval English Queens." In *The Church in Pre-Reformation Society,* eds. Caroline M. Barron and Christopher Harper-Bill, 48–57. Woodbridge, Suffolk: Boydell, 1985.

Crompton, James. "Lollard Doctrine with special reference to the controversy over Image-worship and Pilgrimage." B. Litt. thesis, Oxford University, 1950.

Cronin, H. S. "The Twelve Conclusions of the Lollards." *English Historical Review* 22 (1907): 292–304.

Crouch, David J. F. *Piety, Fraternity and Power: Religious Gilds in Late Medieval Yorkshire 1389–1547.* The University of York: York Medieval Press, 2000.

Cullum, P. H. and P. J. P. Goldberg. "Charitable Provisions in Late Medieval York: 'To the Praise of God and the Use of the Poor.'" *Northern History* XXIX (1993): 24–39.

Dagron, Gilbert. *La Romanité Chrétienne en Orient.* London: Variorum Reprints, 1984.

Daniell, Christopher. *Death and Burial in Medieval England 1066–1550.* London: Routledge, 1997.

Deanesly, Margaret. "Vernacular Books in England in the Fourteenth and Fifteenth Centuries." *Modern Language Review* XV (1920): 349–58.

De Hamel, Christopher. *A History of Illuminated Manuscripts.* 2nd ed. London: Phaidon, 1994.

Delisle, L. "Livres d'Images." In *Histoire littéraire de la France,* t. XXXI, 213–85. Paris, 1893.

Dendy, D. R. *The Use of Lights in Christian Worship.* London: S.P.C.K., 1959.

Denton, Jeffrey. "Image and History." In *Age of Chivalry: Art in Plantagenet England 1200–1400,* eds. Jonathan Alexander and Paul Binski, 20–25. London: Royal Academy of Arts, 1987.

Description of the Great Book of Hours of Henry the Eighth, illuminated by Jean Bourdichon of Tours. N.p., privately printed, 1923.

Despres, Denise. *Ghostly Sights: Visual Meditation in Late-Medieval Literature.* Norman, Ok.: Pilgrim Books, 1989.

Dickinson, J. C. *The Shrine of Our Lady of Walsingham.* Cambridge: CUP, 1956.

Dickman, Susan. "Julian of Norwich and Margery Kempe: Two Images of Fourteenth-Century Spirituality." In *Spätmittelalterliche Geistliche Literatur in der Na-*

tionalsprache, vol. 1, ed. James Hogg, 178–94. Salzburg: Institut für Anglistik und Amerikanistik, Universität Salzburg, 1983.

———. "Margery Kempe and the Continental Tradition of the Pious Woman." In *The Medieval Mystical Tradition in England,* ed. Marion Glasscoe, 150–68. Cambridge: Brewer, 1984.

———. "Margery Kempe and the English Devotional Tradition." In *The Medieval Mystical Tradition in England,* ed. Marion Glasscoe, 156–72. [Exeter]: University of Exeter, 1980.

A Dictionary of Superstitions. Eds. Iona Opie and Moira Tatem. Oxford: Oxford University Press, 1989.

Dictionnaire d'Archéologie Chrétienne et de Liturgie. 15 vols. Paris: Letouzey et Ané, 1913–1953.

Dictionnaire de Théologie Catholique. 15 vols. Paris: Letouzey et Ané, 1924–1950.

Dinn, Robert. "Death and Rebirth in Late Medieval Bury St Edmunds." In *Death in Towns: Urban Responses to the Dying and the Dead, 100–1600,* ed. Steven Bassett, 151–69. London: Leicester University Press, 1992.

Dobson, R. B. *Church and Society in the Medieval North of England.* London: Hambledon, 1996.

Dodgson, Campbell. "English Devotional Woodcuts of the Late Fifteenth Century, with Special Reference to those in the Bodleian Library." *The Walpole Society* 17 (1928–29): 95–108.

Douglas, David C. *The Social Structure of Medieval East Anglia.* Oxford: Clarendon Press, 1927.

Dreves, Guido M. *Ein Jahrtausend Lateinischer Hymnendichtung.* 2 vols. Leipzig: Reisland, 1909.

Driver, Martha. "Pictures in Print: Late Fifteenth- and Early Sixteenth-Century English Religious Books for Lay Readers." In *De Cella in Seculum: Religious and Secular Life and Devotion in Late Medieval England,* ed. Michael G. Sargent, 229–44. Cambridge: Brewer, 1989.

Duffy, Eamon. "Holy Maydens, Holy Wyfes: The Cult of Women Saints in Fifteenth- and Sixteenth- Century England." In *Women in the Church,* eds. W. J. Sheils and Diana Wood, 175–96. Oxford: Blackwell, 1990.

———. "The Parish, Piety, and Patronage in Late Medieval East Anglia: The Evidence of Rood Screens." In *The Parish in English Life 1400–1600,* eds. Katherine L. French, Gary G. Gibbs, and Beat A. Kümin, 133–62. Manchester: Manchester University Press, 1997.

———. *The Stripping of the Altars: Traditional Religion in England c.1400-c.1580.* New Haven: Yale University Press, 1992.

Duggan, Lawrence G. "Was art really the 'book of the illiterate'?" *Word & Image* 5:3 (1989): 227–51.

Dumeige, Gervais. *Nicée II.* Paris: Éditions de l'Orante, 1978.

Dymond, David. *The Norfolk Landscape.* London: Hodder and Stoughton, 1985.

Dymond, David, and Clive Paine. *The Spoil of Melford Church.* Ipswich: Salient Press, 1989.

Dymond, David, and Roger Virgoe. "The Reduced Population and Wealth of Early Fifteenth-Century Suffolk." *PSIA* 36 (1986): 73–100.

Edwards, A. S. G. "The Transmission and Audience of Osbern Bokenham's *Legendys of Hooly Wummen.*" In *Late-Medieval Religious Texts and their Transmission: Essays in Honour of A. I. Doyle,* ed. A. J. Minnis, 157–67. Cambridge: Brewer, 1994.

Erler, Mary C. "Devotional Literature." In *The Cambridge History of the Book in Britain* vol. III, eds. Lotte Hellinga and J. B. Trapp, 495–525. Cambridge: CUP, 1999.

———. "*The Maner to Lyue Well* and the Coming of English in François Regnault's Primers of the 1520s and 1530s." *The Library* 6th ser. 6 (1984): 229–43.

Evans, Joan. *English Art 1307–1461.* Oxford: Clarendon Press, 1949.

Les Exempla médiévaux: introduction á la recherchê. Carcassonne: Garae/Hesiode, 1992.

Farley, Mary Hardiman. "Her Own Creature: Religion, Feminist Criticism, and the Functional Eccentricity of Margery Kempe." *Exemplaria* 11:1 (1999): 1–21.

Farmer, D. H. *The Oxford Dictionary of Saints.* 2nd ed. Oxford: Oxford University Press, 1987.

———. "Some Saints of East Anglia." *Reading Medieval Studies* vol. XI: 31–49.

Farnhill, Ken. "The Religious Gilds of Wymondham, *c.* 1470–1550," *NA* 42 (1996): 321–31.

Ferré, Martin Jean [Louis Leclève]. *Sainte Angèle de Foligno, sa vie—ses oeuvres.* Paris: Plon, 1936.

Finke, Laurie A. "Mystical Bodies and the Dialogics of Vision." In *Maps of Flesh and Light: The Religious Experience of Medieval Women Mystics,* ed. Ulrike Wiethaus, 28–44. Syracuse, N.Y.: Syracuse University Press, 1993.

Finucane, Ronald C. *Miracles and Pilgrims: Popular Beliefs in Medieval England.* Totowa, N. J.: Rowman and Littlefield, 1977.

———. "Sacred Corpse, Profane Carrion: Social Ideals and Death Rituals in the Later Middle Ages." In *Mirrors of Mortality: Studies in the Social History of Death,* ed. Joachim Whaley, 40–60. New York: St. Martin's, 1981.

Firth, Catherine B. "Village Gilds of Norfolk in the Fifteenth Century." *NA* 18 (1914): 161–203.

Fletcher, Alan J. "John Mirk and the Lollards." *Medium Aevum* 56 (1987): 217–24.

Ford, Judy Ann. "Art and Identity in the Parish Communities of Late Medieval Kent." In *The Church and the Arts,* ed. Diana Wood, 225–37. Oxford: Blackwell, 1992.

Fredeman, J. C. "The Life of John Capgrave O.E.S.A. (1393–1464)." *Augustiniana* 20 (1979): 197–237.

Freedberg, David. *The Power of Images.* Chicago: University of Chicago Press, 1989.

French, Katherine L. *The People of the Parish: Community Life in a Late Medieval English Diocese.* Philadelphia: University of Pennsylvania Press, 2001.

———. "'To Free Them From Binding': Women in the Late Medieval English Parish." *Journal of Interdisciplinary History* 27: 3 (Winter 1997): 387–412.

French, Katherine L., Gary G. Gibbs, and Beat A. Kümin, eds. *The Parish in English Life: 1400–1600.* Manchester: Manchester University Press, 1997.

Friedman, John B. *Northern English Books, Owners, and Makers in the Late Middle Ages.* Syracuse, N.Y.: Syracuse University Press, 1995.

Furnish, Shearle. "The *Ordinatio* of Huntington Library, MS HM 149: an East Anglian Manuscript of Nicholas Love's *Mirror.*" *Manuscripta* 34 (1990): 50–65.

Gardner, Arthur. *English Medieval Sculpture.* Cambridge: CUP, 1951.

Gasquet, F. A. "An English Rosary Book of the 15th Century." *Downside Review* XII (1893): 215–28.

———. *The Eve of the Reformation.* 3rd ed. London: Bell, 1905.

———. *The Religious Life of King Henry VI.* London: Bell, 1923.

Giakalis, Ambrosios. *Images of the Divine: the Theology of Icons at the Seventh Ecumenical Council.* Leiden: Brill, 1994.

Gibson, Gail McMurray. *The Theater of Devotion: East Anglian Drama and Society in the Late Middle Ages.* Chicago: University of Chicago Press, 1989.

Gillespie, Vincent. "The Evolution of the *Speculum Christiani.*" In *Latin and Vernacular: Studies in Late-Medieval Texts and Manuscripts,* ed. A. J. Minnis, 39–60. Cambridge: Brewer, 1989.

———. "*Lukynge in haly bukes: Lectio* in Some Late Medieval Spiritual Miscellanies." In *Spätmittelalterliche Geistliche Literatur in der Nationalsprache,* vol. 2, ed. James Hogg, 1–27. Salzburg: Institut für Anglistik und Amerikanistik, 1984.

———. "Strange Images of Death: The Passion in Later Medieval English Devotional and Mystical Writing." In *Zeit, Tod und Ewigkeit in der Renaissance Literatur,* Band 3, ed. James Hogg, 111–59. Salzburg: Institut für Anglistik und Amerikanistik, 1987.

———. "Vernacular Books of Religion." In *Book Production and Publishing in Britain 1375–1475,* eds. Jeremy Griffiths and Derek Pearsall, 317–44. Cambridge: CUP, 1989.

Glasscoe, Marion. "Means of Showing: An Approach to Reading Julian of Norwich." In *Spätmittelalterliche Geistliche Literatur in der Nationalsprache,* vol. 1, ed. James Hogg, 155–77. Salzburg: Institut für Anglistik und Amerikanistik, 1983.

Goldberg, P. J. P. "Women." In *Fifteenth-Century Attitudes: Perceptions of Society in Late Medieval England,* ed. Rosemary Horrox, 112–31. Cambridge: CUP, 1994.

Goodich, Michael. *Vita Perfecta: the Ideal of Sainthood in the Thirteenth Century.* Stuttgart: Hiersemann, 1982.

Goodman, Anthony. "The Piety of John Brunham's Daughter, of Lynn." In *Medieval Women,* ed. Derek Baker, 347–58. Oxford: Blackwell, 1978.

Görlach, M. "Middle English Legends, 1220–1530." In *Hagiographies: International History of the Latin and Vernacular Hagiographical Literature in the West from its Origins to 1550,* vol. 1, 429–85. Turnhout: Brepols, 1994.

Gottfried, Robert S. *Bury St. Edmunds and the Urban Crisis: 1290–1539.* Princeton, N. J.: Princeton University Press, 1982.

Gougaud, Louis. *Dévotions et pratiques ascétiques du moyen âge.* Paris, 1925.

———. "Muta Praedicatio." *Revue Bénédictine* 42 (1930): 168–71.

———. "La Prière dit le Charlemagne et les pièces apocryphes apparentées." *Revue d'histoire ecclésiastique* XX (1924): 211–38.

Graves, C. Pamela, "Social Space in the English Medieval Parish Church." *Economy and Society* 18:3 (August 1989): 297–322.

Gray, Douglas. "The Five Wounds of Our Lord." *Notes and Queries* 208 (1963): 50–51; 82–89; 127–34; 163–68.

———. "Notes on Some Middle English Charms." In *Chaucer and Middle English Studies in Honour of Rossell Hope Robbins,* ed. Beryl Rowland, 56–71. London: Allen & Unwin, 1974.

———. *Themes and Images in the Medieval English Religious Lyric.* London: Routledge & Kegan Paul, 1972.

Green, D. H. "Orality and Reading: the State of Research in Medieval Studies." *Speculum* 65 (1990): 267–80.

Green, V. H. H. *Bishop Reginald Pecock: A Study in Ecclesiastical History and Thought.* Cambridge: CUP, 1945.

Gregg, Joan Young. *Devils, Women, and Jews: Reflections of the Other in Medieval Sermon Stories.* Albany: State University of New York Press, 1997.

———. "The Exempla of 'Jacob's Well': A Study in the Transmission of Medieval Sermon Stories." *Traditio* 33 (1977): 359–80.

Guiette, R. *La Légende de la Sacristine: Étude de littérature comparée.* Paris: H. Champion, 1981.

Hagen, Susan K. "St. Cecilia and St. John of Beverly: Julian of Norwich's Model and Late Affirmation." In *Julian of Norwich: A Book of Essays,* ed. Sandra J. McEntire, 91–114. New York: Garland, 1998.

Haines, Roy. "Reginald Pecock: A Tolerant Man in an Age of Intolerances." In *Persecution and Toleration,* ed. W. J. Sheils, 125–37. Oxford: Blackwell, 1984.

Hall, Donald J. *English Mediaeval Pilgrimage.* London: Routledge & Kegan Paul, 1965.

Hamburger, Jeffrey. *The Rothschild Canticles.* New Haven: Yale University Press, 1990.

———. "The Visual and the Visionary: the Image in Late Medieval Monastic Devotions." *Viator* 20 (1989): 161–82.

Hanawalt, Barbara A. "Keepers of the Lights: Late Medieval English Parish Gilds." *Journal of Medieval and Renaissance Studies* 14 (1984): 21–37.

Harbison, Craig. "Visions and Meditations in Early Flemish Painting." *Simiolus* 15:2 (1985): 87–118.

Harding, Vanessa. "'And one more may be laid there': the Location of Burials in Early Modern London." *The London Journal* 14:2 (1989): 112–29.

———. "Burial Choice and Burial Location in Later Medieval London." In *Death in Towns: Urban Responses to the Dying and the Dead, 100–1600,* ed. Steven Bassett, 119–35. London: Leicester University Press, 1992.

Harding, Wendy. "Body into Text: *The Book of Margery Kempe.*" In *Feminist Approaches to the Body in Medieval Literature,* eds. Linda Lomperis and Sarah Stanbury, 168–87. Philadelphia: University of Pennsylvania Press, 1993.

Harper-Bill, Christopher. "Cistercian Visitation in the Late Middle Ages: the Case of Hailes Abbey." *Bulletin of the Institute of Historical Research* 53: 127 (May 1980): 103–14.

———. "A Late Medieval Visitation—the Diocese of Norwich in 1499." *PSIA* 34 (1977): 35–47.

Harris, Kate. "Patrons, Buyers, and Owners: the evidence for ownership and the rôle of book owners in book production and the book trade." In *Book Production and Publishing in Britain 1375–1475,* eds. Jeremy Griffiths and Derek Pearsall, 163–99. Cambridge: CUP, 1989.

Hart, R. "The Shrines and Pilgrimages of the Country of Norfolk." *NA* 6 (1864): 277–94.

Harthan, Jonathan. *The Book of Hours.* New York: Crowell, 1977.

Harvey, E. Ruth. "The Ymage of Love." In *The Complete Works of St. Thomas More,* vol. 6, part II, eds. Thomas M. C. Lawler, et al. New Haven: Yale University Press, 1981.

Harvey, John. *The Perpendicular Style 1330–1485.* London: Batsford, 1978.

Haslewood, Francis. "Our Lady of Ipswich." *PSIA* 10 (1900): 53–55.

Heath, Peter. *English Parish Clergy on the Eve of the Reformation.* London: Routledge & Kegan Paul, 1969.

———. "Urban Piety in the Later Middle Ages: the Evidence of Hull Wills." In *The Church, Politics and Patronage in the Fifteenth Century,* ed. Barrie Dobson, 209–29. Gloucester: Sutton, 1984.

Heffernan, Thomas J. *Sacred Biography: Saints and Their Biographers in the Middle Ages.* Oxford: Oxford University Press, 1988.

———. "Sermon Literature." In *Middle English Prose: A Critical Guide to Major Authors and Genres,* ed. A. S. G. Edwards, 177–207. New Brunswick, N. J.: Rutgers University Press, 1984.

Herbert, J. A. *Catalogue of Romances in the Department of Manuscripts in the British Museum.* Volume 3. London, 1910.

Heslop, T. A. "Attitudes to the Visual Arts: the Evidence from Written Sources." In *Age of Chivalry: Art in Plantagenet England 1200–1400,* eds. Jonathan Alexander and Paul Binski, 26–32. London: Royal Academy of Arts, 1987.

A History of the County of York East Riding, ed. K. J. Allison. Vol. II. London: published for the Institute of Historical Research by Oxford University Press, 1974.

Hood, John Y. B. *Aquinas and the Jews.* Philadelphia: University of Pennsylvania Press, 1995.

Horsfield, Robert A. "*The Pomander of Prayer:* Aspects of Late Medieval English Carthusian Spirituality and Its Lay Audience." In *De Cella in Seculum: Religious and Secular Life and Devotion in Late Medieval England,* ed. Michael G. Sargent, 205–13. Cambridge: Brewer, 1989.

Hoskins, Edgar. *Horae Beatae Mariae Virginis or Sarum and York Primers.* London: Longmans, Green, 1901.

Hudson, Anne. "'Laicus litteratus': the Paradox of Lollardy." In *Heresy and Literacy, 1000–1530,* eds. Peter Biller and Anne Hudson, 222–36. Cambridge: CUP, 1994.

———. *The Premature Reformation: Wycliffite Texts and Lollard History.* Oxford: Clarendon Press, 1988.

———. "Wycliffite Prose." In *Middle English Prose: a Critical Guide to Major Authors and Genres,* ed. A. S. G. Edwards, 249–70. New Brunswick, N. J.: Rutgers University Press, 1984.

Hutton, Ronald. *The Rise and Fall of Merry England: the Ritual Year 1400–1700*. Oxford: Oxford University Press, 1994.

Ingleby, C., ed. *A Supplement to Blomefield's Norfolk*. London, 1929.

James, M. R. *The Bohun Manuscripts: a Group of Five Manuscripts Executed in England about 1370 for Members of the Bohun Family*. Oxford: Roxburghe Club, 1936.

———. *A Descriptive Catalogue of the Manuscripts in the Fitzwilliam Museum*. Cambridge: CUP, 1895.

———. "Lives of St. Walstan." *NA* 19 (1917): 238–67.

———. *Suffolk and Norfolk*. Bury St. Edmunds: Alastair Press, 1930; reprint edition 1987.

Jankofsky, Klaus P., ed. *The South English Legendary: A Critical Assessment*. Tubingen: Franke, 1992.

Jones, W. R. "Art and Christian Piety: Iconoclasm in Medieval Europe." In *The Image and the Word: Confrontations in Judaism, Christianity and Islam,* ed. Joseph Gutman, 75–105. Missoula, Mont.: Scholars Press, 1977.

———. "Lollards and Images: the Defense of Religious Art in Later Medieval England." *Journal of the History of Ideas* XXXIV (1973): 27–50.

Karras, Ruth Mazo, "Gendered Sin and Misogyny in John of Bromyard's 'Summa Predicantium,'" *Traditio* 47 (1992): 233–57.

———. "The Virgin and the Pregnant Abbess: Miracles and Gender in the Middle Ages." *Medieval Perspectives* 3 (1988): 112–32.

Kent, Ernest A. "The Mural Painting of St. George in St. Gregory's Church, Norwich." *NA* 25 (1935): 167–69.

Kieckhefer, Richard. *Magic in the Middle Ages*. Cambridge: CUP, 1989.

———. *Unquiet Souls: Fourteenth-Century Saints and Their Religious Milieu*. Chicago: University of Chicago Press, 1984.

Kitzinger, Ernst. "The Cult of Images in the Age Before Iconoclasm." *Dumbarton Oaks Papers* 8 (1954): 85–150.

Klapisch-Zuber, Christiane. *Women, Family, and Ritual in Renaissance Italy*. Trans. Lydia Cochrane. Chicago: University of Chicago Press, 1985.

Knowles, David and R. Neville Hadcock. *Medieval Religious Houses: England and Wales*. London: Longmans, Green, 1953.

Knowles, David. *The Religious Orders in England*. 3 vols. Cambridge: CUP, 1948–59.

Kümin, Beat A. *The Shaping of a Community: The Rise and Reformation of the English Parish, c. 1400–1560*. Aldershot: Scolar Press, 1996.

Lachance, Paul. *The Spiritual Journey of the Blessed Angela of Foligno According to the Memorial of Frater A*. Rome: Pontificium Athenaeum Antonianum, 1984.

Lasko, P. and N. J. Morgan, eds. *Medieval Art in East Anglia 1300–1520*. London: Thames and Hudson, 1974.

Lea, Henry Charles. *History of Auricular Confession and Indulgences*. 3 vols. Philadelphia: Lea Brothers, 1896.

Le Goff, Jacques. *The Birth of Purgatory*. Trans. Arthur Goldhammer. Chicago: University of Chicago Press, 1981.

———. "Le juif dans les *exempla* médiévaux: le cas de l'*Alphabetum Narrationum*." In *Mélanges Léon Poliakov. Le racisme, mythes et sciences,* 209–20. Paris, 1981.

Léon, Père. *Lives of the Saints and Blessed of the Three Orders of Saint Francis.* Trans. from *Aureole Seraphique.* 2 vols. Taunton, 1885–87.

Leroquais, V. *Les Livres d'heures.* 3 vols. Paris, 1927.

———. *Supplément (acquisitions récentes et donations Smith-Lesouef).* Mâcon, 1943.

Lewis, Flora. "Rewarding Devotion: Indulgences and the Promotion of Images," in *The Church and the Arts,* ed. Diana Wood, 179–94. Oxford: Blackwell, 1992.

———. "The Veronica: Image, Legend, and Viewer." In *England in the Thirteenth Century,* ed. W. M. Ormrod, 100–06. Woodbridge, Suffolk: Boydell, 1986.

———. "The Wound in Christ's Side and the Instruments of the Passion: Gendered Experience and Response." In *Women and the Book: Assessing the Visual Evidence,* eds. Jane H. M. Taylor and Lesley Smith, 204–29. London and Toronto: The British Library and the University of Toronto Press, 1997.

Lichtmann, Maria R. "'God fulfylled my bodye': Body, Self, and God in Julian of Norwich." In *Gender and Text in the Later Middle Ages,* ed. Jane Chance, 263–78. Gainesville: University Press of Florida, 1996.

Lindberg, David C. *A Catalog of Medieval and Renaissance Optical Manuscripts.* Toronto: Pontifical Institute of Mediaeval Studies, 1975.

Lindberg, David C., ed. and trans. *John Pecham and the Science of Optics:* Perspectiva Communis. Madison: University of Wisconsin Press, 1970.

Lindberg, David C. *Theories of Vision from Al-Kindi to Kepler.* Chicago: University of Chicago Press, 1976.

Lochrie, Karma. *Margery Kempe and Translations of the Flesh.* Philadelphia: University of Pennsylvania Press, 1991.

Lucas, Peter J. *From Author to Audience: John Capgrave and Medieval Publication.* Dublin: University College Dublin Press, 1997.

Maddern, Philippa. "Friends of the Dead: Executors, Wills and Family Strategy in Fifteenth-Century Norfolk." In *Rulers and Ruled in Late Medieval England: Essays Presented to Gerald Harris,* eds. Rowena E. Archer and Simon Walker, 155–74. London: Hambledon Press, 1995.

Maisonneuve, Roland. *L'Univers Visionnaire de Julian of Norwich.* Thesis, L'Université de Paris IV, 1979.

Mâle, Emile. *Religious Art in France: the late Middle Ages.* Trans. M. Mathews. Princeton, N. J.: Princeton University Press, 1986.

Marcus, Ivan G. "Images of the Jews in the *Exempla* of Caesarius of Heisterbach." In *From Witness to Witchcraft: Jews and Judaism in Medieval Christian Thought,* ed. Jeremy Cohen, 247–56. Wiesbaden: Harrassowitz, 1996.

Marks, Richard. *Stained Glass in England during the Middle Ages.* Toronto: University of Toronto Press, 1993.

Marrow, James H. *Passion Iconography in Northern European Art of the Late Middle Ages and Early Renaissance.* Kortrijk, Belgium: Van Ghemmert, 1979.

Marshall, Peter. "The Rood of Boxley, the Blood of Hailes and the Defence of the Henrician Church." *JEH* 46:4 (1995): 689–96.

Martin, Edward James. *A History of the Iconoclastic Controversy.* London: S.P.C.K., 1930.

Mason, Emma. "The Role of the English Parishioner, 1100–1500." *JEH* 27:1 (1976): 17–29.

Matthews, William A. "Thomas Hoccleve." In *MWME,* vol. 3, 746–56.

Matray, Béatrice. "Les Indulgences au XIVe Siècle: Etude des Lettres de Jean XXII (1316–1334) et d'Urbain V (1363–1370)." *Cahiers d'histoire* 33:2 (1988): 135–51.

McDannell, Colleen and Bernhard Lang. *Heaven: A History.* New Haven: Yale University Press, 1988.

McEntire, Sandra J. "The Journey into Selfhood: Margery Kempe and Feminine Spirituality." In *Margery Kempe: A Book of Essays,* ed. Sandra J. McEntire, 51–69. New York: Garland, 1992.

McHardy, A. K. "Bishop Buckingham and the Lollards of Lincoln Diocese." In *Schism, Heresy and Religious Protest,* ed. Derek Baker, 131–45. Cambridge: CUP, 1972.

McKenna, John W. "Piety and Propaganda: the Cult of King Henry VI." In *Chaucer and Middle English Studies,* ed. Beryl Rowland, 72–88. London: Allen & Unwin, 1974.

McNeill, John T. and Helena M. Gamer, *Medieval Handbooks of Penance.* New York: Columbia University Press, c. 1938.

McRee, Ben R. "Charity and Gild Solidarity in Late Medieval England." *JBS* 32 (July 1993): 195–25.

———. "Religious Gilds and Civic Order: The Case of Norwich in the Late Middle Ages." *Speculum* 67 (1992): 69–97.

Meale, Carol M. "'. . . alle the bokes that I haue of latyn, englisch, and frensch': Laywomen and Their Books in Late Medieval England." In *Women and Literature in Britain 1150–1500,* 2nd ed., ed. Carol M. Meale, 128–58. Cambridge: CUP, 1996.

———. "Patrons, Buyers and Owners: Book Production and Social Status." In *Book Production and Publishing in Britain 1375–1475,* eds. Jeremy Griffiths and Derek Pearsall, 201–38. Cambridge: CUP, 1989.

Miles, Margaret. *Image as Insight: Visual Understanding in Western Christianity and Secular Culture.* Boston: Beacon, 1985.

———. "Vision: The Eye of the Body and the Eye of the Mind in Saint Augustine's *De Trinitate* and *Confessions." Journal of Religion* 63 (April 1983): 125–42.

Milhaven, J. Giles. "A Medieval Lesson on Bodily Knowing: Women's Experience and Men's Thought." *Journal of the American Academy of Religion* 57:2 (1989): 341–72.

Molinari, Paul. *Julian of Norwich.* London: Longmans, Green, 1958.

Mooney, Catherine M. "The Authorial Role of Brother A. in the Composition of Angela of Foligno's Revelations." In *Creative Women in Medieval and Early Modern Italy: a Religious and Artistic Renaissance,* eds. E. Ann Matter and John Coakley, 34–63. Philadelphia: University of Pennsylvania Press, 1994.

Moran, Jo Ann Hoeppner. *The Growth of English Schooling 1340–1548: Learning, Literacy, and Laicization in Pre-Reformation York Diocese.* Princeton, N. J.: Princeton University Press, 1985.

Morant, A. W. "Notices of the Church of St. Nicholas, Great Yarmouth." *NA* 7 (1872): 215–48.

Morgan, Nigel. "Texts and Images of Marian Devotion in Fourteenth-Century England." In *England in the Fourteenth Century,* ed. Nicholas Rogers, 34–57. Stamford: Paul Watkins, 1993.

Muir, Edward. "The Virgin on the Street Corner: the Place of the Sacred in Italian Cities." In *Religion and Culture in the Renaissance and Reformation,* ed. Steven Ozment, 25–40. Kirksville, Mo.: Sixteenth Century Journal Publications, 1989.

Myette, Jean-Pierre. "L'image du Juif dans la *Lègende dorèe.*" In *Legenda aurea—la Lègende dorèe (XIIIᵉ-XVᵉ s.), Le Moyen français* vol. 32 (1993), 111–23.

Nichols, Ann Eljenholm. "Books-for-Laymen: the Demise of a Commonplace." *Church History* 56: 4 (December 1987): 457–73.

—. *Seeable Signs: The Iconography of the Seven Sacraments 1350–1544.* Woodbridge: Boydell, 1994.

Nuth, Joan M. *Wisdom's Daughter: the Theology of Julian of Norwich.* New York: Crossroad, 1991.

Oakley, Francis. *The Western Church in the Later Middle Ages.* Ithaca, N.Y.: Cornell University Press, 1979.

Ormrod, W. M. "The Personal Religion of Edward III." *Speculum* 64 (1989): 849–77.

Os, Henk van, with Eugène Honée, Hans Nieuwdorp, Bernhard Ridderbos. Trans. Michael Hoyle. *The Art of Devotion in the Late Middle Ages in Europe 1300–1500.* Princeton, N.J.: Princeton University Press, 1994.

Ouspensky, Leonid. "Icon and Art." In *Christian Spirituality: Origins to the Twelfth Century,* eds. Bernard McGinn and John Meyendorff, 382–94. New York: Crossroad, 1985.

———. *Theology of the Icon.* Vol. 1. Trans. Anthony Gythiel. Crestwood, N.Y.: St. Vladimir's Seminary Press, 1992.

Owen, Dorothy M. "Bacon and Eggs: Bishop Buckingham and Superstition in Lincolnshire." In *Popular Belief and Practice,* eds. G. J. Cuming and Derek Baker, 139–42. Cambridge: CUP, 1972.

Owst, G. R. *The Destructorium Viciorum of Alexander Carpenter: A Fifteenth-Century Sequel to* Literature and Pulpit in Medieval England. London: S. P. C. K., 1952.

———. *Literature and Pulpit in Medieval England.* 2nd ed. Oxford: Blackwell, 1961.

Pagels, Elaine. *The Origin of Satan.* New York: Random House, 1995.

Panofsky, Erwin. "Imago Pietatis." In *Festschrift für Max Friedländer,* 261–308. Leipzig: Seeman, 1927.

Pantin, W. A. *The English Church in the Fourteenth Century.* Cambridge 1955; reprint, Toronto: University of Toronto Press, 1980.

Parker, J. John. *Our Lady of Ipswich.* Ipswich, n.d.

Parkes, M. B. "The Literacy of the Laity." In *Literature and Western Civilization: the Mediaeval World,* eds. D. Daiches and A. Thorlby, 555–77. London: Aldus, 1973.

Parry, Kenneth. *Depicting the Word: Byzantine Iconophile Thought of the Eighth and Ninth Centuries.* Leiden: Brill, 1996.

Partner, Nancy F. "Reading the Book of Margery Kempe," *Exemplaria* 3:1 (1991): 29–66.

Pearsall, Derek A. *John Lydgate (1371–1449): a bio-bibliography.* Victoria, B. C.: English Literary Studies, University of Victoria, 1997.

Pelikan, Jaroslav. *Imago Dei: the Byzantine Apologia for Icons.* Princeton, N. J.: Princeton University Press, 1990.

————. *Reformation of Church and Dogma (1300–1700)*. Vol. 4, *The Christian Tradition*. Chicago: University of Chicago Press, 1984.

Pelphrey, Brant. *Love Was His Meaning: the Theology and Mysticism of Julian of Norwich*. Salzburg: Institut für Anglistik und Amerikanistik, 1982.

Penketh, Sandra. "Women and Books of Hours." In *Women and the Book: Assessing the Visual Evidence,* eds. Jane H. M. Taylor and Lesley Smith, 266–81. London and Toronto: The British Library and the University of Toronto Press, 1997.

Petroff, Elizabeth Avilda. *Medieval Women's Visionary Literature.* New York: Oxford University Press, 1986.

Pevsner, Nikolaus and Bill Wilson. *Norfolk 1: Norwich and North-East.* 2nd ed. London: Penguin, 1997.

Pevsner, Nikolaus. *North-west and South Norfolk.* Harmondsworth: Penguin, 1962.

————. *Suffolk.* Harmondsworth: Penguin, 1961.

Pfaff, R. W. *New Liturgical Feasts in Later Medieval England.* Oxford: Clarendon Press, 1970.

Pfander, H. G. "The Mediaeval Friars and Some Alphabetical Reference-Books for Sermons." *Medium Aevum* 3 (1934): 19–29.

Phillips, John. *The Reformation of Images: Destruction of Art in England 1535–1660.* Berkeley: University of California Press, 1973.

Pollard, Graham. "The Company of Stationers Before 1557." *The Library* 4th ser. 18 (1937): 1–38.

Poulenc, Jerome. "Saint François dans le vitrail des anges de l'eglise supérieure de la basilique d'Assise." *Archivum Franciscanum Historicum* 76 (1983): 701–13.

Pounds, N. J. G. *A History of the English Parish.* Cambridge: CUP, 2000.

Raymo, Robert R. "Works of Religious and Philosophical Instruction." In *MWME,* vol. 7, 2255–2378.

Reames, Sherry L. *The Legenda Aurea: A Reexamination of Its Paradoxical History.* Madison: University of Wisconsin Press, 1985.

Redstone, V. B. "Chapels, Chantries and Gilds in Suffolk." *PSIA* 12 (1904–06): 1–87.

Rees, H. G. St. M. *An Illustrated History of Mildenhall, Suffolk and Its Parish Church of the Blessed Virgin Mary.* Gloucester, n.d.

Reynolds, Susan. *An Introduction to the History of English Medieval Towns.* Oxford: Clarendon Press, 1977.

Richmond, Colin. *John Hopton: A Fifteenth Century Suffolk Gentleman.* Cambridge: CUP, 1981.

Riddy, Felicity. "'Women talking about the things of God': a late medieval sub-culture." In *Women and Literature in Britain 1150–1500,* 2nd ed., ed. Carol M. Meale, 104–27. Cambridge: CUP, 1996.

Riehle, Wolfgang. *The Middle English Mystics.* Trans. B. Standring. London: Routledge & Kegan Paul, 1981.

Ringbom, Sixten. "Devotional Images and Imaginative Devotions: Notes on the Place of Art in Late Medieval Private Piety." *Gazette des Beaux-Arts* 73 (1969): 159–70.

————. *Icon to Narrative: the Rise of the Dramatic Close-up in Fifteenth-Century Devotional Painting.* 2nd ed. Doornspijk: Davaco, 1984.

————. "*Maria in Sole* and the Virgin of the Rosary." *Journal of the Warburg and Courtauld Institutes* 25 (1962): 326–30.

Robbins, Rossell Hope. "The 'Arma Christi' Rolls." *Modern Language Review* 34 (1939): 415–21.

Rosenthal, Joel T. *The Purchase of Paradise: Gift Giving and the Aristocracy, 1307–1485.* London: Routledge & Kegan Paul, 1972.

Ross, Ellen M. *The Grief of God: Images of the Suffering Jesus in Late Medieval England.* New York: Oxford University Press, 1997.

Ross, Thomas W. "Five Fifteenth-Century 'Emblem' Verses from Brit. Mus. Addit. MS. 37049." *Speculum* 32 (1957): 274–82.

Rosser, Gervase. "Communities of Parish and Guild in the Late Middle Ages." In *Parish, Church and People: Local Studies in Lay Religion 1350–1750,* ed. S. J. Wright, 29–55. London: Hutchinson, 1988.

————. "Going to the Fraternity Feast: Commensality and Social Relations in Late Medieval England." *JBS* 33 (October 1994): 430–46.

Rubin, Miri. *Corpus Christi: the Eucharist in Late Medieval Culture.* Cambridge: CUP, 1991.

————. *Gentile Tales: The Narrative Assault on Late Medieval Jews.* New Haven: Yale University Press, 1999.

Rublank, Ulinka. "Female Spirituality and the Infant Jesus in Late Medieval Dominican Convents." *Gender & History* 6:1 (April 1994): 37–57.

Rudolph, Conrad. *The "Things of Greater Importance": Bernard of Clairvaux's Apologia and the Medieval Attitude Toward Art.* Philadelphia: University of Pennsylvania Press, 1990.

Russell, G. H. "Vernacular Instruction of the Laity in the Later Middle Ages in England: Some Text and Notes." *Journal of Religious History* 2 (1962): 98–119.

Russell, J. C. *British Medieval Population.* Albuquerque: University of New Mexico Press, 1948.

Russell-Smith, Joy M. "Walter Hilton and a Tract in Defence of the Veneration of Images." *Dominican Studies* 7 (1954): 180–214.

Ryder, Andrew. "A Note on Julian's Visions." *Downside Review* 96 (1978): 299–304.

Saenger, Paul. "Books of Hours and the Reading Habits of the Later Middle Ages." *Scrittura e Civilta* 9 (1985): 239–69.

Salmon, John. *Saints in Suffolk Churches.* Suffolk Historic Churches Trust, 1981.

Samson, Annie. "The South English Legendary: Constructing a Context." In *Thirteenth Century England I,* eds. P. R. Coss and S. D. Lloyd, 185–95. Woodbridge, Suffolk: Boydell, 1986.

Sandler, Lucy Freeman. *Omne Bonum: A Fourteenth-Century Encyclopedia of Universal Knowledge.* 2 vols. London: Harvey Miller, 1996.

Sargent, Michael G. "Bonaventura English: A Survey of the Middle English Prose Translations of Early Franciscan Literature." In *Spätmittelalterliche Geistliche Literatur in der Nationalsprache,* vol. 2, ed. James Hogg, 145–76. Salzburg: Institut für Anglistik und Amerikanistik, 1984.

Sargent, Steven D. "Miracle Books and Pilgrimage Shrines in Late Medieval Bavaria." *Historical Reflections* 13 (1986): 455–71.

Sawbridge, P. F. *Roof Carvings in Mildenhall Church*. Oxford: Holywell Press, n.d.

Schiller, Gertrud. *Iconography of Christian Art*. 2 vols. Trans. Janet Seligman. Greenwich, Conn.: New York Graphic Society, 1971.

Schmitt. Clément, ed. *Vita e spiritualità della Beata Angela da Foligno*. (Pérugia Serafica Provincia di San Francesco), 1987.

Schmitt, Jean-Claude. "L'Occident, Nicée II et les Images du VIIIe au XIIIe Siècle." In *Nicée II, 787–1987: Douze Siècles d'Images Religieuses*, eds. F. Boespflug and N. Lossky, 271–301. Paris: Les Éditions du Cerf, 1987.

Schofield, R. S. "The Geographical Distribution of Wealth in England, 1334–1649." *Economic History Review* 2nd ser., XVIII (1965): 483–510.

Scott, Kathleen L. "Design, Decoration, and Illustration." In *Book Production and Publishing in Britain 1375–1475*, eds. Jeremy Griffiths and Derek Pearsall, 31–64. Cambridge: CUP, 1989.

———. *Later Gothic Manuscripts 1390–1490*. London: Harvey Miller, 1996.

Shailor, Barbara A. *The Medieval Book: Catalogue of an Exhibition at the Beinecke Rare Book & Manuscript Library Yale University*. New Haven, Conn., 1988.

Shaw, Judith. "The Influence of Canonical and Episcopal Reform on Popular Books of Instruction." In *The Popular Literature of Medieval England*, ed. Thomas J. Heffernan, 44–60. Knoxville: University of Tennessee Press, 1985.

Sheehan, Michael M. "English Wills and the Records of the Ecclesiastical and Civil Jurisdictions." *Journal of Medieval History* 14:1 (1988): 3–12.

———. *The Will in Medieval England*. Toronto: Pontifical Institute of Mediaeval Studies, 1963.

Sheppard, Elaine M. "The Reformation and the Citizens of Norwich." *NA* 38 (1981): 44–58.

Simpson, W. Sparrow. "On the Measure of the Wound in the Side of the Redeemer." *Journal of the British Archaeological Association* 30 (1874): 357–74.

Smalley, Beryl. "William of Auvergne, John of La Rochelle and St. Thomas Aquinas on the Old Law." In *St. Thomas Aquinas 1274–1974 Commemorative Studies*, vol. 2, 11–71. Toronto: Pontifical Institute of Mediaeval Studies, 1974.

Snell, Lawrence S. "London Chantries and Chantry Chapels." In *Collectanea Londiniensia*, eds. Joanna Bird, et al., 216–222. London: London and Middlesex Archaeological Society, 1978.

Somerset, Fiona. "Answering the *Twelve Conclusions*: Dymmok's Halfhearted Gestures Towards Publication." In *Lollardy and the Gentry in the Later Middle Ages*, eds. Margaret Aston and Colin Richmond, 52–76. New York: St. Martin's, 1997.

Southern, R. W. "The English Origins of the 'Miracles of the Virgin.'" *Mediaeval and Renaissance Studies* 4 (1958): 176–216.

Spalding, Mary C. *The Middle English Charters of Christ*. Bryn Mawr, Penn.: Bryn Mawr College Monograph vol. 15, 1914.

Spencer, Brian. "King Henry of Windsor and the London Pilgrim." In *Collectanea Londiniensia*, eds. Joanna Bird, et al., 235–64. London: London and Middlesex Archaeological Society, 1978.

Spencer, H. Leith. *English Preaching in the Late Middle Ages*. Oxford: Clarendon Press, 1993.

Spettman, Hieronymous. "Das Schriftchen 'De Oculo Morali' and Sein Verfasser." *Archivum Franciscanum Historicum* 16 (1923): 309–22.

Stafford, Ann. "Angela of Foligno." In *Spirituality through the Centuries: Ascetics and Mystics of the Western Church,* ed. J. Walsh, 181–97. New York: Kennedy & Sons, 1964.

Staley, Lynn. *Margery Kempe's Dissenting Fictions.* University Park, Penn.: The Pennsylvania State University Press, 1994.

Stargardt, Ute. "The Beguines of Belgium, the Dominican Nuns of Germany, and Margery Kempe." In *The Popular Literature of Medieval England,* ed. Thomas J. Heffernan, 277–313. Knoxville: University of Tennessee Press, 1985.

Stock, Brian. *The Implications of Literacy.* Princeton, N.J.: Princeton University Press, 1983.

Stone, Lawrence. *Sculpture in Britain: the Middle Ages.* 2nd ed. Harmondsworth, Penguin, 1972.

Storey, R. L. "Ecclesiastical Causes in Chancery." In *The Study of Medieval Records: Essays in Honour of Kathleen Major,* eds. D. A. Bullough and R. L. Storey, 236–59. Oxford: Clarendon Press, 1971.

Sumption, Jonathan. *Pilgrimage: an Image of Mediaeval Religion.* Totowa, N. J.: Rowman & Littlefield, 1975.

Sutton, Anne F. and Livia Visser-Fuchs. *The Hours of Richard III.* Wolfeboro Falls: Alan Sutton, 1990.

Swanson, R. N. *Church and Society in Late Medieval England.* Oxford: Blackwell, 1989.

———. "Parochialism and Particularism: the Dispute over the Status of Ditchford Frary, Warwickshire, in the Early Fifteenth Century." In *Medieval Ecclesiastical Studies in honour of Dorothy M. Owen,* eds. M. J. Franklin and C. Harper-Bill, 241–57. Woodbridge: Boydell, 1995.

———. *Religion and Devotion in Europe c. 1215–c. 1515.* Cambridge: CUP, 1995.

Tanner, Norman P. *The Church in Late Medieval Norwich 1370–1532.* Toronto: Pontifical Institute of Mediaeval Studies, 1984.

Tarvers, Josephine K. "The Alleged Illiteracy of Margery Kempe: A Reconsideration of the Evidence." *Medieval Perspectives* 11 (1996): 113–24.

Tasker, Edward G. *Encyclopedia of Medieval Church Art.* Ed. John Beaumont. London: Batsford, 1993.

Theilmann, John M. "Communitas Among Fifteenth-Century Pilgrims." *Historical Reflections* 11 (1984): 253–70.

———. "The Miracles of King Henry VI of England." *The Historian* 42 (1980): 456–71.

———. "Political Canonization and Political Symbolism in Medieval England." *JBS* 29 (July 1990): 241–66.

Thomas, Keith. *Religion and the Decline of Magic.* New York: Scribner's, 1971.

Thompson, Stith and Jonas Balys. *The Oral Tales of India.* Bloomington: Indiana University Press, 1958.

Thomson, John A. F. *Early Tudor Church and Society 1485–1529.* New York: Longman, 1993.

————. *The Later Lollards 1414–1520*. Oxford: Oxford University Press, 1965.

————. "Tithe Disputes in Later Medieval London." *English Historical Review* 78 (1963): 1–17.

Thorndike, Lynn. *A History of Magic and Experimental Science,* vol. 3. *The Fourteenth and Fifteenth Centuries.* New York: Columbia University Press, 1934.

Thrupp, Sylvia. *The Merchant Class of Medieval London.* Ann Arbor: University of Michigan Press, 1948.

Trapp, J. B. "Verses by Lydgate at Long Melford." *Review of English Studies* ns VI (1955): 1–11.

Trexler, Richard C. *Public Life in Renaissance Florence.* New York: Academic Press, 1980.

Tricker, Roy. *Ipswich Churches Ancient and Modern.* 2nd ed. Ipswich: Brechinset, 1983.

Tubach, Frederic C. *Index Exemplorum: A Handbook of Medieval Religious Tales. Folklore Fellows Communications No. 204.* Helsinki, 1969.

Turner, Victor and Edith Turner. *Image and Pilgrimage in Christian Culture: Anthropological Perspectives.* New York: Columbia University Press, 1978.

Vale, M. G. A. *Piety, Charity, and Literacy among the Yorkshire Gentry, 1370–1480.* York: Borthwick Institute of Historical Research, 1976.

Vauchez, André. *The Laity in the Middle Ages: Religious Beliefs and Devotional Practices.* Trans. Margery J. Schneider. Notre Dame, Ind.: University of Notre Dame Press, 1993.

Victoria History of London. vol. 1. Ed. William Page. London: Constable & Co. Ltd., 1909.

Von Nolken, Christina. "Rychard Wyche, a Certain Knight, and the Beginning of the End." In *Lollards and Gentry in the Later Middle Ages,* eds. Margaret Aston and C. Richmond, 127–54. New York: St. Martin's, 1997.

Wallace, David. "Mystics and Followers in Siena and East Anglia: a Study in Taxonomy, Class and Cultural Mediation." In *The Medieval Mystical Tradition in England,* ed. Marion Glasscoe, 169–91. Cambridge: Brewer, 1984.

Ward, Benedicta. *Miracles and the Medieval Mind: Theory, Record and Event 1000–1215.* Rev. ed. Philadelphia: University of Pennsylvania Press, 1987.

Ward, H. L. D. *Catalogue of Romances in the Department of Manuscripts in the British Museum.* Vols. 1 & 2. London, 1893.

Warner, Marina. *Alone of All Her Sex: the Myth and Cult of the Virgin Mary.* New York: Knopf, 1976.

Warren, F. E. "Gild of S. Peter in Bardwell." *PSIA* 11 (1901–03): 81–145.

Waterton, Edmund. *Pietas Mariana Britannica.* London: St. Joseph's Catholic Library, 1879.

Watson, Nicholas. "The Composition of Julian of Norwich's *Revelation of Love.*" *Speculum* 68 (1993): 637–83.

Watt, Tessa. *Cheap Print and Popular Piety 1550–1640.* Cambridge: CUP, 1991.

Welter, J.-Th. *L'Exemplum dans la Littérature Religieuse et Didactique du Moyen Age.* Paris: Guitard, 1927.

Westlake, H. F. *The Parish Gilds of Mediaeval England.* London: Society for Promoting Christian Knowledge, 1919.

White, Helen C. *The Tudor Books of Private Devotion*. Madison: University of Wisconsin Press, 1951.

Whiting, Robert. *The Blind Devotion of the People*. Cambridge: CUP, 1989.

Wieck, Roger S. *Painted Prayers: the Book of Hours in Medieval and Renaissance Art*. New York: Braziller, 1997.

———. *Time Sanctified: The Book of Hours in Medieval Art and Life*. New York: Braziller, 1988.

Williams, J. F. "The Black Book of Swaffham." *NA* 33 (1965): 243–53.

———. "The Gild of St. John the Baptist at Swaffham." *NA* 33 (1965): 2–5.

Williamson, Paul. *Northern Gothic Sculpture 1200–1450*. Victoria and Albert Museum, 1988.

Williamson, W. W. "Saints on Norfolk Rood-Screens and Pulpits." *NA* 31 (1955–57): 299–346.

Wilmart, André. *Auteurs spirituels et textes dévots du moyen age latin*. Paris: Études Augustiniennes, 1971.

Winstead, Karen A. "Capgrave's Saint Katherine and the Perils of Gynecocracy." *Viator* 25 (1994): 361–76.

———. "Piety, Politics, and Social Commitment in Capgrave's *Life of St. Katherine*." *Medievalia et humanistica* n.s. 17 (1991): 59–80.

———. *Virgin Martyrs*. Ithaca, N.Y.: Cornell University Press, 1997.

Wolter, Eugene. *Der Judenknabe*. Halle, 1879.

Woodforde, Christopher. *The Norwich School of Glass-Painting in the Fifteenth Century*. London: Oxford University Press, 1950.

Wood-Legh, K. L. *Perpetual Chantries in Britain*. Cambridge: CUP, 1965.

Woolf, Rosemary. *The English Religious Lyric in the Middle Ages*. Oxford: Clarendon Press, 1968.

Wormald, Francis. "The Rood of Bromholm." *Journal of the Warburg Institute* 1 (1937–38): 31–45.

Yates, Frances A. *The Art of Memory*. Chicago: University of Chicago Press, 1966.

Zeeman, Elizabeth. "Nicholas Love—a Fifteenth-Century Translator." *Review of English Studies* 6 (1955): 113–27.

Zell, Michael L. "Fifteenth- and Sixteenth-Century Wills as Historical Sources." *Archives* 14: 62 (1979): 67–74.

Ziegler, Joanna E. *Sculpture of Compassion: the Pietà and the Beguines in the Southern Low Countries c. 1300-c. 1600*. Bruxelles: Brepols, 1992.

INDEX

Abbreuiaion of Cronicles, 64–5
Abgar, 28, 191
Agnes of Montepulciano, 149
alabaster sculpture, 73–4, 77–81, 91,
    125, Plates 3.1, 3.2, 3.3
Alhazen, 150–2
All Saints, 102, Table 3.3b
Alnwick, Bishop, of Lincoln, 117
Ambresbury, Salisbury Diocese, 121
Angela of Foligno, 131, 145–7, 149,
    153, 192, 193
Anne of Brittany, 169
Apology for Lollard Doctrines, 15, 24, 25
Aristotle, 30–1
Arma Christi, 76, 142, 148, 154, 159,
    169, 172–3, 181–3, 184–6, 193,
    194, Plate 6.5, Plate 6.9
Aston, Margaret, 4, 22, 141
Athenagoras, 15
Atkinson, Clarissa, 141

battle, protection in, 180
Baxter, Margery, 13–17, 20, 27, 41
Beguines, 88–90
Belting, Hans, 57–8
bequests, 8–9, 10, 78, 84–92, Table 3.1,
    Table 3.2, Table 3.3a, Table 3.3b
    of books, 156, 183–4
    clergy's, 87–8
    to friars, 92–3, 95
    to gilds, 95
    to images, 84–105
    men's, 84, 87
    of Norfolk testators, 91–4

    of Suffolk testators, 91–4
    for votive lights, 94–8
    women's, 84, 87–8, 93
Bible, 14, 15, 22, 27, 29, 31, 33, 34, 66,
    160, 183
    see also New Testament, Old
        Testament
Biblia Pauperum, 160
Blomefield, Francis, 104
Bokenham, Osbern, 61–3, 91
bona tractatus de decem mandates, 38–9,
    192
Boniface VI, 169
Boniface, pope, 62
book market, 156–7
Book of Vices and Virtues, 46
Books of Hours, 8, 17, 55, 136,
    155–90
    accessory texts, 158
    cost of, 156
    Hours of the Blessed Virgin, 161
    Hours of the Cross, 161, 169
    images in, 158–90
    language in, 157, 169
    Penitential Psalms, 169, 172
    printed editions, 157, 172, 173,
        179, 186, 188
    suffrages of saints in, 161
    see also indulgences, prayer books,
        prayers, rubrics
Booth, Archbishop, of York, 126, 129
Bordesley Abbey, 184
Bridlington priory, 108–12
Brinton, Bishop, of Exeter, 180

Bromholm priory, 119–20
burial, 98–101
Burton, Thomas, 122
Bydell, John, 188

Camille, Michael, 52
Capgrave, John, 61, 64–67
Carpenter, Alexander, 19, 38, 119, 194
Caxton, William, 17, 49, 139–40, 157
chantries, 72, 77, 93, 94, 114, 117
charms, 8, 10, 180–6, 188, 194
Charter of Christ, 167
Chartier, Roger, 164
childbirth, protection in, 181, 182,
     186, 194
Christ, images of, 189, Plate. 6.1
     Man of Sorrows, 155, 159, 169–72,
          173, 180, 184, 193, Plate 6.4
     Mass of St. Gregory, 159, 169–72,
          175, 180, 184, 186, Plate 6.3
     Passion, 133, 141, 145–7, 154, 155,
          158, 161, 187, 188
     wounds of, 152–3, 159, 164–67,
          173, 182, 186, Plate 6.2
     see also crucifix; Veronica
churches
     architecture, 9, 71–5
     art in, 4, 6, 8–9, 11, 21, 35, 40,
          69–84, 104–5, 112–18, 131,
          141–2, 148, 149, 159, 161, 167,
          173, 193, 195–6: benches 73;
          Easter sepulcher, 96, 97, 117;
          fonts 73, 74, 75; roodlofts, 72,
          76, 86, 103–4, 113, 114, 117,
          167; rood screens 73, 74, 75, 76,
          77; statues 73, 77–84; stained-
          glass windows 73, 74, 76, 195;
          see also alabaster sculpture;
          Christ, images of; crucifix;
          saints; Virgin mary, images of
churchwardens, 8, 90, 113, 123, 195
Cicero, 31
The City of God, 16
Clement of Alexandria, 21
Council of Nicaea (787), 30, 57

Cromwell, Thomas, 195
cross, relics of, 119
crucifix, 9, 13, 36, 81, 121, 162, Plate
     3.3, Plate 6.1
     bequests to, 103
     burial by, 99–100
     in church, 69, 74, 77, 97, 113, 193
     devotion to, 139, 148
     miraculous, 10, 30, 43–4, 55–9,
          122, 192
     in penitential rites, 127
     and prayer, 162, 166–7, 180, 188
     responses to, 9, 11, 70, 133–7,
          140–4, 146, 149, 153–4
     worship of, 28, 47, 49–50, 52

De Idololatria, 16
De Oculo Morali, 150–54
death
     protection against, 180–2, 184, 186,
          188, 194
     vision of Virgin before, 164, 169,
          175, 181, 184
Decalogue, see Ten Commandments
demons, 1, 29, 181, 186
     in images, 13–22, 194, Plate 1.1
     protection against, 180, 181, 186,
          194
Destructorium Viciorum, 19, 38, 119
A Dialogue Concerning Heresies, 191–5
Dives and Pauper, 5, 48–51, 55, 60, 67,
     143
Doctrinal of Sapience, 139
Duffy, Eamon, 91, 181–2
Durham College, 183
Dymmok, Roger, 10, 27–34, 38, 44,
     191

East Anglia, 10, 70–5
     churches in, 75–84
     gilds in, 112–18
     shrines in, 118–26
     see also heresy; Norfolk; Norwich;
          Suffolk
Edward IV, 126

Edward VI, 195
Elizabeth of York, 182
Ely priory, 186
Erler, Mary C., 157
Eusebius, 21
exempla, 5, 7, 44, 54–60, 67, 142, 143, 192

Fitzralph, Archbishop, 119, 194
Foston, Yorkshire, 10, 107–12, 117
Fourth Lateran Council, 43, 112
Fraisthorp, Yorkshire, 108–12, 130

gilds, 9, 11, 72, 90, 92, 94–7, 105, 112–18, 126, 129, 156, 193
    bequests to, 95–7, Table 3.3a, Table 3.3b
The Golden Legend, 17, 30, 54, 56, 61
Greenfield, William, Archbishop of York, 11, 107–11, 117, 124, 128, 130
Gregory the Great, pope, 1, 8, 21, 23, 26, 31, 192

Hailes, 56, 120
Henry VI, cult of, 76, 113, 125–6, 129157,
Henry, Avril, 160
heresy, 3, 12, 13, 14, 15, 17, 22, 24, 25, 30, 34, 39, 41, 60, 64, 71, 126, 127, 128, 132, 138, 144
    see also Lollards
Hermes Trismegistus, 16–17
Hilary, Bishop, of Poitiers, 162
Hilton, Walter, 10, 19, 34–7, 38, 39, 183, 191, 192
Hoccleve, Thomas, 40
Holcot, Robert, 19, 27, 38
Host, 9, 17, 36, 39, 52–3, 55, 57, 73, 97, 116, 130, 144–5, 148, 149, 169, 179–80, 182, 192, 193, 194

iconoclasm, 4, 23–4, 29, 33, 55, 57, 74, 75, 77

idolatry, 1, 4, 5, 6, 10–12, 17, 21, 33, 37, 40, 107, 110–11, 121, 129, 191–6
    accusations of, 3, 10, 12, 20, 22–27, 123, 188
    in Bible, 15, 19
    definitions of, 3, 5–6, 10, 14, 16, 19–20, 23, 32, 38, 41, 45–8, 67, 119
    in exempla, 55
    of Jews, 1, 3, 5, 15, 21, 30, 36, 43, 45, 51, 54, 57, 107, 191, Plate I.1
    of pagans, 5, 21, 55, 60, 61–7
    in saints' legends, 61–7
idols, 1, 3, 5, 12, 13, 15–20, 22, 24, 25, 43, 51, 54, 55, 61–2, 63–7, 191, 194, Plate I.1, Plate 1.1
illness, curing of, 181
image worship, 20, 38, 49, 59
    descriptions of, 49, 50, 52, 87
    dulia 10, 26–27, 32–34, 35, 37, 40, 45–49, 54, 67, 191
    intention in 37, 38, 53, 54
    latria 10, 26, 28, 32–34, 35, 37, 38, 40, 45–49, 54, 65–66, 67, 188, 191
images
    bequests to, 86–105
    as books of the laity, 1, 7, 10, 11, 21, 23, 26, 32, 40, 48–9, 51, 53, 87, 137, 144, 148–9, 158, 160, 161, 187, 189, 192
    burial by, 99–100
    debates over, 3, 9–10, 20–42, 44–54, 186–9, 191–5
    demons in, 13–22
    devotional & mnemonic aids, 10, 11, 30–2, 36–7, 38–9, 41, 46–7, 50, 52–3, 68, 117, 133–4, 139–46, 148, 162–80, 194
    disputes over offerings to, 107–112, 121–4, 129
    economic importance of, 102, 122–3, 129, 195

impotence of, 24–5, 26, 38, 52, 65–6, 127

injunctions against, 195

location, importance of, 112, 118–19, 125, 130

and medicine, 182

miraculous, 5, 7, 10, 44, 45, 49, 55, 56–60, 67–8, 108, 116, 121, 130, 133, 143, 182, 192

names of, 119, 130

in Old Testament 29, 47, 51, 57, 107

in penitential rites, 127–9

relation to prototypes, 27, 31, 32, 40, 45, 47, 65, 67, 127, 145, 191, 192, 194

and sorcery, 182

see also Christ, images of; crucifix; indulgences; lights; Virgin Mary, images of; saints; Veronica

Incarnation, 17, 29–30, 140

indulgences, 7, 10, 120–3, 129, 157, 159, 169–86, 188–9, 193, 194, Plates 6.5, 6.6, 6.7, 6.8, 6.9

Innocent, pope, 181, 182

Jacob's Well, 45–6

Jacobus de Voragine, 17, 61

Jeanne-Marie de Maillé, 147–9, 153, 192

jewels for images, 3, 8, 86, 94, 102, 195

Jews, 29, 30, 55, 60
  as iconoclasts, 30, 55–9, 63
  as idolaters, 1, 3, 5, 15, 21, 30, 36, 43, 45, 51, 54, 57, 107, 191

John Chrysostom, 30

John III, pope, 180

John XXII, pope, 110, 175

John of Damascus, 30, 31, 32, 33, 38

Julian of Norwich, 9, 10, 131–8, 147, 150, 153, 192, 193

Justin Martyr, 15

Kempe, Margery, 9, 10, 70, 90, 131, 137–45, 147, 149, 150, 153, 158, 168, 182, 189–90, 193

Klapisch-Zuber, Christiane, 88

Knighton, Henry, 122, 127

Laity
  literacy of, 3, 7–8, 40, 44, 87–8, 155–7, 168–9, 183–6, 189–90, 192
  as parishioners, 69–75, 76–84, 112–14, 195
  relations with clergy, 6–7, 111–12, 123–4, 128–30, 183–6
  see also bequests, gilds, testators, wills, women

lamplands, 96, 98, 116–17, 130

Langton, Thomas, Bishop of Salisbury, 126–7

Lanterne of Liȝt, 27

Legendys of Hooly Wummen, 62–3, 91

Leontius, Bishop, 30

liber contra xii errores et hereses lollardum, 28–34

Libri Carolini, 21

libri laicorum, *see* images, as books of the laity

Life of Saint Anne, 61

Life of Saint Katherine of Alexandria, 64–7

lights, 3, 9, 24, 69, 77, 86, 87, 88, 92, 94–8, 99, 101–5, 114–17, 126, 127, 128, 130, 193

lives of the saints, 61–7

Lollards, 14, 38, 51, 64–5, 71, 77
  hostility to images, 3, 5, 9, 10, 14–5, 19–27, 40, 45, 48, 50, 53, 54, 59, 63, 66, 68, 84, 104, 123, 126–8, 144, 145, 186, 188, 191, 194, 195
  opponents of, 28–30, 32–4, 40, 57, 60, 160

Love, Nicholas, 140, 168, 183

Lydgate, John, 40–1, 168

magic, 12, 44, 45, 46, 52, 54, 66, 157, 161, 180–3, 186, 194

Marie d'Oignies, 149

Marshall, William, 188
Martianus Capella, 31
Martin, Roger, 69–70, 74, 77, 78, 104,
    195
Mary I, 195
Meaux Abbey, 122–3
meditation, 3, 6, 90, 135, 138–41,
    143–4, 146, 149, 154, 162–8,
    183, 187–8
Miles, Margaret, 88
Minucius Felix, 15
Mirk's Festial, 56, 62, 142, 160
Mirror of the Blessed Life of Jesus Christ,
    140, 168, 183
More, Thomas, 87, 191–5

New Testament, 15, 28–30, 33, 141
Nicholas III, pope, 111
Norfolk, 70–5, 91–4, 117, 137, 138
    Castel Acre, 120
    gilds, 114–8
    Great Yarmouth, 71, 92, 94, 95, 96,
        99, 104, 118, 126, 144
    Great Walsingham, 71, 95, 102, 103
    Horstead, 126
    King's Lynn, 116, 126
    Little Walsingham, 71, 72, 114,
        Table 3.3a
    Shipdam, 113
    shrines, 119–120, 124
    Swaffham, 71, 72–3, 93, 94, 95, 96,
        99, 114, Table 3.3b
    Tilney, 113
    Wymondham, 71, 72, 95, 102
    see also East Anglia; Norwich
Northwood, John, 184
Norwich, 72, 88, 94, 97, 98, 103, 114,
    120, 126, 127, 131, 132, 141,
    142, 144, 156, 195
    bishop of, 120, 151
    Diocese of, 70, 103, 113, 120–1, 128
    heresy trials, 13, 22, 25, 71

Old Testament, 5, 13, 15, 19, 20, 21,
    23, 28–30, 33, 48, 51, 63, 107

Omne Bonum, 17, 20, 186, Plate 6.9
Origen, 21, 33, 150

Paston family, 156
Pecock, Reginald, Bishop, 17
Peter Lombard, 31
Peter of Limoges, 150–4
pilgrimages, 3, 6, 7, 8, 11, 24, 46, 56,
    58, 70, 71, 74, 94, 102, 118–25,
    126–9, 132, 138, 143, 144, 147,
    191–2, 195
    criticism of, 14, 22, 24–6, 33, 68,
        126
poetry, 40–1, 139–40, 167–8
Pomander of Prayer, 155, 158, 168
poor people, as God's image, 25
Pore Caitif, 51–3, 55, 66, 142, 153, 167,
    168, 192
prayer books, 155–7, 160–190, 193
    bequests of, 156, 183–4, 189
    see also Books of Hours
prayer rolls, 173
prayers, 157–8, 162–90
    indulgences, 157, 169–80
    texts: *Adoramus te,* 162; *Agnus Dei,*
        169; *Anima Christi sanctifica me,*
        179; *Ave castissima mater dei,* 179;
        Ave Maria 162, 164, 172, 173,
        175, 184, 187, 189; *Ave principium
        nostre creacionis,* 179; *Ave Regina
        celorum,* 175; *Ave sanctissima virgo,*
        179; *Ave verum corpus domini
        nostri,* 179; *Credo,* 173, 189;
        *Domine Iesu Christi qui hanc
        sacratissimam carnem,* 169; *Gloria
        in excelsis,* 169; *Obsecro Te,* 157,
        181; *O Intemerata,* 157; *Omnibus
        consideratis,* 164, 166–7; *Omnis
        terra adoret te deus,* 175; *Omnis
        virtus te decorat,* 169; *O vernacule,*
        175; *Pater noster* 172, 173, 184,
        189; *Precor te amantissime* domine,
        180; *Quotquot maris sunt gutte,*
        179; *Salve sancta facies,* 175, 189;
        Salve virgo, 162

primers, *see* Books of Hours
printing, 157

Quattuor Sermones, 49–50

Ramsey Abbey, 117
Reading
    as pious act, 8, 11, 139–40, 147–8,
        155–90, 193
    process of, 164–6, 173, 190
    see also laity, literacy of
Redstone, V. B., 117
Regnault, François, 157
relics, 7, 9, 21, 32–4, 120–2, 128, 130,
    148, 160, 182
Reynes, Robert, 94
Richard III, 169
Richmond, Colin, 94
Rolle, Richard, 45, 139, 168, 183
Rood of Bromholm, 119
Rosarium Theologie 13, 14
rosary, 187
Rubin, Miri, 58
rubrics, 156, 162, 164, 166, 168–9,
    172–90, 194

St. Agatha, 62–3
St. Agnes, 62–3
St. Andrew, 61, 101, 113
St. Anne, 102, 179, Table 3.3a, Plate 6.8
St. Augustine, 16–17, 19, 33, 150
St. Barbara, 91
St. Bartholomew, 17, 61–2
St. Bernard, 21–2, 143
St. Bonaventure, 31
St. Bridget, 188
St. Cecelia, 62
St. Christine, 62–3
St. Christopher, 76, 100, 113, 161,
    Table 3.3a, Table 3.3b
St. Dorothy, 62–3
St. Edmund, 76, 116, 118, 121, 124,
    125, Table 3.3a
St. Eloy, 78–81, Plate 3.1
St. Erasmus, Table 3.3a, Table 3.3b

St. Etheldreda, 76, 120, 125
St. Eustace, 61
St. Faith, 63
St. Francis, 59, 99, 147
St. Gabriel, 77
St. Gatian, 148
St. George, 61, 74, 76, 113, 161, Table
    3.3a, Table 3.3b
St. Giles, 87
St. Gregory, 99, Table 3.3b
St. Guthlac, 94, Table 3.3b
St. Helen, 91, Table 3.3a, Table 3.3b
St. Hugh, 128
St. Jacob, 95, Table 3.3a, Table 3.3b
St. James, 115
St. John, 95, 113, 115
St. John the Baptist, 74, 99, 101, 104,
    115, 116, 120, Table 3.3a, Table
    3.3b
St. John the Evangelist, 61, 74, 95, 101,
    167
St. Jude, 61
St. Katherine (or Catherine), 39, 62,
    63, 64–7, 74, 81–4, 91, 95, 99,
    113, 127, 161, Table 3.3a, Table
    3.3b, Plate 3.4
St. Lawrence, 39, 61, 116
St. Leonard, 99, 127
St. Louis, 160
St. Luke, 28–9, 76, 191
St. Margaret, 62, 91, 114, 115
St. Martin, 127, 148
St. Mary Magdalen, 61, 91, 95, Table
    3.3b
St. Michael, 74, 77, 78–81, 121, 126,
    Plate 3.2
St. Nicholas, 95, 99, 102, Table 3.3b
St. Patrick, 17
St. Paul, 15, 29, Table 3.3b
St. Peter, 95, 101, 102, 116, Table 3.3a,
    Table 3.3b
St. Petronilla, 91
St. Philip, 17, 62, Plate 1.1
St. Radegunde, 148
St. Raphael, 77

St. Sebastian, 81–4, Plate 3.5
St. Simon, 61
St. Thomas, 99, 113
St. Thomas Aquinas, 17, 26–7, 32, 33,
    38, 47, 51
St. Thomas Becket, 14, 104, 161, 195,
    Table 3.3a, Table 3.3b
St. Thomas the Apostle, 17
St. Walstan, 113, 124, 125
St. Wulfstan, Table 3.3a
saints, images of, 32–3, 39, 74–84, 88,
    91, 95, 117, 121, 147, 155, 193,
    Table 3.3a, Table 3.3b
    see also names of individual saints
senses, 11, 30–1, 33, 37, 40, 66–7,
    88–90, 131, 134, 135, 140–1,
    145, 150, 153–4, 155, 158, 160,
    168, 179
    see also vision
shrines, 5, 6, 11, 22, 33, 56, 71, 92–4,
    98, 102, 118–25, 126, 127, 138,
    190, 195
sin, remission of, 180
Sixtus IV, pope, 180
Sixtus, pope, 179, Plate 6.6
Speculum Christiani, 46, 55, 60
Speculum Devotorum, 168
Stayner, York Diocese, 121
Suffolk, 70–5, 91–4, 117, 128
    Barton, 116
    Bury St. Edmunds, 114
    Cratfield, 113
    Fressingfield, 173
    gilds, 114–18
    Hoxne, 121
    Icklingham, 117
    Ipswich, 71, 72, 96, 99, 101, 103,
        195
    Kersey, 121, 129
    Long Melford, 69, 72, 73, 77, 104,
        195
    Mildenhall, 71, 92, 93, 101, 113,
        173
    shrines, 121, 124
    Stoke Clare, 61

Stradishall, 114
Walberswick, 71, 72, 94, 99, 101,
    102, 113
    see also East Anglia
superstition, 6, 104, 107, 189, 192, 195

Ten Commandments, 1–2, 19–20,
    22–3, 26, 29–30, 38–9, 43,
    44–54, 127, 183, 186, 188, 191
Tertullian, 15
testators, 84–105
Thomas à Kempis, 133
Thornton Abbey, 122
Tintern Abbey, 121, 125
travel, protection in, 180
Tretyse of Love, 142, 143, 168
Trinity, images of, 29, 34, 81, 99, 116,
    Plate 3.3
Twelve Conclusions of the Lollards, 26, 32

Valor Ecclesiasticus, 118
vernacular manuals, 43–54
Vernicle, see Veronica
Veronica, veil of, 28, 58, 136–7, 159,
    160, 175, 189, 191
Virgin Mary
    images of, 5, 10, 11, 13, 17, 44, 55,
        56, 58, 59, 60, 73, 96, 101, 102,
        104, 105, 113, 117, 120–1, 122,
        125, 128, 147, 148, 162, 164,
        167, 179, 184, 187, 188, 192,
        Plate 6.8: Annunciation, 95,
        Table 3.3b, 161; Foston Virgin,
        107–112, 117, 128–30; Our
        Lady of Arneburgh, 92, 94,
        115, 120; Our Lady of
        Halberton, 102; Our Lady of
        Ipswich, 71, 118; Our Lady of
        Walsingham, 6, 24, 71, 93–94,
        118, 124–5, 138; Our Lady in
        the Sun, 179, Plate 6.6, Plate
        6.7; pietà, 9, 11, 41, 58, 69, 90,
        95, Table 3.3b, 101, 131, 139,
        142, 144, 154, 155, 159, 173,
        181, 193, Plate 6.5

vision
  acts of beholding, 139, 140, 142,
    146, 149–50, 160, 168, 173, 179,
    180, 183, 187, 189–90, 193
  relation between spiritual and
    physical, 134–7, 140–2, 144–5,
    147, 152–4, 168
  superior to hearing, 30–1
  theories of, 10, 150–4

wills, 84–105, Tables 3.1, 3.2, 3.3a, 3.3b
  executors 103–4
  men's, 84
  from Norfolk 91–4
  from Suffolk 91–4
  women's, 84, 87–8, 193

  see also bequests, women
women, 113
  bequests of, 87–8, 91, 93, 156, 184,
    101, 102, Table 3.1
  as book owners, 156, 184, 189
  literacy of, 87–8, 137, 141, 146,
    147, 148–9, 189–90, 193
  responses to images of, 87–91,
    122–3, 131–154, 195
  wills of, 84, 87–8, 193
woodcuts, 155, 159, 167, 173, 179, 182,
  Plate 6.5, Plate 6.7, Plate 6.8
Worcester priory, 184
Wycliffe, John, 23, 87

Ziegler, Joanna E., 88–90